The Moors

A Comprehensive description

Budgett Meakin

Alpha Editions

This edition published in 2020

ISBN : 9789354158629 (Hardback)

ISBN : 9789354159039 (Paperback)

Design and Setting By

Alpha Editions

www.alphaedis.com

email - alphaedis@gmail.com

To

the Memory of

My Father,

who loved the Moors:

and to

those Noble Men and Women

who have devoted,

or who will hereafter devote, their lives

to spreading the Truth of the Gospel among them,

this volume is

with admiration

dedicated.

Hampstead,

January 1902.

PREFACE

IT was with no intention of "making a book," but only for the convenience of personal study, that on arriving in Morocco in 1884, on what was intended to be a few months' holiday, I commenced at once to post and classify the facts I learned by observation and enquiry, or gleaned from every available work. But as my visit lengthened—developing eventually into six years' residence,—and the incomplete and unsatisfactory nature of what had already been published became apparent, I decided to enter the field myself.

Accordingly, in 1888 I remodelled the scheme under which my notes had been arranged, in such a manner as to form a definite plan for a standard work on Morocco. The position I then occupied, in charge of "The Times of Morocco," which my father had founded in 1884, afforded me peculiar facilities for coming into touch with everything Moroccan, and having made myself acquainted with the colloquial Arabic of the country, I had already determined to pass in the interior the time I might have spent in returning to England.

During those journeys, which embraced the chief points open to Europeans, without attempting anything by way of exploration, my object was always to get as close as possible to the people. Adopting the native dress, and to a certain extent a native name—Ṭahar bel Mikki,—for the most part in company with a faithful Moor, I was enabled to mingle with all classes to a degree impossible in European costume, just as for a Moor free social life in England would be impossible while retaining his picturesque attire.* Those who know the East best will agree with me that there is almost always a point beyond which Oriental and Occidental cannot go together, but until one of them adopts as far as possible the life and customs of the other, that point is never approached. The facility afforded by this plan for visiting spots forbidden to all but Muslims, though by no means the least interesting feature in a pleasant past, is not to be compared to its opportunities for unrestricted intercourse with every rank and type.

Finally, after six years' study of the Moors on the spot—prolonged by my determination to see through the press the first English-Arabic vocabulary published for Morocco†—I returned to England, having at least learned how inadequate my powers were for the task before me, and how little I really knew about it. My plan was to complete a course of reading at our National Museum, and then to bury myself in the interior of Morocco till I had emulated Lane in Egypt, that, after visiting kindred countries to know what was really Moorish and what was not, I might produce a work which might be relied on. I offered several London publishers to devote the next few years to its completion in the manner described, if they would publish the work of which I presented the scheme, provided it came up to their expectations; but all they wanted was something light and picturesque, which I refused to consider until I had accomplished something of real value. Later, in despair, I did make the attempt, but gave it up as futile, with such wealth

* For some account of my experiences see *The Land of the Moors*, ch. xxii.
† London, Quaritch, 6*s*.

of matter in hand. I also offered to undertake the preparation of a Morocco Arabic version of the Bible at my own cost, in Fez, if the British and Foreign Bible Society would publish it should it prove satisfactory, but they would not then depart from the eastern standard.

I had already offered to explore the Central Atlas, probably spending a year there to study the Berbers, if either the Royal or the Scottish Geographical Society would lend me the requisite instruments on my depositing their value, and would instruct me in their use, but neither accepted the offer, so this ideal also remains unattained.

I therefore decided to spend another year in Morocco, writing a still unpublished story of Moorish life, and then set out on a systematic series of journeys which have taken me into some sixty countries, commencing with the footsteps of the Moors in Spain, and the remaining parts of Barbary; eventually embracing all the important Mohammedan lands. Having kept the subject fresh by repeatedly writing and lecturing on it, I returned to my adopted home in 1897 for the purpose of collating and completing my voluminous notes. After another visit to the Atlas, several months were spent in this work, every note being read out in Arabic to a representative group of natives for their criticisms and additions. Many of the most interesting and popular "facts" regarding the Moors which had found place in previous works on the subject, several of which I had myself unsuspectingly employed, had to "go by the board," which will account for some apparent omissions now, though many other items have been added in their stead.

From that time to the present I have been engaged continuously for the greater portion of my time in re-writing and completing one or other of the series of three volumes which have grown out of my original plan for one. Another year spent in reading was required to amplify the history of "The Moorish Empire," the first to appear, and "The Land of the Moors" was only produced with extensive local co-operation by correspondence. The present volume should have held the foremost place, but its publication was deferred to render possible a second revision in Morocco, which has been effected this summer. The gifted and generous friend to whom the final revision of the previous volumes owed so much has again rendered invaluable assistance, this time as my wife, my indebtedness to whom I cannot attempt to express, or what I also owe to my mother for her careful revision of the text, as well as to the inspiration of her interest. Nor can I enumerate all the kind friends who have contributed new facts or checked those already obtained. Suffice it to say that I have laid under contribution almost every likely acquaintance, and only fear that I must have sadly tried many a patience with interminable queries and proofs. Nevertheless, I have one more favour to ask of each, that every error discovered, however slight, may be reported to me, not so much for my own sake, as *pro bono publico*. I am unable myself to feel the satisfaction of those kindly critics who, while recognizing the motives and labour required to produce these works, have not been qualified to realize their defects.

When, twelve years ago, single-handed and unprepared, I set myself a task requiring both resources and experience, I was equipped with neither. By study and travel

I endeavoured to repair my qualifications, but it has never been in my power to devote myself to my object as I could have wished. The result is therefore a disappointment, and publication at this stage confession of failure. I only launch these imperfect volumes because I feel they are needed, as occupying a field in which as yet they have no rival, and because, if this occasion be not grasped, I fear lest crowding duties and fresh interests may render the completion, even of a part, impossible and out of date.

Had any one of the authorities to whom I appealed in my youthful ardour on my first return to England given me encouragement or accepted the offers I made, the result would have been far different, and I do not think they would have had cause to regret it. I therefore with peculiar pleasure record the encouragement afforded me by Mr. W. T. Stead, who recommended my proposals to Messrs. Cassell and Macmillan; by the late Sir W. Kirby Green, who recommended them to the late Mr. Murray; by Lord (then Mr.) Curzon, who recommended them to the University Press; and above all by the late Dr. Robert Brown, who did not hesitate to point out how much was required in a student facing so great a task, and who lent ungrudging assistance in spite of his own busy life.

I have also to thank the many friends who have lent me photographs, notably Dr. Rudduck, my companion on my last tour in the interior, who secured a large number of special subjects for these three works; and Mr. C. H. Read, of the Ethnological Department of the British Museum, for permission to reproduce the drawings of Moorish objects in that collection, most of which I brought from Morocco myself for Sir Wollaston Franks.

To Messrs. Sonnenschein & Co., too, I feel that my readers as well as myself owe a debt for their enterprise in publishing such expensive volumes on a subject not in the public mind.

Personally I claim no more of my readers than the indulgence due to one who has done his best to lay in order the facts he has been able to glean regarding the Moors, their Land, and their Empire.

Oak Park, near Chicago,
August 1900.

BUDGETT MEAKIN.

ADDENDA.

TABLE OF EXPORT DUTIES, p. 187.

Since this table went to press the following products have been added to the list, as subject to a duty of 5°/o:

Bananas, green peas, onions, potatoes, tomatoes.

All of these, save onions, are of recent introduction from abroad, but are capable of great development.

THE SPELLING OF ARABIC WORDS

IN such a work as this the question of transliteration calls for remark, and its importance has secured its most careful consideration. The system followed is that adopted by the Beïrût missionaries in 1838 and confirmed in 1860, modified to suit the singularly pure and classical Maghribin pronunciation under the advice of several well-known Arabic scholars, and as the outcome of many years of experiment. Since each Arabic letter is distinguished by a dot or other sign, the original form of a word can be at once reproduced; and since Arabic is written phonetically, the correct pronunciation can be arrived at by anyone acquainted with the values of the original characters. In my Morocco-Arabic Vocabulary this system was strictly adhered to—printer's errors excepted,—but in a work intended to present native words in a form for popular use, it has been deemed essential to make certain modifications for the sake of simplicity.*

These modifications have, however, involved me in a maze of difficulties, and have failed to satisfy either party, the pedantic or the slovenly, so critics attack them from either side. I am nevertheless convinced that no other course than a via media would have suited my purpose, and since the publication of *The Moorish Empire* further modifications with this view have been introduced. These I trust will meet some objectors, but I see that the correction of the proofs having taken place amid pressure of other matters, several discrepancies and variations have been overlooked, for which I must ask my readers' indulgence.

* This does not of course apply to Arabic names of objects, phrases, etc., which are transliterated strictly.

In this volume ʽaïn is represented throughout by ʽ instead of â, and I have discarded "ee" and "oo" almost altogether, in favour of î, ï, or û, retaining the former only in words of one and two syllables when the accent falls upon it, for the convenience of ordinary English readers; the final yá (î) of adjectives derived from names is also modified to i. The final h is usually omitted from feminine proper names (students will remember that it always follows an unaccented a, becoming t for euphony when the following word begins with a vowel). The accent ʹ denoting the initial álîf or "vowel prop" is omitted when the initial vowel is a capital. The dots which distinguish consonants unknown in English (ḍ, ḥ, ḳ, ṣ, and ṭ), the tie-dash beneath letters which can only be approximately rendered by two characters in English (dh, gh, kh); and the sign ʹ (representing the hamzah), necessary to enable students to identify the words, can always be omitted in popular use; but it is strongly recommended that, with the exception mentioned, the accent be always retained, as on it so much depends. The standard is throughout the local spelling (and therefore pronunciation) of the educated classes, to obtain which special pains have been taken.

It is the hope, therefore, of the writer, who has made large concessions in this matter to the views of others, that he has not expended this labour for his own works alone, but that he has provided a standard of spelling which will be adopted by future writers. It may be added that these renderings are in accordance with the principles adopted by the Royal Geographical Society, the Foreign, India, Colonial, and War Offices, the Admiralty, and the Government of the United States, all of which will here find their authority for Moorish names.

(An index of place names is appended to *The Land of the Moors*, and a glossary of common words to the present volume.)

Every letter is pronounced: Consonants as in English, single vowels as in Italian.

a ´ niṣbah, short open sound, as "a" in "can," sometimes "ŭ" as in "but."

á, ا álif with niṣbah, longer open sound, as "a" in "far."

à, ى limálah, or álif maksoorah, as final "a" in "papa" (always final).

b, ب bá, as in English.

d, د dál, ,, ,,

dh, ذ dhál, ,, ,,

ḍ,* ض ḍád, strongly articulated palatal "d."

dh,* ظ dhá, thick "dh," something like "th" in "thee."

e, ´or ˍ niṣbah or khafḍah, short English "e."

ee, ـِيـ yá with khafḍah, as in English.

f, ف fá, as in English.

g, گ gáf, ,, ,, hard.

g, ج jeem, ,, ,, ,, (g).

gh,* غ ghaïn, deep guttural.

h, ه há, as in English.

ḥá, ح ḥá, ,, ,, like "hh."

i, ˍ khafḍah, as in English.

í, ا álif with khafḍah, like the first "i" in "India."

î or ï, ي yá, as in English.

j, ج jeem, ,, ,,

k, ك káf, ,, ,,

ḳ, ق ḳáf, peculiar hard "k" low in the throat, as "ck" in "kick."

kh,* خ khá, rough guttural sound as in Scotch "loch."

l, ل lám, as in English.

m, م meem, ,, ,,

n, ن noon, ,, ,,

ŋ, ً or ٍ (doubled final short vowels) ,, ,,

o, ُ rofâh, ,, ,,

ô, و waû, ,, ,,

oo, وُ ,, with rofâh, as in English.

r, ر rá, as in English.

s, س seen, ,, ,,

ṣ,* ص ṣád, ,, ,, hard, like ss.

sh, ش sheen, ,, ,,

t, ت tá, ,, ,,

ṭ,* ط ṭá, short palatal "t."

th, ث thá, as in English "three," but rather more of the "t" sound.

u, ُ rofâh, as in English.

ú, ا álif with rofâh, as in English "up."

û, و waû, Continental "u" sound, as in "pull."

w, و waû, as in English.

y, ي yá, ,, ,,

z, ز zaïn, ,, ,,

ʾ* ع ʾaïn, guttural, far back in the mouth, as in the "baa" of a sheep.

ء hamzah, showing that the preceding vowel is cut off short, and a slight pause made.

ʾ shows that a letter is elided in the pronunciation, generally "a" in ordinary conversation. In past participles it is generally "u" which is elided.

· is placed between two letters which *might* be sounded as one, to separate them.

* The correct pronunciation of these letters is only to be acquired from a native: the nearest possible English rendering being given, no difficulty will be experienced in connecting them with their Arabic equivalents.

NAMES OF PLACES

For	A'sfî	Saffi.
„	El 'Araish . . .	Laraiche.
„	Fás	Fez.
„	Ḥajrat N'kûr . . .	Alhucemas.
„	Jazaïr Zafrán . . .	Zaffarines.
„	Melilîyah	Melilla.
„	Miknás	Mequinez.
„	Rîbaṭ	Rabat.
„	Sibtá	Ceuta.
„	Slá	Salli.
„	Ṭanjah	Tangier.
„	Tettáwan	Tetuan.

COMMON WORDS

For	A'l or él	El.
„	A'llah	Allah.
„	'Aráb	Arab.
„	Banî	Beni.
„	Ḳáïd	Kaid.
„	Muḥammad (or Moḥammed) .	Mohammed.
„	Mûlâï	Mulai.
„	Seedî (more correctly Seyyidî) .	Sidi.
„	Sulṭán	Sultan.

TRANSLITERATION OF HEBREW WORDS

A	א	K	כ	P	פ	Ṭ	ט
B	ב	Ḳ	ק	R	ר	W	ו
D	ד	Kh	ך	S	ס	Y	י
F	ף	L	ל	S	שׂ	Z	ז
G	ג	M	מ	Ṣ	צ ץ	'	ע
H	ה		ם	Sh	שׁ		
Ḥ	ח	N	נ ן	T	ת		

THE MOORS

CONTENTS

PART I.—SOCIAL

PART II.—ETHICAL

PART III.—SUPPLEMENTARY

LIST OF ILLUSTRATIONS

THE MOORS

INTRODUCTION

"The poor misguided Moor that raised my childish fears."
HOOD.

STRANGE as it may seem, this familiar word "Moor" is unknown in Morocco itself save to Europeans, and cannot even be said to be derived from the name of the land which the Moors inhabit. From early times we read in the classics of *Mauri*,* North African tribes who were probably Berbers, from whom the North Western districts came to be called by the Romans Mauretania, just as the name of the *Ifrikis*, a Tunisian tribe, the nearest to Rome, had been given to the central portion of that coast, and ere long was applied right and left, until the Continent of Africa became indebted to them for its appellation.

The Word "Moor."

As we use it, the word "Moor" is loosely applied to any native of Morocco, but in its stricter sense only to the townsman of mixed descent. The aboriginal inhabitants, as far as we can trace them, are the Berbers, common to all the North African countries, who have lent their name to Barbary

* Cf. Hebrew and Phœnician *mahur*, western; and Greek μαυρός (*mauros*) dark.

(Spanish, *Berbería*), which includes the Empire of Morocco, the French possession of Algeria—erstwhile a dependency of Turkey, the French-"protected" Turkish beylik of Tunis, and the Turkish province of Tripoli. Of these, the Moorish Empire alone has throughout retained its independence, and even made itself for several centuries a Power feared in Europe. This distinction is due to the predominance among its people of Berber blood.

The majority of the Berbers still inhabit the mountains, retaining customs and speaking a language more or less common to all of their race, but altogether distinct from those of the plains, where the Arabs roam. These Arabs are not, as some have supposed, descendants of conquering hordes from the East, but are peaceful nomads who for many centuries have wandered on till in this *cul de sac* they have accumulated, face to face with the Atlantic. Nor were they the hosts who ruled in Spain, for those were Berbers with an Arab creed and code, who adopted Arabic names, and whose leaders were often genuine Arabs. The descendants of that mixed race are the Moors of to-day.

Berbers.

The pure Morocco Arab still lives in his tent on the plains, and has few wants unknown to his ancestors. His gun and its accessories, his tea, his sugar, his candles, with a few foreign textiles and nick-nacks, sum up the innovations with the exception of which he lives the life of Abraham, Isaac and Jacob.

Arabs.

There is a large mixed agricultural population, partly Berber diluted with Arab, partly Arab diluted with Berber, generally belonging to tribes retaining the name of their original stock or home, and especially proud of the former. It has long been the practice of Moorish sultans to transport whole tribes or families to distant provinces for misbehaviour, and though

Moors.

hundreds of years may have passed since the change, so strong is their clannish pride that they continue to use their original name. Even in some of the tribes where the Berber element predominates, daily exigencies and the introduction of Arab wives have made Arabic the common tongue, though many will send, as the patriarchs sent, to the distant home-land for wives for their sons. These are known in northern Morocco as Hillsmen *(Jibálà)*, since they usually dwell upon the lower hill-sides, and the ranges separated from the Atlas, where the true Berbers live. Like the mixed races which people the towns, these are also sometimes distinguished by Europeans from the pure Berber or Arab as "Moors," otherwise a term of very general application.

The Moors a White Race.

One popular misconception must always be met when treating of Moors. A strange idea pervades the English mind that they are black, and the old-time expression "Black-a-Moor," to say nothing of Shakespeare's erroneous description of "The Moor of Venice"—who was evidently no Moor at all, but a Negro—assists in its perpetuation.* Both Berbers and Arabs are white like ourselves, though often sunburnt and bronzed for generations, and both their children and those who have lived in the cities might pass anywhere as Europeans. The mulattoes and octoroons are of course no more typical Moors than typical Yankees, though doubtless sometimes taken by strangers as such. No one could mistake the negroes, imported from Guinea or bred in the country, for their white masters.

* Shakespeare, however, only endorsed a popular misconception of his times, and Marlowe also speaks of Moors as "coal-black." Juvenal, too, long before had written "Mauri celeres et Mauro obscurior Indus."[1]

[1] *Satire* xi., l. 125.

There is still one race in Morocco deserving of notice, though not to be classed with the Moors, the oppressed yet progressive Jews. Everywhere they play a leading part, observable or not, and everywhere they are despised and hated. On the coast their principal language is Spanish, as they are there in great measure descendants of those expelled from Spain, but among the Atlas Berbers, a peculiar, broken Arabic and Shilḥah—as the local Berber dialect is called—are their tongues. Restricted to special costumes of black or dark hues, they are conspicuous in every crowd, and as they hold the reins of commerce they are indispensable.

Jews.

Chiefly in the coast towns there reside between six and seven thousand Europeans, of whom over five thousand are Spanish colonists in Tangier.* The pursuit of wealth engrosses the majority, but the officials of foreign Powers form a conspicuous proportion.

Morocco is not a land of statistics, and any attempt to estimate the numbers of these various races, or their total, can be little more than guess-work. It must therefore suffice to quote the figures calculated by a few of the leading writers, and leave the reader to form an average for himself.

Population.

Jackson,	15 millions.	Lanoye,	6 to 7 millions.
Bonelli,	10 ,,	Hellwald,	6½ ,,
Urrestarazu,	9½ ,,	Chenier, copied by Lemprière,	6 ,,
Réclus,	8 to 9 ,,	Olivié,	5½ ,,
Gråberg,	8½ ,,	Klöden.	2 ,,
Cervera, copied by Calderon,	8¼ ,,		

* The census of 1901 showed the British subjects in Tangier, including visitors in hired houses, but not those in hotels, to number 750, and

There are only three inland cities properly so-called, Fez with perhaps 150,000, Marrákesh with perhaps 50 to 60,000, and Mequinez with perhaps the same or less, but these too are guesses, although in the case of towns there are more data.

Capitals.

With these exceptions the only great centres of population are on the coast, namely, to enumerate them from East to West:—

Ports.

	Estimated Population.
Tetuan	25,000 (?)
Tangier	30,000
Laraiche	7,000
Salli	20,000
Rabat	30,000
Dár el Baïda	20,000
Mazagan	10,000 (?)
Saffi	15,000 (?)
Mogador	25,000 (?)

In these cases their smaller size and greater familiarity to Europeans render the estimates more reliable, but doubtless they are yet far from the mark. In most of them the Jews alone number a fifth or a fourth of the total.

The only other important towns are Tarudant, capital of the rich Sûs province; Oojda on the Algerian frontier; Táza, mid-way between that and Fez; Shefsháwan, south of Tetuan, forbidden to Europeans; El Ḳaṣar, half way between Tangier and Fez; Wazzán, south of El Ḳaṣar; Mulai Idrees on Zarhôn, near Mequinez, holiest and most unapproachable in the Empire; and Damnát, up in the hills to the East of Marrákesh.

Inland Towns.

those resident elsewhere in Morocco 375, total 1125, the majority being Gibraltarian, but including a few Maltese. The number of Spaniards in Tangier on the books of their consulate is 3300, but the total colony is estimated at over 5000, and it has been higher.

The remaining towns are only of local importance, though judged from our standpoint their fame and influence are often quite out of proportion to their population. Some are government centres; some, from the possession of a saint's shrine, form the attraction for thousands of pilgrims, while others have a name for, or are the marts of, some crop or manufacture of repute. In many instances, however, a name which looks important on the map, or which is heard in everybody's mouth in the country, turns out on being visited to be not that of a town at all, but of a district with a rambling group of dwellings round a fortress as the central feature.*

Minor Towns.

Excepting in the vicinity of these towns, and in certain mountain districts where the villages cluster on every hill-side, the population is extremely sparse, though for the most part spread out wherever the soil is good, in consequence of the allotment of the land to tribes, each of which endeavours to make the best of its own possession. Few vast districts remain for Arabs to roam in, and north of the Atlas there are no deserts, but the villages are often far apart, and cultivated areas are separated by wide stretches of pasture or brush-wood. Morocco could, indeed, support several times its present population, were an enlightened government to encourage the development of its natural resources, and to assure justice to its subjects.

Population Distributed.

The native name for Morocco is المغرب الاقصى† El Maghrib el Aḳṣà,—"The Furthest West" or "Sun-set,"—a name imported by the Arabs, since the land seems to have been nameless as a whole when they came.

* As Tafîlált, Tádla, Tifnût.

† Written from right to left; the ḳáf being dotted in accordance with local custom, not as in the East. See chapter xviii.

In the country itself El Maghrib—"The West"—is considered sufficient, but in the Orient the whole of Barbary is apt to be so designated, hence the need for a distinctive epithet. Tripoli is then distinguished as Trablûṣ el Gharb, and Tunis and Algeria as El Gharb or El Maghrib el Jawáni or—"The Nearer West;"—Algeria, when distinguished from Tunis (pronounced Toonas), retaining its name of El Jazaïr—"The Islands,"—of which its modern name is a corruption.

The Word "Morocco."

Our English word "Morocco" is curiously descended from the name of the southern metropolis, Marrákesh, through the Spanish corruption "Marruecos," their present name for the whole country. As the Andalucian Spaniards almost drop their final "s" in conversation, we, having learned it from them, have made of it "Marocco" and "Morocco,"* while the French have still further clipped it to "Le Maroc," and other nations have only borrowed the English with varied spelling. The first "o" in our popular form is apparently due to a hazy idea that the word "Moor"—in French "Maure," in Spanish "Moro"—was in some way derived therefrom, a sort of attempted reconstruction not unknown in other literary lines.

"Moros" or "Moor-men."

The wide-spread use of this word "Moor" is likewise due to the Spaniards, to whom all Orientals were "Moros," since the true possessors of the name were the only ones they really knew. So it was with the Portuguese, the two nations carrying the misnomer with them round the Cape to western India, to Ceylon and the Malay Peninsula, where a hideous

* Unsuccessful attempts were made some years ago to establish the former spelling, as one letter nearer to the original, but it would be idle to attempt the correction of a single vowel without restoring the termination, especially as the word, if rightly spelled—Marrákesh or Marrákusha, applies to the city of that name only, not to the country.

English translation, "Moor-men," still survives as the designation of the local Mohammedans, in reality descended from Arabian colonists. A parallel is found in the description of North American tribes as "Indians." It is probably from some confusion such as this that the "Black-a-Moor" misconception arises.

FEZ DISH.
(Blue, on white ground.)

PART I—SOCIAL

ON A MOORISH MARKET.

(Outside the Walls of Dár el Baida.)

CHAPTER THE FIRST

"THE MADDING CROWD"

IT lacks but half an hour to noon: high noon of a Morocco May. It is warm, as one might expect from the time of year, but not unpleasantly so, and the bright streaming light which pervades the scene, with all its colours and contrasts, serves to lessen the heat, in fancy at least. Were the costumes around us of sombre hue, or were the sky filled with cloud, how truly hot it would seem! Yet here, beneath this wayside fig-tree, we can almost discover a breeze. There is room for it, too, on this open space outside the Thursday Gate* of Marrákesh, on the day after which it is named, when the famous market is held.

A Morocco Market.

From early morning country-folk have gathered here from all the districts round, bringing in produce and live-stock for sale. Many a weary mile have some of them trudged, since long before dawn, women as well as men bowed down beneath burdens more suited to quadrupeds. Some have even arrived over-night, and spent it rolled in their woollen tunics, white or brown, like so many chrysalides, notwithstanding a belated spatter of rain that had overstepped the wet season. Perhaps that is why the morning seems fresh, and bargaining brisk, as it certainly is, but it requires much heat to turn a Moorish appetite for trade.

* Báb el Khamees.

So here, too, are some hundreds of townsmen on business bent, though going about it as no European ever would, except in the sunny South. Between them arises a deafening din, loud vociferation interspersed with high-pitched feminine calls and expostulation, in rivalry with which donkeys bray, dogs bark, and horses maintain a lively discussion. Any chance there might be of momentary interval or lull is done away with by the lusty salesmen who perambulate to advertise their wares or publish the latest bid, and shout or sing according to taste, while the peripatetic water-seller jingles his bell and hoarsely exclaims, "'Lîkhaṣṣ-hu 'l má'! 'lîkhaṣṣ-hu 'l má'!—for him who wants water! for him who wants water!" as though his life depended on it; or if he has had his skin-full paid for to be given as alms, he cries: "Sabeel Allah! Sabeel Allah! Măï! Măï! Măï: bi la shaï! A'shráboo' ya'l 'aṭshá-neen—The way of God! The way of God! Water! Water! Water without price! Drink, ye thirsty!" And indeed one would almost like to drink, did one not know whence came the water, for the dust is rising, and the air grows parched as noon draws near.

The Din of it all.

Overhead the deep blue firmament is cloudless, and yonder rises the Atlas, snow-clad. Against the background of the city walls, red, crenellated, crumbling, everything seems silhouetted, for the crowd is mostly clad in soft wool-white, so that the few in black or brown or colour show up clearly. Pointed hoods, broad hats, red caps, blue head-kerchiefs and turbans intermingled, ever moving, like a sea of full-grown locusts, give an air of bustle to the scene, such as one hardly looks for in the sleepy East. One scarcely knows where to commence its description.

Its Colours.

As to massing and grouping, the artist must be consulted, detailed figures and their actions alone come within

A FEAST DAY IN SAFFI.

Photograph by Edward Lee, Esq.

the scope of the pen, as one by one they detach themselves from that busy throng, it may be only for a "kodak shot." From all parts of the Empire representatives are here, white, bronzed and black; of Berber, Arab, Negro, Jewish, stock, but

Constituents.

INTERESTED IN THE FOREIGNER.

Photograph by Herbert White, Esq.

never a Nazarene. There are indeed a few inside the walls, engaged in preaching the Gospel or courting trade —a mere handful, all told,—but so seldom to be met with here that the crowd before us is entirely, typically, native.

The ever-changing scene is a kaleidoscope of Eastern fancy: 'Ali Bábá and the forty thieves, Blue-beard,

Aladdin and the Grand Vizier—all in succession pass before us. Possibly, too, under that all-concealing blanket is some fair Sháharah-zádeh—if you can pronounce her name, but do not try to, for in Morocco jealous guardians are not to be trifled with – and who knows but that Al Rasheed and Shah-zenán and Shah-riár are not among the surging crowd? At all events their slaves are here, great, fat, important-looking eunuchs, hard-worked porters, all as black as Africa can make them, but right in heart, and thoroughly good-natured. See, here is one of their race who has obtained his freedom or been born to it, dressed as any Moor might be, in flowing gauze-like robes of rain-bow hues. No other can this be than that Othello whom fair Desdemona won, who, having told a traveller's tale, found little difficulty in extending it to make himself a Moor, a lie that lives.

The Negro Element.

But others take us further back, for with his string of camels here comes Eliezer of Damascus, and behind him Isaac, seated on his ample mule, a barrel-bodied beast that seems to know the weighty character he bears. Surely no more graceful or picturesque costume was ever invented than Isaac wears. Beneath a semi-transparent toga of wool, glimpses of luscious hues are caught, crimson and purple, deep greens and orange—"sun-of-the-afternoon-tint" they call it,—salmons, and pale, clear blues. Although it is warm, his costume is hardly thin, for over his shoulders is loosely thrown a dark blue selhám or cloak of one piece. His turban is of goodly proportions and glistening white; his slippers are bright lemon yellow.

The Well-to-do.

Side by side with this picture of comfort stands a tattered negro who has had his eyes put out for robbery, a punishment now fortunately rare. His sightless sockets turn appealingly to this and that one as they hasten by, his footsteps guided by a little child. Most are importuned in vain, but here and there one gives, for the Moors believe in alms as steps to Paradise, and no excuse or refusal is taken unless couched in the phrase "Yajeeb Allah! May God bring it!"—from which the beggar infers that the speaker at least will give nothing.

The Ne'er-do-well.

"Ah Mulái Idrees! Ah ḥalawát!—Oh my lord Idrees, O sweets!—Ah ḥalawa-á-a-t!"—It is the voice of an itinerating sweet-seller, whose laden tray of stickiness is hardly freed from hovering swarms of flies by his busy swish, ever and anon descending right or left upon some shaven pate beneath which eyes look longingly, and feet suspiciously approach.

The Sweet-seller.

Yonder stalwart form, contrasting strangely with the lighter hues around him, in a thick, stiff robe of goat-hair, fringed, shaped like to an extinguisher, with tasselled hood to match; jet black except an assegai-shaped patch across the back about the level of the knees—the patch bright-yellow with designs in red or black,—that form is an Atlas Berber, a Shlûḥ. He represents the original Moor: no mixed blood in him, but a pride of independence dearly bought, and still to some degree maintained. He might be Mephistopheles, to see him stalking there, his bare and bony shanks beneath that curious robe, thrust into leather bags now brown, that once were heel-less yellow slippers. One arm alone is visible, the right, which, holding back the corresponding cloak-flap, is employed in violent gesticulation, for its owner would purchase a mule at half the price asked, and is stoutly swearing that its complicated ailments and defects reduce its value to far less than he is offering. A crumpled, unwashed, cotton bell-sleeve flutters loosely in the breeze,

The Mountaineer.

2

and the garment to which it belongs is seen to be girt at the waist by a leather belt.

A Mule Sale.

Meanwhile a lusty auctioneer endeavours to persuade him to bid for another. Up and down a narrow space amid the crowd he is pacing a distracted bare-backed beast, whose head is held back by a cruel bit forcing open its foaming jaws; its flanks made gory by the use of a single-point spur. Hear him cry-

HORSE AND MULE MARKET OUTSIDE MARRÁKESH.
(The tent is that of the Revenue Officer.)
Photograph by Dr. Rudduck.

ing the bids. "Wa meeátaïn wa khamseen, thláthá—and two hundred and fifty-three!" Surely this is famine price, but it will rise, for Morocco auctioneers know well the gain of beginning low, where time is no object. The bids are in metkals or ducats, worth about three-pence, and rise by fives, for there is no hurry, though the sun be high. Presently they cease, and the auction-eer, dismounting, throws the end of the halter into the hands of the highest bidder, proceeding to parade another animal. But the sale is far from complete, for the apparent purchaser has only gained the right to drive a private bargain with the seller, who, retaining the right to refuse the bid, invariably does so, and stands out for better terms. These having at last been fixed, a visit is paid to the so-called "vet," more properly the farrier, who, for a consideration, discovers faults, each of which is an excuse for claiming a reduction in price, while the vendor claims as his right "ḥaḳḳ Allah" or "God's due" in addition to what he has agreed to take. When at last the transaction is ended, the necessary documents exchanged, and the market dues paid—after further haggling—it is already past noon, and feeling hungry, we turn to the town.

Method of Auction.

This, however, is more easily said than done, as we laboriously thread our way through the surging mass, in which each individual behaves as though only his or her business were of the slightest importance, jostling, vociferating, gesticulating and cursing. But in the noise they make the women excel the men. The young and good-looking wrapped in their blankets, so that only the eyes—perhaps one alone—can be seen, the old and faded with a mere pretence at concealing their features—the coquettish letting a corner fall from time to time "by accident,"—they move about like animated sacks, or squatting on the ground beside their wares, drive bargains with the best. Here is a group surrounded by panniers of charcoal, hard by are others with bundles of wood and grass which they cannot lift unaided, but which they have brought in on their shoulders. Others have before them vegetables, pottery, or home-spun and ready-made garments.

The Women.

"How much? Why, ten metkáls, and cheap at that!"

"Ten metkáls? Art mad? Everywhere else it is sold for five! But I'll give thee six; never mind."

"Never mind! I like that. Clear out! I'll take nine and a half or nothing."

A Bargain.

"Yes, and thou'dst like to, no doubt. Thou old miser! Think thyself lucky if thou canst get six and a quarter; it's all I'll give."

"Then what dost thou want with me? Thou knowest it cost me nine, may God curse the liar!"

"God burn thy father! It cost thee five!"

"Well, what if it did? My last price is nine and a quarter."

"Then get it! In peace!"

Turning on his heel, the possible purchaser directs his attention to the wares of a rival trader, adding as a parting fling: "Six and a half is all I possess!"

He has scarcely commenced a similar process there, when he hears himself re-called, but hardly deigns to return.

"Hi, Uncle Pilgrim!"

"Yes, my Mother! Well?"

"Look here, take it for eight and three-quarters: I don't mind losing a little by so good-looking a man. Say nine less a fourth?"

"Pooh! That's all rubbish. Thou'dst be glad to get seven, but I'll make it six and three-quarters; come now, thou'dst not be hard!"

"Hard? I should think not, when I make a sacrifice to gratify a fancy. Now—prayers be on the Prophet—acknowledge that thou art prepared to give eight!"

"Not for a moment: seven's the highest price I could dream of."

"Well, if thou wilt not, thou wilt not: so be it." Thus the matter drops, both sides requiring the relief of an armistice wherein to take breath, during which their thoughts apparently wander with their tongues to other things, as each engages in conversation with some one else. After a while the customer remembers it is time to move on, and as he turns to go asks languidly, "Give it me for seven and a half? I can't be bothered bargaining longer."

"No, eight less a quarter is the furthest I can go."

"All right then; I'm off."

So, seeing that he really is off this time, the old woman exclaims in despair, "Where's thy money? Take it and leave me to starve!"

"At seven and a half?"

"No, seven and three-quarters."

"Seven and a half was all I bid."

"Then pay it and begone!"

Some Moorish Types.

But articles in common use, of which there are many sellers, fall to what is practically a fixed price, so that it is only with some object out of the usual size or run that the Moor's love of cheapening can be indulged to the full. The purchaser we have been watching was a stalwart plainsman from the central provinces, Dukálla, maybe, or Rahámna, Shaweea or Ḥaḥá: known by his coarse white ḥaik or blanket, loosely wrapped about him, draping freely, and his slovenly turban, also once white, beneath which his bronzed cheeks and limbs tell of an out-door life. In contrast to him stands close by a native of the valley of the Dra'a, across the Atlas to the south, a short, thick-set mulatto with a rag for turban and a tattered cloak of undyed brown,—quite different in race, a mixture between the Berber and Negro,—representing an important province. With him is engaged in deep conversation a neighbour from Sûs, the province which includes the southern spurs of the Atlas, a fair-skinned Berber, also in white, a cotton shirt with a red leather satchel, and a camel-hair cord round his shaven skull; short like the Dra'wi, but keen-eyed and active, sharp in trade and clever in craft. He and his friend are talking in Berber,—Tamazeeght they call it—a curious-sounding, guttural, sibilant medley, the real language of Morocco, though its dialects vary considerably from province to province.

A Jewish Group.

Under a tree in the shade, as we pass along, sit a group of Jews, sombrely clad in black or blue cloth robes or dark woollen cloaks like some of the Moors, but not for a moment to be confounded with them, even apart from their greasy black skull-caps and slippers, or the kerchiefs of white-spotted blue which most have tied over their heads. Their features, their peculiar pronunciation, their cringing behaviour, all stamp them as down-trodden Hebrews, able though they be to out-wit their oppressors in money matters. Here they are among the principal traders: yonder grey-beards in shabby garb, seated on unloaded panniers, are among the leading merchants of the place, who for a sufficient percentage will advance you any sum you may have reasonable hopes of returning. Those others, in Berber cloaks like that worn by the buyer of the mule, but with great tufts of curly hair below each temple, come from the Atlas, where each one is tributary to a Berber under whose protection he lives, and without whose permission he dare not travel.

A Trading Encampment.

Many others we might stop to notice, had we time; in most cases we might tell the province, if not the town, whence they came, by their dress or their features. So we pass on rapidly, and merely spare a glance for the pottery sellers with their primitive, elegant wares displayed round their extemporized tents; then at the dealers in spices, with more elaborate shelters, and a multitude of trays and boxes spread out before them, containing not only the seeds and roots used in cooking, but also those sold as drugs, the gums for incense, the tea and sugar, the scents, and the poisons so convenient to jealous wives. For a penny we may buy corrosive sublimate or arsenic enough to put an end to the household—just a little in their tea! Fruit there is too, oranges piled up in abundance, and apricots just coming in, sold in cane-work crates.

The Slaughter Field.

Less inviting is the butcher's quarter,[1] where are hanging carcasses galore on tripods of branches, the soil beneath so saturated that when a breeze blows our way after rain the odour is unbearable. So on we hasten to the city gates, where the crush grows greater, the noises are louder, the stenches are stronger, and the crowded colours seem brighter, as seething masses pour in and out amid herds of cattle and droves of sheep, here making way for some important-looking dignitary, there anathematising a careless slave on the tail of a bare-backed mule, lashing it with the halter and making his way through with a clatter and cry of "*Bál*-ak! bál-ak!! bál-*ak!!!—Mind* out! mind out!! mind *out!!!*"

[1] See p. 93.

A CITY GATE, RABAT.

CHAPTER THE SECOND

WITHIN THE GATES

LIKE the portals of their houses, the Moors build their city gates with a double turn, presumably in this case to prevent the inrush of enemies, by causing them to lose their impetus.* So even in time of peace there is always a crush at the main city gates, the sides of which are torn and worn by the continuous stream of loaded animals. In the crenellated mud-built walls most typical of Moorish towns, deep-red or brown, or in the white-washed, stone-built walls of the coast, the frowning gateway is the one relieving feature, which imparts an air of majesty to what would otherwise be gloomy and uninteresting. Frequently surmounted by a battery, or ornamented by stone-work or tiles, the effect is good in the rudest examples, and here before us is one of the best. Cautiously stepping amid the throng, we follow the passage, first to one side and then to the other, till we emerge in the wider thoroughfare beyond, wide, that is, for Morocco, where, as in most Oriental countries, streets are only arranged for pedestrians, and where even beasts of burden may block the way. In the gate itself is often an alcove, occupied by an authority administering justice, or it may form the office of the tax-collectors.

The City Gate.

* The Chinese similarly erect short blank walls opposite entrances, the object in view being then the exclusion of evil spirits, who, unlike those of the West, are understood to be unable to proceed except in a straight line.

The street in which we find ourselves is cobble-paved, if paved at all, with disused mill-stones down the centre covering the sewer.* At night it needs some local knowledge and care to pick one's way

Streets.

A CITY GATE.
(Marshán Gate of Tangier Citadel.)
Molinari, Photo., Tangier.

about, for the streets are unlighted, and wayfarers or their servants who need light must carry their own,

* As in some of the older streets of Prague.

huge lanterns generally furnished with candles. The street is lined on either side by cupboard-like shops, the floors of which are raised above the ground waist high, the fronts being made to open horizontally in two flaps, one hanging down to the ground with the step affixed, the other propped up to form a sun-shade, from which are often suspended articles for sale. These also line the sides and all but cover the floor, in the centre of which squats the owner, demure and reserved, not seldom asleep, as he composes himself comfortably on his wares. When a customer appears he will be wide awake enough, if there is business to be done, though he may still abstractedly mumble his rosary prayers, as he defends himself against attempts to bargain. To stop and investigate these dark recesses one by one would take weeks: to do so we must seat ourselves on the ledge in front left bare for customers, our feet dangling over the street, and take our time, for nothing is to be done here in a hurry, and the cheapening we heard on the market goes on also in the shops.

The Shops.

As we pass through the city we find that most of the trades have sections to themselves. Just now we were in Grocers' Street, surely this is that of the drapers, and yonder are the silk-plaiters. A deafening din of hammering announces that we are approaching the haunt of the copper-smiths, and round the corner are the shoeing-smiths. For silver-smiths and tin-smiths we must visit the filthy melláḥ, or Jewry. Here, however, are the carpenters, hacking away with hoe-like tools for all sorts of operations, and close by the turners employ toes as well as fingers, spinning the object in hand between two fixed points with a bow drawn back and forth. For apprentices they have mere children, bright lads, though, and full of promise of which their fortune is not likely to permit the fulfilment.

Trade Centres.

In an adjoining street the weavers sit at their primitive looms, in which the shuttles are thrown to and fro by hand, while beside them lads reel off the hand-spun threads and fill the spools. Just beyond is the street of the dyers, everything in it splashed with colour, great vats steaming, skins and cloth hung out to dry, and a matted, vine-clad trellis overhead to ward off the sun. Many of the busy streets

Weavers and Dyers.

STREET OF THE DYERS, MARRÁKESH.

Photograph by Dr. Rudduck.

are thus protected, to the great comfort of passers-by who elsewhere are exposed all day to the sun.

Next we light upon the felt-maker, boys combing wool into small square pads which, skilfully laid on one another and soaked with lather, become one piece, some in flat sheets for saddle-cloths and praying rugs; some in moulds for caps, which will be calendered with burrs from bushes outside the walls. Saddlers working in red leather and cloth, shoe-

Wool and Leather Workers.

makers beating out yellow leather on stones, satchel-makers, belt-makers, all are inspected in turn, not one craft without its special interest and primitive accessories. Then a grateful odour of mint leads us to turn our steps to the cool, well-watered fruit and vegetable market, always a refreshing retreat in Summer. * Down the centre the mint, which the Moors take in tea, is piled up by the donkey-load, fresh and green, in enormous quantities, while other sweet herbs in abundance add to the pleasant fragrance. Coriander, cummin, parsley, marjoram, verbena, celery and sage scent the air in turn, and one lingers over the delicious oranges which are too tempting to be passed untasted.

Vegetable Market.

Surely this is the place to pause and feast our eyes, too, on the interlacing streams of colour, as they eddy before us, all with a strange unconcern as to time, purchasers and passengers alike sedate in their movements; with an occasional camel, or string of camels, passing through, with long necks swinging from side to side in calm, supercilious observation. The charm of the Arabian Nights is upon us; we have eaten of the lotus, and would fain forget the bustling West. The very Babel of sounds has something subdued and pleasing about it. There is neither scope nor need for shouting such as we heard just now upon the market, though half the people seem to be talking at once, and it is only now and again that a voice rises out of the chorus, some lad who shouts across in not unmusical tones, or the deep bass "bálak" of some "grave and reverend seigneur" or his henchman, as they thread their way with dignity. The sunlight, streaming in patches, tells of the strong glare outside, and renders us more thankful for this pleasant

The Charm of the Streets.

* For an illustration see *The Land of the Moors*, p. 295.

shade, and for the coolness of the freely-sprinkled water. But we must pass on. Though loth to abandon this grateful shelter, we will enter yon handsome portal, so out of repair, for it seems, by the constant going and coming, to be some public building.*

A Fandak or Store.

So it is, a fandaḳ, or public store, with rows of offices and wholesale shops.† Packing-cases from Europe litter the central court-yard, and one wonders how the large ones got here. But see, another is arriving, carried by eight stalwart porters,

A TYPICAL MOORISH GROCER'S SHOP.
Photograph by Herbert White, Esq.

each pair bearing between them a bending pole from which the bulky package is swung by ropes. Poles creaking, men shouting, it is borne in and dumped down, as its bearers "stand easy" and wipe their brows with their sleeves. In the stores around us sales are being effected of woollens and cottons, goods from Manchester

* For an illustration see *The Land of the Moors*, p. 303. † Ditto p. 257.

and Birmingham, from Antwerp and Trieste, all with the leisurely disregard of time which is everywhere noticeable. Tea, sugar, candles, prints, satins, silks, muslins, broadcloth, braids and calicoes; tea-pots, tea-glasses and tea-urns—all of styles unknown in England although often manufactured there, the last-named being the Russian samovar;—knives, looking-glasses, locks, nails, screws and trinkets; a varied, if not an extensive, assortment; all are here, and represent the chief imports from Europe.

The Upper Floor.

Reached by a dirty and broken-down staircase, a sort of verandah surrounds the court-yard, serving as a passage for the upper storey. Here we find a better class of stores, where greater quiet reigns, but few save the important dealers require more than one small store for their modest display, though they have warehouses elsewhere. Many of these fandaḳs are devoted to some special class of goods, while others are the resort of merchants from some special city. Here, too, Jews have stores and offices, while living in the Jewry, and there was a time when each of the foreign nations trading with Morocco was allotted one of the fandaḳs, in which the merchants resided under their several consuls.

Caraván-saráïs.

The name fandaḳ is, however, applied equally to any caraván-saráï or hostelry, the plan of which is always a series of rooms round a court, "good stabling for man and beast." In the door-way is a little coffee shop, and here we halt for some refreshment, though coffee is not the cup of Morocco, where tea reigns supreme. This man, however, knows how to make it in Arab style, so we are glad to seize the opportunity. Toasting a spoonful of berries over the fire in a ladle, he replaces this by a tiny, long-handled, lidless copper pot, filled with water, and while it boils, he pounds the fragrant coffee which he next puts into the pot. Letting it boil up a second time, he withdraws it, tapping it on the "hob" to settle the grounds, and having let it boil and settle again, he pours it out, a vivifying beverage such as we seldom taste at home.

AN "OLE CLO" SHOP.
(Outside the gate of Tangier.)
Photograph by George Michell, Esq.

The Kaïsarîyah.

In many of the larger towns there is another class of business centre, a ḳaïṣarîyah, or covered mart, surrounded by gateways or bars, and consisting of a somewhat better class of shops in better paved streets, into which beasts of burden are not admitted. These are either the property of the Government or of some mosque, and are fairly well looked after. Those of Marrákesh and Fez are especially fine, and of an afternoon are usually thronged. There sales by auction take place, certain articles on certain days, when the shops are replenished from the stock of home-made goods brought in by country folk. Nowhere throughout the Mohammedan East,—either in Baghdád, Shiráz, Samarkand, Bokhára, Peshávar, Delhi, Agra, Lahore, Haïdarabád, Muscat, Baṣrah, Damascus, Constantinople, Cairo or Tunis,—have I seen more picturesque and animated scenes than may be witnessed day by day in Morocco, and thither should the student of the Orient repair, if he would drink in its spirit.

Sub-divisions.

Once again emerging into the narrow, winding streets of constantly varying width, some paved, some littered with garbage amid which mangy curs are poking hungrily, we notice the gateways here and there which shut off the various quarters and most of the many blind alleys at night, to prevent the perambulation of evil-doers. After dark we should all carry lanterns, and shout for the porter at each of the gates; great men send their servants on ahead to have them all ready. In the residential quarter which we are now approaching the shops grow rare, except for small clusters of the poorer sort here and there, and the blank, resounding walls on either side of the way lend an aspect dismal and gloomy in contrast to what seemed just now so gay.

Residential District.

It is only when these walls are broken by the entrance to some mosque, into the tesselated court of which we surreptitiously peep for a moment and then pass on, or a way-side drinking trough—here called by courtesy a "fountain"—sometimes beautifully decorated, that there is any relief from the window-less, prison-like look of the place. Moorish dwellings are designed for the seclusion of the women, and wherever there is a small window, it is closely barred.

Little decoration is expended outside, save on palace doors. Many of the finest private residences are approached by filthy, dark, serpentine *culs-de-sac*, across which rooms are built at will, excluding light and air, and rendering them really dangerous at night. There is little of the picturesque about the outside of this class of Moorish dwellings.

CHAPTER THE THIRD

WHERE THE MOORS LIVE

"HOME," with all its associations for us, is hardly the word to apply to most eastern dwellings, though no doubt to their inmates—as representing the centre of all they know of family life—they do possess a charm of their own, notwithstanding that no special word may exist which conveys the same meaning.* Home-life, however, does not depend on the form of the dwelling, though some of the features of Moorish houses are the outcome of the peculiar social arrangements of Islám. For instance, the almost universal absence of outside windows, and the double turn of the entrance passage, are for the purpose of secluding the women from public gaze: the division of the larger houses into separate suites—almost independent dwellings—being for similar reasons, as well as to accommodate the various wives of the wealthy. The open central court-yards, the flat roofs and the narrow rooms, are governed by the climate and available materials for building.

Not "Homes."

The typical Moorish house consists of an irregular quadrilateral, on three sides of which run long rooms not more than ten or twelve feet wide, the fourth being occupied by the kitchen, of similar width, but shorter, having the entrance-passage, stairs and insanitary convenience in the corner. The central court thus formed is usually open to the sky, but surrounded

A Typical House.

* The nearest approach to it in Morocco, wakr, is almost exclusively used of the lairs of wild beasts.

by a covered colonnade which supports a second, if there is an upper storey, as is often the case in towns, and a third but seldom. The court is paved with tiles of some artistic merit, unless it is of plaster, red- or white-washed; or in the coast towns, particularly in houses inhabited by Jews, paved with black and white marble;

COURTYARD OF A POOR MAN'S HOUSE IN TETUAN.
Molinari, Photo., Tangier.

or an imitation, in which case the stairs are also white marble, and sometimes the dado, though cheap Spanish tile-work is now used commonly on the coast.

Tile-Work.

In strictly native buildings the dado is of Fez or Tetuan tiles, the difference between the two being that the former are squares cut down to the requisite shapes, while the latter are made of the shapes required, with much less effect. * Cold colours exclusively are used in the tiles, which are each of one colour only, except

* See chapter xi.

in the case of inscriptions, and as the white employed is always more or less tinted, the effect is most agreeable. A fountain often gurgles in the centre, surrounded by orange-trees, or in less pretentious dwellings the inhabitants literally live under their own vine and fig-tree in the yard. The pillars round this are of plaster or marble, in the latter case of foreign importation and workmanship, and support horse-shoe arches, often elegantly scalloped, across which wooden stays are not considered unsightly.

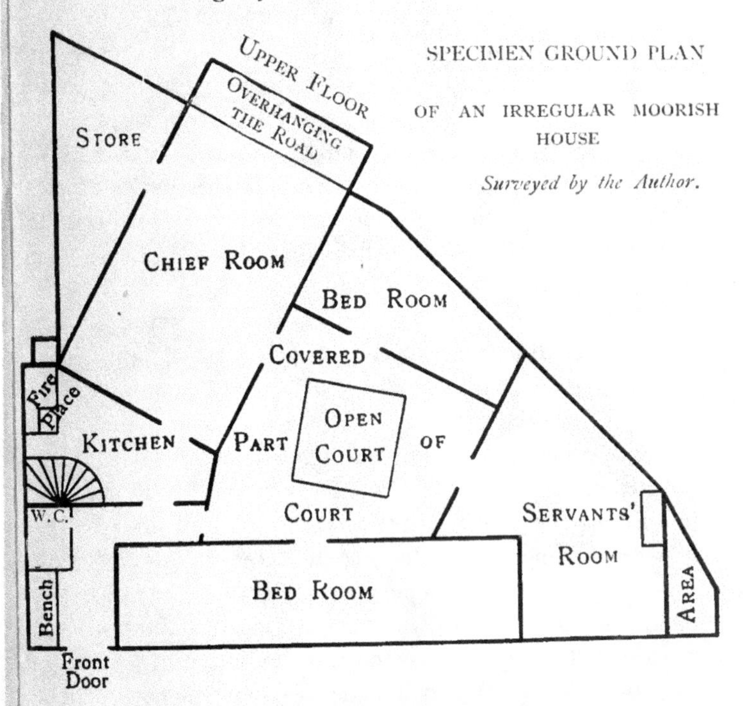

SPECIMEN GROUND PLAN OF AN IRREGULAR MOORISH HOUSE

Surveyed by the Author.

One of the most notable peculiarities of Moorish domestic architecture is the absolute irregularity of the whole. It is not too much to say that except by accident no two lines are ever parallel or horizontal: the shape of the house generally follows the shape of the ground, whatever that may be, the angles of the walls inside reducing the shape of the central court to something approaching a square, but if this be impossible, a second court and surroundings may be introduced to serve as quarters either for the servants or for a favourite wife, or as a suite of guest-chambers with separate entrance, such as is often introduced as a mezzanine floor above the kitchen near the entrance. This is almost invariably an "L" shaped passage, so that no one from without can look into the court, a striking contrast to the Jewish houses, which frequently have a front-door leading directly on to the "patio," generally open during the day.

Irregularity.

Entrance.

The Moorish front-door, most jealously guarded, is a massive-looking construction studded with heads of great nails in rows, and ornamented with a gigantic ring for a knocker.* The lock is in proportion, and the key becomes a formidable weapon on occasion.

When a visitor knocks he hears the patter of bare feet inside, and is presently answered by a piping voice within—probably that of a little slave-girl—"Who's there?" But on learning the name, instead of opening the door, she patters off to inform her master, who, if his guest be of sufficient importance, will most likely come himself to give admission, calling as he does so to his women-folk, "Make way! Make way!" Then, throwing wide the door, he offers his hand with all the customary salutations and greetings, leading the visitor into an apparently deserted dwelling, in which no females except slaves are seen. Crossing the courtyard, they pass up the narrow, steep, tiled stairs with wooded edges to the treads, and so to the principal chamber,—dining-room, drawing-room, bed-

Reception of Visitors.

* For an illustration see ch. xvi.

room and work-room in turn,—over the entrance to which, instead of shutting the huge pair of doors, a cotton sheet is let down as a curtain which must not be approached or lifted till the host has again given notice to the women "Make way!"

HIGH-CLASS INTERIOR, FEZ.
(First-floor gallery round courtyard, showing entrance to a reception-room, with servants' recess on the right.)
Molinari, Photo., Tangier.

Each of the rooms has a single doorway in the centre to match, of height and width sufficient to admit all light required, which is not much in this bright atmosphere, where all walls are white-washed. Additional air, and of course some light, are sometimes admitted by a delicate plaster fret-work over the door-way, and more commonly by narrow, unglazed slits high up on the walls, a foot or a foot and a half by two or three inches, like loopholes widely splayed inside. The doors are huge and two-leaved, often carved and painted in arabesques, and swing clear of the arch on the outside, the hinges being simply the side pieces lengthened top and bottom, and fitted into sockets. Each of the leaves of a large door is provided with a smaller horse-shoe door for use when they are closed. If the rooms are very long, light arches are often thrown across at about a fourth from each end.

Doors and Windows.

Most Moorish rooms are furnished in the same style, varying only according to the owner's fortune. The floor is covered with rush matting or hand-made carpet, or both, which must not be walked upon with shoes, so they are removed at the threshold. When receiving Europeans, Moors, in their politeness, will often entreat them not to remove their boots, and strangers are sometimes ill-advised enough to yield, but do not hear the subsequent remarks, or realize how far attention to the reasonable native prejudice in matters of this kind will go in assisting friendly relations. Round the walls are placed mattresses covered with print or coloured cloth protected by semi-transparent cotton, sometimes embroidered across the ends in silk. These are the only seats provided, and serve also as beds, though frequently there are also big brass bedsteads at either end of the room, more often for show than for use, except that in many homes the tea-things are kept beneath them. Some of the poorer houses have wide wooden shelves across the ends of the room to serve as bedsteads.

Furniture.

The post of honour is the centre of the wall facing

the door-way, the seats right and left ranking next. The host will either seat himself on the end, or if of lower rank, by the door on the carpet. Servants or inferiors admitted and told to be seated, do so on their heels against the wall, in a position of restful balance difficult for Europeans to acquire. Thick round cushions of embroidered leather or cloth, and pillows covered to match the mattresses, are placed about for convenience, often being used across the knees for the elbows to rest upon, and so relieve the back as one sits cross-legged. Nothing else is placed upon the floor but candle-sticks and dining-table, and these only when in use. The walls are usually hung with a dado of rush-mat or cloth (ḥaïṭi), if not tiled, the favourite pattern representing a series of horse-shoe arches. Above this it is the fashion to hang a number of cheap German mirrors and clocks, the latter by preference of the musical variety, set to any odd times. No room is considered well furnished without a pair of "grandfather's" clocks as well, one on either side of the door-way. Undoubtedly the style of furnishing, as well as the etiquette observed, owes most of its features to the tent-life of the Arab, but though as dwellings these moveable homes are therefore the most typical, they must be dealt with separately. *

Seating the Guests.

Walls.

The ceilings, which in the larger houses are very lofty, either show the roughly trimmed boughs which support the successive layers of boards or brushwood—rammed earth and plaster or tiles forming the upper floor or roofs—or are decorated in arabesques with or without boards. In palaces the well-known "stalactite work" of wood is employed, the effect being produced, not by carving great blocks, as would at first appear, but by binding together a number of

Ceilings.

* See chapter ix.

pieces of varying lengths, according to the design, and carving only their points. The colours used in ceiling decoration are invariably warm, and afford a grateful relief to the eyes from the surrounding brightness. The walls above the dado are always left white, though in palaces often covered with incised plaster in geómetrical patterns, called naḳash el ḥadeed. The flat roofs are generally white-washed, and in the case of high buildings surrounded by a protecting wall, as they are the only promenades of the women, and are therefore strictly forbidden to men. If repairs have to be done, it is necessary to notify the police of the quarter and the neighbours, that their women may retire.

Water Supply.

Though called flat, these roofs generally sag in the centre, from which grooves are cut to the edge and fitted with short pipes to throw water clear of the wall into the street or inner court. Rain-water is collected in tanks beneath the courtyards of many houses, a mosquito-haunted, well-like aperture taking the place of a fountain in the centre: many houses also possess wells. Nevertheless, in dry seasons it is often necessary to purchase water for drinking, if not for household purposes, the precious liquid being brought in goat-skins or barrels from wells and springs in the gardens outside, as the Moors rightly attribute great effects to good or bad water, and will sometimes incur considerable expense to secure a satisfactory supply. In the larger towns, the sites of which were chosen with a view to this convenience, the better houses are all furnished with running water, usually admitted first to a raised tank on one side of the court, supplying a fountain in the centre, not a jet such as we understand, but a pleasantly gurgling flow which only rises a few inches.

Drainage.

Drainage in Morocco is about as bad as it could be: no traps are employed, and

TILED "FOUNTAIN" IN A FEZ COURT-YARD.

Photograph by the Rev. E. L. Hamilton.

the conduits are constructed of brick and stone roughly laid, ventilated often by openings to the street. The orifices in the houses are but square holes flush with the ground, on which stones or lids are laid.

Baths.

Only the very large houses have baths of their own, invariably steam-baths (ḥammám), heated by a furnace and cauldron (bormah) below, for there are plenty of very cheap * public baths, which are open from 1 p.m. to sunset for women, and the rest of the time for men, while in the cities there are some exclusively devoted to either sex. On entering, *right* foot first, † exclaiming, "God deliver us from the spirits!" ‡ the bather undresses on one of the raised alcoves (dukkánah) round the lobby, handing valuables to the attendant (gillás), and hanging up his clothes. In this apartment (el bárid) there is often a fountain (hassárah) or tank of cold water, and a supply of pattens (ḳabáḳab) to raise the feet from the heated floor inside, beneath which pass and re-pass the flues of the furnace. Rough stones, (m'ḥaḳḳah) smoothed on one face, are also sometimes provided, wherewith to rub the skin down after the bath.

Steam Bathing.

Wrapping a towel round him, the bather proceeds first to the warm dry room, then to that heated by the steam escaping from the door of the hot room (es-sakhûn) beyond, which he enters after a short pause. This is filled with steam from an open cauldron from which buckets are drawn and tempered with cold water from a tap, wherewith to wash in one of the recesses, the towel having been removed. An

* The general admission fee in Fez, etc. is two mûzûnas (about a Spanish centimo each), or in Tangier five to ten mûzûnas. The rent of a ḥammám for a private party ranges from a peseta to two dollars.

† In Egypt the *left* is put forward.

‡ 'Allah yataḳ-ná min el jinûn."

attendant or friend may give the bather a thorough soap down and a good scrub with halfa grass, after which he is treated to a rude but effectual massage (kibs) with limb-twisting and joint-cracking (tartak), the effect of it all being delightfully refreshing, and far more pleasant than the Turkish hot-air system.*

Public Baths.

But the Moorish public baths are very poor and dirty compared with those of the East, with which I have had an extensive acquaintance, though the best even of these do not compare with those of Europe. Those of Morocco are strictly closed to all but Muslimîn, and my experiences have been gained at some risk in that guise. The scene in the hot rooms, dimly lit by coloured glass "eyes" in the vaulted roof, or by spluttering oil-lamps, is one not to be forgotten; swarthy figures moving slowly through the steamy atmosphere amid the splash of water and the crash of wooden buckets on the pavement, and resounding deadened voices.

Gardens.

Whenever it is possible, a Moorish house has a garden, not an expensive pleasaunce such as the well-to-do like to have outside the town, to which they can ride of an afternoon, or where they can picnic, but a small walled-in enclosure crowded with leafy creepers and shrubs interspersed with masses of hardy flowers, the commonest being geraniums, roses, jessamine, violets, lilies and pinks. Trellis-work covers the tile-paved walk, and water bubbles into an open tank, at times containing fish. Cut flowers and plants in pots are seldom seen in houses, but balsams and sweet herbs are frequently cultivated in cafés.

Moorish kitchens are fitted with low tiled benches with holes for charcoal fires (kanûn), a funnel-shaped

* The Moorish and the Russian baths are on the same principle, but the steam is in the latter case produced by throwing water on the heated stones.

chimney stretching out over the whole. This is supplemented by earthen braziers (mijmár)—more convenient for handling, and therefore in more common use—on which pipkins of stew are left simmering all day long with marvellous results. Otherwise there are no fire-places in a Moorish house.

Kitchens.

A MOORISH GARDEN.
(Kaid of Damnát's.)
Photograph by the late Joseph Thomson, Esq.

The material of which these Moorish houses are constructed is chiefly a sort of mud concrete, tabîa, made by ramming certain stony soils moistened with water only, in a frame-work on the walls. The durability of this material is shown by the condition of the Alhambra at Granáda, which was so constructed centuries ago, and indeed takes its name, which means simply "The Red," from the colour of the earth employed, which is also that of the buildings

Building Materials.

on the Marrákesh plain, locally known from the large admixture of ferruginous ochre, as "Blád el Ḥamarr, The Red Country." Where lime or gypsum can be obtained, these are used to finish the surface, inside at least, or the outside is simply white-washed, if it can be afforded, or left its natural colour, with a little plaster where the water from the roof runs down.

CENTRAL MOROCCO HOMES.

Photograph by Dr. Rudduck.

The peculiar appearance of weather-worn tabîa wall, covered over with what look like pigeon-holes—and often serve as such,—is produced by the falling away of the inferior mud with which the "put-log" holes and those made by the binders of the frame-work are stopped.

Country Dwellings.

Out in the country the style of dwelling varies from province to province, and only the homes of the wealthy or the fort-like residences of the governors—ḳaṣbahs—are at all of the style described, though whenever possible they approach it, at least in furnishing. Throughout the northern portions of the Empire the prevailing country residence, apart from the tent of the nomad, is an oblong, rectangular thatched hut,* while in Central Morocco the shape is more generally that of an English bee-hive, but pointed. † As the mountainous districts are entered, the mud and stone-built dwellings of the Berbers are observed, the roofs of which over-hang, the upper storeys being left as open verandahs. ‡ And in the Atlas itself the war-like tribes inhabit fortress-like erections which must be described when describing that people. §

* Worth about $30 or £5 complete, with two rooms. A single chamber is sometimes set apart as a mosque for about $5.

† For illustrations see *The Moorish Empire*, p. 46, and *The Land of the Moors*, p. 425.

‡ Ib. p. 25.

§ See chapter xxii. and *The Land of the Moors*, p. 384.

MOORISH INDOOR DRESS.

Photograph lent by the Baron Whettnall.

CHAPTER THE FOURTH

HOW THE MOORS DRESS

FEW Oriental costumes are more picturesque or better adapted to the life of those who wear them than the simple garb of the Moors. Of art sartorial it cannot be said there is any display in Morocco, where the skill to be admired consists in the ingenious methods by which that art is dispensed with, and the best effect still secured. A fully dressed Moor of the upper classes is a sight worth seeing, with his flowing garments of abundant white and colour, harmonizing beautifully, and imparting remarkable dignity. First and foremost among the components of his apparel is the lordly k'sá, the most effective and elaborate covering ever worn, although the simplest. Its cream-white, gauze-like texture surmounts the turban and shields the sides of the head from sun and wind, this ample head-piece being perhaps the most effective part of it all: other folds form abundant skirts and liberal sleeves, while the whole is held in place by a silk-striped, long-fringed end which crosses the breast and hangs gracefully down the back. It is surely the survival or descendant of the famous Roman toga. When taken off, this costume, complete in itself, is found to be but a plain piece of hand-woven woollen material, about six and a half yards by one and three-quarters, with a fringe at each end, and a few silk stripes, also white, at one end.

Suitability and Elegance.

To don the k'sa, a right-hand corner is brought over the left shoulder to near the waist, that edge being passed behind the back, under the right arm, across the waist, leaving the lower edge free to fall like a skirt. The upper edge is now brought loosely behind the back and over the head, being so adjusted that the free end nearly reaches the ground in front. The upper part of the section thus left loose behind the back is next plucked forward by the right hand over the left shoulder, and a similar hitch is made beneath the left arm if required. Then the free end is deftly gathered together by the right hand in folds on which the ultimate grace of the garment greatly depends, and the edges forming the head-piece being held in place beneath the chin by the left hand, the free end is thrown over the left shoulder with a slight twist which catches its edges beneath its folds, which are left to drape the figure. The finishing touch consists in loosening the hood-piece at the sides without affecting the edge, and gathering it slightly behind the ears, to finally adjust the part over the turban.

Donning the K'sá.

The Moors do not, like the Algerians and the Arabs, bind their head-dress to their heads, but leave it loose, which greatly adds to their appearance. Women of the better class, however, who in riding wear a selhám as over-all, sometimes do so. Worn without a turban, as by the youth of the wealthy, the k'sá is shorn of half its effect, and without a beard a turban is seldom used, unless, as the native proverb puts it, "from lack of modesty." So much depends upon the ease and grace with which the k'sá is worn, that it is almost always possible to tell those who are "to the manner born" from those who are not, and it was not until I had studied and practised it well in private that I ventured to appear with it in the

Local Peculiarities.

streets, where I was often complimented on the natural way in which I wore it. * Some dandies even study the

MOORISH GENTLEMAN.
(Wearing k'sá and selhám.)
From a photograph by Herr W. Brauer.

effects of its graceful draping on figures of cane, when the results are certainly unsurpassed.

Moorish women, and country-folk of both sexes, em-

* For illustration see *The Land of the Moors*, p. 422.

ploy a similar piece of material of much coarser texture, called a ḥáïk, which the women of the coast wear after the same fashion as the men, with the exception of the final fold: instead of bringing the loose end over the shoulder they double it on itself for about a couple of feet, and bring back the folded edge

The Ḥáïk.

MOORISH LADY IN WALKING COSTUME.

Photograph by the late Joseph Thomson.

across the forehead, where it is stretched just above the eyes, then folded down each cheek with a twist that keeps all in place, like the hood of a nun. Before men the right side fold is held up horizontally beneath the eyes, leaving only an oblong aperture through which to peep, which has to be kept open by finger and thumb at each end. When one hand is needed elsewhere, the aperture assumes a triangular shape, and when both hands are required, the edges are caught in the mouth as best they may be. Thus the face is almost completely hidden, and will continue to be so though occasion may arise for every other part of the body to be uncovered, as when fording a river.

MOORISH LADIES OUT FOR A WALK.
(On the beach at Dar el Baida.)
Photograph by Dr. Rudduck.

Fási Women.

In Fez, however, the women drape their ḥaïks after quite another fashion. One-half of it is doubled along its length, selvedge to selvedge, the doubled edge being pinned round the waist to hang in pleats like a skirt, meeting at the back. This is suspended by a strong strip of cloth selvedge, or a specially woven cord, passing round the neck and pinned on either side in front, like braces. The remaining half of the ḥaïk (which is *not* folded) is then brought up over the head from behind, and doubled back from the face, falling on either side to drape shoulders and arms. A white muslin veil – lithám—about a yard long and fourteen inches wide, sometimes with embroidered edges, carefully folded lengthwise, is bound round the face, the exact centre of the fold passing over the ridge of the nose, and the ends being brought round so that each covers the forehead—leaving only the eyes visible,—they are fastened behind. Their indoor head-dress consists of a silken kerchief (ḥamtûz) mounted on a foundation of stiffened paper, rising up like a wall in front, and sloping off behind. These women wear black slippers (biláḡhî) with thin soles, and although their feet are bare, they encase each leg separately in white calico (rajlîn es-serwál). A piece about a yard long is sewn together at the edges, with a gusset at the top, and this, being too long when drawn on, is twisted round to keep it in place. In the country women engaged in field-work protect their calves by binding on leather with palmetto cord.

The ḥáïk and a pair of red leather slippers (masháïat) constitute a complete out-door costume in the coast towns, the calves being bare, as is the case also with the men, though coarse woollen socks (taḳashîr) are sometimes worn by elderly people in very cold weather.

Foot-gear.

The slippers of the men are yellow, of slightly varying patterns, practically always worn with the heels down, which is easy enough after practice. The soles of those worn by the women out-doors (ruáhî) are three-quarters of an inch in thickness and have straight sides. Tetuan is famous for a good class shoe for men, called bilḡhah (*pl.* biláḡhî), with round toes and thick soles, but the neatest, called siráksi, with pointed toes, thin soles and waists, are chiefly of Fez manufacture. For riding, both men and women use a soft leather stocking, called t'mág, which is often tastefully embroidered, as are also the velvet or leather slippers (shrábel) worn by the women in-doors, on which gold and silver thread are commonly used. In the rainy season the people of the level inland towns go abroad in pattens, often inlaid, called ḳabáḳib (probably an onomatopœic word), with long metal points to prevent them from falling. The Jews wear black shoes and caps.

Head-gear.

Hats (tarázát) are only worn by Moors in the country, and are not general even there; they are usually broad-brimmed, high-crowned constructions of palmetto, sometimes in tasteful patterns, or adorned with little tufts of silk, the brim being supported from the crown by an adjustable rigging. With this exception the Moors are deeply prejudiced against all hats, which they consider to be Christian emblems. The so-called "Fez" caps used in Morocco are not now to a very great extent made in that city, their place having been usurped by a cheaper and inferior article from Austria and elsewhere. The genuine Fez cap (sháshîah) is made by hand, of a solid wool felt, dyed a rich crimson, pointed at the top like a sugar-loaf, and surmounted by a deep-blue tassel (shûshá) of floss silk, sold by weight, as distinct from the cap. Literary and religious fashion favours a low cap of this shape, usually almost hidden by a turban, while the civil officials and police are known by its height, the ordinary policemen (makhazni) seldom wearing a turban. Common soldiers, and in the ports the youth of the lower classes, wear the cheap foreign cap like a truncated cone (tarboosh),* though some prefer the round-topped Tunisian shape. Country lads also crochet for themselves wool skull-caps of divers colours, or tie camel-hair cords round their

* A Turkish word, from the Persian "sar-poosh"—head-covering: *cf.* "ba-boosh" from "pa-poosh"—foot-covering or slipper.

heads, somewhat after the Arab style, or they merely wrap round it the red cloth case of their flint-lock when in use, a practice of highly artistic effect. All well-dressed Moors wear under the sháshîah a white cotton "perspiration cap" (araḳîyah) which can be washed. The felt caps themselves are cleansed with gall.

Turbans.

The turban, which to many is the distinguishing feature of an Oriental costume, though by no means so universal as is generally inferred, is in Morocco almost always white, the size corresponding to the wearer's idea of his own importance, but also a fair test of his actual position, since one arrogating too much by his turban would soon suffer at the hands of the mob. The only exceptions are a few green turbans worn by members of the Darḳáwi brotherhood. Turbans are not supposed to be used by unmarried youths. In donning the turban, the art consists in tightening the edges of the folds by twisting them at the back, precisely as in bandaging. When travelling, the supply of cloth or rope which a turban affords is often most useful, whether needed to dress a wound, to strain the milk, to replace a girth or tent cord, to lengthen the rope at the well, or to serve as clothes-line. Besides this, the voluminous folds of the turban—called in Morocco rozzah or 'amárah—though a trifle irritating to the novice, are a splendid shield from the sun, and altogether there is much more to be said in favour of this head-gear than of that crowning barbarity of civilization, the "top-hat" or "stove-pipe."

The Jelláb.

But in Morocco the most practical protection for the head is the hood (koob) attached to two of the most common garments, which may be worn over turban and all, or serve as a pocket. The most typical of these two garments is the jelláb, a woollen cloak made of a rectangular piece of stuff joined down the front, the upper portion being cut and ingeniously joined to form the hood. Arm-holes slit in the upper corners are supplemented by sleeves a few inches long, made out of the pieces cut out to form the hood. As the width of the made-up garment exceeds the length, the total length of the sleeves is ample, and the draping is perfect.* There is usually a small pocket inside the front seam, and in North Morocco those of native cloth are frequently decorated, like the hats, with tufts of silk, if not with embroidery. The jelláb is a decided improvement on the ábá of the Arabs and the Persians, which has no hood, and is open in front.

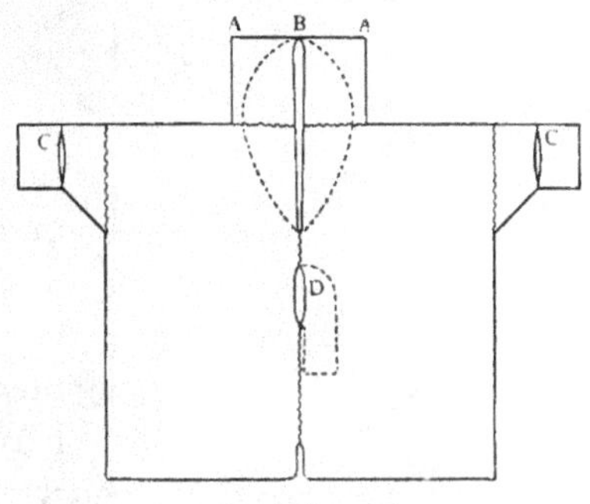

PATTERN OF JELLAB.

One width from top of hood to bottom, the shoulders being cut and seamed, and the sides of the hood turned forward from A to meet at B, the front edges becoming thus continuous with the breast flaps to which they are sewn, in use lying open, as dotted lines. The sleeve and cuff pieces are cut from the adjacent corners. C C are openings for the hands when the cuffs would be too long. D is an inside pocket.

The Selhám.

The other hooded garment is the selhám, known in Algeria as the burnûs, also made from one rectangular piece, but with the lower corners of the front edges, which are not joined, cut round, and with a hood made out of these trimmings. Neither of these garments requires any fastenings, and the front of the latter is only caught together for a couple of inches to keep the hood on the head. The selhám is a more aristocratic garment than the jelláb, and, made of native white or foreign blue cloth, may be worn over the k'sá in cold or wet weather. It is the regulation official dress, which alone is permitted before the Sultan, and both hood and left end must be thrown

* See illustrations on p. 75, etc.

back across the shoulder in the presence of a superior. It is this cloak which is given by the Sultan as a sign of honour, sometimes of investiture, and which is sent with his rosary to make an offer of pardon to rebels. For chiefs to send their selhâms to the Sultan is a declaration of rebellion, but it is said that if a cloak can be thrown over the Sultan's shoulders, or on the ground before him, he may not refuse the petition with which the act is accompanied, It is a common practice to throw the corner of the selhâm over the feet of a person whose protection is sought, when it would be considered more than churlish to refuse assistance. Another variety of the selhâm, called the khaïdûs or ákhnîf, is distinctive of the Berbers of the Central Atlas. Its peculiar feature is the yellow or red decoration on a ground of black, which often takes the form of an assegai, or "eye," across the lower part of the back, though sometimes confined to a narrow border by the style of which the various tribes can be distinguished, though this distinction is not strictly adhered to.* Some of these cloaks are brown, and a few white, the darker varieties being woven of goat-hair, and the white, called ḥaddûn, of wool.

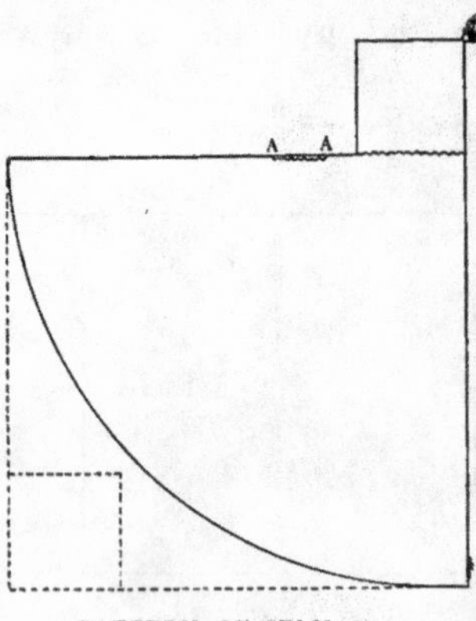

PATTERN OF SELHAM.

Made of double width cloth, the fold being down the back, and the edges fastened together from A to A, across the chest. The dotted lines show original shape of cloth, and whence the hood is cut. Tassel and braid of same coloured silk.

The Khaïdûs or Ákhnîf.

In under garments there is almost as great a similarity between those of the men and the women as in the outer. The tshámîr or shirt is usually a rectangular

* For illustration see chap. xxii.

sack with slits for neck and arms, though these openings are sometimes sloped and embroidered. The serwál, or drawers, are of the same design, unless for riding, when they are forked and very short. Otherwise the width will be as great as the outstretched arms of the wearer, the length that from waist to knee, a mere bag with a running cord (tikka) at the top, and holes in the lower corners for the legs, bound with white silk braid. Over these is commonly worn a ḳamîs or ḳandûrah, a tunic of cotton with wide bell-sleeves, buttoned to the waist by small knobs in the stitching and braiding. A very pretty open-work collar of silk or cotton is often attached, and an opening over the left shoulder to permit of pulling it on without unbuttoning the front, is drawn together by a silk cord forming an ingenious running noose. The kamîsah may be surmounted by a ḳafṭán or farrajîyah of wool, felt, or sateen, which, if of a bright colour, will be masked by a third (farrajîyah m'jarwán or manṣurîyah) of semi-transparent cotton, all three garments being of the same pattern, except that the first has no slits at the sides. The costume formed by the three is styled manáṣar. The ḳafṭán of the women differs from that of the men only in being rather longer. It is open down the front, and its sleeves are

Under Garments.

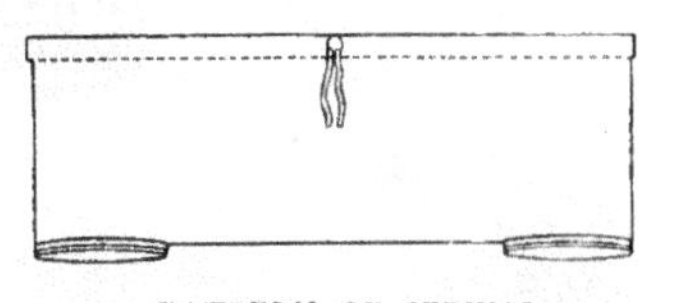

PATTERN OF SERWAL.

Cotton, with white silk or cotton braid at knee-holes, and coloured cloth selvedge or silk running cord.

PATTERN OF FARRAJÎYAH.

(Worn by men and women.)

The zigzag lines represent seams. Silk braid and buttons of same colour as cloth, white if on cotton.

sometimes cut narrow and buttoned, while the farrajîyah opens but to the waist, and has bell-sleeves.

Girdles.

Such a costume, when worn by men, is girt with a silk-embroidered leather belt (m'dammah), but the girdle of the women (hazzám), which is distinctive, may be a foot or more in width, and long enough to go round twice or thrice. It is made of stiffened silks, and often has four patterns, so that either may be folded outside. As these patterns are constantly changing, the wealthy dispose of those out of fashion by sale, and the economical employ a modification with two patterns only, the concealed half being merely of covered paste-board, for a good one in gold will cost as much as $40 or $50. Sometimes two of the patterns are in gold brocade—skalli—and two in silk. For the sake of display the hazzám will often be so wide—right up to the wearer's armpits—that she can hardly move.

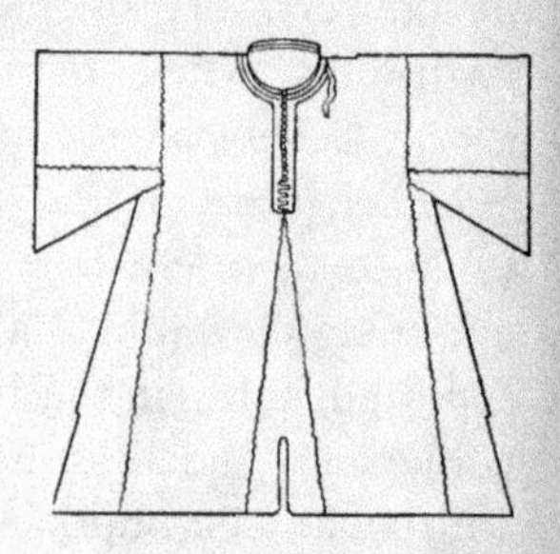

PATTERN OF KAFTAN.
(Worn by men and women.)
The zigzag lines represent seams. Silk braid and buttons in front of same colour and cloth.

Pockets.

By way of pocket, working and middle class Moors carry a leather satchel (shakárah) at the left side, slung by a silken cord (mijdûl), but men of leisure scorn such a convenience, and if they need to carry anything do so in the prayer-carpet which they tuck beneath the left arm, and it is marvellous what this will hold. A short curved dagger (ḳûmîyah) is also often slung at the side, and likewise, on a separate cord, a small Ḳor'án or some devotional book, in a leather or silver case.

Men of the merchant class often wear a less strictly Moorish garb of foreign felt cloth; baggy drawers, tight waistcoat, (badaïyah) and short jacket (jabadûr) with tight sleeves of which the cuffs are lined with gay silks to turn back. Waistcoats are also made for women in similar style, but with elaborate embroidery in gold and silver, which is not permitted to men. So particular are the latter in this respect, in accordance with the teachings of their religion, that though they are glad enough to carry watches, they

Merchant Costume.

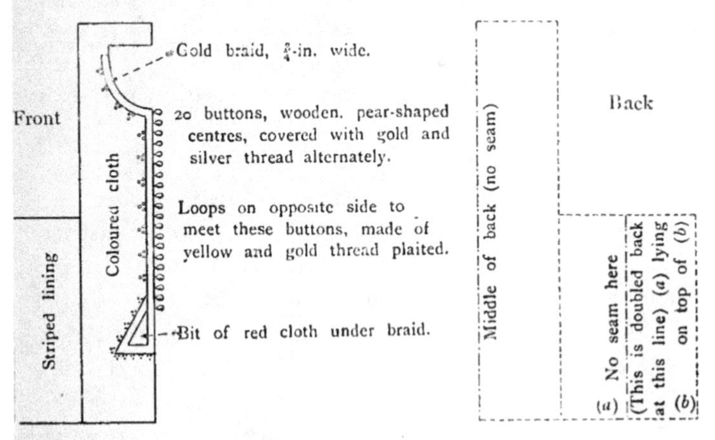

PATTERN OF A BADAÏYAH.

eschew watch-chains, substituting cords of silk, though for a man to dress in silk would be considered quite as improper as for him to wear gold.

Consequently they wear no jewellery, leaving that to the women, who make a show of all they can get, chiefly silver bracelets (dibálj), flat ankle-bands (kh'lákhil), finger-rings (khawátim), gigantic earrings (m'fátil), necklaces, chiefly of coins, and frontlets of coins, which while so used are secure from the husband's creditors. The country-women also wear

Jewellery.

SILVER ANKLET.

brooches (b'zaïm) of a peculiar pattern,* a pair at a time, one on each shoulder, to retain in place their ḥaïks or a sheet called eezar, thrown over the shoulder.

SILVER BROOCH.

Other articles peculiar to the costume of the ladies are: the ridá, a piece of fancy material thrown over the head and shoulders indoors; the d'fûn, a tunic of figured muslin work worn over bright coloured things; the m'shámar or taḥmîl, cords worn over the shoulders to support burdens, or to tie back the sleeves while at work, and the dh'faïr, imitation hair-plaits, by which their own queues are lengthened. Variations of these costumes are to be observed in almost every district, but those described are the most characteristic, and most generally to be seen in towns.

Feminine Attire.

Tailoring in Morocco is the work of men, but it is only required in the towns, and there only for certain costumes. Much felt cloth and sateen are imported from England and Austria, the quantity from the latter country steadily increasing on account of the low price at which an inferior article can thence be furnished; but these cloths are supplied of special hues to suit the taste of the Moors, chiefly dark-blue, plum-colour, white, brown, salmon and orange, and black for the Jews: a still poorer quality of red is also provided for the military uniform and women's tunics.

Tailoring.

Of course the original spinning and weaving fall to the lot of the women, as also the carpet-making and some of the open-work and decoration of the cotton "towels" (fûtát *s.* fûtah) for which Tetuan is especially

* Strange to say, similar brooches have been dug up in the bogs of Ireland, and may be found in the Dublin and other museums.

famous, much of which is highly effective. In some parts of the country two of these towels make a complete costume for a young girl, one tied round the waist to form a petticoat, and the other thrown

Country Garb.

MOORISH GIRL.
(Clad in fûtahs.)
Photograph by W. W. Hind-Smith, Esq.

across the head like the end of the ḥáïk, also, if need be, folded like it over the face. About Rabat these fûtahs are of well blended tartans.

Further south, an imported blue cotton fabric called khunt is generally worn by the women.* This material

* "Blue Selampore." For an illustration see p. 297.

is made for the most part in England in imitation of a better quality from the Ṣûdán. But in other parts, where only wool is worn, as among the Idá oo B'lál, the women appear in a black veil nearly a yard long, with a tassel on each corner, something after the Bokháran fashion.

The more primitive among the Berbers are content with a far simpler costume than that described. For them a plain piece of uncut home-spun suffices, knotted at the corners, so as to save even sewing, for the people of Morocco are poor tailors, and the majority of them only make use of needles, when they can get any, to extract thorns from their flesh. The Moorish method of sewing is just the reverse of our own, which they consider most absurd. All their seams are on the outside of the stuff, first run and then back-stitched, in the direction opposite to that followed by English women. What little sewing is done, falls to the lot of the men who make it a profession, except in towns, where ladies spend their time in fine embroidery in silk. This is the same on both sides, and is used for curtain ends, mattress covers and pillow slips.

Sewing and Dressmaking.

At night the Moors remove little, if anything of their in-door costume, wrapping themselves in their cloaks or blankets if need be, the latter being provided only in better class houses. Any change required is usually made in the morning, when ablutions are also performed, but the poorer classes change their clothes very seldom. For washing purposes the favourite emollient is ghasûl, a variety of fullers' earth found in certain districts, and forming one of the exports to the East, but an excellent soft-soap is also used.

Sleeping.

The washing of their clothes is performed by the Moors with the same soft-soap, made of wood-ashes and olive oil. This being smeared over the damp garment, it is folded up and danced upon by

Washing.

WASHING DAY IN MOROCCO.

Photograph by Herbert White, Esq.

the side of a well or stream, water being poured upon it all the time. Obstinate spots are thrashed out with billets of wood. But dirty clothes will often be put on again after a bath, and the odour of sanctity is sometimes acquired by washing neither body nor clothes till the latter fall to pieces *in situ*.

Although the popular idea of the Moors may not connect their name with over much nicety in either dress or toilet, they have their canons, and are quite as strict in their adherence to them as we are to ours. A brilliant writer[1] has described the Moorish women—though how he got to know we do not ask—as "antimony black beneath the eyes, vermillion on the cheeks, white lead on the neck, carnation on the nails: a palette, neither more nor less." Not a pleasant picture, according to our way of thinking, certainly, and somewhat over-drawn, though to the list of adornments might have been added tattooing on the chin and neck, and a brownish tint imparted to the gums by the use of walnut root or bark (sûák) for the cleansing of the teeth. This it accomplishes admirably, the frayed end being rubbed up and down.*

Cosmetics.

Care of Teeth.

The white-lead above alluded to is an invention, but a foreign preparation called bîádh el oojah is employed to whiten the cheeks, and antimony (k'hôl) is used, as throughout the East, to blacken the edges of eye-lids, and to alter their appearance to the coveted, languishing almond-shape.† The powdered antimony is kept in a little bottle-shaped vessel (mukáḥlah) into

Eyes.

* The sûák burns the lips so that the women commonly draw the back of a knife dipped in oil across them to relieve the pain.

† The amount of paint permitted on the face is regulated by strict etiquette, and in the case of young married women indicates approximately the length of time since their nuptials.

[1] De Amicis.

which a probe (mirwad) is introduced as a stopper, and the probe being moistened serves to apply the collyrium. * The rouge for the cheeks is either a preparation of ochre ('akkár) from abroad, or a local preparation of cochineal (kashiniah), which is either spread on sheets of paper ready to be transferred to the skin by application after being moistened, or is sold painted on earthenware saucers, and it is sometimes laid on in sharply defined patches. The so-called "carnation" on the hands and feet is the dye produced from the leaves of the *lawsonia inermis*, or Egyptian privet (ḥenná), of a deep-orange colour, and is the only "cosmetic" allowed to unmarried women. It is imparted by spreading over the part to be dyed a paste composed of the pounded leaves with water, † and then, having carefully dried it over a brazier, binding it up for the night at least, after which oil is sometimes rubbed in. The parts so treated are the soles of the feet, the insides of the hands, the toes and the top-joints of the fingers, the nails appearing of a considerably brighter hue. It has, of course, to be renewed from time to time, as it wears dull and disappears. Fingers and toenails are also sometimes tipped with a black pigment called harkos, prepared from wood ashes, pitch and spices, which is likewise employed to arch the eyebrows and unite them above the nose, and to trace with a stick a lace-like pattern on the backs of the hands, which imparts almost the appearance of mittens. Patches, also, are occasionally employed. The

Rouge.

Paint.

* Sometimes nitrate of silver is used, prepared with equal parts of sulphate of antimony and sulphate of copper pounded with cloves and finely sifted. This gives to the skin a blue-black colour, but a pure black is produced by the addition of smoke-black from a candle, collected on a plate. [1]

† Alum and the juice of a lemon are occasionally added.

[1] OVILO, p. 169.

tattooing (ûshám or sîálah) is usually confined to a series of small stars and dots in a line from the chin downwards, and a few similar designs on the toes and the fingers.* To produce it, gall-nut, smoke-black, gunpowder or indigo is worked into prickings done with a needle, which are afterwards rubbed over with the leaves of beans, or a plant called bûk'nînah, and verdigris and saffron are occasionally employed. The hair of the head is allowed to grow long, and is often dyed with ḥenná, but women remove all other hair from the body by the application of a depilatory composed of yellow arsenic (zarnîkh) soft-soap and lime; the men, however, prefer the exclusive use of the razor, and shave all over but the moustache and beard, both of which they keep neatly trimmed. Well-bred Moors keep their nails very short, which saves trouble in cleaning, and is more convenient when the hands are used in the dish.

* Instances are sometimes encountered, however, of elaborate designs on the chest, which, strange to say, include crosses. See the chapter on Christian Influences, *The Moorish Empire*, p. 309, note.

MOORISH WOMAN GIVING WATER TO SLAVE-WOMAN AND CHILD.

Cavilla, Photo., Tangie

CHAPTER THE FIFTH

MOORISH COURTESY AND ETIQUETTE

IN contrast to some of our northern nations it is hardly too much to say that the Moor, of whatever class, is born a gentleman, for there is such a grace about the humblest, such an easy bearing, that whenever circumstances place him in positions calling for the exercise of courtesy, he very seldom fails to respond, and thus it comes to pass that in a democratic nation in which every man of ability—cunning, perhaps, would be the better word—may rise to the highest place, even though he start life as a slave, the self-proclaiming parvenu is practically non-existent. This is not, however, to imply that the vulgarity and unpleasant manners which come from evil dispositions or stupidity are unknown, for unfortunately the life led by the average Moor is one which dwarfs refinement of instinct, as it does development of mind, and the vices to which the majority succumb in early life too often stultify the most promising commencement. Probably much of the graceful deference of the younger Moors is due to the respect they are taught to pay to their elders, but something must also be due to their unconstrained life and limbs, and to their costumes, while the very slowness of their actions lends an air of dignity.*

General Courtesy.

Its Causes.

* El Makkári tells the story of a ḳaḍi in Spain who refused to hurry even when the king had summoned him on important business. When asked what had detained him, taking a stick from one of the attendants,

Salutation.

Two elderly, dignified Moors saluting form a pretty picture, as with measured pace, the eyes of each fixed on those of the other, they approach with a slight inclination, holding their right hands somewhat advanced. On meeting, without removing their gaze, they press their finger-tips together, and commence a volley of prescribed enquiries, greetings and salutations, hardly pausing to insert replies or ejaculate "God be praised!" Then each presses the finger-tips which have been honoured by contact with those of his friend, first against his own lips, with perhaps an audible kiss, and then on his heart, as he raises his head, redoubling his salutations.

Greetings.

To every fellow Muslim the greeting is given "Es-salámu 'alaïkum"—"Peace be unto you,"* to which the answer is "wa 'alaïkum es-salám"—"and to you be peace"—though to the unbeliever the nearest approach to this permitted is "'Alà 'salám'tak"—"On thy peace," which might mean anything. The way to speed the parting guest is to exclaim "Allah îsallam-ak"—"God give thee peace," or, more curtly, "B'ís-salámah,"—"In peace," though to those whose presence has never been desired, it is usual to exclaim in tones sufficiently explicit in themselves, "Allah îhann-ak"—"God protect thee!" On arrival it is customary to exclaim to the guest "Marḥabbá bi-k,"—"Welcome to thee," or "Marḥabbáṇ, áhláṇ wa sahláṇ,"—"Be wel-

the learned judge assumed the attitude of one about to run, holding up his skirt in his hand. "What's this?" asked the king.

"This means, my liege," answered the ḳaḍi, "that I am preparing to assume my new office, for on my way hither, from the manner in which the messenger wished me to quicken my pace, it appears that I am now to be a soldier in the noble body-guard, instead of a judge." On this the king had the good sense to burst into laughter, and never again expected a ḳaḍi to hurry.

* The unusual use of the plural pronoun implying salutation also to Mohammed.

come, at home, and at ease." Then fall thick and fast the queries, "How art thou? Thy house?"—the nearest approach permitted to enquiry after a man's wife. "The relatives? What news? Is nothing wrong?" To which each replies, if there is nothing special to complain of, "All right, thank God. All are in prosperity." Or, if bad news has to be given, "God knows; everything is in the Hand of God."

MY SERVANT DIRECTING A WAYFARER IN WINDY RAHAMNA.
(Both wearing jellábs, but of different thicknesses.)
Photograph by Dr. Rudduck.

When a Muslim meets a European accompanied by a Moor, though the latter be the servant, he not infrequently ignores the presence of the foreigner, and offers the salute to his co-religionist only, but if he passes a mixed company of Moors and Jews or Christians he exclaims "Peace be on the people of Islám," or if two such parties meet on the road, "Peace be to those accompanying the Jews," or "the Nazarenes," and it is sufficient for one of each party to give and return the greeting, though in the country several often do so. Inferiors saluting superiors usually kiss the hand, shoulder, top of the turban, or feet, or the knee or stirrup of a horseman, according to the terms on which they approach. The more abject forms are only used to implore a favour, under which circumstances they are also employed even to Europeans, and sometimes the very feet of one's horse are embraced. But it is customary to sharply withdraw the hand about to be kissed as soon as it is touched. To accentuate the ordinary greeting on equal terms, the hands, after the first finger-tip touch, will be brought together as in an English hand-shake, and then, after a moment's pressure, each will remove his fingers to the other side of his friend's wrist, still keeping the thumbs locked together. This is sometimes repeated, backwards and forwards, many times. Hands are commonly struck together in concluding a bargain or enjoying a laugh. The old custom, too, of falling on one another's necks, is still in vogue between friends long separated, and notwithstanding that in this country men and women restrict their greetings in public to words, I was once, when returning to the country after some years' absence, somewhat startled by the sudden embrace of a negress whose freedom my father had been the means of obtaining. The kisses on such occasions are, however, fortunately delivered in the air or on the shoulder. It is customary to exclaim at meetings of this sort "I have been desolated for thee!"

Greeting non-Muslims.

Kissing.

To judge from the exclamations ever on the tongues

of the Moors, they might be an extremely pious people, and no doubt there are among them those who really mean what they say, but the most pious phrases have long degenerated into empty repetitions. Such are the constantly used expressions "B'ism l'llah,"—"In the Name of God;" "I'n shá A'llah,"—"If God will;" and "El ḥamdu l'I'llah,"—"Praise to God;" or "Yá A'llah!"—"O God!" Similar pious wishes are continually being expressed without thought,* as "The blessing of God be on thee," "May God increase thy welfare," and "God repay thee," used in the sense of "Thank you," "May God bless thee," or "bestow on thee a blessing," "God help thee," said to people at work; and "God preserve thee," "guide thee," "protect thee," "lengthen thine age," "satisfy thee," and "give thee strength;" not to tabulate all the elaborate curses which fall almost as freely, such as "God curse thee," "burn thee," "thy father," "thy mother, the abandoned creature," "thy grand-parents, the unbelievers," or "thy people and their religion, thou son of the other liar!" This last is an attempt to kill two birds with one stone. As an Englishman might exclaim "Well, I never!" and in just the same tone of surprise, a Moor will cry "Sallî en-nabî!"—"Bless the prophet!" but if desirous of acting cautiously he will declare "A'stághfir Allah el 'Adheem!"—"I ask pardon of God the great!" and at any time of trouble or anxiety, or embarkation on important business, as in making war, one or a party will repeat the beautiful opening prayer of the Ḳor'án, the Fátiḥah. When about to repeat any portion of the Ḳor'án or prayers, the petition is commonly uttered, "I seek refuge with God from Satan, the stoned," and when

Pious Expressions.

Common Sayings.

* For the Arabic rendering of these see my *Introduction to Morocco Arabic*, Part 5, as also for a collection of common proverbs, etc.

anything great or alarming occurs they exclaim, "There is neither might nor power, save in God, the High, the Mighty!" Quotations from the Ḳo'rán are also freely introduced in conversation by the learned, as by the generality of Moors are proverbs and sayings, a knowledge of which is a great help in conversation. In this connection, however, I cannot refrain from quoting one such proverb: "The uninstructed man who joins in the conversation is like the deaf dog who barks because he sees others barking."

Several minor social usages of Moorish life deserve attention, if not confined to Morocco, such as the exclamation to one who sneezes, "Nejjak Allah,"—"God hasten thee," *i.e.* to escape; or "The forgiveness of God be on me and on thee," to which the reply is "Justice and praise to God!" or the sneezer merely exclaims, "Praise to God!" and is answered by those present with "God have mercy on thee!" If a man who yawns in public does not put his hand to his mouth,* anyone speaking to him may place his own hand there, remarking, "I seek refuge with God from Satan the stoned," for the devil is accredited with performing an unpleasant operation in yawning mouths.

Sneezing and Yawning.

On the other hand, anyone wearing a new garment, or looking specially spruce, or having performed some clever or meritorious act, receives the compliment "Bi saḥḥ't-ak,"—"In thy strength!" But if occasion should arise for the mention in polite society, or before a superior, of a woman, a pig, or a Jew, it is incumbent to make use of an apology, "Ḥásh-ak!"—"By thy leave!" In referring to one recently dead it

Compliments.

* Although it is correct to place either the palm or back of one's own right hand before one's mouth, the back only of the left hand may be so employed.

is the custom to add "May God have mercy on him!" Strangers to whom occasion arises to speak in the street or elsewhere, are commonly addressed, according to relative, age and sex as "My Father!" "My Brother!"

MOORISH WOMEN INDOORS.
(The one to the left betrays negro blood.)

"My Mother!" "My Sister!" while those who have performed the pilgrimage to Mekkah are commonly addressed as "Am el Ḥáj!"—"Uncle Pilgrim!" Men who look well-to-do are usually spoken to as "Yá el Foḳîh!"—"O Learned One!" while Jews and Europeans are addressed as "Tájir!"—"Merchant!" But a female relative or acquaintance must never be accosted by a man in the street, unless engaged in selling or work.

Enjoying a Joke.

When a Moor is treated to a good joke he knows how to enjoy it to the full, and seated on the floor he sways backwards and forwards without restraint in his laughter, a common practice being for the speaker and listener so to enjoy it together, raising their right hands far above their heads as they roll back, and then, with a sweep round, bringing them together for a hearty shake: there never was invented a grander way of enjoying a joke. The women, when happy, give vent to their feelings by a shrill ululation produced by the soft palate: "Yoo yoo, yoo yoo, yoo yoo yoo!" which it would be difficult for untrained women to produce, and out of the question for men to attempt.

Jubilation.

Superstitious Etiquette.

Among the minor points of etiquette in vogue may be mentioned the prejudice against handing cutlery, which is always placed on the ground for another to pick up, since such things take life. A kindred feeling prevents the use of a knife to cut bread, or the mention of lead or fire. The former, because of its use to destroy life, is described as "khafîf," "light" (in weight), while for the latter word, on account of its connection with the abode of the wicked, is usually substituted the word 'aáfîá, "comfort." Some such superstitious feeling, doubtless, prevents the Moors from blowing out candles, which are gracefully and deftly extinguished by a rapid closing of the hand with the middle finger close to the flame.

Bread, as the staff of life, is almost venerated, and any piece which falls in the street is carefully picked up and placed in some cranny; paste made of flour even is refused by the shoemakers, lest it should be trodden on, and is replaced by raw spleen. No one who can help it thinks of eating in the street, and although when offerings of milk are made it is customary for the recipient to dip in a finger-tip and place it to his tongue, it is not etiquette to take refreshment publicly. Thus the Sultan, when he makes excursions to saint's shrines etc., may not even take a glass of water, and has also to abstain from food for nine or ten hours at a stretch. There are, however, abundant eating-stalls and cook-shops at which the humbler classes may refresh themselves, but even they sit down, and would be horrified at the idea of *déjeuner à la fourchette*.

Eating Abroad.

It may seem paradoxical to speak of table etiquette in people who eat on the floor, but nevertheless the Moors do indulge in tables of a sort, maintaining etiquette thereat as strict as our own. Naturally, when these tables are but a foot or six inches high, and those who make use of them sit round on the floor, tailor-fashion, eating with their fingers, the ceremonies attendant thereon must considerably vary from our own, but they are none the less refined, and are much better suited to the people and their surroundings than any others could be. It must always be remembered that it is the habit of the vast majority of mankind to eat with their natural forks and spoons, for it is only a few of the western nations who have lost that art, and have been reduced to the employment of mechanical substitutes, as a few of the eastern nations have descended to the invention of chop-sticks.

Table Etiquette.

All others use the means that God has provided, considering our habits clumsy and vulgar. "Poor things!" say the Moors, "they don't even know how to eat: look at their awkward manœuvres; and that disgusting implement they put into their mouth! Ugh! Yesterday was it not in somebody else's mouth?

Fingers versus Forks.

6

Bah! We use only our own for our own mouths!" When it is remembered that the fingers of the eater do not actually enter even his own mouth, and are scrupulously washed before and after the meal, the objections to the fingers of another in our pie disappear, especially as our own food is so much handled in the kitchen before we see it. Moreover, the exceeding gracefulness with which a well-bred Oriental conveys the food to his mouth is not to be approached with spoon and fork, and a little experience in a well-ordered native house soon dispels the prejudice in which we have been brought up.

Eating with Hands.

Another noteworthy feature with regard to hand-eating is that it can only be accomplished satisfactorily on the floor, so that spoon and chop-stick nations alone have had recourse to chairs (or *vice versâ*), and of the latter class indeed, only the Chinese. So a Moorish feast is conducted on the time honoured lines of the majority, well worth attention.

Preliminaries.

Previous to the announcement of dinner or supper there is always, on important occasions, a preliminary round of the favourite beverage, tea. This is usually ushered in by the passing round of an incense-burner (mubikhrah) on to the glowing coals of which the host has thrown a few chips of aromatic wood or gum.* The resulting smoke is fanned by each of the guests beneath the hood and folds of his garments, which for several days retain the scent. Then follows round the room a long-necked vessel (m'rashshah) with a fine hole or holes at the top, containing rose or orange-flower water, which by a quick jerk of the wrist is directed

INCENSE BURNER.

* As aloes-wood (aôd el k'márî), gum-benjamin (jáwî), gum-lemon (hasalobán) or aromatic pastilles (nidd).

over the face, neck and hands, and under the turban, being left to evaporate, a most refreshing operation in a hot and stuffy room, producing a most welcome coolness. A little slave-girl having attended to these preliminaries, the tea is brought in—now the national drink, though as late as 1670 both tea and coffee were unknown, and a European resident apparently had to discuss them from hearsay.[1]

MOORISH KAID MAKING TEA IN GARDEN.

Photograph by Edward Lee, Esq.

Before the host or his deputy there is placed on the ground a large brass tray on which are arranged many more tiny glasses and cups than there are guests, with a pear-shaped metal tea-pot, one long-handled spoon, and a tumbler larger than the rest, wherein is now a bundle of mint, verbena or lemon thyme, or a bundle of each for successive brews, but which afterwards serves as a slop-bowl. Then comes in

Tea-making.

[1] CHARRANT, *Réponse*, p. 115.

a steaming samovar of brass—quite the Russian article, —a painted tin tea-caddy, and a basin of chunks of loaf sugar, broken with a hammer specially kept for the purpose.* The operator having measured a certain amount of the tea in his hand, it is placed in the pot, and a little hot water is poured on to wash it lest the Nazarene dealers should have added colouring, for it is almost always green. This being quickly poured off, the pot is filled with sugar, and the water is added. After a minute or so sprigs of mint are placed under the lid, with the stalks protruding, and it is left a few minutes to brew.

Tea-drinking.

Tasting a little in a glass, the host pours back what remains, and if need be adds one or other of the ingredients, proceeding to fill the glasses and cups. This is performed in a specially graceful manner, bending forward each time, then rising and almost replacing the pot on the tray before repeating the operation. Passing the glasses one by one to the guests, the most honoured first, these hold them by the top and bottom between the right fore-finger and thumb, and take the longest and most audible sips they can. Although the sound produced is unpleasant to ears trained as ours, the effect is not only to cool the tea, but also to increase the enjoyment of the flavour, and certain it is that taken in no other way does the Moorish tea-and-mint-syrup taste so good. Three of these tiny tumblers are *de rigueur* if no excuse be made, and then the tea-things are removed. Ambergris ('anbar) is sometimes used by the wealthy to add fragrance, a small scraping being melted in a cup with hot water, and the oily drops as they rise to the surface transferred to the

* In the country the sugar is sometimes brought in as a loaf in blue paper, from which the host breaks off what he needs with the house-key at his girdle.

glasses of tea. Occasionally, too, the glasses are previously fumigated with mastic (miṣṭkah), as is also done to flavour cold water. Coffee is but little used in Morocco, and when it is, it is badly made with much sugar—and, perhaps, toasted chick peas,—the method and cups of Arabia being seldom employed.

HAND BASIN (ṬÁṢ) and EWER (BU ÎDDU), of brass or copper.

Hand-washing.

Hitherto the guests have remained sitting round the room on mattresses against the walls; a slave-girl now places before each in turn a broad brass basin (ṭáṣ) usually covered with a grating in the centre of which is a raised soap-dish. * Having poured a little water over the right hand into this, the attendant passes to the next, the guest drying his fingers on a towel across his shoulder. As every well-bred man will have come with clean hands and nails, the soap is not used on this occasion. Scarcely is the basin removed when the table (maïdah) is placed in front of the most important guest, and the others are requested to cluster round, several tables being brought if necessary, as only six or eight can sit with comfort round one, unless of large size. They stand from four inches to a foot from the ground, and are seldom above three feet across, as the food must be within reach of all, and sometimes they are surrounded by a high rim.

Tables.

In the middle is placed a large basin, usually full of stew (tájin), and loaves of bread are distributed round the table, sometimes also pounded herbs and salt—as cummin with roast mutton, which is excellent,—or salads

* In the country soft soap, if any, is used, but in the towns small European tablets or moulds, highly scented, a favourite form being a coloured model of the "Tangerine" orange, imported from France.

or fruits to form part of this course. Taking up the loaves one by one, the host now breaks them into quarters by making a series of indentations with the right thumb-nail, on account of the superstitious feeling referred to. The first taste of each dish is always accomplished by dipping a sippet of bread in the gravy—the way in which all the gravies and stews are eaten,—and it is the duty of the host to take the first sop, as he drinks the first glass of tea, to make it evident that he knows of no poison in it. His next care is to hand a sop to the chief guest, and similar honour is shown by the presentation of choice morsels to one another throughout the meal. But before the first sip or mouthful is taken each mutters by way of grace, "B'ism I'llah"—"In the Name of God!" The close of operations is signified by the withdrawal of the hand and the corresponding ejaculation, "El ḥamdu l'I'llah"—"Praise be to God!"—which is repeated frequently after a good meal as a wind-up to a series of "inarticulate ventriloquial noises" which form the only really disgusting feature of a Moorish meal, though even to them one grows accustomed in time.

Breaking Bread.

The Sop.

But for the stranger it is always the method of conveying the food to the mouth which is the interesting part, for with our unskilled notions we are apt to imagine something very bungling and inelegant, if not fatal to shirt-fronts. Nothing is, however, farther from the fact, for by a plentiful use of bread, and always imparting to his arm that graceful half-turn which as children we were taught to give to the treacle spoon, the spilling of a single drop is avoided, and what we imagine to be a barbarous performance becomes a polished and elegant action. It is the impossibility of properly accomplishing this unless the head can lean forward and the arm can take the requisite curve,

How to use one's Fingers.

that makes it necessary to sit on the ground when using the fingers for food, and renders unsuccessful all attempts to do so at a high table or on a chair.

Disposal of Liquids.

When broth or some preparation of hot milk forms part of the meal, it is either drunk direct from small bowls, or wooden spoons are provided, wherewith all help themselves from a common dish. Water is passed round as requested, in a basin which may be left floating in a pail, but the Moors are not great drinkers at meal-times, and after their meals the chief occasion of thirst is avoided by the excellent custom of rinsing the mouth. When the last dish has been removed the washing basin is again brought round, the water on this occasion often being hot, and used with soap; with it both hands are carefully washed. The soapy forefinger of the right hand is employed to polish the teeth, and thrice the mouth is filled with water which after a brief agitation is expelled with some force. Then comes tea again, three cups as before, followed by scented water and incense, the entertainment concluding as it began, although sweetmeats or small pastry (ḥaláwát, bishmát, fiḳáḳis, etc.) are often served with the second tea.

As a specimen Moorish dinner menu I may quote one from my notes:

Specimen Menu.

Stewed mutton with almonds, spices and hard boiled eggs; sliced oranges and split radishes as salad.

Stewed beef with artichoke stalks (khershûf) and other vegetables.

Minced beef, stewed with potatoes and capsicums.

Fowls boiled in butter with black olives etc.

Pieces of liver and fat threaded alternately on skewers, grilled with spices (ḳoḍbán).

The crowning "lordly dish" of kesk'soo, with a rich stew turned out on top.

Eating Kesk'soo.

The eating of this last preparation is an art in itself, requiring special skill. A portion of the granulated paste being scooped up in the fingers, it is deftly manipulated into a ball which is transferred to the mouth from the back of the thumb, much as a school-boy puts an alley into the ring. This is easy enough, but the puzzle is to prepare the ball, since the slightest excess of pressure causes the grains to fall apart, and the only way is to keep giving the wrist a partial turn. Particles adhering to the fingers are removed by the tongue before washing, and the correct thing is so to treat first the little finger, then the middle finger, then the thumb, and finally the third and the first fingers.

Meal-times.

Such a meal as that described would only be eaten in the evening, about an hour after sunset, or perhaps at noon, these being the general meal times. In the morning little or nothing is taken by way of breakfast, seldom more than a cup of coffee or hot milk and a biscuit, or perhaps some soup (ḥarîrah) or gruel (ḥasûwah). In the Atlas gruel is quite an institution, being made of barley or wheat, and so is its relative porridge, there often made of maize and poured out into a broad wooden trencher, with a lump of butter in a hole made in the centre. This is the national dish of the Berbers—'aṣîdah—than which I have never tried a more satisfying diet.

CHAPTER THE SIXTH

WHAT THE MOORS EAT AND DRINK

THE food that other nations eat is always an attractive subject to the curious, and one which often well repays investigation, but it is strange how few European travellers give fair trial to the cooking of Orientals. This arises generally from inherent prejudice and misconception, yet in almost every country the staple dishes are the outcome of experiences handed down for generations, as the most suitable provision for its race and climate. Morocco has unfortunately shared the effects of this neglect, its people being popularly supposed to exist on all sorts of unpalatable, if not disgusting, viands, which is so far from the case that English cooks, if not too ignorant to profit by example, might glean many wrinkles from the Moors. To begin with, it is quite a common practice with prejudiced travellers who do secure the opportunity of trying a Moorish dinner to "make sure of a good meal before they start," as they feel sure that they will not relish the few things they may dare to eat, with the inevitable result that their experience bears out their forebodings. How many English dinners would stand such a test?

Prevalent Misconceptions.

The average inexperienced Englishman has only to be told that most of the Moorish cooking is done in oil, for the whole thing to be steadfastly tabooed, but the few who have had the good fortune to experiment in first-class Moorish houses with a healthy appetite, will bear me out in the assurance that the oil explains half the success, and is open to no objection when really good. The difficulty is for those not intimate with the people to secure admission to such tables, and of course it is unfair to judge from the fare of the poorer classes, especially as exemplified by the vain attempts of the foreigners' servants, who scarcely ever understand the preparation of native dainties. In good Moorish houses this department is in the very capable hands of negress slaves—not to be obtained by Europeans,—some of whom, with proper training in the culinary art, command high prices.

Difficulty of Experiment.

The typical dish of Morocco is the famous kesk'soo, of the name of which an able writer on the gastronomy of Morocco [1] has declared that "the mere sound of the syllables is musical, with a sweet sibilance suggestive of twin kisses united to the coo of the turtle-dove and the note of the cuckoo." But without indulging in such rapture over its name—only to be explained by the qualities of the dish described —I do unhesitatingly assert, from an exceptionally wide and appreciative acquaintance with native cookery the world round, that I do not know a dish at the same time more nutritive, more wholesome, more simple and more tasty. Its basis is the nourishing granular nodule or germ found only in wheat grown in comparatively poor, dry soils, which from the difficulty of grinding it is known as *se-molina*, *i.e.* "half-ground:" on the Continent this is used in the form of macaroni and other pastes, and in England it is advertised as "Vitos" or "Hovis" and kindred prepared breads. The Moors, who call it smee<u>dh</u>, make also from it a delicious white or macaroni-coloured bread. For the preparation of kesk'soo or, as the country-

The National Dish.

[1] G. D. Cowan, in *Moorish Lotus Leaves.*

folk pronounce it, siksoo, the grains of smeedh are moistened and rolled in fine flour till they form pellets about the size of buck-shot, the smaller being considered the best. After being steamed and dried in the sun, it will keep good in a bag for many years, and a few days since I partook of some which I procured from Fez eight years ago. For eating, the kesk'soo is again steamed, this time over a bowl of rich stew which is served on top of it, heaped in the centre of a big basin, sometimes with the addition of stewed quince or other fruit. But before serving the grains are carefully separated by rubbing in butter, some portion of which, called smeen, has been preserved till it has acquired a sort of Gorgonzola flavour. Too strong a dose of this at first is apt to repel the novice, but if tested gradually, this, more than anything else, renders Moorish dishes attractive, for it whets one's appetite, as assafœtida does in an Indian curry or "Yorkshire relish."

Flavourings.

Not that the Moroccan cuisine depends on its green-streaked smeen, which has perhaps been buried in an earthen jar for twelve months—a little of which then goes a long way,—for with a liberal use of capsicums ("red peppers") and the usual Oriental spices, coriander, cummin, sesame, fenugreek, cinnamon, carraway, cloves and nutmeg, there is no lack of flavour, but the Moors are not fond of "hot" things. A speciality of their kitchens is rather the use made of raisins, dates, etc. in their meat stews, with most excellent results. After kesk'soo, their stews are their strong point, and right tasty and tender they are, whatever the age of the creature supplying the meat, as they needs must be, when they have to be carved with the fingers and thumb of one hand.

This perfection is achieved by the use of oil instead of water, permitting the viands to be cooked at a very much higher temperature than would otherwise be possible without either boiling or burning. The oil or melted butter being heated till it will at once brown anything plunged into it, is removed from the fire and allowed to simmer for hours over a gentle heat. Naturally the result from an English point of view depends upon the pureness and the freshness of the oil, and the poorer Moors and Jews content themselves with a very inferior rancid article of a most nauseous, ineradicable taste, while the best oil imparts no taste at all, and the abundant flavourings, together with the large amount of bread consumed therewith, counteracts any feeling of richness. Englishmen usually prejudice themselves against Oriental dishes by disposing of them as we might of our own stews, instead of regarding them more in the light of condiments with the assistance of which to feast on bread or rice, or kesk'soo.

Cooking in Oil.

Little meat is eaten in the country, though the wealthy townsman consumes far too much of it. The mountaineers have to club together to kill an occasional ox, but the Arabs with their flocks and herds indulge more frequently, at least once a week. The Moors prefer mutton to beef, but often pass off goat for the former, so that practised housekeepers demand to see the tail on a carcass from which they purchase. Camel's flesh is also eaten on occasion, and I have found it much like coarse beef. Then, too, in the country wild boar is sometimes consumed, in spite of the koranic prohibition: so also are porcupines, neatly described as "pigs disguised in pen-holders." Foxes, jackals and hedgehogs enlarge the bill of fare in some parts, but one may live years in Morocco without a chance of trying anything but mutton, beef and "chever." When fresh meat is plentiful, as after the "Sheep Feast," the superabundance is cut in strips, sun-dried and packed

Varieties of Meat.

A MOROCCO MEAT MARKET.

Drawn by Herr Romberg.

away in jars with melted butter. In this condition, known as khalîa', ît will keep for years,* and is in great demand for travelling. Of game the Moors eat most varieties within both their reach and the Mosaic limitations as adopted by Mohammed, and the same may be said of fish. Fowls are everywhere to be obtained, and a favourite dainty is "squab" or unfledged pigeon in pastry,—"basṭîlah." Snails are sometimes stewed or fried in oil by the poor, and so are locusts, boiled half an hour with salt or vinegar, and fried with pepper, while in some parts a big stag-beetle is eaten. In order to be ḥalál, or lawful, animal food must not only be from an acknowledged "clean" animal, but it must be slaughtered in such a manner as to get rid of the blood, as by cutting its throat, and this is always done even with game, which if secured when already dead, is prohibited, ḥarám.

Dairy Produce.

Milk, eggs and butter are staples in the country during spring, and very fair cream cheeses are made, but they do not keep. Fresh milk can only be obtained at the moment of milking, for it is stored in unscalded jars, or even mixed with the sour milk in house, very much preferred to fresh all over the East. Honey is often to be had, but is by no means as plentiful as it might be; in these details every district has its own peculiarities. The vegetables grown by the country Moors seldom include anything beyond pumpkins, cucumbers, broad beans, onions and turnips—the last-named being eaten dried in the mountains,—but in the towns there is always a good supply, the favourites being artichokes—of which the stalk (khershûf) is eaten, and it is delicious—carrots, truffles, egg-plants, "ladies' fingers," tomatoes, and radishes. Roasted green corn, date-palm shoots, palmetto roots and

Vegetables.

* Jackson said he had known it thirty years old (p. 349).

barley sprouts are also in vogue at certain seasons, and all fruit that can be obtained is eaten, which away from the towns is not much. Several other excellent vegetables comparatively unknown in England are used in Morocco, such as egg-plants, kohl-rabi, and beet-root tops (an excellent substitute for spinach).

Pastry and Bread.

In the matter of sweets and pastry the Moors are fairly clever, but their productions do not always tempt Europeans. Their pastry when well made is exceedingly rich and flaky, being first kneaded, then cooked with oil, and they make a delicious sort of short-bread cakes to take with tea. Sponge fritters (sfinjes), are made to perfection, and they are a favourite breakfast dish. For travelling they turn out a good solid biscuit which will keep a great length of time, but their bread, unless specially baked, is best eaten fresh. Most families knead their own, employing natural leaven, and send the flat round cakes like big buns to the public oven, where a certain proportion is retained in payment, and sold to those who have no one to make it for them. To collect the bread, lads are sent round the streets with boards on their heads, making their presence known by uttering a shrill incomprehensible cry; house-wives requiring their services, on the other hand, loudly rap the knockers on their doors, their persons carefully concealed within, and only a fat arm showing.

Public Ovens.

The ovens consist of long low tunnels, on one side of which are wood fires, and the cakes are put in and turned with long shovels, not being allowed to brown or form a hard crust. In the country, where often not even an attempt at such an oven is to be found, bread is quickly made—often of barley or maize—on an earthenware pan, in a cake (ragh̲îfah) about half an inch thick, which though heavy when cold, is very palatable fresh, with butter—and an appetite.

Although from necessity the Moors are generally frugal in their habits, and often almost vegetarians, it certainly cannot be said that they are so from choice, as whenever they do get a chance, they indulge to such an extent that cash and corpulence are almost regarded as synonymous, and in woman at all events, beauty may be estimated by weight. Their great meal, at which, if possible, kesk'soo makes its appearance as the crowning dish, is soon after sunset, and that over, they are fit only for sleep.

Over-eating.

In order not only to convey a more exact idea than would be possible by mere description of the food of the Moors, but also to enable English housekeepers to gather what they will from them, I append a few recipes which I have tried myself, and found good. I must, however, quote the remark attributed to a lady, who, on furnishing the recipe for Banbury cakes which made her table famous, added, "This will produce excellent Banbury cakes if your cook knows how to make them." So let not those who flatter me by trying these dishes be too hasty to condemn the Moors or myself if unsuccessful.

Specimen Recipes.

On shaking up semolina in a tray, the coarse grains (fá<u>kh</u>ar) are taken off as they rise, a double handful being thrown into a broad shallow earthenware pan (gessa') and a tablespoonful of water sprinkled over it. Then a handful of finer semolina is thrown on, then a little more water as before, and more fine flour, the manipulator all the time rolling it over the bottom of the pan with the palms of the hands, so that each original grain grows into a minute ball the size of No. 4 shot. The whole is then sifted in a coarse sieve to remove the larger particles, which are rubbed in the hands to break them up, and put back in the pan

Kesk'soo or *Siksoo.* (In Spanish, *couscousou.*)

to be worked by the hands as before, while fine flour is sifted on. When ready, the grains are placed in a steamer over water, and steamed till all are separate, which can be ascertained by inspection. If the kesk'soo is to be kept in house, it must now be spread on a sheet in the sun to dry, and occasionally worked with the hand to separate any granules which may have stuck together.

POTTERY SELLERS, MARRAKESH.

Photograph by Dr. Rudduck.

Before cooking old kesk'soo, wash it in water and steep it in fresh cold water till soft, say half an hour. Then cook as if just made. Place it in a steamer (keskás) over a stew, described separately. See that *all* the steam passes through the grains by securing the joint with dough or a cloth. Steam until quite soft, and when ready to serve, heap up in dish (makhfîyah), working in sufficient butter, fresh or preserved, or both, to cover each grain, without causing them to stick together, or leaving melted butter in the bottom of the

Final Cooking.

dish. The making of a good dish of kesk'soo is a dash of good old smeen, which may be prepared at home by keeping unsalted butter till it becomes rancid, and then boiling it down. When the heap is ready, place the meat from the stew in a depression in the centre, and pile the big vegetables first, with the onions, raisins, etc., on top. It may then be sprinkled with cinnamon, if fancied.

Another way to serve kesk'soo is to work it up with fresh butter only, and cover the heap with a thick layer of powdered sugar, cinnamon being plentifully sprinkled over all.

*Stew for Kesk'-soo (Kûdrah).**

Put salt into the bottom half of the steamer, with an ounce or two of butter; add sliced onions and pepper, ginger, nutmeg, coriander, allspice, turmeric, and saffron if desired. Pound or grind the spices together. Chopped parsley, marjoram, and green coriander may be added if in season. Now put in the meat. Leave it to simmer, and then add enough water to submerge the onions, etc. Cover close, and put on slow fire, after stirring well. When the water boils away add more, hot or cold. When the meat is tender and the stew boils, place the top half of the steamer on with the kesk'soo in it.

Slice some more onions, and simmer in gravy from the stew with a little butter or smeen, and spices—perhaps a little saffron. These are put on top of stew when served on kesk'soo. Raisins may be added, or quinces may be boiled separately and served on top. Broad beans, when fresh, may be added to the stew, or any vegetable but potato, though not in large quantities.

Boil 1 lb. oil in a stew-pan till it smokes, then add lb. butter, and put a fowl in, ready trussed and

* May be made of fowls, mutton, or beef.

stuffed, with a little salt rubbed into it. Turn it occasionally, over a moderate fire, till it is brown and tender. The latter point can be ascertained by touching with the finger, but beware of a scald! An excellent stuffing is made with chopped almonds, raisins, bread-crumbs, eggs and spices.

"Roast" Fowl.

Beef or mutton may be cooked like the fowl, with spices to taste added to the gravy When the meat has absorbed most of the oil, add water, hot or cold, to make the required quantity of gravy. Keep close covered, and turn, taking care that the fire is not fierce enough to burn it. If onions or other vegetables are fancied with the meat, some of the gravy is poured into a separate vessel to stew them and they are served round the joint in the same dish Chopped carrots, etc., may be poured out over it, stewec in this way.

Joint of Mutton or Beef.

This is often accompanied by salad on a separat plate, and with mutton—of which the breast and shoulde are the favourite portions,—a plate of pounded cummi and salt mixed forms a most agreeable relish into whicl to dip the meat as it is plucked from the joint. Olive are often added to the gravy, or apples, and are del cious thus.

For a stew boil oil till it smokes, and add two tabl spoonfuls of pounded capsicum. When boiling add ha a pint of water. When cold pour off the cle oil from the top into a stew-pan. Add tw or three heads of garlic, and when boiling put in th meat, cut up. Stew till tender.

Stew (Tájin).

When nearly ready add the vegetables, leaving the long enough to cook, according to what they ar any sort being suitable, but potatoes least of all so.

Fowl and Olives (very good).

Stew a fowl (cut up) in butter and oil, with pepper, salt and allspice (all in powder), the butter to be put in first, and the oil poured on when melted.* The meat should be first rubbed with salt, and left so ten minutes, after which the salt is washed off, just before putting it into the pot. Cook a quarter of an hour. Then replace the lid for ten miuutes, after which put in the onions, cut up, and pour on a pint of water: boil till nearly all this has evaporated. Stew till no moisture comes out when a fork is stuck into the

MOORISH BEE-HIVES.
Photograph by Dr. Rudduck.

meat. Now add the raisins, and in five minutes add the olives and grated nutmeg, as much as a pea of the latter. Leave it near the fire for a quarter of an hour. Serve with plain boiled rice, like a curry. It should take altogether an hour and a half to cook.

* For one fowl use: Olives, 3 doz.; Butter, 2 oz.; Onions, 3; Spanish Oil, 3 tablespoonfuls; Raisins, 2 oz.

The following recipe will make good soup for four persons. Chop up the onions very fine, with pepper, salt, and green coriander. Put into a pan with 1 oz. smeen, and add ½ lb. meat, cut into dice. Leave all to simmer about half an hour, watching that it does not burn. Then fill up with a pint and a half of water. Leave it to stew slowly till the meat is tender. Then add 2 oz. vermicelli. Mix 2 oz. flour and leaven or lemon into a smooth thin paste with water, and pour it in. Boil a quarter of an hour longer, and remove from the fire; at that moment pour in two eggs well beaten up, and serve. Parsley may be substituted for coriander if the latter is unobtainable, but it is not so good.

Egg and Coriander Soup. (Harîrah, hasûwah, or f'toor.)

Half a dozen mackerel or large herrings, or an equal quantity of any fish, prepared in the following style, form a favourite dish, especially among the Jews.

Boil 4 oz. oil in a frying-pan over a slow fire. When bubbling, add ½ oz. sweet red pepper powder and a little water. The fish being prepared on the bottom of a stew-pan, cover them with chopped green coriander, three heads of garlic, bread-crumbs and salt; pour half a pint of water on the oil, and let it boil ten minutes. Cool and pour into a stew-pan, careful not to wash off the bread-crumbs, etc. Do not pour out the red pepper sediment; throw it away. The dish will be ready in twenty minutes to half an hour, if kept covered up. See that it doesn't burn. A slow fire is preferable.

Fish in Garlic.

Cut ½ lb. lean meat* across the fibres into pieces the size of a shilling, a quarter of an inch thick, and ¼ lb. fa

* Liver is very good this way, and sure to be tender. It is the called "kabáb."

into pieces half that size. Roll all in spices and coriander,* and thread alternately on skewers. Broil over a slow clear fire, preferably of charcoal, and beware of smoke or flame. Revolve occasionally to ensure equality in cooking. Serve on the skewers, very hot, and eat with new bread. †

Meat on Skewers (Kodbân).

Mince raw meat, and 6 oz. fat, mixing in well and equally a small onion, pepper, salt, bread-crumbs, with cummin, parsley, marjoram, green coriander, and mint, chopped fine. Press a handful round each skewer, and broil as above.

Mincemeat. (Kiftah).

Another excellent way is to roll it into balls, and stew very gently for two hours in plenty of butter, over a slight fire. When nearly ready to serve, fill up with ready boiled peas. In default of peas, hard-boiled eggs may be added at an earlier stage of the cooking.

The next recipe is a great dish of the hillsmen, who put cabbage into it and eat it with bread.

Bring a quart of water to near boiling-point, and add a pint of split broad beans, leaving them to boil for half an hour, removing the scum as it rises. If they are then tender, take them off the fire, which should not be too fierce, but if still hard keep them boiling till done. Then stir well with a wire whisk till the whole is reduced to a paste. Now add a pod of red pepper, (or if pounded ½ oz. or less,) a head of garlic, salt, and pounded cummin. Oil or butter may be added if fancied. If salt is put in the water first the beans will not become tender.

Bean Porridge (Baïsar).

* Green coriander leaves, chopped, or in default, parsley, pepper, salt, and cummin seed pounded together.

† Mashed potato goes very well with them.

Frumenty (Herrbel).

The standard New Year dish of the monntaineers, practically our frumenty ("frumity"), is thus prepared. Put a pint of new wheat in hot water in the afternoon, and on the morning of the next day but one, pound it in a wooden mortar sufficiently to remove the husk, which should be cleared away. Put it into a quart or more of boiling water, and boil for three or four hours, till quite soft. Then add a little salt and half a pint of milk, boiling a quarter of an hour longer, after which put in six ounces of fresh butter, and stir well.

Sponge Fritters (Sfinjes). *

Knead 1 lb. flour into a stiff dough for half an hour, with warm water and 1 oz. leaven, keeping on till it bubbles; then commence to thin down by adding warm water in small quantities, and kneading well till it is reduced to a thick paste, sufficiently stiff to remain in a long thread from the finger to the trough when a piece is pulled up with the hand. Leave it to ferment for a quarter of an hour, or more if necessary, till bubbles rise freely. It is then ready to fry.

Take hold of a piece in the hand, and break off a ball the size of a hen's egg. Pierce this with the fore fingers and thumbs of each hand, and drawing it out into a ring, drop it into *boiling* oil, turning it over when one side is browned. These are deliciously light and appetizing, and may be eaten either alone or with salt, sugar, honey, etc.

Prepare dough as for sfinjes. Clean an earthen pan by well rubbing with soft soap and drying. Place it on a slow fire till very hot. Then drop in a spoonful of

* Evidently the Greek word *σπόνγος*, (spongos) a sponge.

COUNTRY WOMAN CARRYING WATER.

the thin dough. When the face is set, turn the pikelet thus formed, being careful that the fire is not fierce enough to burn it to the bottom. In case it does, scrape the pan well, butter and soap as before.

Pikelets (Hartaïtahs).

Serve very hot, and eat with butter, or butter before serving. More or less salt should be added to the dough, according as they are intended to be eaten with fresh butter or sugar or honey.

Drinking Customs.

Of what is understood by drinking customs the Moors have few, since they adhere with creditable strictness to the prohibition in the Ḳor'án of the use of alcohol. Although a number do infringe this law, chiefly among the highest and the lowest classes, it is done in secret, for to be known as a tippler in Morocco would be a greater disgrace than to be known as an adulterer in England, since the relative ideas of the immorality of moderate drinking and loose living as observed in Morocco and England are exactly reversed. Moors, too, like most people to whom the habit is new, never use strong drink to allay thirst only, or as a medicine, but only as an actual intoxicant, so that when friends do meet together to have a bout, it is to "go the whole hog." Formerly the chief supplies of those who indulged in this practice depended almost entirely on the products of Jewish vats and stills,* to which they yet have recourse, sometimes supplying the grapes or raisins or figs for some Jewish employé to manufacture the liquor they love;†

Sources of Supply.

* James (vol. ii., p. 33) speaks of white and red varieties resembling Burgundy, produced in Tetuan and sold for next to nothing.

† Mixed grapes are pounded up and boiled to half their original bulk in about twelve hours, and added to an equal quantity unboiled, being then left a month to ferment, when the liquor is skimmed and bottled. Some prepare a thick syrupy variety called ṣámit, much used at feasts in

but now-a-days, with increasing trade, and consuls fostering this branch, increasing quantities are being introduced from abroad by smuggling or under private permits, for the right to prohibit its importation is exercised by the Moorish government. *

Smoking.

As compared with most Orientals, the Moors are by no means great smokers, but the habit was introduced as far back as the close of the sixteenth century by the tribute bearers from Timbuctoo, which in 1590 fell for a time under Moorish sway. At first the penalties imposed to prevent the use of tobacco were severe, but ere long they broke down, till in 1887 they were revived by Mulai el Hasan III. † The doubt as to the lawfulness of narcotics which had always existed in this country had led the Moorish Government to reserve in all its treaties the right to prohibit their introduction, or to farm as a monopoly the trade in them and everything used in their preparation or consumption. In the year named, therefore, on the expiration of the lease of the monopoly, its renewal was refused, and all existing stocks were taken over at a valuation and destroyed, huge bonfires being erected outside the gates, and surrounded by soldiers until consumed.

Opposition.

Numerous imprisonments for the use of the weed followed, but the heart of the officials was not in the work, so by degrees the habit revived. Europeans have obtained sufficient permits to introduce whatever they needed for their own consumption, to be able to abuse this privilege and supply the Moors as

the mountains. Spirits are distilled by the Jews from raisins, figs, dates etc., generally flavoured with anise-seed.

* Drastic punishments for drunkenness are heard of from time to time, such as hanging a man by his feet with a skin of wine tied to his neck, as was done in 1680.[1]

† For account see *Times of Morocco*, March 10th and 17th of that year.

[1] Godard, p. 532.

well, at prices lower than before. Several factories have in consequence arisen, and Tangier-made cigarettes are sold at ten or twelve a penny. A good deal of tobacco is also grown in the country, chiefly on the lower slopes of the mountains, but for lack of care and cultivation it is poor in quality. The Moors always speak of "drinking smoke," and seldom spit while smoking. The use of water-pipes is practically unknown.

Hemp Smoking.

Indian hemp *(Cannabis Indica)* is more extensively grown, and perhaps more extensively used, for tobacco has as yet made no general headway in the interior, being universal only in the coast towns, where it is almost exclusively used in the form of cigarettes. Sometimes hemp and tobacco are smoked together in a tiny pipe with clay bowl

PIPES FOR SMOKING HEMP.

(1) Carved and filled with wax of various colours.
(2) Outlines of design cut, and the whole stained green and yellow.

(shkaf) and wood stem (sibsi), hemp being seldom consumed alone. In this form it is known simply as ḥasheesh —"grass"—or by its own name, keef, but it is also consumed as a sort of sweetmeat ball called m'ajoon—"kneaded." Its immediate effects are commonly exaggerated in description, the smoker passing into sleep filled with sensuous dreams, but its ultimate effects are only to be appreciated by those who have had to employ its victims, and have learned how utterly untrustworthy and useless the habit renders them. No one willingly employs a "kiyaf," who is readily detected by his pasty face, his half-closed eye, his listless attitude. Opium also is slowly making its way into Morocco,

Opium. being chiefly eaten—never smoked—by rich men in the capitals, who would scorn to be found using hemp, or even tobacco.

Snuff is the form, or rather preparation, in which tobacco is most generally used inland, were few Moors of middle age who can afford it are without their snuff-nut, but neither snuffing nor smoking have grown general among the women, who are kept on too short commons for such indulgence. Moorish snuff is usually made of about equal quantities of tobacco, pounded walnut shells and wood-ashes, and it is fairly pungent withal. It is snuffed up from a train laid along the ridge formed by the metacarpal bone of the index finger, half with each nostril. It is kept either in genuine young cocoa-nuts with ivory probes for stoppers, attached by silver chains, or in smaller holders of similar shape turned in ebonized walnut-wood, often tastefully inlaid with silver wire, beaten in, and then polished.

Snuffing.

"POWDER-PLAY."

Drawn by Warwick Goble.

CHAPTER THE SEVENTH

EVERY-DAY LIFE

AS soon as the arrival of a little one in a Moorish house becomes known there is no lack of visitors, for whose entertainment preparation is often made months in advance. While the mother gets in a store of flour, semolina, butter, fowls, honey and eggs, and makes a plentiful supply of biscuits, the father purchases a sheep or ram, and lays by towards expenses. Great cries of joy announce the birth of a boy, and sometimes, not to interfere with the feasting, the sex of a girl is concealed until the day comes for naming, as otherwise there would not be the same occasion for festivities.

Birth-Feast.

Amid a crowd of female visitors the new arrival is rubbed all over with oil and henná, its eyes are blackened with antimony, and eye-brows are painted in, while walnut juice and oil are rubbed into its mouth. Meanwhile the mother drinks honey and oil flavoured with cummin, or "holy water," rendered so by some "saint" dipping in his finger! For the first week the child is not washed, and wears only old clothes, but on the eighth day, called in Morocco the seventh, both mother and child undergo the prescribed ablutions, and are dressed in new clothes for the naming.* During this time, when the means of the parents allow it, there has been daily feasting, all women visitors being supplied with bread and honey or tea and cakes, the men also being fed apart in the morning, if the child is a boy.

* Sometimes, however, this takes place on the seventh day.

Over night, a cruse of water with a little salt and fennel seed mixed has been placed by the child's head for luck, and the water having served for the first bath in the presence of the company, it is passed round on a tray, on which the guests place coins for the nurse, while the salt and fennel are thrown on the floors, with the exclamation that they are for the envious. By pounding a mortar close to the child, and by shaking it in a sieve, it is supposed to grow inured to noise, and to life's ups and downs. After this ceremonial bathing the child gets no proper washing for a twelve-month, lest its health might suffer,* but the mother, who is purified at the steam-bath before the naming, revisits that institution fortnightly. On the fortieth day she takes the babe with an offering to the shrine of a dead saint or the house of a living one.

The First Bath.

On the morning of the name-day the father or nearest male relative slaughters the sheep, exclaiming as he cuts the throat, "In the Name of the Mighty God for the naming of so-and-so, son (or daughter) of so-and-so," referring to the mother, who is asked to give the child a name. In the evening a feast is made of the sheep, the nurse receiving as her perquisite the fleece and a fore-leg, with perhaps a present of cash besides, in return for her presence for seven days. The mother sits in state on a special chair brought by the nurse.

The Naming.

The names in vogue in Morocco are extremely limited in number, and are very simple, the elaborate combinations known in the East never being used and honorifics very seldom. Nearly all are classical Arabic names, those of Berber origin having grown rare. Of all, Moḥammed is the favourite, being

Boys' Names.

* A prejudice by no means confined to the Moors. A French woman assured me that she had never yet ventured to bathe her two-year old boy for the same reason, though a healthy child.

most frequently conferred on the first-born son, while variations of it, such as M'ḥammed, Aḥmad (or Ḥámed), Ḥamîd and Maḥmûd, are sometimes distributed among the brothers. Next in order of favour comes 'Abd Allah ("Slave-of-God"), and hardly less popular are 'Abd el Ḳáder, 'Abd er-Raḥmán, 'Abd el Karîm and 'Abd es-Salám, meaning respectively, "Slave-of-the-Powerful," "of-the-Merciful," "of-the-Generous," and "of-Peace." Kindred, though less common, appellations are: 'Abd el Málik, 'Abd el Laṭîf, 'Abd el Azîz, 'Abd el Majîd, 'Abd el Gháni and 'Abd el Waḥid, meaning "Slave-of-the-King," "of-the-Gracious," "of-the-Beloved," "of-the-Glorious," "of-the-Rich" and "of-the-One,"—all, of course, referring to God, but used as equivalents of Mohammed, to whom it is claimed they all belong. Then come 'Ali ("Noble"), El 'Arbî ("the Arab"), El 'Abbás ("the Lion"), Musṭafà ("Chosen"), 'Drees, (Enoch), El Mukhtar ("the Selected"), 'Allál, Sulaïman, Es-Sâïd ("the Fortunate"), Kasem, El Ḥasan ("the Handsome), El Ḥosaïn (diminutive of Ḥasan), El Háshmî ("the Liberal"), Eṭ-Ṭáhir ("the Pure"), 'Bû Sha'ib* ("Father-of-Travelling-Bags"). 'Bû Selham ("Father-of-the-Cloak"), 'Bû Shtá ("Father-of-Rain"), Melûdî ("Birthday-One")—commonly bestowed on children born at the feast of Mohammed's birthday—Ibrahim and 'Omar. Others are but rarely employed.

YOUNG MOROCCO.
From the Author's Kodak.

* The Arab name for Jethro: Sha'ib=Hobab: cf. EWALD, *Gesch.* II., 58, n.

The names for girls are still more restricted, the most common being: Fáṭimah or Faṭûmah ("Weaner"), 'Ayeshah ("Mother-life"), Khadîjah, Raḥmah ("Mercy"), Maryam, Raḳîah ("Charm"), Es-So'dîah ("the Fortunate"), Zaïnáb (an aromatic tree), Zobîdah ("Marigold"), Azîzah ("Beloved"), or Manánah ("Kind")

Girls' Names.

To slaves a distinct set of appellations is given: for the men, Fataḥ ("Victory"), Marzûk ("Provided-for"), Mesa'òd ("Fortunate"), Mubárak ("Blessed"), Manṣûr ("Conqueror"), Bellál ("Benefit") etc.; and for the women Mubárkah ("Blessed"), Mesa'ôdah ("Fortunate"), El Yaḳût" ("Ruby"), Johrah ("Pearl"), Gha'liah ("Incense"), Záïdah ("Increase"), Amînah ("Trustworthy"), Yamînah ("Right-Hand"), Rabḥah ("Gain") and Ḥabîbah ("Dear").

Slave-Names.

Such a name is known as the ísm, and is personal, there being in Morocco very few family names (konîah), usually adjectives derived from professions or localities, or else imported from Spain.* So in defining a certain person it is generally necessary to mention the name of the father,† or his trade, or place of abode, though reference to personal peculiarities may be made for this purpose without insult. Moors are no[t] referred to as the fathers of their children—*e.g.* Ab[u] Isháḳ ("Father-of-Isaac")—as are Syrians and others.

Surnames.

Once thus fairly ushered into the world and named solicitude is not apt to be wasted on the little Moo[r] whose days are chiefly spent slung in a she[et] like a hammock, with perhaps a hole throug[h] which to observe his surroundings. If a town baby [he] may enjoy the superiority of a cradle (m'had), but

Babyhood.

* *E.g.* Torres, Perez, Garcia, Moreno, Aragon, Barráda, Rozini, Barg[as] (Vargas), Deleiro, Calderon, Crispo, Blanco, Camiro, Grandino, Palami[...]

† *Surnames* beginning with Ben ("Son of") are common in Fez, [...] Ben-A'ni, Ben-Nees, Ben-Zakor, Ben-Shikrán.

"BROTHERS, WE."

Molinari, Photo., Tangier.

one or other he howls to his heart's content, till he learns that crying is useless, and thereafter is a model of silent good behaviour. When his mother or big sister—often very small for the burden according to our ideas—takes him abroad, it is first in a sheet slung across her back, and then astride of her hip, with his little bare pate exposed to the broiling sun. This latter method is most favoured by the Arabs, the former by the Jibálà or northern hill-tribes. Moorish women suckle their children either until the supply ceases, or is required for another.

Hair-Cutting.

The first hair-cutting is the occasion of a special feast called 'aḳîḳah, and the family barber will sometimes shave a youngster's head gratis for years in the hope of securing continued custom, with a handsome reward when he is asked to preside at the youth's wedding. Occasionally a little brother may be brought in to be shaved towards the close of a wedding-feast, that an opportunity may be afforded for a special collection for the barber, all present being constrained to press a silver coin on the child's forehead.

Certain little tufts are left unshorn, according to local custom or fancy, a habit which goes back at least to ancient Egyptian times. A patch left to grow on the top is called a g'ṭi or guṭṭáïah, a tuft at the side a garn, and a narrow line from front to back an 'orf.* Otherwise the heads of boys are shaved all over, a little water only being used with the razor; but little girls, and not infrequently very small boys, have their hair simply brushed out from the centre and clipped all round like

* Douls describes the custom in the far south of leaving these locks, which are cut off one by one on the occurrence of some great event in the youth's life, the middle one at the top being left to the last (p. 14). The Arabs of these districts, like those of southern Arabia, butter their hair. (Paddock, p. 258.)

that of the Russian peasants, reaching in front to about the eyebrows, and behind to the nape of the neck. It is common with girls, and sometimes with boys, to dye the hair with ḥenná – Egyptian privet,—which produces a rusty red.*

For the first few years of their lives the boys and girls have much the same experiences, often being difficult to distinguish by their dress, which may be either of the scantiest, perhaps no more than one small shirt, or may consist of two or three gowns, one over the other, with a girdle at the waist. Both receive a fair share of parental interest, but the boy will probably be made a little more of, as more promising, according to the Oriental standard. The Moors are by no means destitute of affection for their children, and a father may often be seen playing with his youngsters of both sexes at the door of his house or stable, yet without the freedom we allow ourselves, for one of the first principles inculcated is deferential bearing towards the parents, and especially the father. On being bidden to enter the apartment in which he is seated—and Moorish children would not venture to do so without permission—they respectfully kiss his hands and those of any guests who may be present, maintaining a respectful silence: it is very seldom that a boy is permitted to eat in the presence of his father, and even men and women practically never eat from the same dish, the viands being sent out to the women when the men of all grades have had their turn.

Dress.

Manners.

The boys in due time go to school, as will be de-

* In the East, especially in Persia and among the Muslimîn of northern India, men whose hair has begun to turn grey adopt this practice, subsequently using indigo, which with the ḥenná produces a good jet black, though apt to turn red if neglected.

scribed elsewhere,[1] to learn at least to recite some portions of the Ḳor'án, if not to read it, or to write. School hours in Morocco are so arranged, in the country at least, that after it is over in the early morning, the lads may tend the flocks till sunset approaches, and in this they often have the assistance of their sisters. The great event of the boy's childhood is his circumcision festival, which occurs in towns while yet of tender years, but in the country is frequently postponed till twelve or thirteen, usually taking place at the feast of the Maôlûd.[2]

Schooling.

As children, both sexes play together without restraint, but about the age of eleven or twelve the girls commence to be secluded and veiled, earlier in town than country, where considerable laxity prevails, even with grown women. It is sufficient for a damsel to be discovered making use of a mirror for her parents to take warning and cover her up.

Games.

The games in which the youngsters indulge are neither many nor varied. The principal one is a kind of foot-ball,—more akin to that of Siam and Burma than to that of England,—known as la'ab el kôrah, played by an irregular group who kick a leather ball about four inches in diameter, stuffed with wool, as high into the air as they can, the object being to keep it up like a shuttle-cock. The la'ab el ḳisrah b'il 'aṣà (game of cork-with-stick) is easily recognizable as hockey of the unscientific sort, the object being to drive a piece of cork into a hole; and la'ab el ḥajár is simply stone-throwing, so dear to all boyish hearts. In the coast towns tops have been successfully introduced. Leap-frog (subsubîyát) is sometimes met with, and so is blind-man's buff (la'ab ghamîḍ el 'aïneen), in which the great thing is to strike the ground with a slipper and remain at that point till the

[1] Ch. xviii. [2] See ch. xiv.

"blind-man" approaches, and then escape. Elder youths indulge in wrestling ('abbáz), and fencing (áshḳár b'îl 'aṣá), while at the time of the Great Feast a special game is in vogue called bû j'lood, in which one of the players, whose arms and legs are protected by leather,

MOORISH COUNTRY WOMAN.
(In Ḥaïk and Fûtah.)
Drawn by Herr O. Schulz; from a photograph.

repays with thongs the blows which he receives from others with slippers.

The chief amusement of the adults of Morocco is the "powder-play" (la'ab el bárûd), which not only affords a spectacle and test of horsemanship, but also serves as cavalry drill, representing the tactics of the Moorish horse-soldier. It consists of foot and horse-back exercises in which long muskets have taken the place of the lances for which they were designed. It is generally held in the afternoon, sometimes for several days in succession, and attracts large crowds, for the Moor is pre-eminently a horseman. At one end of a space left more or less clear, a line of gaily caparisoned steeds is reined up, tight and prancing, by a line of riders as richly clad, the abundance of colour in their flowing garments being toned and heightened in effect by the prevailing wool-white of their cloaks or shawls. As a signal from the leader in the centre sets their bridles loose, and lets their sharp-cornered shovel stirrups or spurs descend upon their horses' flanks, each rider waves above his head a gleaming flint-lock as his forefather did his spear; and away they charge at a furious gallop, nothing heard but the thud of hoofs, all voices hushed and all eyes strained in their wake. At another signal a volley is fired, and the steeds are reined up on their haunches by brutal bits just when seeming about to tear through the crowd, or to charge a wall. Then turning, all walk back as sedately as if they had never exerted themselves, the methodical, dignified way in which all has been performed being a feature of the spectacle.

"Powder-Play."

The sight of their gaily caparisoned steeds, their flowing, many-coloured garments, and their burnished guns, is picturesque in the extreme, and the exhilaration of the rush is ample to account for the favour in which la'ab el bárûd is held. *

At other times the "powder-play" takes place on foot, a group of men forming into a circle, and after

* For another illustration see *The Moorish Empire*, p. 145.

spinning their guns in every direction, firing them all at the ground, unless, as sometimes happens, one has charged his piece with ball to settle some old-standing feud. This pedestrian method is more often seen in the country, or at weddings, or when bringing offerings in for some saint, the players advancing as they re-load, then halting to re-form the circle and fire again. The best "powder-play" of all is to be seen wherever the Court is stationed, for thither at each great feast the governors repair with their retainers, and hundreds perform at once on the finest of horses.

Variations.

On great occasions special feats are performed with the flint-locks, which are fired in every attitude, or riding in some apparently impossible manner. To the horses the shock of the sudden halt is most prejudicial, straining especially the hind-legs, which in Barbary steeds are often weak from their having been so employed when too young.

A ZERWATAH with side view of guard.

The chase, too, is always popular among the Moors, but they are seldom good shots, and are not very scientific in their methods. Rabbit hunting is conducted by boys with curved sticks ('okkáz or zerwátáh) which they are able to throw with some skill Hawking is indulged in by a few of the wealthier ķaïds of the great plains, but the birds have now to be imported.* Fishing is not looked upon as a sport.

Hunting.

In-doors the Moors have few amusements, chess being indulged in by a small proportion of the better educated only, † though draughts are more common, being played in coffee-houses with astonishing

In-door Games.

* See *The Land of the Moors*, p. 73.

† At Shiraz the ķáḍi expressed to me his horror at such a practice,

rapidity, accompanied by voluble remarks not always complimentary. Spanish playing-cards and dominoes, although forbidden by Islám, are being introduced by the drinking-shops with which the ports are becoming

JUGGLERS ON THE JUMU'A EL FANA, MARRAKESH.
Photograph by A. Lennox, Esq.

infested, and are making their way all over the country, along with a taste for the drink of the Europeans.

first alleging that chess was prohibited as a game of chance, and then, when I showed him that it was not so, declared that the murderers of Ḥasan and Ḥosaïn played it before committing the deed, so that it had become abhorrent to all Shî'ís.

Entertainments

Other recreations much in favour in Morocco, rather to be classed as entertainments, are music and singing, story-telling, dancing, jugglery, snake-charming and acrobatic performances. Moorish music cannot here be dealt with fully, but it may be summed up as monotonous, irregular, and enharmonic, chiefly minor; most unpleasant to the ears of strangers from the West, but not at all unpleasing when one has become accustomed to it.* As instrumental music is seldom employed alone, the droning nasal singing it accompanies must always be considered with it, and as there are few professional musicians, the average attainments are not high. Most Moors seem to think that they can strum a ginbrî, as their two-stringed mandolins are called, and the women at feast times beat earthenware ágwáls or earthenware drums. While a song is in progress everyone present joins in with snatches of words as he can, adherence to the tune not being essential, as indeed would be impossible on account of its constant variations, for neither words nor notes are committed to writing. Among those who go about to play at feasts a good many Jews are found.

Music.

The story-tellers who beguile the closing hours of the day on the market-places are, on the other hand, always Moors, and very effective they are, with their abundant action and their tambourine accompaniment. Few sights in Morocco are more effective than the intent and wide-mouthed group which a skilful raconteur will assemble round him on the market-place of an afternoon, as he thrills and tickles them alternately with tales of love and adventure, enlivened with gross humour and local touches, interspersed by appeals for collections "just to show their interest," and pious exclamations in which all join, stroking their

Story-Tellers.

* For further details see ch. xi.

MOORISH SNAKE CHARMERS.

Albert, Photo., Tunis.

faces with both hands the while. Most of the stories told would to satiated western ears seem tedious, but Orientals never tire of their old favourites, which always come out in fresh guise at each re-telling.

Moorish dancers—from whom some derive the name "Morris-dancers"—are all women of a dissolute class, who perform the well-known voluptuous "stomach dances" of the East, the art in which consists in moving as many of the muscles as possible independently of the others, especially those of the abdomen, while the feet remain unmoved. So skilful do some of these women become, that with a tray of teacups on her head, an adept will go through her dance, and finally sit down on the ground without shifting a cup. Moors never dance for their own amusement. "Why should we," they ask, "when we can afford to pay others to do so for us?"

Dancing.

Moorish acrobats generally come from the province of Sûs, and belong to the religious brotherhood of Sîdî Ḥamed û Mûsà. They are not very common, but are expert enough to be in request for the great circuses of Europe and America, where there are always several troupes *en tour.* I have come across them in Chicago at the great World's Fair, and in the shows of "Buffalo Bill" and Barnum and Bailey. Both acrobats and jugglers do more talking than performing, and the same may be said of the snake-charmers, for they all rely on what they can excite the crowd around to give in hopes of hurrying on the performance. None of the tricks I have seen displayed were of a special merit or peculiar nature, and there is more to disgust than attract in the so-called charming of snakes. Although an offer will sometimes be made to try the effect of a bite on any animal that may be brought, the challenge is seldom accepted, and is

Acrobats.

Snake-Charming.

then not free from suspicion of *leger-de-main*. But the performer—usually a member of the 'Aïsáwà brotherhood, who has a coil of presumably poisonous reptiles about his neck, and clears a space around him by for a moment turning one loose, or swinging it round by its tail, contents the onlookers by swallowing all but a few inches, and letting it bite the back of his hand or his tongue till the blood comes, all accompanied by a continued performance on the tambourines and oboes of his orchestra.

Condition of the Women.

All this may be very entertaining to the European visitor, but in considering the life of the Moors it is impossible to overlook the state of their women, sad, like that of all Mohammedan women, and one of the causes which most powerfully militate against national development. Treated from childhood as inferior beings; imbued with no ideal higher than the power of tempting passion; left in ignorance and servitude; they are an effectual clog on all progress. Accustomed to be either worshipped or driven, according to the favour or disfavour in which they may be regarded; often having to share and contend for the husband's attentions with a "partner," or perhaps with a house full of female slaves; covered up from the gaze of all in the street; unlettered, untrained, untrusted; the life of a Moorish woman is not far removed from that of a slave, though she be called free, and so what little one generation learns is lost for lack of the training that only a mother can give.

THE SLAVE-MARKET IN MARRAKESH.

CHAPTER THE EIGHTH

SLAVERY AND SERVITUDE AMONG THE MOORS

ALTHOUGH nothing that can be advanced in extenuation of the traffic in human beings which still flourishes in Morocco can justify its continuance, no advantage is to be derived from painting only its dark side, and intensifying even that, as so many writers have done. It is as well to make clear from the outset that the treatment of slaves in Morocco in no way compares with that meted out to the victims in years gone by on plantations owned by Englishmen. To begin with, the Moor, although he considers himself justified by the colour of a brother man to take from him his dearest privilege, his liberty, to subjugate him to his every whim as he might a brute beast, nevertheless regards him still as a man, and one who, once made free, is capable of taking his stand by the side of white men without presumption, for in Morocco no amount of negro blood is regarded as a social drawback. The consequence is that while some cruel natures abuse the power they wield as owners of their fellow-creatures, just as they ill-treat their beasts, the majority treat their slaves well, so well that many cling to their masters as their only friends. It was doubtless the position held in the State by emancipated slaves which led our forefathers to fancy the Moors were black, as instanced in the classical misrepresentation of Othello.?

Absence of Race Hatred.

It would be difficult to estimate with accuracy

The author points out that the Moor is not like the Englishmen But fails to realize that he is still framing his work through the lense of an Englishman Thinking and stating that their would be something such as "Negro" blood for as stated "The Moor, although he considers himself justified by the colour of a brother man..." "Nevertheless regards him still as a man."

meaning that if this slave come from among the Moors the slave himself would be also a Moor or of some Tribe, nation or clan, but would not be consided a negro.

Again the author says ~~control~~ contradicting statements that to me show that he is trying his hardest that the "Moor" and "Negro" are not one in the same.

He says "for in Morocco NO amount of negro blood is regarded as a social set back" - Now why would that be? other than the reason ~~as the being~~ the social class of a Negro is a European construct of White supremacy they borrowed the word. Next he clearly even states how the slave was taken from specific places or were taken in "local" warfare

Numbers of Slaves.

what proportion of the population of Morocco belongs to this class, and accounts of the numbers imported each year vary too much to afford a basis for calculation, but it may be taken that the proportion is extremely small, as except in the large towns there are very few slaves, and the number introduced depends entirely upon the facility of transport and the peaceful or disturbed state of the country. Almost all are brought when young from across the western Ṣûdán by caravans which also trade, and carry over the mountains and desert great slabs of rock-salt wherewith to purchase children from their captors, who have either obtained them by ambush or in local warfare. So great is the value of salt in those districts, that the piece some six or seven inches thick on which a lad can stand is said often to be given as his price, called "ḳeemat el milḥah," a term used in reproach. Grown men and women are seldom imported, although able-bodied youths and comely maidens are in constant demand.*

Supply.

Of all the evils that may be charged against the Morocco slave trade, after the separation of the captured children from their parents, one of the worst is the terrible journey over the Sahara and the Atlas. Two or three children are packed in each pannier on the back of a mule, so that they cannot move, and are given barely enough food to live. For much of the way the journey is performed by night, the caravan hiding by day, and the pace is slow, as the adults are driven on foot.† Arrived at the markets of

Importation.

* Tindûf is a great distributing centre for the Timbuctoo caravans. Douls here met 200 of both sexes mounted on camels whose water skins had been emptied (p. 24).

† Side by side with this picture it is only just to the Moors to show how the Anglo-American marts were supplied within a century. The

Marrákesh or Sûs, where first they change hands—though many have succumbed by the way,—the survivors are better fed and are taught a little Arabic, together with the ceremonial duties of Mohammedans. Hitherto their language has been that of the Guinea coast, Ginâwah, which they always continue to speak among themselves,—and their religion, on which they merely superimpose some notions of Islám, a sort of spirit worship. They

story is told by Mr. John R. Spears in *Scribner's Magazine*, September 1900, under the heading of "The Slave Trade in America." Beside his narrative even the brutalities inflicted on European slaves by such a wretch as Mulai Ismá'îl lose their peculiar horror.

"Having been captured in the midst of fire and bloodshed, the slaves of the interior were hurried to the sea. *En route* they saw their relatives and friends hacked to pieces for lagging. They were herded in pens on the beach, where they saw other friends and relatives perish under hard treatment. They were sold, not by families, but by chance, and so members of one family went on board different ships, separated for ever. Here they saw some of their numbers rejected for physical defects, and the rejected ones were often murdered before the eyes of the others. They were stowed in loathsome holds, bound to a region of which they could know nothing, and of which they could imagine only the most fearsome evils.

"'The ships,' said Dr. Alexander Falconbridge, of the slaver *Tartar*, 'were fitted up with a view of preventing slaves jumping overboard.' There was a netting stretched above the rails, but an opening was left in one place that refuse might be dumped overboard, and through this many a slave, suffering from home-sickness, plunged to his death. They stole rope-yarns that they might hang themselves. They refused to eat, that they might starve to death. The first care of the slavers was to prevent revolts, but little less was the vigilance needed to prevent suicide.

"In connection with this vigilance we find further tortures. Because the slave often refused to eat, the tube-like instrument which surgeons use in feeding lock-jaw patients was carried on almost every ship. Hot coals and red-hot irons were used by more cruel shipmasters to open the stubborn mouths, and lest this seem incredible, I must remind the reader that branding slaves was as common then as branding cattle is now, and that the civilization of even this age is not likely to end the torture of cattle for many years to come....

"The truth is that by a fair interpretation of the laws of England in 1781, the murder of the slaves was 'a case of throwing over goods; for to this purpose and the purpose of insurance they are goods and property.' The Solicitor-General, Mr. I. Lee, used the words quoted."

are also allotted a special set of Arabic names, the commonest which have elsewhere been enumerated.

Girls with any promise of beauty are carefully fattened, and others are instructed in household duties; one who has been trained under a first-rate cook commanding a considerable price. I once saw a girl just purchased for about £13, for whom the dealer hoped to receive £25 when she had been trained by a

Prices.

SLAVE-WIFE AND SON.

Photograph by the late Joseph Thomson, Esq.

cook for whom he was asking £33 10s. The prices obtainable vary too much from season to season, fluctuating with supply and demand, for any set of prices to serve for more than an indication of the relative values of different classes. I once saw a batch disposed of by auction when business was dull in Marrákesh, in which two small boys fetched £5 and £5 10s.; a full grown white girl, £24; black girl of twelve to fifteen, £9 to £10; a stalwart negro, £14; and so on. A beauty, the dealer told me, might just then fetch £130 to £160, but such prices would be altogether exceptional. In a slack season I have known a man with his wife and child sold for £6 10s., a girl of eight for £3 10s.; an able bodied woman for £10; and a mother with two boys of a few months and six years old respectively for £3 15s.; while about the same time £30 was all that could be obtained for a father and mother with three children, and £28 10s. for a woman with three children; so these lots were withdrawn.

Slave Auctions.

Of the details of these auctions, conducted precisely as are those of cows and mules, often on the same spot by the same men, it is needless to speak at length: suffice it to say that the human chattels are subjected to just the same treatment as cattle would be under similar circumstances, being personally examined in the most disgusting manner, and paraded in lots by the auctioneers, who shout out their attractions and the bids. Sales usually take place on the afternoons of stated days, affording a lounge for a certain class who discuss the "goods" offered, and look out for bargains. In response to the representations of European philanthropists this public sale of slaves was abolished in the coast towns some years ago, but sales are still conducted from door to door, sometimes even in the market-places, in defiance of the regulation.

Another way in which the Europeans have been frequently outwitted is by the importation of Circassian and other slaves and eunuchs from Turkey viâ Gibraltar or Algiers in foreign vessels, usually entered as members of the family of their master. Notwithstanding the nominal prohibition of the trade in the Turkish Empire, there are houses on the Bosporus where young children are trained for the ḥareems by instruction in music and dancing, and even in English and French, as well as in the degrading arts by which the women of these lands endeavour to secure the favour of their lords. These, too, are sometimes brought to Morocco, where they fetch high prices, if offered at all to the public; as much, sometimes, as a couple of hundred pounds or more, of which they are very proud. The mother of the present sultan was one of these women, bought from the ḥareem of a well-known pasha of Cairo by a friend of mine—along with two others whom he kept for himself—and presented by him to the late sultan, with whom she speedily became a favourite, securing for her son a continuation of favour which gained him the throne. This is often the case with white concubines, who are in great demand, even if natives. Consequently white girls are frequently kidnapped, and in time of war openly sold, to be trained by dealers in this special article, but though, if report is to be credited, some do occasionally yield to the temptation to sell their own daughters by slave-mothers, such a proceeding is not only illegal, but in the highest degree abhorrent in native eyes.

Slaves from the East.

Many of the black slaves in Morocco are the offspring of slave parents, for their masters can mate them with whom they like, though they may not afterwards separate a couple whom they have married, and a slave is not supposed to have more than two wives. The children of such unions are the property of their parents' owner, and are saleable, but the children of a master by any of his slave-women, of whom any number may be concubines, are free, and

Marriage and Manumission.

their mothers may not be sold, but become free on the death of their master. To manumit a slave is considered a meritorious act; sometimes this is promised by the master's will,* or a slave is allowed a certain amount of

A MOROCCO SLAVE.

Molinari, Photo., Tangier.

liberty that he may earn enough to purchase his freedom. But without papers of manumission they are liable

* The unfortunate part of this cheap way of laying up "merit" is that frequently the liberated slave, especially if a woman, finds it almost

to be seized and sold like stray cattle, and cannot marry or acquire property.

Cruelty.

The power of their owners over their slaves is such that they may even take their lives with impunity, and instances are not wanting among well-known living men in which this has been done, in one notorious case even under British protection.* There is therefore no limit to the cruelties which may be, and at times are, inflicted on their slaves by inhuman masters, and I could easily fill pages with most harrowing descriptions of authenticated instances. I have myself seen the stumps of a poor woman whose feet had been burnt off by her being set to knead unslacked mortar therewith. Eunuchs are, however, very seldom made in Morocco, and then only for the royal palace.

General Treatment.

As has been already pointed out, the majority of owners, whether men or women, treat their slaves with comparative kindness, for it is in their own interest to do so, and on the whole it may be assumed that with the exception of occasional cases of brutality, the lot of the average slave in Morocco is no worse than that of the so-called free wife, or the unprotected labourer. It must be remembered that the slave has at least his natural wants provided for without anxiety, for as soon as his owner cannot feed him he is sold to raise money, as a horse would be, and when he has been brought up in captivity his aspirations after freedom must be very slight. Within six or eight days

impossible to make a livelihood, often from mere age. The condition of such is most pitiful, and in Tangier an effort is being made by some resident English ladies to provide for urgent cases, contributions towards which may be remitted to Mrs. Brooks, Tangier, or to the Anti-Slavery Society, 55, New Broad Street, London, E.C.

* Christians and Jews are by the laws of the country prohibited from owning slaves, a prohibition which the laws of Europe extend to foreign-protected Mohammedans.

of purchase a slave may be returned if the slightest bodily fault not proclaimed at the sale be discovered, or even if he or she be unable to perform the work expected. At the sales they are usually decked in at least one garment of showy print, and when installed in good homes the girls are arrayed in gorgeous if inexpensive colours, the choice of their race, and exceedingly handsome they look when well kept, with their good-natured features and their kindly dispositions, which always secure them friends among the unprejudiced.

Domestic Service.

So much of the household work of Morocco is done by the slaves, since all but the poorest find it cheaper to purchase a fellow-creature than to hire one; and so much is done by the women of the households themselves, that there is very little room left for domestic service. Indeed, for a free woman to serve in the home of another except as a wife would be considered quite improper, unless she were either a mere child or an elderly married woman, though among the poor much neighbourly service is constantly rendered. Men and boys, however, have no such objection, but the latter cannot enter the women's quarters, and can only be employed in the stables, on errands, in bringing water and such like offices. The lot of labourers who till the ground is but little removed from that of their employers, and there are few of those social distinctions which count for so much in the West. But agricultural labour falls under another category, that which follows.

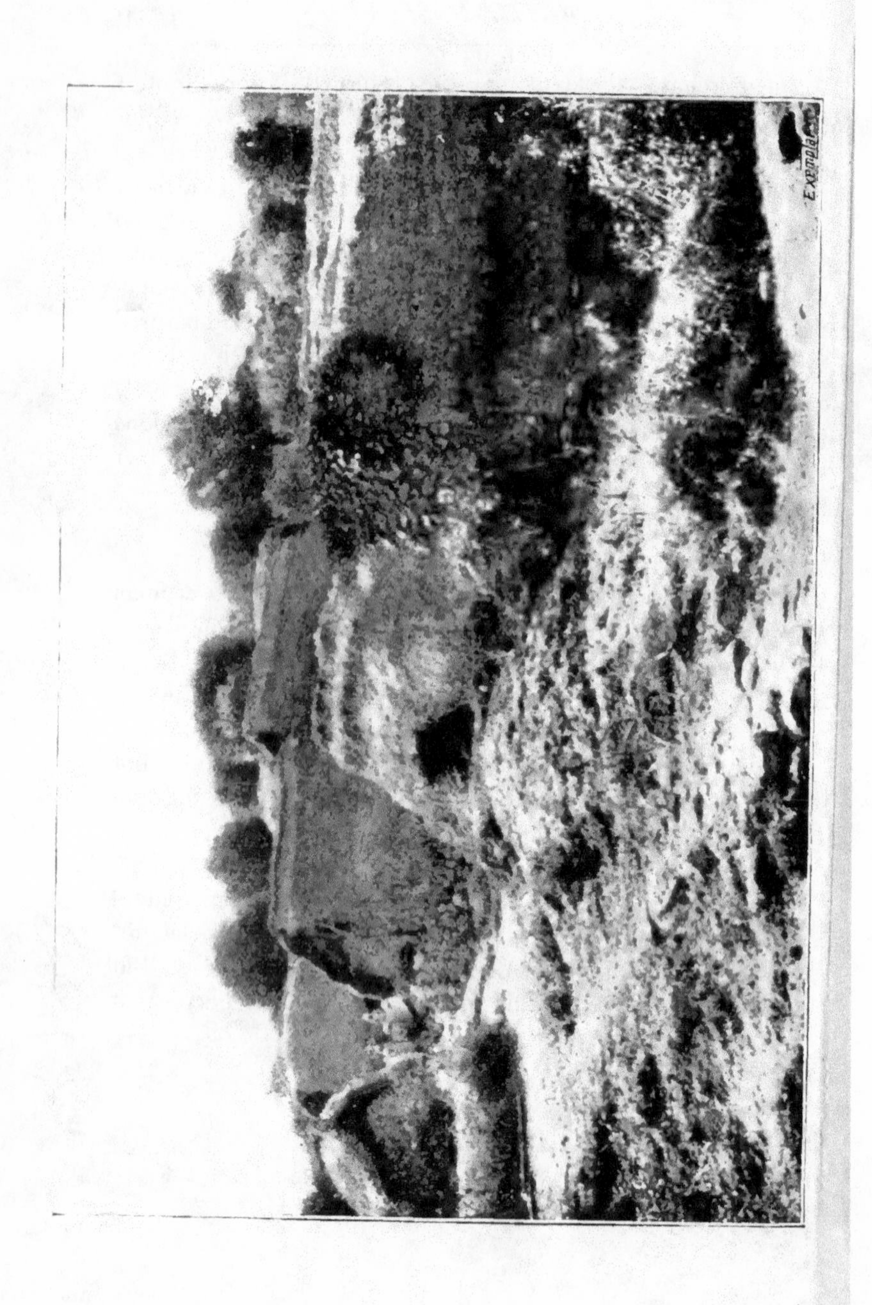

CHAPTER THE NINTH

MOORISH COUNTRY LIFE

CONSIDERING the large proportion of the Moors who still dwell in tents, when compared to those who inhabit houses in towns, and the much larger proportion who occupy settled villages of huts and mud-built cabins, it is strange that writers on this country have devoted so little attention to these classes. Much has, indeed, been written on their picturesque aspect, and somewhat too on their unfortunate condition, but a serious study has yet to be made of their inner life, and the points wherein their habits and institutions differ from those better known in the towns.

Neglected Features.

Unfortunately, after one's first interested glances at the Moorish country-folk, what little attraction there is in them disappears, as they are found to be, in the words of a skilful writer,[1] "simply pastoral, simply poetical, simply filthy," but the people themselves, underneath the dirt, would well repay the closer attention of a sympathetic student. Another reason for their neglect is the assumption that the life of the Arab nomad, wherever found, is practically identical, and that the difference is slight between countrymen and the townsmen. Both these suppositions are to a certain extent correct, but there still remains sufficient originality in the North African country-folk to repay the attention of one conversant with the life of their eastern

Reasons of Neglect.

[1] W. B. Harris: *Land of an African Sultan.*

counterparts. In Algeria much has already been done in this direction, but in Morocco the task has not yet been attempted.*

Treatment of Foreigners.

Foreign visitors, though seldom treated with incivility along the main tracks, are never made warmly welcome unless old friends. No race is more easy to get on with when humoured a bit, like so many children, but none is more ready to return kindness for kindness or spite for spite. In villages removed from the main tracks there is more bigotry and fanaticism to lead the people to resent intrusion, while in those more frequently invaded, familiarity has bred contempt, and hardly courtesy is shown to Europeans entering their precincts. This is not, however, from any ill-will, but from wisdom born of experience that the less they have to do with foreigners—Nazarenes they call them indiscriminately—the better for themselves.

Unwelcome Guests.

The more Europeans they see the less they are welcome, because some bring letters from the authorities which they construe into orders for provender not to be paid for, though supplied by people on the verge of starvation. Strangers can well afford to despise the dwellings and customs of the natives as they stroll inquisitively round the village, poking their noses unceremoniously here and there—if they do not hold them too high in the air—criticizing their novel surroundings in a way that is evident enough to disgust even those who know not a word they say, yet when it comes to paying for what they have been so ready to eat (not to speak of tea and candles) too often they find that they cannot afford that!

* The nearest approach is the excellent work of Lieut.-Col. Villot, since wisely appointed head of the "Bureau Arabe" in Algeria: *Mœurs, Coutumes et Institutions des Indigènes de l'Algérie*. See also *Les Mystères du Peuple Arabe*, by Ch. Richard.

Picturesque and poetical though it may be, the life of the nomad is not an ideal life. The very freedom from restraint, and the constant restlessness, preclude encouragement in art or science, or development in social administration, stability being indispensable for the growth of civilization. Men whose struggle with the elements is severe and unceasing, whose migrations are uncertain and frequent, cannot be expected to pay much attention to the refinements of life, or to the accumulation of unnecessary property, and it is not to be wondered at that the lesson taught by the nomads is how much we can do without.

Drawbacks of Nomad Life.

After the in-gathering of the crops, and the conclusion of the other agricultural operations of the season, the encampment may at any time be changed. Every belonging having been loaded on the backs of beasts of burden, or even of human beings, the whole tribe will set off in search of pastures new, to settle at a spot already selected. As Morocco contains few large unappropriated districts, and the sphere of each tribe has been limited by custom and its neighbours, these migrations are not often to great distances, and are chiefly undertaken in search of pasturage or to avoid a foe. Two or three days' journey is generally the limit, as the country is fertile, and often the only motive for a change is to secure a clean camping-ground. In spring moves are commonly made northwards, or nearer to towns for the disposal of produce, but the Arab thinks nothing of a day's journey in search of water, so long as grass is plentiful. When a desirable spot becomes a bone of contention between two tribes, they do not hesitate to "let the powder speak," and often by their kinships and alliances inflame a whole province.

Migration.

It is a mistake to suppose that the nomads of Morocco

owe their existence to the Mohammedan invasion in the early years of the eighth century. Even the genuine Arabs among them are not descendants of the invaders, but of tribes imported in the eleventh and twelfth centuries of our era,* and according to native authors, many, if not all, of the Berbers themselves, were originally nomadic; it is probable that they had not all become stationary when the

Origin of Nomads.

APPROACHING AN ARAB DÛAR OR VILLAGE.
(Across waste of palmetto scrub.)
Photograph by Dr. Rudduck.

first Arabs arrived. Large numbers of the Berbers, as we know from the same sources, became "Arabicized,"† and it is possible that some of the tribes now speaking Arabic only, are in part, if not altogether, of Berber blood. There are, however, no great nomad tribes in

* See *The Moorish Empire*, pp. 32, 33, and LEO, (Hak.) p. 396.

† "*Must'arab*," corrupted by Europeans into "Mozarab."

Morocco of a strength to defy the settled power, as the policy of the Moorish Government has always been their subdivision and dissemination, so that to-day one encounters fractions of the principal tribes in all parts of the country, and the majority know no tribal cohesion.

The Patriarchal System.

The Arab tent is a most wonderfully comprehensive institution, often sheltering beneath its simple roof not only its owner's immediate family, but sometimes a considerable circle of relatives. Thus I have known a patriarchal native and his wife sharing their abode with three daughters—one a widow with two sons, one with a husband and two daughters, the third with a husband, three daughters and a son—fifteen in all. Cases sometimes occur in which a man with four wives has about a dozen married children, but unless among the very poor, these usually manage to make homes for themselves. Thus the number of immediate relatives with which each is surrounded is appalling, but such numbers mean strength and protection, and the Arab household is self-contained, depending on very little outside its own circle.

Possessions.

Each well-to-do nomad possesses all the requisites of life, food, clothes and transport. "His camels not only carry his wives, children and tent, but feed them: his cows enable him to sell two or three jars of butter, and his fowls a basket of eggs weekly: his sheep will give him twenty-five lambs annually beyond what he consumes: the wool from them gives him from four to six ḥaïks and a carpet: his barley feeds his cattle when vegetation ceases, and some of it is sown to produce and make his kesk'soo."[1] When travelling, he leaves his grain stored in maṭmôrahs beneath the ground, or in the hands of people settled in ḳ'ṣûrs, who retain a tenth as their remuneration, and he goes

[1] DAVIDSON.

off with a light heart seeking for pasture. The real nomads of the south do not plough, and carry little grain with them, the only Arab agriculturalists being those of the north, where there are also fixed tent villages.

Encampments.

Few of the encampments of Morocco—called dûárs or "circles"—are of great size, such as may be met with in Arabia, consisting rather of detached groups of a dozen or twenty tents, or in exceptional circumstances up to a hundred, acknowledging a sheïkh or elder as common head and ḳáïd over the whole tribe. For purposes of taxation these authorities are recognized by the Government, but some of the tribes are under the jurisdiction of the provincial governors, as is usually the case also with the Jibálà or Hillsmen (*s.* Jibli). Most of the encampments are found off the main tracks, if possible in a hollow, or on some gentle slope sheltered from the wind. From the distance they appear mere black lines on the horizon; their roofs are so low that one has to approach fairly near before the individual tents can be distinguished.

Arrangement.

The Morocco Arabs are not to be feared by strangers who would visit them; such will find them hospitable and agreeable, although if they saw a chance of robbing any who were not their guests, they would not hesitate to seize it. On drawing near to a dûár, its shape is seldom found to be regular, but the tents are always grouped with their open sides towards a common centre, in which are tethered or herded at night their four-footed possessions. Loud-barking watch-dogs do the patrol, except when a foe is known to be near, when a regular watch is maintained. Often at night it is only the yelp of distant dogs that guides the traveller to the encampment, and by the time he approaches, their noise is deafening, in spite of the blows and curses of their owners, intended to silence them. Between sunrise and sunset scarcely any but women, children and old men will be found at home, all others being at work in the fields, or away with the cattle or sheep.

The Tents.

Their tents are not inviting residences. The broad roof of home-spun cloth, a brown-and-black mixture of goat- and camel-hair, palmetto and other vegetable fibres, rough and coarse, is stretched out from twenty to forty feet across a ridge-pole and

MOORISH TENT-DOOR SCENE.
(The woman seated inside is watching the stew on a fire indicated by the smoke.)
Photograph by Dr. Rudduck.

two lower side-poles to strong stakes in the ground, which it does not reach. The back and walls are of similar material separately stretched, supplemented by bundles of brush-wood and thistles standing on end, outside which is piled a circle of brambles. When the wind and rain beat in from the front, the inmates hang up blankets to protect themselves, but it is generally left open by day. One half of the interior is almost always reserved for the women, a partition against which is piled the family baggage being stretched across the centre. The cost of such a dwelling in northern Morocco will only be $20 to $30, say £3 to £4, so each married couple secures a separate establishment, if nothing more than an extension of the parent tent. Sometimes a hut (nûállah or ḳabbûsah—"caboose") beside the main tent will serve this purpose.

Furniture.

The contents of the average dwelling (khaïmah) are neither numerous nor valuable. The largest and most important article is the upright loom against the partition, an extremely primitive affair at which one or other of the women works most of the day. Near the entrance a few blackened stones by an ashy hole mark the fire-place, if a good-sized pipkin (bormah) be not simmering upon them, while hard by are the hand-mill, and a wooden trough (gessa') for the preparation of kesk'soo. A few more jars and basins, a sieve or two; a tiny three-cornered lamp of clay, a spindle and distaff; perhaps also a brass tray with glasses and tea-pot; a leather-covered trunk of best clothes, a few leather bags (mizwid) * used as cushions; at night a wooden plough and occasionally a few hoes and sickles: these complete the furniture. Coin or valuables usually find a place quite underground, but butter is kept in yonder goat-skins (shikwan), and corn in those sacks (sullah). †

Such are the objects in view, not to speak of the half-clothed urchins rolling about, or their elders busied in household duties, and fowls making free of the

* In the South frequently a gazelle's skin.

† The jibli or mountaineer would use a great earthenware jar (tanjîah) for oil, and a mud-coated cane basket (sullah) for corn.

whole. Calves, lambs and donkeys also sometimes share the sleeping accommodation, the only special provision for the bipeds being palmetto mats on heather or brushwood laid on the trodden earth floor. Many villages are to be found in which huts have begun to supplant the tents, or tents to eke out the huts. The better class huts or tents are distinguished by the introduction of small luxuries in imitation of the towns, such as brass trays, copper kettles, tea-things, cushions, mattresses and crockery.

Inmates.

From sunrise to sunset, often before and after as well, the inhabitants are at work, for they have little temptation to over-sleep in the quarters described, and without anticipated recreation of mind or body they see no reason to hasten their tasks. As soon as the cock crows for the third time during the night the Arab housewife knows it is the hour to rise, and praises God, because taught by the doctors of Islám that when a cock crows it has seen an angel, and that the interpretation of its cry is "Commemorate God, O ye negligent!" Soon all will be bustle and noise, except where her husband slumbers apart, wrapped in his woollen mantle. If a donkey wishes his friends good day, she duly exclaims "I take refuge with God from Satan the stoned," because taught that when the donkey brays he has seen a devil. Then begin her duties for the day.

Occupation.

First she has carefully to count out the flocks to the shepherds, among whom are her elder sons and daughters, if the former are not attending school. One or two of them probably carry reeds of their own munafacture, or equally primitive banjos, to while away the time, for the Moor is essentially musical. The elder girls have their spindles and distaffs, wherewith to spin the handfuls of wool tucked into the openings of their dresses. Away they go, in different directions, fasting, but with a lump of bread for lunch: for water they have the brooks and wells they pass, and when they return at night they will find ready for them the one square meal of the day.

Housekeeping.

When they are despatched, their mothers light the fire and boil the barley meal, or make the bread in large round cakes, all heavy and scorched, cooked in earthen pans on the fire. Then they have their weaving to do, to make new garments for their families, or perhaps a new roof for the home.

AN ARAB VILLAGE.
(Showing hedges of cut thorns and thistles.)
Photograph by Dr. Rudduck.

Presently the husband awakes, and as the sun rises eats his scanty breakfast before going out to work. It is the duty of the men to sleep but lightly during the night, to be ready at any moment to sally forth when the bark of the dogs bespeaks danger, so that their best sleep comes when the others are stirring. Well know they from long years of practice what is about if the dogs give warning, whether a distant foot-step or a prowling beast, or whether a robber discovered close at hand, when their loud vociferation wakes the whole village.

An Arab Toilette.

Left alone, the ladies snatch a moment for their toilette, without which even a Moorish woman would not be happy. A hasty rinsing of face and hands, a little antimony laid along the eyelid and drawn out to give the eye an almond shape: a little yellow-red henna-leaf paste on the finger-tips, and then sometimes their pearly teeth are given a rub up and down with the frayed end of a piece of walnut root,—but never across, as too many unenlightened English folk do, for do not the Arabs know that Satan brushes his teeth that way? Now for a peep in the little tin-backed mirror so highly prized, with which a Moorish woman on no account likes to part, and the toilette is complete. For the last few weeks they have not undressed, so their clothes do not give them much trouble, the most they need at such times is a careful hunt in one another's heads and garments for troublesome visitors, and our friends are "dressed for the afternoon."

Relaxation.

When the feasts of their religion come round, or someone is born, or married or buried, or when some official jubilation takes place, the Moorish country-folk unhesitatingly leave their work,—for cannot to-day's be done as well to-morrow?—and enjoy themselves like children freed from school, for they are of simple natures and easily pleased. Without books, without art, their whole relaxation consists in these occasional feastings, except for the slight dissipation of market-day, which visits each district in turn, week by week. As Morocco villages, whether of tents or huts, very seldom contain any shops or resident mechanics, the farmers wait till a market is held near them to dispose of their produce, or transport it to the coast, and also to purchase foreign stores and cloths. Here, at these weekly markets, meet Arabs and Berbers, and in the North the nondescript hill-tribes or Jibálà.

The Jibálà.

The last-named live in huts and houses, and their villages are of a more permanent character than those described, for their way of living differs much from that of the Arabs. They are of mingled races, and probably represent the Berbers first Arabicized in the eighth and ninth centuries. They are distinguishable by their dialect as well as by peculiar customs, and are said to have in each tribe a different way of pronouncing Arabic, which they never learn to speak like Arabs; it is alleged by natives that they are more successful with European tongues, while those of Zarhôn and of the Mirmûsa tribe in the Rîf are declared to speak like the Jews of Fez.* Space will not permit of a detailed comparison of their customs with those of their neighbours, but they would doubtless repay investigation. While Arab customs vary in detail from tribe to tribe, the Jibli customs are universal. The Jibálà are cleaner by far than the Arabs, and in matters of religion less fanatical, but more strict in its observances. The Arabs, with a ḳaïd for each tribe, are in closer touch with the government than the Jibálà, whose sheïkhs are nominated by the bashá of the nearest town. The Jibálà generally confine their cultivation to gardens or to crops required for their own consumption. The actual work of the field is done chiefly by labourers, called khamás, who receive in addition to their food, a cloak and a pair of slippers or sandals at the Great Feast, and a fifth of the wheat or barley raised, or a fourth of the beans, chick-peas, dra' or vegetables, the straw being common property. Sales of horses, mules and camels are recorded in formidable documents which describe the appearance

* Concerning the peculiarities of their dialect, see ch. xviii.

of both vendor and vended most minutely, and the same accuracy of detail is observed in the records of agricultural partnerships or any other transaction witnessed on paper.

Out in the fields the villagers of both races lead much the same existence. Soon after the rains have thoroughly soaked the ground in the later autumn the ploughing begins, the usual primitive Eastern

Agriculture.

PLOUGHING IN MOROCCO.

Photograph by Herbert White, Esq.

ploughing with a home-made wooden plough drawn by oxen or whatever beasts the farmer can muster; it may be camel and donkey, or perchance, having only one ass, he sets his wife to pull by its side! The area a pair of oxen can plough in a month—a jûjah *—is the only measure of land, so much of which goes uncultivated that except in the vicinity of towns it may almost be had for the tilling. No hedges are planted between the fields, or walls built, except when trees or vegetables are to be grown, when cattle must be kept out. In the open country only a few loose stones, if as much, mark the limits of each cultivated patch, so that to remove a neighbour's land-mark in Morocco is a very easy task. Having so much available ground, the Moors shift their cultivation from point to point to avoid impoverishing the soil, and allow it abundant rest.

In the dry ground wheat, barley, peas, beans and lentils are sown, in the damp ground maize and millet.

A Curious Custom.

Barley is planted first, then wheat, and maize comes last. About the middle of February, when the corn has sprung up, the women of the Jibli villages make a large dressed figure called Máta, covered with ornaments to which all contribute. This they carry in procession round their fields, singing a peculiar ditty. The figure is borne by the foremost woman, who must give it up to any other woman who can get in front of her, which leads to much racing and contention. When the women have had their turn, the "guy" is given up to the men, who are all mounted on horse-back, and jump over the figure, eventually galloping over the young corn, each trying to secure possession of it. At sunset the "Máta" is burned. In spite of the damage done to the crops by this sport, it is believed to bring good luck; its origin would be an interesting study, as it undoubtedly savours of heathendom.[1]

* Villot reckons this as 20 hectares on the plains, or 10 on the hills say 15 on an average.

[1] Cf. Hay, p. 45. and Godard, p. 85.

The rainy season should commence in the end of September, when the prevailing winds change from east to south west, and, heralded by a sudden coolness of the atmosphere some days before, showers fall at night, the intervening days being bright and fresh. Then the former rains come down in earnest, and as they soak in ploughing and sowing begin, often during several weeks of almost fine weather which are truly delightful, till the latter rains set in, and the country is deluged. April usually sees the end of the rains,* when maize (Turkiah), sown in March, is planted out, for along the coast, where dew and breeze are plentiful, it is not dependent on the rain, like wheat and barley, which by this time are well up, and will be ready for the sickle in May and June.†

The Seasons.

Harvesting then demands every available hand, and all turn to in the field, the men with small, saw-toothed sickles, when the demand for labour is such that whole families make it an occasion for their summer holiday, and go into the country, reminding one of the hop-season at home. The grain, which ripens at the height of eighteen inches or two feet, is cut off close to the ear, the reaper drawing the sickle across it to-

Harvesting.

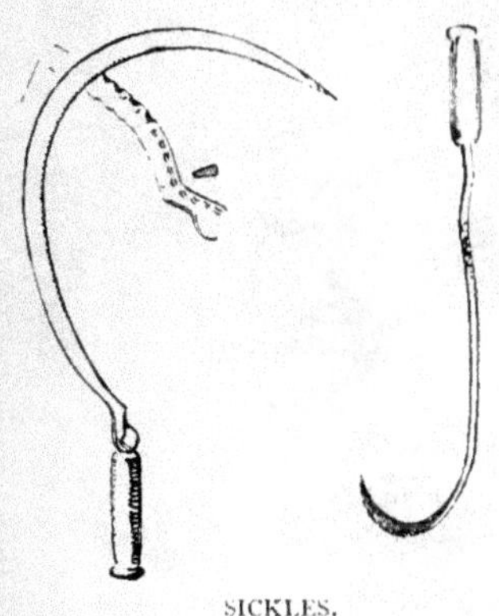

SICKLES.

* It is considered bad luck, however, if there be no rain from May 7th to 19th, and if none falls from April 18th to 24th or from October 12th to 18th the farmer considers himself undone. From August 23rd to 27th is considered "the furnace of the year."

† The author of *Raôḍ el Ḳarṭas* declares that he saw corn sown on April 15th, 1291, and reaped in the end of May, 45 days later, after an almost continual east wind, and no rain after April 12th.

wards himself,—and the remaining stalks are left to return to the soil. The corn is trodden out upon the threshing floor of earth by oxen and other animals, frequently donkeys and mules, or threshed with flails, or a rude construction of rolling logs is dragged over the ears, the grain being afterwards winnowed with shovels. A curious practice is the sowing of canary-seed (zûál) with the grain, and its removal during this process.

MOORS WINNOWING CORN.

Photograph by Herbert White, Esq.

The Grain Trade.

Grain is usually brought to town by the cultivators themselves in sacks, and, if not already paid for, is sold at the doors of the foreign merchants at a price which the latter have fixed. By them it is stored, until shipment in great warehouses (heri), or by native purchasers in underground cells (maṭmôrah), circular, bottle-shaped pits dug beneath a peculiar stratum of tufa which covers most of the Morocco plains, and is impervious to damp.* Groups of these pits are found at some spot (meri) by each village, in charge of a keeper (merrás) who, for a fixed proportion, measures it in and out and gives a receipt. Thus preserved, the mouths of the pits being sealed, wheat and barley are kept for years, and even though after a great length of time it turns black, and the bread made from it is sour, it is not considered less wholesome. In time of war these stores are as eagerly sought for as carefully hidden, and some claim to be able to detect them by their scent. In the hills, where they do not exist, their place is taken by large baskets of wicker or cane (sullah) covered with thatch, as in upper Egypt.

Fruits, etc.

Fruits and vegetables are not much cultivated except in the neighbourhood of towns, and their nature has been treated of elsewhere.† Figs and raisins are largely dried, especially for use when travelling. The method of preparing the last-named is to make a clear lye of ashes and lime, and mix it with oil: into this the bunches of grapes are dipped, and then dried in the sun.

Travelling Arrangements.

In their travelling arrangements the Moors, as well as the Arabs, are far behind the Persians, who, while working on identical principles, have introduced numerous little refinements, such as superior trappings, bells, and caravan-sarais. Camels are ill-adapted to mountain journeys, and in wet weather on clayey soil are liable to constant slips from which they cannot recover, so the popular beast of burden is the tough and sturdy mule, higher in price, as a rule, than the horse, but requiring less attention. Its load is only a couple of hundred-weight, about the same as that

* Diodorus Siculus mentions similar stores as in use among the ancient Britons.

† See *The Land of the Moors*, p. 49.

of a mare, and except when carrying merchandize, it is provided with a pair of roomy panniers (shwárî) across a straw-filled canvas pack-saddle (bardah, or, if of light Sûs make, áḥlás).

Loading.

When loading a pack beast, the general rule is to pile on the weight till it becomes unsteady on its knees as it stands, and then to mount on top of the load, it being well-known that a larger load can be carried when in motion than when at rest. The same principle is applied to the loading of women with grass, straw, charcoal, fire-wood, and other articles of which they bring tremendous bundles many miles into town.

Method of Riding.

Perched on the top of the pack, the rider sits dangling both legs against one side of the creature's neck to make it go. But this is not the only method of urging its pace, for in his hand he usually carries, as more effectual than a stick, something sharp, a splinter, a packing-needle, or an aloe point, wherewith to goad the animal in the shoulder, where there is almost always an open sore. The saddles are usually badly padded, so that under them there may often be found a great raw patch as big as a soup-plate, but the Moorish mind is inured to such sights, and cannot understand our sympathy for these dumb sufferers. Whether they employ rich riding-saddles, mounted on a dozen or more felt cloths of different colours, or only the rude packs of goat-hair cloth stuffed with wool, or of canvas stuffed with straw, all are huge, solid, ungainly things, so it is little wonder that few beasts are to be found with whole backs. The case is still worse with the donkeys, which are numerous and for the most part small, seldom carrying more than a hundred-weight—and so cheap that they receive scant attention.

Mares are the favourite mounts of the farmers themselves, and they are often highly prized. Horses are invariably used unmutilated, and they are sometimes of a fine strain. Their saddles (sarj) are great heavy constructions covered with red cloth, distinguished from those intended for mules by their more elegant construction and lighter shape, the military pattern having a high back and pommel from between which it is difficult to fall. Those of the mules (sarîjah) are merely modified pack-saddles. Both are furnished with large, high-strung shovel-stirrups, the corners of which serve as spurs, if these are not worn, but if they are, they are single spikes of considerable length. The bridles also are cruel inventions, that of a horse (lijám) being a tremendous lever curb by which the mouth may be forced open, that of a donkey (sarîmah) being a simple ring on the lower jaw, and that of the mule, like the creature itself, between the two. Saddles of all sorts are secured in place by broad chest-bands (dîr) and buttock bands (d'fár), but the girths are often quite inadequate, and cause much suffering.

Saddlery.

STIRRUP.

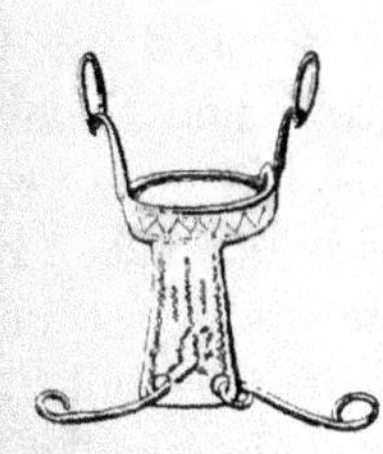
A MULE'S BIT.

The lower jaw passes through the bit, shown here as seen from beneath, so that by drawing the reins the mouth may be prized open. The upper rings are for the cheek straps.

At night the steeds are picketed in rows before the tents, one leg or both fore-legs being attached to a rope between pegs on the ground, and so they stand without shelter, eating the barley and straw which form their principal fodder. In Spring a few beans are given to fatten them, and to brighten their coats, and so is grass (ḥasheesh), especially barley-grass (kaïl), and sometimes fenugreek and sullah, a sort of wild lucerne. New barley is not given until after midsum-

Treatment of Steeds.

mer, or when it is, the mouths are washed with pitch to prevent the rough grain from making the gums sore. Old butter is given to horses in summer. When grazing, one fore and one hind foot are shackled together by a short rope (shikkel), and they are turned loose. They drink only at noon, or at sunset after a journey: then comes the one good meal of the day, barley, followed by crushed straw, with perhaps a handful of barley in the morning, and a nibble by the way at midday. Sand is used as litter.

Farriery.

The shoes employed in Morocco are thin, almost triangular plates, pierced in the centre, and slightly turned up behind. The hoofs are pared to fit. An English gentleman, desirous of showing what our cart-horses were like, drew on the ground the size of one of their shoes: "Ay," replied the farrier, "but go up country, and you will find that our lord the Sultan—God send him victory!—has horses with hoofs so big!" and he drew one twice the size. Not to be beaten, the foreigner sent home for a specimen shoe. On presenting himself with this in hand, the farrier quietly offered to make one twice the size, if he would pay for the trouble. Finally the Englishman sent home for a good-sized cart-horse skull. On taking this to his friend, all the answer he received was: "Now you've beaten me. I can make a shoe of any size, but I can't make skulls—that's not my trade!"

Moorish Breeds.

The 'Abda, Aït Z'dig, M'tûga and Haïáïna breeds are the most celebrated in Morocco. The M'tûgi has a larger crest than the 'Abdi, but more slanting hind-quarters. Well-bred colts and fillies reared by Europeans with a little care and knowledge develop into beautiful creatures, but the country stables of the natives generally contain gaunt, underfed animals, only beautiful by reason of their trappings.

The important question for the farmer everywhere is water, first as to the season and amount of the rainfall, then as to irrigation from rivers during the summer, for northern Morocco at least is not deficient in water-supply. In the mountainous districts

Water-Supply.

MOORISH WATER-WHEEL AT WORK.
(Turned by the donkey.)
Photograph by Herbert White, Esq.

irrigation is extensive and efficient. Every little stream is carried off along the slopes at high level, in mud-banked channels, which are often marked for miles by rows of walnut trees, all being verdant below and parched above. At intervals these conduits feed primitive undershot water-mills, each pair of stones being separately housed and turned by the stream direct, quite one of the features of the Atlas scenery. Below them the hill-sides are terraced like the Himálayas or the Alps, and wherever there is a level patch there is exquisite sward amid olive trees.

Further down, on the plains, where the fall is less, the irrigation channels grow less frequent, and the supply of water is but temporary. As the turn of each cultivator comes round, the precious liquid is conveyed successively to every patch, the area under cultivation being divided into sections surrounded by slight banks of mud, so that each may be equally flooded and left to soak. The course of the stream is deflected from one patch to another by shifting the mud of the banks with the foot. In this way a large area can soon be treated, and waste avoided. Drought, nevertheless, comes at intervals, and on the plains causes famines which a more extended system of irrigation would prevent, since there are plenty of rivers, and the hotter the summer the greater the extent to which the eternal snows of the Atlas melt, and consequently the greater and cooler the flow of the rivers they feed.

Irrigation.

Yet there is still a greater enemy than drought for the Moorish farmer, and that is the locust, which in its search for green pastures too often accompanies drought. At such times myriads cross the Atlas, breeding many myriads more on the fertile plains, which they unsparingly devastate, the attempts made to exterminate them being hopelessly unsystematic and inadequate. In former times the sultans used to pay the Berbers of the Atlas to kindle large fires in the colder altitudes, to which the locusts were attracted by the warmth and burnt.[1] It is only of late years that the Government has yielded to the advice of foreign officials and consented to purchase all eggs collected and brought to the coast for destruction, but the way in which the collectors are cheated greatly minimises the effect of this measure. When the locusts fly into the sea, their putrefying bodies, washed up by the waves,

Locusts.

[1] Riley, p. 531.

have been collected in such numbers as to cause sickness.[1] The only solace to be obtained from such a visitation is that some of the people use them as food, as we would eat shrimps, which they strongly resemble.[2]

Misrule.

In Raḥamna the crops are sometimes also attacked by armies of rats from the hills, and everywhere, what locusts and rats have left, ill-paid officials prey upon. Such is the injustice and oppression of the Moorish Government, that in the very best of years little wealth can be amassed, and the Moorish farmers are not to be envied. Whatever they may be able to save in good years is more wisely buried than spent in display which would only tempt some rapacious official, so unless some sort of protection can be obtained, even the well-to-do will clothe themselves in rags and wear the garb of misery.

Agricultural Partnerships.

Large numbers, on account of their poverty, are obliged to enter into relations, often most disastrous, with capitalists, Jewish or European, who advance them money for the purchase of cattle or seed, going into "partnership" it is called, a practice which is regulated by traditional customs varying from district to district. But those prevailing in the northern provinces may be described as a specimen of the whole.* The fellàḥ or farmer there undertakes to tend and feed cattle, sheep or goats for from a fifth to a half of the profits after deducting all expenses, besides presenting his sleeping partner with twenty of the fifty pounds of butter each cow is expected to give,† while he keeps the milk himself. Half the price of the sheep and the goats, if

* For a minute account of these customs see Cuevas' *Estudio General del Bajalato de Larache*, a translation of which I published in *The Times of Morocco* of April 21 and 28, 1887.

† The lb. of butter there weighs 24 Spanish dollars.

[1] Hay, p. 62. [2] See p. 95.

not of the cattle, has to be repaid by the Moor at a given date,* but should he fail in this, the speculator takes possession of the whole. Till this debt is discharged the capitalist may take over all the produce,—young, wool, skins, etc.—and if when a reckoning is made there is found to have been a loss, the farmer has either to make his share good by borrowing money for the purpose elsewhere at usurious interest, or to consent to a renewal of the arrangement on terms which as often as not render him ere long the slave of his partner, on whom also he is dependent for protection from the Government, so that he dare not rebel.

Horses are bred and tended by such partners in return for their use at certain times, as those of ploughing and threshing, and camels for a fourth share in the profit from their hire.†

* Or the opposite arrangement may be made, and the townsman may pay off half and take all.

† Formerly a stallion was provided in each village for public use.

CHAPTER THE TENTH

TRADE IN MOROCCO

WERE it not for the innate love of trading shown by the Moors, and their desire to secure in exchange for their superfluous produce some of the luxuries afforded by other lands, it is probable that the bigotry and narrowness of their religion would still have maintained intact the barrier of prejudice with which they were so long surrounded. It is a striking fact that while their vessels prowled the seas in search of foreign merchantmen as prey, they offered greater privileges than they enjoyed themselves to foreign merchants who made a home among them, or who brought their vessels to Moorish ports.* And now the foreign merchants in this country find themselves so vastly better off than the natives, that to escape the wholesale oppression that reigns throughout, high and low are fain to seek their protection.†

Commercial Instinct.

So eager indeed are the Moors to obtain immunity from the abuses of their own officials, that instead of a merchant paying commission to a native broker for his work, it is often the broker who pays for a post which by treaty carries with

European Protection.

* Thus Mulai Ismá'īl decreed that European vessels coming to trade in his ports should not be taken in sight of Morocco, and on their return should not be taken till they had touched at a foreign port.[1]

† The existing conditions of the foreign trade of Morocco are treated of in *The Moorish Empire*, pp. 406—413.

[1] THOMASSY, p. 192.

it protection from injustice. When one hears of so-and-so going into "the cattle business," for instance, with a native partner, it is always understood in Morocco that a large proportion of the European's share in the concern is represented by the value of the protection afforded.

Methods of Business.

The actual business done by the majority of foreigners resident here is more or less influenced by the demand for protection, and a few only maintain sufficient import or export trade to qualify for the issue of protection papers, since those alone whom the Customs authorities recognize as wholesale merchants have the right of protecting native brokers. This is not the place, however, to deal with the vexed question of the protection system as such,* but it must needs be referred to in order to explain one of the peculiar conditions of trade in Morocco. Inland the business is almost entirely transacted by brokers or semsars who often purchase crops before they are sown, thus enabling the farmers to buy the seed, and it is these men—most of them Jews—who really need and obtain the protection of the foreigners employing them.

Trade Advances.

The system of advances is one, however, which leads to numerous abuses of a serious nature. In the first place, the farmers in bad years become so bound to the traders by their inability to fulfil obligations, that they have to agree to part with the next crop at ruinous rates, and are often quite as much reduced by this as by unjust officials. In the wool, cattle, and other trades the same thing occurs, but although there is much to be said on behalf of the Moors in this matter, it should also be borne in mind how many European firms have eventually come to grief over long credits to Moors, whom failure of crops and

* Fully dealt with in *The Moorish Empire*, p. 414, *et seq*

the disordered state of the country have prevented from meeting their liabilities.

Collection of Debts.

The most curious detail of the arrangement is that instead of each debtor being summoned direct by his creditor, as in any other country, it is the custom to present such claims to the Moorish Government for collection, a practice which opens the door to still further abuses. Thus it often happens that while the rich, who really could pay, are able to get off by "squaring" their officials, the poor, who cannot, are thrust into gaol as proofs of diligent activity, only to be released by death, or their discharge at the hand of some humane foreign official, satisfied that they really have no possessions.

Usury.

Closely interlinked with this method of transacting business is the system on which the payment of usurious loans is secured. As by Mohammedan law no interest can be claimed, and it is difficult to recover debts of any sort, the difficulty is evaded by making the borrower execute a receipt for a round sum which includes both principal and interest, as the price in advance of so much specified produce which he undertakes to deliver at a certain place on a certain date, or else to return the money. The price at which the calculation is effected is usually so low that it is much more advantageous to "return" the money. But if this is not forthcoming, the document has to be at once renewed on similar terms, the "fair and purely philanthropic" rate of interest being 5 per cent. per mensem, but the actual rate charged frequently running to cent per cent. for six months, or even more, when the debtor is already in gaol, and can get out only on the lender's terms. Such loans are usually secured by sureties, who are of two classes: dáman el wajah ("face-surety") who agrees to present himself at a certain place as a substitute for the debtor, should he fail, and dáman el mál ("treasure-surety")—the most common—who can only be proceeded against for the amount if the debtor fail. In

CHARCOAL SELLERS, MAZAGAN.
Photograph by the late Dr. Robert Brown.

trade, however, the books of the seller are often the only proof, but they suffice.

In a country which so swarms with Jews, it is natural that they should be well to the front in this business, but it must not be imagined that they are the sole, or, from a comparative point of view, the worst, offenders, for not only do rich Moors sometimes entrust Jewish partners with capital, and support them in pressing their claims, but Europeans, for whom there is no excuse, have been known to do the same. The Jews, moreover, have a large share in the trade of Morocco, both internal and external, and in many of the mountainous districts they are almost the only commercial link between hostile tribes. It is they, too, who mostly frequent the country markets which are held on certain days of the week at certain spots a short journey apart throughout the Empire, conveying European luxuries from one to another, as well as offering their services as craftsmen, cobblers, tin-smiths, silver-smiths, shoeing-smiths, etc., or as muleteers.

Jewish Share.

These markets take their names from the days of the week on which they are held, coupled with the name of the local tribe or saint, or some neighbouring geographical feature,* for they are often held far away from human dwellings. The only sign of the where-abouts of such markets on other than market-days is the grass-less state of the plot of ground, on which perhaps the parings left by the

Country Markets.

* Such as:

Ḥád Ḳorṭ	held on	Sunday.
Thaneen tát Shtûka	„ „	Monday.
Thlát Amzmiz	„ „	Tuesday.
’Arbáh tát Aôlád ’Amrán	„ „	Wednesday.
Khamees Beni ’Arôs	„ „	Thursday.
Juma’ Sidi ’Aïsá ben Ḥasan	„ „	Friday.
Sebt Aôlád Bû ’Azîz	„ „	Saturday.

These are names of actual markets, taken at random to show the class of name by which they are known. Sundays and Thursdays seem the most usual days, and Fridays and Saturdays the least common. The word Ṣôḳ, or market, is not used as part of the names, which run simply as: "Saturday of the Children of the Father of the Precious"—the last instance given above,—these worthies being a tribe so-called.

cobblers, and the tripods of rough branches used by the butchers, are the only indications of use, though occasionally rows of ill-built hovels await their tenants on the appointed day. At these centres not only is the business of the nation transacted, but here the political and religious movements of the people take their rise and spread, and here the farmers come for entertainment. There is nothing in Morocco more picturesque or more instinct with life than such a scene in time of peace during the busy hours before noon in fair weather; a vociferating, seething mass of human beings, quadrupeds and feathered things.

Objects of Trade.

At these markets are to be obtained native woollens and other simple manufactures for which there is a demand among the country-folk, such as pottery, baskets and sieves; Manchester goods, such as prints, and figured muslins, turbans, and in the South, blue selampore, or khunt; coloured felt and sateen, hank-silk, green tea, white sugar, composite candles, native oil and argan oil, rancid butter, dried raisins, figs, honey and pitch,—this last for washing out water-skins and jars. When fruit is in season, it is here that it is to be found, with a few vegetables, chiefly onions, and here alone is meat to be obtained, unless a sheep be killed at home to mark some notable event in the "humdrum" lives of the country-folk. Cheap European hardware and nick-nacks, such as small, bright-coloured basins, rough diminutive tea-glasses, beads, trinkets, Continental padlocks, chains and nails, are also exposed for sale. Domestic animals of all sorts are here bought and sold, while such public resorts are naturally favourite grounds for a whole army of itinerant "medicine men," story-tellers, acrobats, conjurors and snake-charmers, who find a willing audience and easy dupes in the ignorant rustics.

As one travels through the country and nears the

locality of one of these markets on the day on which it is held, a busy string of road-farers is encountered going to and from it, some mounted on asses or horses, but the majority walking sedately and unconcernedly behind the loaded packs which contain their stock-in-trade. Sometimes it is the lord and master who rides the already heavy pack, while his "better half" strides heavily along behind, under the weight of a considerable burden, or perchance a child, whose shaven crown toasts in the noon-day sun. Occasionally a long drove of tiny donkeys comes along, each with a double grain-sack slung across its back, or a train of stately camels, dirt-begrimed and sore, pacing the distance with measured tread, soft as wool or india-rubber on the beaten track. "Sure and steady" is the apparent motto of these desert ships, and the distance they can cover in a long day's march is greater than would at first sight appear, for although their pace is far behind that of the other beasts of burden, in the long run its steadiness tells. The average load for a camel is about five hundred-weight, generally consisting of a couple of securely bound-up packages, so corded together that they may with ease be slung across its hump, as it obediently though grumblingly kneels, but quickly makes known by its cries when the "last straw" has been imposed.*

Market Traffic.

"Ships of the Desert."

There are no roads in Morocco but the tracks made by traffic, and there are very few bridges, most of them in bad condition, so that in many parts travel is almost suspended during the worst of the wet season. When rivers have to be crossed

Internal Communication.

* Camels are very particular in feeding, and are supplied with a "tablecloth" on the ground. The Arabs declare that the female camel will miscarry if she observes another camel fed before her. A male camel under similar provocation snorts violently.

this is accomplished more often than not by fording,* even on the large water-ways, but at a few points along the main routes rough boats are to be obtained, into which, after a vast display of obstreperous kicking, and with no little damage to goods, the caravans are transferred, or the passage is made on a rude raft of branches on inflated goat-skins. De Foucauld mentions a crossing of the Wád el 'Abeed, at a width of twenty-five to forty metres, by means of cords from tree trunks fixed in cairns on either bank.[1]

Night Quarters.

With the exception of an occasional official halting-place (n'zálah) at which a guard is provided, but which consists of a foul enclosure bounded by a hedge, there is no provision for spending the night, so that travellers have to provide themselves with tents, or sleep in the open air. It is only in a few of the more dangerous passes that proper caravan-sarais (fandaḳs) have been erected, dirty comfortless yards surrounded by rows of cells for travellers, which each occupant must clean and furnish for himself. The general custom in travel is to make at night for some village, the inhabitants of which are at their own risk bound to watch over the safety of their guests, providing a guard (ássás).

Provisioning.

Met with on the road, the inhabitants of such a village might be thieves, but at home they are hosts, who, notwithstanding their customs of hospitality, know how to drive a bargain with their visitors if they are ordinary travellers. Barley, fowls, eggs, and in the spring milk and butter, are the only things which one can rely on purchasing from them, for they seldom have meat except on feast or market days. If necessary in troubled districts, a guard may be obtained

* For an illustration see *The Land of the Moors*, p. 7.

[1] Page 74.

CAMPING OUT IN MOROCCO.

Photograph by Herbert White, Esq.

from the authorities as well as from the village, but this guard is really a spy, and a clog on one's movements, and is never supplied when there is any real danger. Yet, in theory, unless a guard (makházni) is taken, the Moorish Government does not hold itself responsible for any interference with the foreign traveller or his belongings.

Europeans are, however, seldom molested, even when the country is disturbed, for fear of possible consequences, and throughout the lower levels they may travel in times of peace with as perfect security as in Europe. It is only where the authority of the Sultan is weak or disputed—which is the case generally among the mountains,—that it is not safe for Moor or Jew or European to travel without local protection, and not always with that when it can be obtained. This has kept the Atlas practically unknown to the outside world, notwithstanding its proximity to the centres of civilization.

Safety of Travel.

The great caravans which formerly accomplished journeys between Timbuctoo and Morocco, and along the North African coast to Egypt* and Mekka, linking there with caravans from every part of Asia, are things of the past.† The modern sea-routes of the Nazarene

* Visitors to Cairo may still visit, as I have done, the Ṣôḳ el Magharbà —"Westerners' Market"—in which these caravans used to put up.

† In a special report of 1789 the British Consul at Tangier stated that the annual Moorish caravan to the East used then to start from Tadla or Fez about the beginning of March, passing thence via Táza, bearing to the south of Tlemçen and Algeria, taking about two months and a half to reach the salt-pits of Tripoli, whence they followed the coast for some fifty more days to Alexandria. But the sultan was discouraging this ancient route as much as possible, even hiring vessels to divert the trade with Egypt through his ports where he could charge duties. The annual value of the caravan trade in this direction was, however, estimated still at some two million Mexican dollars a year. The Timbuctoo caravans, consisting of from 100 to 300 persons, still continued to prosper, taking

have rendered them superfluous, and with them one of the most picturesque features of Eastern life has disappeared. But their memory lingers, and there is still an important trade conducted by this means across the western Saḥara, though by no means what it once was, since the French and others have tapped the sources of supply from the West African coast.* Yet these expedi-

55 days from Tatta to Timbuctoo, crossing on the way one desert in four days and another in nine. For every horse brought the king of Timbuctoo gave from twelve to twenty eunuchs, and some 4000 slaves were annually imported, though many of them were passed on to Algeria. Public Record Office, F. O. Docs., Morocco, vol. 17.

* That even now considerable quantities of goods are regularly exchanged by means of these caravans, will be seen from the following list of what one brought to Marrákesh in the Spring of 1887, which is given by M. Zerbib of Mogador, in the *Anti-Slavery Reporter* for May of that year.

"40 loads Ostrich feathers, worth at Mogador 75 to 30 fcs. per kilo.
85 „ Ivory (some tusks weighing 30 lbs.) worth 800 fcs. per 54 kilos.
120 „ Giraffe skins, sold at Tindûf at 90 to 100 fcs. per 100 kilos. (These skins go to the Atlas, and not to Mogador.)
30 „ Incense, a kind of aromatic resin, of which there are two qualities—white and black, worth 400 to 600 fcs. the 100 kilos.
20 „ White and blue jellábs of linen and of cotton, very well made; and also piece goods of camel's hair for tents and selháms. The load is worth about 500 or 600 fcs.
35 „ Camel's hair and goat's hair, value 100 to 140 fcs. per load.
225 „ Gum arabic, worth 100 fcs. per 54 kilos.
45 „ Wax worth 90 to 100 fcs. per 54 kilos.
50 „ Camels laden with water, provisions, etc.
650 „ Camels.

"The caravan which arrived 2nd February, consisted of 350 men with 650 camels and 520 slaves, the majority girls of from 8 to 16, and boys of from 6 to 12. A camel load is generally 300 lbs., which is not excessive, but their owners do not overload them, so as to be able to mount the slaves when necessary.

"I could not ascertain the quantity of gold dust brought, as, not being ordinary merchandise, it is carried on the person; but I reckon that each of the 350 men of the caravan had 1 to 4 parcels containing 30 to 40 metkals each parcel, worth 13 to 14 francs the metkal, which weighs a little less 15 francs in French gold coin.

"I calculate the total value of the merchandise and slaves by this caravan at about three million francs ($120,000)."

tions have lost their glamour, and their way-worn members attract but little attention, being hardly distinguishable from an ordinary band of casual travellers. Were it not for the slaves who are brought over by most

POTTERY SELLERS, MARRAKESH.
Photograph by Dr. Ruddock.

caravans, and for whom there is a steady demand with no other source of supply, it is probable they would cease altogether. *

One of the chief reasons for the diminution of the

* In a report on the trade of N. W. Africa the late Col. Mathews, U. S. Consul at Tangier, and an authority on Morocco, estimated the total value of the merchandize annually transported from Morocco by the great caravan to Timbuctoo at $100,000, and that of other smaller caravans together at $13,000.

Timbuctoo at one time formed part of the Moorish Empire, having been annexed in 1591 by Ahmad V. (Ed-Dhahebi), but having regained its independence, tribute was again collected by Mulai Ismá'íl.

trade of Timbuctoo with the North is the falling in price of the commodities formerly brought that way, by reason of the development of new countries in various parts of the world, whence the same articles can be shipped and brought to Europe at far less cost than they can be transported across the sandy wastes of the Saḥara. A considerable and increasing trade is carried on, too, between European traders on the Gold Coast and in Senegal and the natives in the very heart of the Continent. Although the white people have direct dealings only with tribes in their immediate neighbourhood, each tribe barters with one farther inland, and so the trade with places inaccessible to foreigners is carried on as effectually, if not in such large proportions, as if the traders could themselves penetrate "up country."

Reasons for Decline.

Time was, when, like the people of Iceland, the inhabitants of Timbuctoo bore an otherwise unparalleled character for honesty and uprightness, but how that may be to-day it is difficult to ascertain. Old writers[1] assert that the traders from Morocco were accustomed, on arrival at their destination, to spread out their wares in lots on the ground, and then retire, coming forward shortly afterwards to find a pile of gold or other valuables for export opposite each lot, which was the price the natives were willing to give. If this were deemed sufficient, the bargain was concluded, the gold was carried off, and the natives were at liberty to remove their purchases without having conversed with the foreigners. Should the amount offered be considered too small, the traders would again retire, when the natives would come forward and add to the pile or withdraw it, according to whether their bid was the highest they would make or not. However

Honest Trading.

[1] *E.g.* PELLOW, p. 286; TORRES, p. 470; "RO. C." and others.

this may have been, the story had without doubt some foundation in fact, and it seems quite certain that the demoralized inhabitants of the more civilized North found the honesty of these sons of Ham a remarkable trait.*

Dangers of the Journey.

In those days almost the whole trade used to be monopolized by a rich company, or rather association, of Fez merchants, who made a very good thing out of it, notwithstanding the heavy expense of the desert caravans, and the still heavier burdens of occasional losses from drought or robbers. Those two dangers were and are the chief ones to be considered in crossing the vast sea of sand which separates the southern confines of Morocco from the northern limits of Timbuctoo. Although all the water is carried that can be found room for, during a long journey over arid or sandy wastes it is apt to run short, even when dealt out most carefully and sparingly, if for any unforeseen circumstance the time occupied by the journey exceeds the expected limits.† Sometimes the guide will lose his way, probably in a sand-storm; sometimes hostile tribes or roving bands of wild Arabs will cause delay by their plundering raids, when the dangers are increased tenfold. For protection against plunder it is customary for the caravans—which before crossing the deserts unite in one vast host—to pay black-mail to certain tribes whose territory has to be crossed, and who undertake to convey them safely through it

* A similar character has, however, been given to the Fîlâlîs (inhabitants of Tafîlâlt), who are said to make use of no locks.

† Jackson[1] gives the time as 130 days including stoppages at El Wahs (the Oases), about 25 miles being covered each day. From Fez to Wad Nûn, Tatta or Akka, 18 days, then a month's rest: Akka to Taghassa, 16 days and 15 of repose: thence to Taudeni, 7 days and of repose 15, and like spaces of travel and repose to Arawan, whence Timbuctoo is 6 days, making 54 in all on the road. Sometimes the total journey was effected in 82 days.

[1] p. 285.

to the next tribe. The common starting-points are Tafilált and Tindûf, whence they make for Akka and Tatta, taking great slabs of salt, woollen shawls, sashes, arms, tobacco, tea, sugar, looking-glasses, beads, knives and other European nick-nacks.*

Postal Services.

Internal communications being so poor, there is small cause for wonder that no regular postal service is maintained by the Moorish Government. Several foreign nations have nevertheless introduced courier mails along the coast, and to centres reached by European trade, to say nothing of numerous private services established rather with a view to furnishing collectors with rare stamps than for the conveyance of letters. The only Moorish services are of a semi-private nature, linking a few of the chief towns, for which no stamps are issued, but a "post-mark" is stamped on the letters when payment in cash is made. All inland letters are conveyed by couriers on foot, who make most creditable time for minimum charges. The distance from Tangier to Fez, about 150 miles, is covered by one of these runners in three days and a half,† and from Tangier to Tetuan, 40 miles, I have sent a man and received an answer in twenty-four hours, for a dollar, worth then about three shillings. Wearing very little clothing, and supporting themselves on a supply of parched flour carried in their waist-bands, these men are a tough and hardy lot, but scarcely to be envied.

* For the overland trade between Morocco and Algeria, see the *Rapport . . . sur le Commerce . . . de l'Algérie* by De Forçade la Roquette, Algiers, 1863.

† Campou records a journey on foot with a foreign minister's message from Tangier to Fez and back, between Friday at noon and Monday at noon, though this is incredible. When it was over the courier slept for thirty-six hours, at the end of which he ate for two hours, consuming five dishes of kesk'soo and twenty cups of tea![1]

[1] p. 98.

Commerce in Morocco, as is so often the case in the East, is also sadly hampered by the lack of a satisfactory currency, though things are now much better than they were. Till within recent years all sorts of disused and debased European coins were in

Currency.

WOMEN SORTING WOOL, AT SAFFI.
Photograph by the late Dr. Robert Brown.

circulation under the nominally Spanish standards of dollar (riál), peseta (basîtah) and real vellon (billion), but these having been refused on the coast, with the exception of Spanish coins current also in Spain, Moorish coins of equal value have been struck in France and Germany, at times exchanged at premium or discount. The interior still continues to be a happy dumping-ground for coins of depreciated value, the ignorant natives being too glad to get anything that they can spend to ask many questions, although when once bitten, they often refuse the best of coins if a trifle unfamiliar. Being unable to read, they learn to distinguish one from another by such descriptions of the designs as "with—or without—guns" (i.e. the pillars on the arms of Spain), "baby-face," "old-woman," "young-woman," "whiskered" or "bearded." One method by which they are duped is to import a quantity of some discarded issue, passing it at first perhaps at a discount, till it gains credit and circulates freely, and then to refuse its acceptance unless at a very low rate. Both Europeans and Jews appear to manipulate this class of business.

Moorish Coins.

Of genuine Moorish coins there are very few in circulation, though in times past, as the collections extant in the British Museum and elsewhere show, there was an extensive series, including gold, now extremely rare.* Some of these are round, some square, and most are thin; many bear interesting genealogical information. An extremely debased and ill-struck mintage of bronze, called flûs, is all that is now issued. The unit or fils is no longer coined, the smallest being two flûs: three flûs are about equivalent to a Spanish *centimo*, of which a hundred are worth from 6d. to 9d. according to the rate of exchange. Weights and measures, although known by the same names,—the rotl (or pound) as the standard of weight, divided into okîahs (ounces), and the mudd as that of capacity—vary from town to town. For length, a man's forearm is an approximate cubit, dra', and any piece of old iron or stone may pass muster as shop-weight †

* Numerous illustrations of these are given in *The Moorish Empire.*

† In former times English people were equally careless, and stones were frequently used as weights.[1]

[1] Cf. PLUMPTON, Corresp. 21; Public Health, ii., 30, and GREEN'S *English Life in the Fifteenth Century*, ii., 28.

Although the trade of Morocco is no longer hampered by monopolies as it once was, the prohibition of the export of wheat and barley, or even its transport coast-wise by sea, is a serious check on the expansion of which it is capable, while in the absence of practical routes the latter restriction often leaves one district starving while superabundance rots in another. In consequence, large fertile districts remain uncultivated, and famines recur periodically, when terrible havoc is wrought, and food-stuffs have to be imported, while the rich are made to open their grain-stores.[1] The scenes at such times baffle description, and one "year of hunger" is still fresh in the minds of many, when the sufferers were stated on good authority to have in some cases become cannibals, and when a Mansion House Fund was opened for their relief.*

Famines.

In addition to arms and ammunition of war, the Moors reserve by treaty the right to prohibit the introduction of all intoxicants or narcotics, and of articles used in their manufacture or consumption. The narcotic monopoly was abolished in 1887, but tobacco and intoxicants are now introduced in growing quantities on the plea that they are needed for the use of Europeans.† Leeches, formerly exported in great quantities to Spain, are also a monopoly in name, and though in 1858 permission to export them was sold for $50,000, to-day no one can be found to bid for this

Prohibited Imports.

* Mulai Sulaïman attributed the famine of 1817 to the large number of public women and boys in Mequinez, of whom he arrested over five hundred and had them lashed in public. The women were either then sent back to their husbands or distributed among his body-guard.[2]

† Just as has been the case with the opium traffic forced on the Chinese, this innovation, so detrimental to the hitherto abstemious Moors, is encouraged and gloried in by some of the foreign consular officials, as shown by their published reports.

[1] See *Kartas*, p. 133; Campou, p. 50, etc. [2] Gråberg, p. 214.

privilege. The under bark of the cork tree, used for tanning, was likewise formerly a monopoly, being chiefly furnished from Laraiche, as were also the leeches.*

Regulation.

In 1853 the importation of tea, sugar, coffee, cochineal and dye-wood was prohibited, and in 1854 the exportation of oil, measures which hastened the British treaty of 1856, abolishing all monopolies and restrictions save those specified, and forming the basis of all subsequent conventions. Horses, cattle, mules, donkeys, goats, sheep and bones are only permitted to be exported from time to time by special permission, and there seems to be a strong objection to allowing any female animals to leave the country. All other articles of Moorish produce pay export dues on a scale agreed upon with the Diplomatic Body, and with

Import Duties.

the exceptions specified all imports are supposed to pay a cash duty of 10 per cent. *ad valorem.* Jewellery of gold or silver, precious or imitation stones, gold lace, manufactured silks (pure or mixed), tinned meats, wines and spirits only pay 5 °/₀, and tobacco, per 112 lbs., if in leaf, 40 rvn; cut, 60 rvn, and in the form of cigarettes, 100 rvn

The following table shows the present export tariff. Among the articles of importance which have disappeared from this list, but which were once exported in considerable quantities, are ostrich feathers and elephant tusks from the Ṣûdán, as also sugar, honey, ginger, capers, cotton, silk, indigo, walnuts, gold dust and lead ore.

(Articles in parentheses are only allowed to be exported occasionally.)

* See p. 207.

Article and measure.	*Duty* Rvn. *
Almonds, per 112 lbs.,	15
Annis Seed, „	10
Antimony, 110¼ lbs.,	5
Bark, 112 lbs.,	6
(Barley), 73 lbs.,	6
Baskets (palmetto), 100 lbs.,	8
Beans, 113 lbs.,	10
Blankets (wool),	5%
Brushes (palmetto), 112 lbs.,	1·5
Canary Seed, 112 lbs.,	5
Carpets,	5%
Cheese, 112 lbs.,	20
Chick-peas(garbanzos)122lbs.,	10
Carraway Seed, 112 lbs.,	8
Cochineal, 112 lbs.,	10
Copper Ore, 112 lbs.,	5
Cords (goat-hair), 100 lbs.,	10
Cork, 112 lbs.,	6
Coriander, 112 lbs.,	10
Combs for wool (wooden), 100,	2
Cress Seed, 112 lbs.,	10
Cummin Seed, 112 lbs.,	6
Cushions (embr. leather),	5%
Dates, 112 lbs.,	20
(Donkeys), each,	100
Eggs, 1000,	25
Esparto Grass, 112 lbs.,	2
Fennel, (nigella), „	8
Fenugreek, „	5
Fish (salted), „	20
Flax, „	16
Fleeces (cured), „	18
(Flour), „	17·5
Fowls, dozen,	10
Fullers' Earth, 112 lbs.,	7·5
(Goats), each,	8·8
Goat Skins (cured), 112 lbs.,	18
Gum Ammoniacum, 112 lbs.,	10
Gums in general, „	8
Gut, 112 lbs., „	10
Haiks (shawls),	5%
Hair, camel and horse, 112 lbs.	15
Hair cloth,	5%
Hares, each,	1
Hemp, 112 lbs.,	16
Henna, „	6
Hides, „	18
„ parings, etc., (for glue)	4
Horns, 1000,	8
Iron Ore, 112 lbs.,	2
Jellábs (cloaks),	5%

Article and measure.	*Duty* Rvn.
Lemons and Limes, 1000,	4
Lentils, 119 lbs.,	10
Linseed, 112 lbs.,	5
Maize, 118 lbs.,	10
Marjoram, wild, 112 lbs.,	4
Mats (reed),	8%
Millet, 119 lbs.,	10
(Mules), each,	500
Oil, „	25
Oranges, 1000,	4
Orchella (lichen), 112 lbs.,	10
Ores, other than iron or lead, 112 lbs.,	5
Osiers, 112 lbs.,	2
Ostrich Eggs, each,	0·5
„ Feathers, 18 oz. Eng.	18
Palmetto, 100 bundles,	8
„ Fibre, 112 lbs.,	2·5
Partridges, each,	1
Pears, 112 lbs.,	10
Peas, 119 lbs.,	10
Porcupine Quills, 1000,	2
Rabbits, each,	1
Rags, 112 lbs.,	5
Raisins, 112 lbs.,	10
Rice, 112 lbs.,	9⅜
Rose Leaves, 112 lbs.,	10
Sarghînah (root).† 112 lbs..	5
Sashes (woollen), 100 lbs.,	50
Satchels (leather),	5%
Sesame Seed, 112 lbs.,	10
(Sheep), each,	20
Sheep Skins (cured),	18
Sieves,	5%
Skins (tanned),	50
Slippers,	5%
Socks (woollen),	8%
Stirrups (iron),	5%
Tákaût (gall-nut),‡ 112 lbs.,	10
Tallow, 112 lbs.,	23
Thread (cotton),	8%
Timber, half camel load,	6
Tortoises, 110 lbs.,	2.5
Trays (brass),	8%
Walnuts, 112 lbs.,	8
Wax, purified, 112 lbs.,	60
„ crude, „	50
(Wheat), 98½ lbs.,	10
Wool, washed, 112 lbs.,	40
„ in grease, „	27·5

(All payable in cash, percentage ad valorem.)

* Reals vellon of 25 centimes, 20 to the Spanish dollar, of which about six go to the sovereign.

† Either *Telephium imperati* or *Corrigiola telephiifolia*, used medicinally and in the preparation of perfumes.

‡ Presumably from the tamarisk; brought from the Sahara.

[illegible] PALACE, MARRAKESH

[illegible]

CHAPTER THE ELEVENTH

ARTS AND MANUFACTURES

A MOST erroneous notion prevails as to the comparative positions of mediæval and modern art in Morocco. It is commonly assumed that the Moors have almost entirely lost the skill and taste which they evinced some centuries ago, and that they are now incapable of reproducing the remains we have of their halcyon days, but this is quite a mistake. In the first place the popular estimate of their achievements when masters of Spain is very much exaggerated,—sufficient allowance not being made for the employment of foreign workmen and the bleeding of a subject nation,—and in the second place sufficient allowance is not made for the repressive influence of a corrupt and mercenary government on all exercise of either skill or taste.

Mediæval Achievements.

It must also be remembered that in eastern lands there has seldom been any wide encouragement of private enterprise in art, except where a luxurious Court, maintained by tributary peoples, has set the example, and it is worthy of note how few relics of the past which we possess have been the creations of individuals unconnected with Courts. It is doubtful if the mass of the people have in any of these lands been better off than they are to-day. Of Morocco it may be asserted without hesitation that there never

Lack of private Enterprise.

was found here more inherent or latent art than there is at present, though there may have been in its history periods when successful monarchs, by subduing and exhausting its neighbours, have afforded scope for display, employing every available workman on their palaces and mosques and gate-ways, or in manufacturing articles of vertu such as were never in common use.

Early Ideals.

Among existing monuments of ancient Moorish architecture, the sister towers of Marrákesh, Rabat and Seville, all erected about the year 1200, are at once the earliest and finest specimens of anything elaborate,* but in the mosques of Córdova † and Fez (the older parts of the Ḳarûeeïn) ‡ are to be found examples of the original mosques of Islám, as also in those of Ḳaïrwán § and Old Cairo. ** It is the primitive "horse-shoe" arch in an undecorated wall, resting on plain, square pillars, as is still retained in the Moorish type, for in Morocco there has never been that elaboration which prevailed in Spain towards the close of the Moorish epoch. ††

What the origin of this most elegant arch may have been it is of course impossible to say with certainty, but no one wearing the hooded cloak of the country and facing the wind could fail to be struck by the precision with which the arch misnamed the "horse-shoe" is outlined before him, and it is a curious fact that no

* For illustrations see *The Moorish Empire*, pp. 64, 77 and 83.

† Rebuilt in the time of Charlemagne, A.C. 786.[1] For illustration see *The Moorish Empire*, p. 43.

‡ Founded, A.C. 859. See *The Land of the Moors*, p. 267 *et seq.*

§ Founded A.C. 670.

** Id. A.C. 642—700.

†† See "Die Mittelalterliche Maurische Kultur," von Gustav Diercks, *Monats Hefte Westermann*, Jan. 1892, Heft 424.

[1] El Makkári, vol. ii, p. 86.

amount of setting out by the established rules for drawing curves is successful in producing it. The native architect, who is still as successful as ever in obtaining the correct curve and proportions, does so entirely by eye, and the constantly present ideal which this requires is not far to seek. The result is that no two arches nominally of the same size coin-

Origin of Arch.

COURTYARD OF A MOORISH HOUSE.

Molinari, Photo., Tangier.

cide exactly, and that the two halves of the same arch are seldom identical. An ingenious writer has surmised that the tracery on the Ḥasan Tower at Rabat was inspired by the forms in which the coloured sands of the Sebû are thrown by the Atlantic waves.[1]

The period of these three sister towers, and of the building of Rabat would appear to have been unique in the employment of carved panel stone-work, such as decorates the faces of the towers, and those of several

[1] URQUHART, *Pillars of Hercules*, p. 195.

gate-ways in Rabat and among the neighbouring ruins of Shella. Most of these are built, as well as faced, with stone, a style quite foreign to Moorish art proper, and accounted for by the thousands of Spanish captives who were set to work on them.

Stone Epoch.

ANCIENT ARCHWAYS OF THE KÛTÛBÎYA, MARRAKESH.
(Walled up.)

Molinari, Photo., Tangier.

The designs, indeed, are arabesque, but it is probable that the details were the work of foreign artists, confined to the style already set. The koranic prohibition of the portrayal of animal life is sufficient in itself to account for the development of a high class of geometrical designs, and it is evident that their elaboration is almost entirely due to foreign influence, under which the chaste severity which marks the earlier examples and gives them their value is entirely lost amid an overwhelming minuteness of detail. The marble pillars

Foreign Influence.

introduced even in the earlier examples are always foreign* or imitations of such, and when sugar was grown in Morocco we read that it was exchanged weight for weight against Italian marble. The huge sectional columns of the unfinished Ḥasan mosque at Rabat have nothing Moorish about them.†

A much more distinctively Moorish work is the facing of glazed tiles or large mosaics still employed in palaces and residences, as also in mosques, shrines, fountains and sometimes on gate-ways, as on the beautiful specimen at Mequinez, that of Manṣûr el 'Alj, built in 1732.‡[1] This is by no means a lost art, and only requires the encouragement of demand to revive. The colours are good; blue, black, white, green and yellow, and another artistic green is used for the glazed tiles of saint-shrine and mosque roofs. The warmer tints of the ceilings and wood-work need the softening hand of time to lend them beauty, but the designs, although not numerous, are good, and the effect is usually heightened by a little carving-out of certain portions.

Tile-work.

Between the tile-work of the dado and the cornice of the ceiling nothing but pure white is permitted, yet in the Alhambra the Spaniards have attempted to improve on this, and their misconceptions led away even Sir Inigo Jones, whose beautiful copies of Moorish wall designs are altogether marred by being fancifully coloured, whence the misleading nature of all

Colourings

* Thus of the 1200 columns which once stood in the Córdova mosque (now reduced to 854) 115 were from Nîmes and Narbonne, 60 from Seville and Tarragona, 140 from Carthage (presented by Leo, emperor of Constantinople). They include specimens of jasper, porphyry, verde antique, etc. The white marble Corinthian columns of the Tangier Palace are presumably of Roman origin.

† For illustration see *The Land of the Moors*, p. 173.

‡ For illustration see *The Moorish Empire*, p. 165.

[1] EZ-ZAÏÁNI, p. 71.

$1 per 1000

Each tile 1¼ inch long, ⅜ inch wide at narrow part.

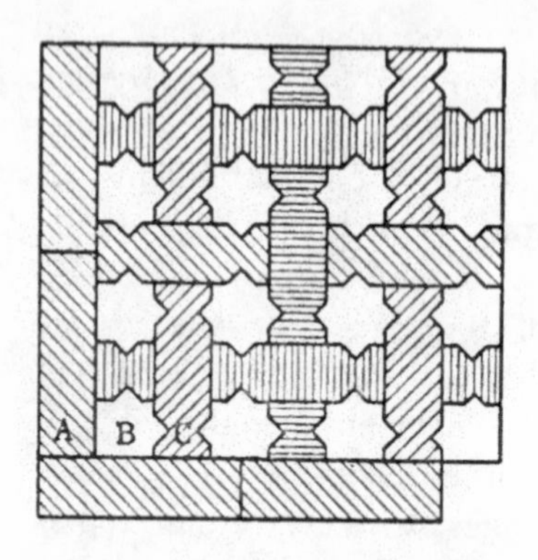

A. $2 per 1000
B. „ 1 „ „
C. „ 3 „ „
Pattern without border, 6½ ins. sq.

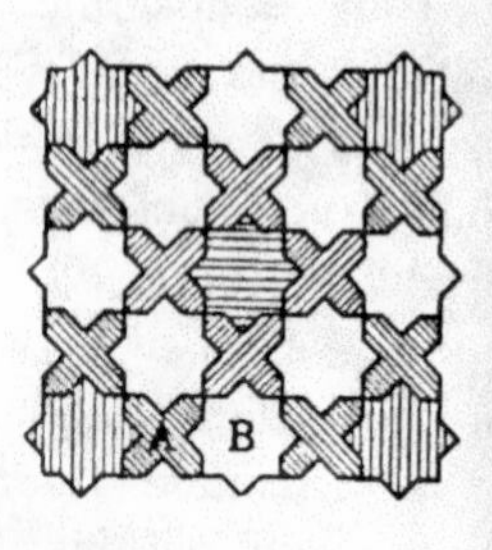

A. $1 per 1000
B. „ „ „
3 tiles to 2¾ inches.

Large size, $2 per 1000,
3 tiles to 4 inches.

|||| = black; ≡ = yellow; //// = blue; \\\\ = green.

COMMON DESIGNS OF MOORISH TILE-WORK MADE IN TETUAN.

(Prices of 1887.)

attempted reproductions of the Alhambra, such as that at the Crystal Palace, which have his work as their pattern. It is true that ignorant and ruthless Moorish servants cover much of the most beautiful work with white-wash, often till even the outline of the incised pattern is obliterated, so that beneath the rough and scaling surface of many an old Moorish wall there lurks unsuspected delicate tile-work, and marble columns are often similarly disguised. In the blending of colour the Moors show remarkable taste, a striking contrast to their Jewish neighbours, by whom gaudiness and brightness are more appreciated.

Morocco Leather.

In manufactures the Moors are best known to the outside world for their leather, once famed as "Cordovan," whence our "cord-wainer" and the French "cordonnier." Now, however, although the same excellent quality continues to be produced in Morocco, the taste and requirements of the present time have brought about the manufacture in other lands of a so-called "Morocco leather," but the goat-skins from which some of it is prepared are in truth exported raw to France and to the United States. That which is still tanned in Morocco is in local demand for slippers, belts, bags, harness and book-binding, while for various fancy purposes a smaller quantity is also tanned green, brown and white. It is seldom exported, except in the form of slippers sent to Egypt.

Qualities of Leather.

By far the best real Morocco leather is the yellow, which is well prepared, soft and rich: after this comes the red, though I have seen specimens of brown equal in quality to the yellow. White, brown, black and green come next, but the blue is usually poor. The best yellow is prepared in Tetuan, Marrákesh ranking second in its manufacture. It is used chiefly for slippers, but is too light for lasting wear, soon turning dark, though the better the quality, the longer this is delayed. Red leather of an excellent quality, and stouter than the yellow, is produced at Marrákesh, Fez and Tetuan. The best is used

DRYING GOAT-SKINS PREVIOUS TO SHIPMENT.
(Messrs. Murdoch and Butler's Store, Saffi.)
Photograph by the late Dr. Robert Brown.

for satchels and women's outdoor slippers, inferior qualities serving for saddlery, belts, etc. The brown comes almost exclusively from the mountains, where it is used for satchels and shot-pouches. Black is made only in

Fez for the women's slippers peculiar to that city, worn elsewhere by the Jews alone. White is used for cushions and slippers, but is poor, being usually sheep-skin. Green and blue are rare, and are chiefly employed for ornamental work. The best of the former is from Tafîlált.

Special Varieties.

The leathers of Tafîlált have a better name in Morocco than all others, and are so highly esteemed that they are sold by the pound. As they have to be transported across the Atlas, their price limits their sale. They are usually smooth, while the best qualities from other places are beautifully grained. All the best leather is made from goat-skins, and is finely marked, that from the back of the animal being most highly prized. Sheep-skins are comparatively poor, and are often prepared for use with the fleece on. Ox-hides are employed for soles, and for these Rabat is famous. Lion and panther-skins when procured, which is but rarely, are tanned a beautiful white.

Incised and coloured design on a leather wallet or purse intended to roll up.

The excellence of the tanning of Morocco is ascribed to the use of certain plants cultivated for the purpose, but those interested are naturally chary in supplying information on these points.* A plant called "uzza," found in the Atlas, is said

* From an Algerian source I am informed that the method of tanning Fîlâli leather is as follows:

First bath: cold rock salt brine for 7 or 8 days, renewed every 24 hours; then washed and dried in shade.

Second bath: Water saturated with fresh date juice, for 6 to 10 days. Each day pressed dry to open pores.

Third bath: Water and sea salt, to restore tenacity, 2 days, dried during the night.

Fourth bath: Warm solution of various roots of doubtful utility. Dried to make the leather soft,[1] and fuller's earth is sometimes employed.[2] Either sea-water or fresh may be used in the process, but the latter is preferred.[3] The seeds of the *acacia gumifera* and the branches of the *euphorbium* cactus are likewise utilized in this art,[4] as also the scented fir and the rind of the pomegranate.

Tanning.

In dyeing silk and wool the Moors are very skilful, and some of their silk embroidery is most effective. The blending of colours in some of their home-spun cottons likewise shows great taste. Their carpets no longer hold a foremost place, as they are entirely the output of private looms worked without supervision, the result being a rough, irregular, odd-shaped rug, very inferior to the better-known products of the East, but no less artistic and durable. Rabat is held in best repute for their manufacture, but they are made in several other towns, notably in Casablanca, which of late years has obtained unenviable notoriety for the employment of aniline dyes in place of the vegetable dyes hitherto exclusively used. Nevertheless good carpets are still obtainable, and the faded relics of bygone generations command high figures. The bare feet of the Moors produce a very different effect

Carpets.

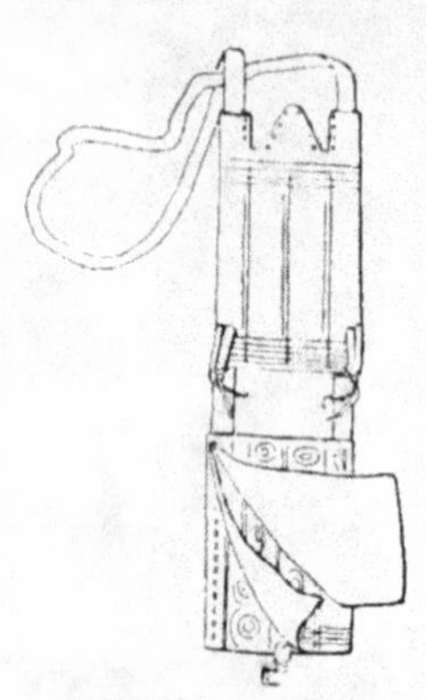

LEATHER POUCH.

Ingeniously and securely closed by sliding down the envelope over the flaps. Used to carry hemp, tobacco and change.

in shade, after which follow many more washings.

It is then dyed by being sewn into bag form and filled with liquid containing wood ashes, with which they are filled ten times for 24 hours. Finally they are dried slowly in the shade, and sprinkled occasionally to keep them soft.

[1] JACKSON, p. 49. [2] Ib. p. 78, [3] DE CAMPOU, p. 236. [4] JACKSON, p. 81.

from the boots of the Nazarenes, imparting to these well-worn specimens a beautiful softness instead of kicking them into holes. There is another class of rug, less known abroad, woven with little or no nap, in broad stripes, chiefly yellow, or, among the mountains, dark red: these are not to be surpassed for camp use, and both wash and wear well. *

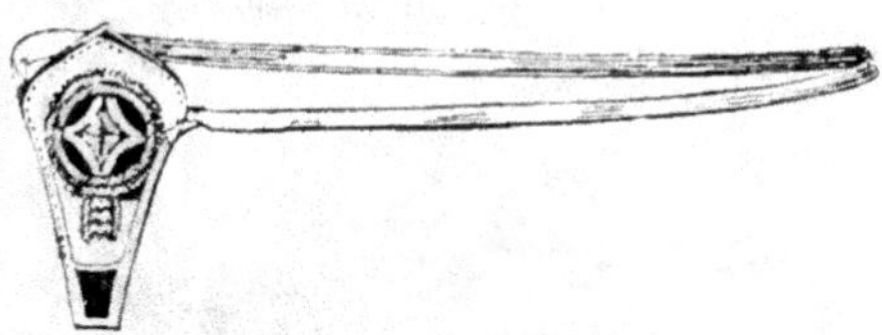

LEATHER HOLSTER FOR PISTOL,
(Embroidered in silk.)

Weaving.

With the exception of the white woollen k'sás or shawls worn by well-dressed men, which are often of a gauze-like fineness—and in the case of those from Ibzû in the Atlas resembling crêpe—most of the materials woven in Morocco are coarse and substantial, the finer classes being rapidly ousted by importations from Europe. The most primitive looms are employed, and the threads, which have been spun between the fingers and thumbs of shepherdesses watching the flocks, may be seen in the country stretched out to form the warp, over the sward, on two poles before the tent door.

* In Algeria the principal dyes used are:—
Red: madder, which grows wild in the South; but for scarlet cochineal.
Blue: imported indigo, as also woad—*Isatis tinctoria* (pastel).
Yellow: wold—*Reseda luteola.*
Green: indigo, gall nuts and wold.
Black: indigo, gall, sulphate of iron and wold.
Violet: indigo and cream of tartar.
Dyes used warm, and fixed with alum: blanched with soda boiled in water, or with much soap.
In the Saḥara wool is made milk white, and the grease removed, by gypsum pounded and suspended in cold water.

Felt is only made for "Fez" caps and saddle- or prayer-cloths, and is never of very fine texture.

Pottery.

The pottery made in Morocco, often excellent both in colour and design, is very crude in execution, and is chiefly confined to basins and bowls for food, water-jars and lamps. Fez and Saffi produce the best, but a perfect piece is seldom to be obtained: green and blue are the prevailing tints.

FEZ DISH.
(Blue on white ground.)
(In the British Museum.)

Gun-making.

In the mechanical arts the Moors do not excel, yet in whatever they do produce, good taste is shown, and only lacks encouragement. For some centuries past they have known how to manufacture flint-lock guns of clumsy construction and coarse workmanship, but generally well decorated by inlaying with ivory, silver, etc.* The best are made in Tetuan, and the most highly ornamented—with chased barrels and richly inlaid stocks, recognizable by a hoof-shaped butt,—in the province of Sûs, which boasts the best workers in metal which this country contains. The Rîf province has also a name for its guns, the butts of which are shod with a long transverse shoulder-piece, while those of Tetuan have a much smaller butt. The barrels sometimes run to four feet long, and the total length of a gun may be six feet, but still more clumsy blunderbusses are also made. The art of making barrels from twisted metal is said to have been imparted to the Moors by a Portuguese taken captive at the battle of El Kaṣar in 1578.† Extreme subdivision of labour is employed in their manufacture, the making of stocks, locks and barrels being independent trades.

PRIMING HORN.

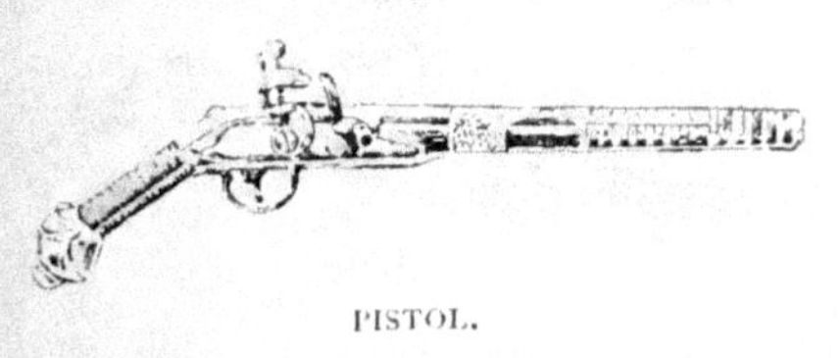
PISTOL.

Metal Workers.

As copper-smiths the Moors show average skill, principally in cooking utensils which are tinned inside, and embossed or engraved trays which hold their place among those of the East. The scabbards of their swords and daggers are often similarly decorated in brass, silver or gold, but the blades are now mostly of German manufacture, while the sheet brass comes from Birmingham. As carpenters or turners they

* For illustrations see *The Moorish Empire*, pp. 242, 246.

† Hay, p. 154. The story goes that a Moor discovered the trick while in the guise of a Jew white-washing the gun-smith's shop.

have little to show beyond occasional stalactite ceilings, beaded architraves and the well-known style of lattice called

Carpenters.

"mushrabîyah" work, from its employment in Egypt to protect shelves on which stand water-coolers. The native jewellery, though artistic, is coarse, but this, with most of the minor mechanical arts, is chiefly in the hands of the Jews, so much more ready to adapt themselves to changing requirements and innovations.

In the manufacture of musical instruments, rude though most of them are, it may be said that the Moors show

Musical Instruments (Stringed).

more skill than in their performances on them. The most common is the ginbrî, a diminutive two or three stringed guitar, so simple in its construction of rough wood and skin that many rustic players make their own, and may be encountered

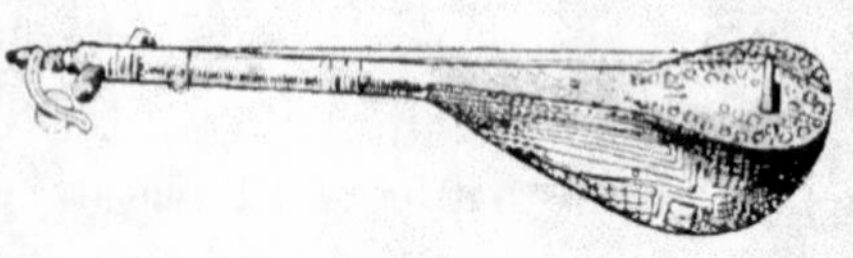

A GINBRI.

A GINBRI.

droning languidly beside their flocks with monotonous accompaniment on this instrument. Much more important looking is the full-sized 'áûd (lute) or mandoline, closely resembling that of Spain, with four pairs of strings, tuned to the *g*, *d*, *a*, and *d* of the treble clef, which is played with a plectrum of whale-bone or horn. A third stringed instrument—the rabáb, played chiefly by Jewish musicians—is a clumsy sort of fiddle of two strings tuned to the *c* and *a* of the treble clef; the effect produced on it is excruciating. The European variety of the violin, an imitation of it, is known as the kamanjah.

Wind Instruments.

Of wind instruments the Moors make most use of the oboe or g͟haïtah, players on which, with distended cheeks, lead most religious processions. A cane flute, shabábah or shiffárah (whistler), is also used, and in Ramaḍán a long horn (nafeer) is blown from the mosque towers during the night. The Rifîs and others also make rude cane pipes of two reeds in which are inserted two smaller ones split at the side, and a picturesque instrument (zummárah), constructed of two curving horns, side by side, fitted to reeds, sometimes attached to of a bag-pipe.

GHAÏTAH.

ZUMMARAH.

Skin Instruments.

But them ost popular instruments are of the drum class, headed by the drum proper (tabil), beaten on one side with a thick nobbed stick, and on the other with a switch. Then there is the plain tambourine, bindar or dîf, with two strings across the centre against the skin,* such as are also introduced in other instruments of this class. Tambourines, called ṭar, of a more elaborate make, with cymbals in the rim, are used by the Jews, and story-tellers fa-

TABIL.

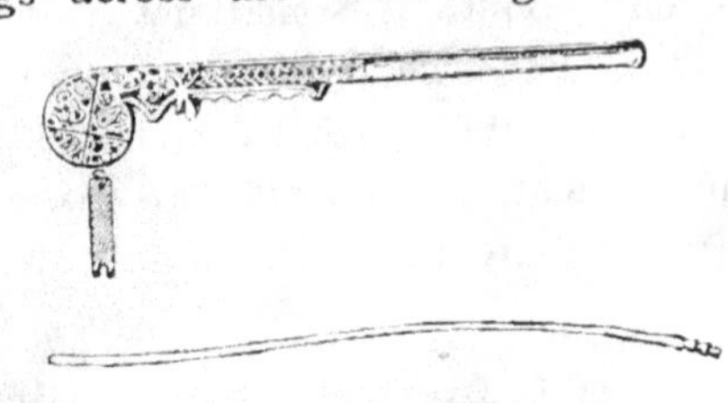

PAIR OF DRUM-STICKS
with section of the head of one.
(Larger scale.)

* Rabbit, goat or lamb skin is most commonly used.

vour a kind of double tambourine, square, with skin on both sides, the bandîr. The most common instrument of this class, however, is the ágwál or darbukkah, a short clay cylinder of varying size, often gaily decorated, with skin and perhaps strings. Great numbers of these are sold to the women and children at feast times, as also are tin castanets, ḳaráḳab. Many original patterns come from Guinea, and the genuine negro minstrel is a common object in Morocco, decked with cowrie shells, buckles, brace-buttons and other European "curios," and armed with formidable mandoline or castanets. Nothing pleases a Moor so much as to tap rhythmically with his finger-tips upon a tambourine or drum, as he hums or intones a nasal air of a few indefinite, wavering notes.

Moorish Music.

His music is based, like that of the Orient generally, on the pentatonic scale, which it is necessary for the untrained European to practise before being able to appreciate the native intervals and divisions. Without this key it is as idle to discuss eastern music, as foolish to condemn it. The use of this scale appears to have been almost universal at one time, and it is that which lends the ancient Scotch and Irish airs their peculiar charm.* It is similar to the modern diatonic major scale with fourth and seventh omitted, sometimes called the "Scotch scale," and to produce it instruments of five and ten strings were invented. Its subdivisions are impossible on our mechanical instruments, so eastern tunes should be reproduced by the voice or on a violin.

* One Indian pentatonic tune familiar to us is "There is a happy land," but the very fact that it can be played on an octatonic instrument indicates that it lacks the distinctive pentatonic subdivision.

CHAPTER THE TWELFTH

MATTERS MEDICAL

IN spite of the fame for medical skill achieved in mediæval Spain* by a few of the Moors, their descendants are in no way better off in this respect to-day than the neighbouring nations, and whatever knowledge of the healing art may once have been theirs, has long since been lost. In all Morocco there does not exist a single native doctor deserving the name. Even those who practise quackery instead are in most cases natives of the East. On the other hand, every European is supposed to possess some knowledge of physic, if not control over sundry evil spirits who torment men's lives. Dr. Rohlfs considered this belief directly traceable to Christ as the Great Physician.

Anatomy.

The only serious practitioners among the Moors are the barbers, who, in addition to shaving, are prepared to bleed or circumcise. Of anatomy all are profoundly ignorant, as the mutilation of a human corpse by dissection is held by them to be almost sacrilege. In consequence of this ignorance many internal ailments are erroneously attributed to the heart. Thus, "my heart aches" means to the Moor "I have a pain in my stomach;" while "his liver is in his mouth" describes a state of intense trepidation.

* It is probable that more of the so-called Arabian Scientists of Spain were Jews than is generally supposed, the confusion arising from their adoption of Arabic names, and in some cases of the Arabian religion also.

Although few Europeans live long in the country without a touch of some form of fever, the greater portion of Morocco is extremely healthful, and with due precaution the foreigner need have no more fear for his health here than at home. Indeed, the climatic attractions of Tangier and Mogador are such as to render those points favourable health-resorts, which only need development to rival those as yet more famous on the coasts of the Mediterranean. During a continuous residence of six years, passed for the most part in Tangier, but including some travel, the writer suffered from nothing worse than colds, or headaches induced by overwork. Yet the effect of mild winters is unquestionably enervating in the long run, and it needs a busy life and determination to maintain even average energy.

Health of Foreigners.

Diseases are generally classified by the Moors under two heads: those productive of heat, inflammation, or increased activity, and those productive of cold, of a loss of feeling or force, or of atrophy. Fevers of course fall into the first class, and they are very prevalent. The scanty precautions taken against changes in temperature and consequent chills, rashness in camping or living near marshy places, and a variety of other causes, render many prostrate with what they simply call "heat," as well as with a variety of intermittent fevers and agues. The most prevalent form of fever is enteric, sufferers from which are left almost without food, and with very little water, until the struggle ends one way or the other.

Classification of Diseases.

The chief time for fevers is October, especially when the rainy season,—which opens in that month and lasts until March or April—sets in gradually, causing unhealthy vapours to rise from the superficial filth accumulated during the Summer. A heavy rainfall,

Fevers.

which soaks things thoroughly and washes the ground, usually remedies this. Some attribute their sufferings in this way to the over-eating of melons grown in swamps. In June, July, August and September intermittent fevers are common, but they prevail in some parts most of the time. For influenza, which here takes a mild form, few lie up, or if they do so, it is seldom for more than a day.

In the interior dysentery is a greater enemy to the stranger than even fever, but the exercise of sufficient care in boiling and filtering my drinking water, and in carrying with me a pure supply for a day or two in case of meeting only with suspicious wells or streams, were, I believe, my bulwarks against this enemy, while I always sought an elevated spot for my camp, in order to avoid malaria and mosquitos. At the same time I was careful as to diet, relying entirely, however, on native produce and cookery, and strictly excluding both intoxicants and narcotics. I know of none of my friends who added spirits to their water, or who smoked on account of evil odours, who had so successful a health record.

Drinking Water.

Although the natives will drink water of almost any degree of opacity, so long as it is running, I do not think that they suffer greatly in consequence; yet dysentery often attacks them. Both they and the animals are perhaps more troubled by evil results from imbibing leeches. The abundance of these creatures in Morocco may be inferred from the fact that for many years—till the European demand died out—the right of exporting them was a government monopoly, as it still is in name, the contractors agreeing to supply any one in Morocco free of charge. Leeches may still be so obtained, as it is against the law for anyone to make a charge for them.

Leeches.

In consequence of their extreme carelessness, worms very frequently trouble the natives. Tape-worm is expelled by a purge of aloes, sulphur and senna-leaves, after a tablespoonful of dry powdered Indian hemp-leaves has been administered to give it a quietus. An ordinary vermifuge is a decoction of rosemary, thyme and broom leaves.

Worms.

The Moors firmly believe in the existence of a minute creature of undefined form, called a *midd*,* which may be swallowed in the water at a size invisible to the naked eye—at all events when the water is thick,—but which afterwards grows tremendously, attacking at discretion throat, brain, heart or legs. In fact, in its vagaries they find a sort of joint personification of internal worms and a score or so of rheumatic and other pains.

Almost every spring there is an epidemic, more or less pronounced, of small-pox, and the number of pitted faces is very large. Mothers are anxious that their children should pass through the ordeal early, and with this end in view place them in the way of contagion. I knew one poor woman who had a pet son of perhaps eight or ten. One day she came like Rachel, sorrowing and not to be comforted for his loss. "O God!" she cried, "What can I do? God knows it was not my fault that my boy did not take the disease in time: for three successive years I borrowed the blankets in which others had died of the small-pox, directly they were buried, and it was only this year he took it. Now he is gone, and I am left alone! Help me, O God, help me!"

Small-pox.

One native method of inoculation is to rub a raisin in an open small-pox pustule, and give it to the child to eat. Vaccination seems, however, to have been more

* An idea probably based on the Guinea worm.

or less known for some time, the vaccine being taken directly from the cow, never from a human being, and inserted between the fingers of the right hand.

Inoculation.

I have never come across this personally, though I have heard of inoculation of small-pox itself, but I give it on the authority of Rohlfs, himself a medical man. A more primitive alleged preventative is to stuff the nostrils with pitch.

AN ENGLISH MISSIONARY LADY EN ROUTE.
Photograph by W. W. Hind-Smith, Esq.

In the interior a child who has had small-pox is said to have had "God's small-pox;" if it has been inoculated by a Jew for a fee the parents say "we bought small-pox for it;" and when it has been vaccinated by a missionary, they say "it has had the 'Tabîbah's* small-pox.'"

Europeans—missionaries and other philanthropists—

* All lady missionaries in Morocco are addressed by the Moorish as Tabîbah, "Doctress."

are now introducing vaccination widely. Much has been done to overcome the prejudice against its practice by the English wife of the late Shareef of Wazzán, who has for twenty years past vaccinated large numbers of Moorish and Jewish children, probably 1500 to 2000 in the course of a year. She has introduced the practice in Tangier, Tetuan, Fez and Wazzán, and many come long distances for treatment by her.*

Vaccination.

Hydrocele is common among the Moors, but rare among the Jews, and by the natives in Tangier is attributed to the local water. Beyond tapping, where possible, by any method which may suggest itself to the amateur, I am not aware of any special treatment for this complaint. The nature of the water in many parts of the country is answerable, doubtless, in a measure, for the many cases of stone in the bladder which are encountered. From the same cause the people of some districts suffer from chalk stones in enlarged glands in the neck. Dr. Kerr of Rabat records having removed from a man such a stone, the size of a large hen's egg. The use of imperfectly cleansed brass kettles, an inordinate consumption of green tea, the national beverage, and sundry other peculiarities of life in Morocco, are unquestionably the cause of much illness. Lumbago, rheumatism and sciatica are common, but the life led by the poor renders it remarkable that they are not more prevalent. The "bone-ache" of which one hears so much, is generally rheumatism, if not syphilitic in its origin.

Hydrocele, Stone, etc.

The national disease of Morocco may be said to be syphilis, called the "great sickness" or "women's sick-

* As a result several of the villages round Tangier pride themselves on having no small-pox at all, and there has been no epidemic of it, as so frequently occurs in other parts, for the last sixteen years.

ness," and unjustly attributed to the Jews expelled from Spain by the Inquisition. As a matter of fact the Jews are, on the contrary, wonderfully free from this scourge, as also from white spots and inflammation of the eyes, which are, to a great extent, syphilitic. One medical practitioner assured me that during four years he had met with only two cases among the "chosen people," and they were so notorious as exceptions to the rule that all the other Jews of the place knew of them. On the other hand, an English doctor travelling in the country has surmised that among the Moors every other man, woman or child is tainted with this disease in one form or another. One in every five patients at a medical mission in Tangier came to be treated for venereal diseases. The only native recommendations which I have come across have been to adopt a vegetable diet for forty days, meanwhile drinking sarsaparilla, or to fast entirely except that each day a piece of bread the size of two fingers is allowed.

The National Disease.

There are many cases of white spots, but leprosy is not very common. Rohlfs considered the disease called by the Moors j'dám, usually described as leprosy, to be rather constitutional syphilis arrived at a stage unknown in Europe. There are one or two leper towns in the Empire, but of these I have visited only that outside Marrákesh. The cases I saw there did not present by any means the loathsome appearance already so familiar in syphilitic subjects who promenade the Moorish streets, nose-less or lip-less, or with hideous running sores on head or limbs. They complained, however, that damp air caused them to "ache all over." Compared, too, with cases which I have seen in Burma, Cashmere, the Himálayas, Calicut, and other countries, the effects of this disease in Morocco are much less loathsome. A case encountered in Sibe-

Leprosy.

ria reminded me most forcibly of those seen in this country.

Some make a plaster for the sores, of henna-leaves—*Lawsonia inermis*, or Egyptian privet—with clay, and others recommend as a specific for leprosy a decoction of argan leaves to be used internally and externally. This is the *Elcodendron* or *Syderoxylon argan*, a tree peculiar to Morocco.* The oil prepared from its fruit in many points resembles that from the olive, but is not to be confounded with it, and is very much preferred for culinary purposes, though against it there is a groundless supposition that in some way it predisposes to leprosy.† On the other hand, a foreign official in Morocco early in the last century‡ was convinced that copious draughts of this oil were a cure for the bubonic plague,—the terrible disease known as the "black death," which had recently visited the country,§—so he printed Arabic circulars to enlighten the people, and made great efforts to induce them to adopt the remedy. Olive oil is also recommended as a curative beverage and unguent in typhus fever, or, as a substitute for it, saltless butter, to be eaten in considerable quantities.

Prescriptions.

Elephantiasis is frequently met with, both in the simple form and in that distinguished as *Arabum*. I used to know a negro musician who accompanied the clanking of his iron castanets and the jingle of the buttons and shells strung in his hair, with the big-drum-beat of his elephant-foot on the ground, thus pressing even disease into his service in a novel way.

Elephantiasis.

Apart from these special forms, there are a number of

* See *The Land of the Moors*, p. 40.

† Leo had this idea: perhaps therefore, as a remedy, it may claim to be homœopathic.

‡ G. G. Colaço, Portuguese consul at Laraiche in 1818.

§ Introduced, it is said, by an English vessel with pilgrims from Mekkah, which resulted in the loss of perhaps a fifth of the inhabitants.

NEGRO MINSTREL IN MOROCCO.
(A Victim of Elephantiasis.)

Cavilla, Photo., Tangier.

prevalent skin diseases from which few escape, including ring-worm, favus, scabies and others. It has been stated by one medical writer that almost all boys in Morocco are attacked by ring-worm at one time or another, but that it usually dies out about the age of puberty: it is seldom found in girls. The indiscriminate shaving of the healthy and the diseased with the same razors presumably accounts for this, and the complaint itself is little noticed. The natives treat scabies successfully by rubbing in soft soap and sand in equal proportions.

Skin Diseases.

Inflamed eyes and ophthalmia, though by no means so common or so distressing as in Egypt, are as prevalent as the habits of the people can make them. It is said that ophthalmia is less prevalent among the women than among the men, on account of their use of antimony to blacken the eyelids. A favourite remedy is to blow powdered sugar and canary-seed into the eye.*

The Eyes.

Although ceremonial washings do much to counteract the complacency with which the Moor regards filth, they are generally too perfunctory, with the exception of the great purification, usually performed in a steam-bath, where disease is easily transmitted. Even this loses half its value when the oft-times lively garments are replaced, for even religious injunctions have failed to inculcate the *principle* of cleanliness. At the same time it is only fair to say that among the upper classes the natural refinement of Oriental civilization has brought about a much better state of things, and there no greater faults can be found than among ourselves. Of all the prescriptions of cus-

Are the Moors Clean?

* One of Pellow's adventures consisted in substituting cayenne for canary-seed when so treating a Moorish highwayman, from whom he thereby escaped.

tom on these points, perhaps that which causes the males to shave all over except the beard and mustache, and the females all but the head, is one of the most closely obeyed, and one of the most salutary. In some districts the heads of the youngsters, which have been shorn of their natural protection, are temporarily covered with pitch before they are again let loose in the broiling sun, as was still the custom in the Grampians two centuries ago. Pitch is in great repute for all skin diseases, and is supposed to add a virtue to water contained in skins or jars which have been washed with it. It is sold in the markets tied up in sections of sheeps' intestines, or kept in bulk in a stomach.

Lungs, and Heart.

Athough the climate is not favourable to the development of tubercle, and the Jews almost entirely escape by a rigid adherence to the Mosaic laws, it is found among the Moors, who readily eat both cattle and fowls, which suffer from it widely. Heart diseases are not frequently found in Morocco,.

A Strange Complaint.

Of all the diseases to which the Moor is heir perhaps the most curious is one described by the natives as "clay-cold," which is said to display itself in an irresistible desire to eat clay, alone or with food.* Genuine lunatics are common enough, and a premium is placed on counterfeit insanity by the reverence in which it is held. When it is considered necessary to restrain a madman, he is usually chained in a sort of dungeon known as a morsṭán. The patients there usually live naked on a stone floor in the midst of unutterable filth. Hydrophobia has been stated to be unknown, and Rohlfs adds that here dogs fed on raw meat are in no danger of going mad, but rabies is really common in some parts, as at Rabat, where a European doctor had to kill as many as six mad dogs in one year.

* Reported among the Beni Miskeen.

Nevertheless, on the whole the physique and general health of the Moors in the face of so many foes is astonishing, and nothing speaks more for the cleansing power of the sun than their comparative freedom from epidemics resulting either from the absence or defective condition of drainage which allows poisonous gases to flood the streets. There, as often as not, is thrown all the offal from the kitchen, and dead dogs, cats, rats and chickens soon afford familiar sights and smells. Horses, mules and donkeys, when their working days are over, are generally thrown on the huge rubbish heaps outside the city-gates, and it would be considered little short of a crime to despatch them in order to put an end to their sufferings. After the "Sheep Feast," when every household has a ram slaughtered at its door, the entrails are left to putrefy in the narrow streets. In addition to this, many of the towns are situated in hollows or at the foot of hills which serve as cemeteries, the site having been chosen on account of some attractive spring, soon to become tainted by the burial of the dead on the heights around, even if the water is withal more sparkling.

General Health.

But the greatest enemy to health and long life in Morocco is, undoubtedly, the unrestrained gratification of sensual proclivities. Moorish lads are not to be surpassed in good looks or promise, but from the age of eighteen or upwards they rapidly deterioriate, till they are old men at forty, ancients at fifty. With women married at twelve the effects are still more marked. At thirty they are old; at forty to fifty, hags. Possibly the way they become wrinkled from thirty upwards is attributable in some measure to the fattening process to which they are subjected previous to entering the marriage market. After each meal they are supplied with boluses of zammitah,

The Radical Evil.

(parched flour) and honey flavoured with anise, or with spoonfuls of olive oil and sesame.

*Child-birth.**

Although I have known of a case in which a Moorish woman has gone forth in the morning to her reaping or to her washing at the well-side childless, and at night has returned with a new-born infant on her head or hip, things do not always work so smoothly, even in this land of unrestricted growth and development. Males are, from the nature of the social conditions of a strictly Mohammedan country, rigidly excluded from all share in attentions on womankind, and it has only been on occasions of rare confidence or enlightenment that even European medical men have been trusted in such matters. That this arises, however, from no delicacy of feeling is evident from the unrestricted way in which a Moorish woman will converse on all her troubles and experiences with a man.

Diseases of Children.

Among children, one of the most prevalent diseases is that of "falling sickness." Infantile mortality is very high, but not remarkably so in view of the way in which the children are neglected. It is a common sight to see youngsters hardly able to toddle, naked from the waist down, sitting about in puddles on the cold, tiled pavement of a rich man's courtyard or in the mud of some village "square." It is indeed a case of the survival of the fittest.

Pharmacopœia.

A list of the various objects employed by the Moors to cure or to kill would be hardly credible, and would only be outdone by a list of those used by the Chinese. Poisons are more in request than even remedies, and corrosive sublimate or arsenic may be secured for a trifling sum as easily as salt, and both

* This subject not being capable of popular treatment, I would refer those interested to a paper which I contributed some years ago to *Modern Medicine*, of Battle Creek, Michigan. U. S. A., 1895, p. 101.

are found useful, being easily administered in tea. Perhaps the most painful death is that caused by mixing finely-chopped horse-hair with the victim's food; but merely to cause injury the pounded bones of a dead man, or a hyæna's brain, may be administered. The latter prescription is also mentioned as a suitable purge for horses, and may be seen dried in the spice-shops: its effect on human beings is supposed to drive them crazy. *

MOORISH CHILDREN IN RAHAMNA.

Photograph by Dr. Rudduck.

When a Moor does take physic he likes it strong, and speedy in manifest action. Nothing is therefore in greater request than violent purgatives. Epsom salts, when they can be procured, are indulged in by the heaped table-spoonful, and a Moor

Drastic Remedies.

* In the desert, the urine of camels is credited with wonderful powers. It is there used to wash the Arab brides before marriage.[1]

[1] DOULS, p. 21.

will take with satisfaction a dose of croton oil that would all but put an end to an Englishman. On one occasion I remember mixing a good strong dose and a half of Epsom salts and quinine for a mother and child who had come to me tortured with ague, directing the former to drink two-thirds of the nauseous mixture, and the latter the rest. But on the child's refusing her share after tasting it, the mother abused her roundly as a "daughter of sin," the "offspring of a wanton woman," and cursed all her ancestors, at length growing so exasperated at her stubbornness that she drank the remainder herself.

Surgery.

In surgery the Moors are even farther behind than in medicine. The utmost they can do is to extract shots and bullets from living subjects, under which operations the patients display a remarkable degree of fortitude. There was once a family renowned for bone-setting, but they were not large-hearted enough to found a school, or to pass on the secrets of their art. Some do, nevertheless, know how to set fractures in bandages stiffened with the starch which they prepare from wheat. Other families have gained a name for operations in cases of cataract, with an instrument like a needle, introduced sideways, but they have no knowledge of cures for other eye complaints. On the other hand, one hears of a gun being brought in to assist in the extraction of a ball which had been fired from it.

Evil Spirits.

The Moors are firm believers in possession by evil spirits, which I have known cast out with great success by liberal doses of tartaric acid and bicarbonate of soda, one after the other. Indeed, Morocco offers a wide field for the charlatan, but very little pay, which is, perhaps, its salvation.

A much more common practice is to brand a patient

somewhere in the neighbourhood of the diseased part, an operation borne with unflinching fortitude in the public street, or wherever may be most convenient. A favourite spot is the small of the back, or it may be near the shoulder-blades, for complaints of the stomach or lungs. Any hot iron will do, and the local smithy is considered as suitable a scene as any, while amid an interested and enthusiastic crowd the patient is held down upon the ground for the performance. Rohlfs tells how he gained no little fame by introducing the use of caustic instead, a treatment described by the natives in contradistinction as "cold fire." Personally, I have found oil of cantharides in great request for raising blisters behind the ears to relieve inflamed eyes, but the trouble was that half the village would apply for similar treatment on one pretext or another, as the owner of the blister was the man of the hour.

Firing.

But more common still is the practice of bleeding, performed by every barber, often on the open market place, and always recommended for headaches and fevers. The simplest method is to draw half a pint or a pint of blood from the arm by means of an incision in the vein, after carefully binding the upper part. Or regular cupping may be practised on the back of the neck, where a series of fine scratches are made with a razor. The only other instrument employed is a brass or tin cup with a long thin tube from near the top, which serves also as a handle, the end of which is wrapped in a piece of leather, closing together and forming a valve when moistened. Through this tube the air in the cup is exhausted after pressing it against the skin, the patient bending in such a way that the cup hangs down as it fills. Dry-cupping is also practised, the air in any suitable vessel being exhausted by clapping it on to the desired spot over a piece of burning

Bleeding.

tow, fibre or shavings, an "elegant" blister resulting. Massage is of course employed in the steam-baths, but is hardly looked on here as medical treatment.

Dentistry.

Dentistry is practically unknown, the highest achievement in that direction being the extraction of a painful tooth by the barber with an antiquated key-wrench, such as was in use a century ago in our own land, and which is still manufactured for these countries in France.

Faith Healing.

After all, however, Morocco is a land of faith healing, and few cures are effected by any other agency. The blessing of a shareef or noble of Mohammed's descent, or even oil or water from his tomb, is more highly valued than any medicaments, and an amulet is more relied upon as a preventative of disease than any precaution suggested by science. The explanation of this is that all disease is supposed to result, directly or indirectly, from the exercise of the "evil eye," an influence to be successfully combated only by the exercise of some restraining good influence, whatever means may also be used. Charms are therefore worn by all women, and by a great many men, and may be either general or special. The former may consist merely of a rudely modelled hand or some sacred earth or stone, or of a "writing" carefully protected by a leather or silk case, * and worn suspended from the neck or over the affected part. Many make a livelihood by preparing these documents to order, their contents being usually an extract from the Ḳor'án, but also sometimes a rambling incantation. For some utterly inexplicable complaint, such as indigestion, for instance, a favourite remedy is the phrase "and only God is the Healer," written out a score or so of times on a piece of paper, which is to be torn into so many equal parts,

Amulets.

* For illustration see ch. xix.

and these taken, rolled up, with a little water, night and morning. Love philtres and aphrodisiacs are in great request, and are frequently furnished in this form. But the Moor is always careful to ascribe all praise to Him to whom it is due, and whenever he hears of sickness he exclaims "Lá bás"—"No harm!" or "Allah îshafhu"—"May God heal him!" A three days' sickness is held by some Muslim teachers to render the faithful pure as new-born infants, for they believe that during illness the recording angels take no note of evil deeds, but give double credit for good deeds.

Veterinary Methods.

Veterinary skill among the Moors is at about as low an ebb as their other sciences, though they certainly practise some drastic, and not always unsuccessful, measures. As with human beings, the favourite remedy is the hot iron. If the tendons of the foot are swollen or stiff, a circle within which a cross is inscribed is branded thereon, and so on. When on the ulcerated back of a beast of burden from which the saddle has not been removed for a week or two—to prevent the irritated beast from rolling in the dirt—the proud flesh commences to be odoriferous, a seton is usually inserted over the shoulders. This consists merely of a piece of cord threaded through about six inches of skin with a pack-needle. Small sores under the saddle are considered a positive advantage, as rendering the animal more restive and less liable to lag. Pitch or black soft-soap seem to be the only remedies applied.

It frequently happens that when the barley which forms the staple food of the horses, mules, camels and donkeys, is new, considerable irritation and swelling are caused in the palate; to remedy this native farriers are wont to make incisions therein, which generally have a favourable result.

Among the remedies administered internally, the foremost place is contended for by rancid butter and gun-powder. The former is given chiefly for colds, and the latter for stomach complaints, though both are considered as near panaceas as possible. The gun-powder is made into a paste with soft-soap prepared from olive oil and wood ashes. Rest, and half a pound of melted butter three days following, is a favourite prescription for unaccountable thinness, and the Moors can usually tell by the look of their steeds when they ate or drank last.

Internal Remedies.

But the Moors are not the only strange horse-doctors in Morocco, as the following instance will show: a favourite horse of mine had a bad fall, and while its wounds were healing got into a generally disordered condition. The local European chemist was called in, a man who prided himself on being a practical horse-doctor. His prescription was, all the fresh grass it could eat, a bottle of port wine, and a bottle of hot senna-tea. The last two I saw him administer consecutively, but with no result. Next day a consultation was arranged with the local European farrier, who advised the substitution of bran mash for green food, which he considered absolutely dangerous under the circumstances. His remedy was a pint or two of olive oil and exercise. This having likewise failed to secure improvement, a third European expert arrived on the scene, an advocate of bottled beer and barley grass. After two bottles of the former and a day's trial at the latter, the horse succumbed, and there only remained the bills to pay.

Rival Practitioners.

PART II—ETHICAL

THE CREED OF ISLAM.

لا اله الا الله و محمد الرسول الله

"Lá ílaha íl' Al'ah, wa Mohammed er-Rasûl Al'ah."

(There is no god but God, and Mohammed is the Apostle of God.)

Inscription from over entrance to shrine of Sîdi 'Ali el Bárakah, Tetuan.

CHAPTER THE THIRTEENTH

SOME MOORISH CHARACTERISTICS

NO task falls more heavily upon the writer on a foreign people who would "nothing extenuate nor set down aught in malice," than the effort to delineate their character with brevity and accuracy. To the transient impressionist it is a pleasant occupation to record such features as chance uppermost, and which, from their apparent truthfulness, secure him credit, but to the student with a feeling of responsibility the summing up of all the little traits in his experience becomes a weighty undertaking. Few qualities, whether good or bad, are not to be found somewhere in a nation, wherefore it is possible only to touch upon the manner in which this or that presents itself, without dogmatic assertions as to the proportion of the people by whom it may be exhibited.

Difficulty of Task.

Among the Moors the master-passions may perhaps be set down as self-love and cupidity, supported by self-satisfaction and religious pride. It is this which militates most strongly against progress, and precludes improvement from outside. "God doth not change the condition of a people till their minds are changed," runs a koranic saying, and it exactly applies to the Moors. At the same time their supreme contempt for Nazarenes, although tempered to some slight extent by the forced acknowledgment of

The Master-Passions.

their superior inventive genius, hinders them from learning where they might, and the very fact that any good thing comes out of Nazareth is its condemnation in their eyes. Their self-love, too, prevents the exercise of public spirit, and accounts in a great measure for the hopelessly corrupt state of the government. It is the old story over again, every man's hand against his neighbour, every man for himself, even to the dividing up of families, although as children much parental affection is often enjoyed, and much deferential respect is shown. Courtesy and dignity remain with most through life, and imperturbability is practised as a mark of good breeding. Nothing that occurs can move the well-trained Moor to betray his feelings, or to exhibit surprise or alarm, hardly even the unexpected report of firearms close by, or any sudden catastrophe, which will only cause him to ejaculate some pious phrase ascribing power to God, or blessings on the "prophet."

Self-Control.

The belief of the Moor in predestination, like that of all Mohammedans, amounts in many instances to apathy, for what good is there in man proposing if God has already disposed? The expression "if God will," or "what God wills," is introduced at every reference to the future, often even when granting requests with a mental determination that in this case God shall not "will." Thus whatever happens which does not actually cause him suffering, the Moor preserves a calm exterior, and being of a light-hearted and recuperative disposition, soon regains his balance and displays a cheerful countenance, as children do. But, although the men exhibit considerable fortitude in grief, the women, lacking self-control just as much as their lords possess it, give way to extraordinary and unreasonable demonstrations, and are easily upset. The death-wail, for instance, is almost entirely confined to their

Fatalism.

sex, and their ebullitions of joy are quite as marked as their shrill but meaningless cries.

Endurance.

In bearing pain, even where it might be avoided, the Moors show so much endurance that there need be little hesitation in attributing to them a less keen sensitiveness than experienced by us thinner skinned folk. This is in some measure attributable, no doubt, to their out-door life, and to the rough-and-ready treatment of the young which results in the survival of the fittest only. This characteristic is evidenced by their silent submission to corporal punishment which might be avoided by the payment of money or by divulging a secret: by the way in which they will bear the pain of surgical operations without anæsthetics, as I have witnessed myself: by the readiness with which they will handle live coals, or continue at work with open sores; to say nothing of the long day's fast of summer Ramaḍáns, or the way they sleep out-of-doors in bad weather, or ride on, hour after hour, when travelling.

That they possess great natural courage cannot be questioned, but their bravery is supported by this quality of endurance, as well as by their belief in predestination. Many stories might be told of Moorish courage, and European military instructors in Morocco speak in high terms of the fighting qualities of the recruits. Obstinacy, however, is one of their characteristics, and here again come into play the qualities described. To the same callousness must be attributed a great deal of what seems to strangers innate cruelty, exhibitions of which on man and beast are encountered at every turn. Notwithstanding all the brutal acts which could be proved against them, I cannot think the Moors as a nation cruel or

BRASS-MOUNTED DAGGER.

Cruelty.

hard-hearted. In Morocco, as everywhere else, evil is wrought just as much by want of thought as by want of heart, and it is the training rather than the disposition that is at fault.

Fellow-Feeling.

Sympathy they do not often show, but it is there, and cases of most touching nature might be cited. It would almost seem as though in the down-trodden and oppressed the tender virtues flourished, but that acquisition of power meant their loss, and their replacement by cold stony-heartedness: the probability is that under the existing régime only those succeed in office who are conscienceless. Gratitude is usually found among the lower orders, overwhelming gratitude when further favours are anticipated, but often sincere beyond doubt. They are liberal, too, exercising hospitality as a religious duty, yet not often without a suspicion of self-interest.

Integrity.

The commercial instinct is strongly marked, though the Moors are no match for the Jews, and while as a whole they cannot be commended for honesty, Europeans trading with them can give abundant instances of wonderful integrity. In Tunis the inhabitants of Sûs have such a name for trustworthiness, that to them before all others is entrusted the guardianship of warehouses, shops and railway stations, and in this respect Moors generally bear a high character in the East. * It is usually, however, only in transactions with individuals with whom it is their interest to maintain credit that the Moors live up to such a character, and often the man who has the greatest reputation for fidelity with his employers will be known by others as

* Lane, for instance, recorded, "I have never heard any particular nation thus honourably distinguished except the English and the Maghribîs, or Western Arabs, which latter people have acquired this reputation by being rather more veracious than most other Arabs."[1]

[1] *Modern Egyptians*, p. 303.

an unprincipled rogue. Thus few Europeans can be found to agree as to the honesty of any specified Moor, although almost every resident or traveller becomes attached to at least one "faithful retainer."

MOORISH BOYS
(From Mission Orphanage at Tangier.)
Photograph by David J. Cooper, Esq.

Lying.

Truthfulness is not a quality which need be sought for in Morocco, for the Moors have no conception of what we understand by that term, any more than Orientals generally.* Protestant Christian countries alone have developed the high ideal on which their religion is based, and this has made "the word of an Englishman" the best description of a truthful statement known to the Moors. Lying comes as second nature to

* "Falsehood was *commended* by their prophet when it tended to reconcile persons at variance with each other; also when practised in order to please one's wife, and to obtain any advantage in a war with the enemies of the faith, though highly reprobated in other cases." [1]

[1] Ib., p. 304.

the unregenerate man, and will remain a characteristic of the Moors, as of all others, until they learn the Way of Truth. The strongest asseverations have to be employed in daily intercourse, and few expect to be believed without an oath: a mere imprecation upon liars and the father of lies more often than not emphasizes a lie.

It is therefore necessary in all dealings with Orientals to consider whether any statement made is likely to be to the speaker's advantage, or what reply it would best serve him to give. For a similar reason their promises can never be relied on, and no expectations should be entertained on that account alone. Cunning in diplomacy is greatly aided by their freedom from these trammels, and if the Machiavellian-Jesuitical system be admitted as the standard, the Moors must rank high. "Do they think me a dog of a Nazarene, that I should be bound by my word?" was the typical expostulation of a Moorish sultan, called on to fulfil the stipulations of a treaty, and it is only fear of consequences which prevents the existing conventions from being broken wholesale.

A Word to the Wise.

The extent to which sensuality pervades the Moorish character could not here be told, but it is no wonder in view of the low ideals of enjoyment inculcated from their earliest years, both in women and men. The women have to be shut up, not only for protection, but also for restraint. Thus the strength of the nation is sapped, there being in their religion no constraining spiritual power to check the impulses of nature. This is the saddest feature of life in Morocco, where natural vice is respectable, and unnatural vice is winked at.

Sensuality.

Although the Moorish code of manners is so strict that women are never mentioned in polite society without an apology, and are not considered fit subjects for conversation with strangers or superiors, when a Moor feels himself at home among his friends, there is no more favourite theme than the fair sex and doubtful dealings therewith. It has been urged by apologists for Islám that it has at all events kept its women moral, but it has only done so in so far as it has succeeded in degrading them to the level of captive subjects for the lusts of men, as the native pro-

Position of Women.

MOORISH "WOMEN OF BURDEN."
Photograph by W. W. Hind-Smith, Esq.

verb has it, "slaves by day, and queens at night." It would hardly be going too far to say that no woman in Morocco is chaste who has it in her power to be otherwise, and that no man loses the slightest chance of gratifying his lust.

Indolent and lazy the Moors unquestionably are, for "why," asks a native adage, "should one run when walking will do; or walk when there is no necessity; or stand when one might as well sit; or sit when there is room to lie? And why, when lying down, keep one's eyes open?" Yet, paradoxical though it may seem, as workmen the Moors are active and diligent: it is rather in their ingrained procrastination that they show their laziness. "Never do to-day what can by any means be postponed till to-morrow," might be taken as the never-varying motto of the nation. But Morocco would lose its greatest charm in a rush, and in business its inhabitants would still procrastinate—"to-morrow, if it please God, to-morrow!"

Indolence.

Time, with any idea of saving it, is of no account whatever in Barbary, though much pains are taken to dispose of it. The greatness of Moorish officials is to be measured by the length of time they succeed in keeping suitors dancing attendance upon them, continually excusing themselves, temporizing, postponing, and protracting things generally. From the Sultan downwards it is the same. The standing policy of the government is to promise all things, performing nothing till driven to it by necessity. "Ghaddá, in shá Allah," *pro cras*, "to-morrow, if it please God": that is the unvarying answer of rulers and ruled,—the saving clause expressive of dependence on God being specially insisted upon. It matters not what may be the urgency of the affair in hand; once a Moor has made up his mind not to bother about it to-day, it is useless to urge; it is worse than attempting to drive the most stupid of asses. Creditors are constantly robbed by continued procrastination, and many a native suitor dies of that sickness which results from "hope deferred." In everything it is the same, the Moors preferring to jog along in their own tardigrade fashion, vegetating where they find themselves, with folded hands; taking things easy as they drag along a sluggish life, everlastingly hanging fire and dawdling where prompt action is demanded,

Procrastination.

wasting their lives in passive inaction, living and dying like snails.

Good Humour.

Easy-going good humour is much more a Moorish characteristic than vindictiveness, the custom of the vendetta notwithstanding, for the task of avenging blood is looked on in the light of religious duty rather than of personal revenge, and were it not for the opprobrium of public opinion, blood-money would be accepted far more often than it is. They are after all light-hearted and child-like: no one appreciates a tale or joke better than do the Moors, and it is good to see them laugh in their unrestrained way. It is really wonderful how much they will put up with from their officials, for they are a remarkably submissive race upon the plains, but the mountain Berbers are very different, as will be elsewhere described.* On the whole it is noteworthy how similar in character the mixed race known as Moors are to the Arabs everywhere, as, among others, to the modern Egyptians described by Lane.

POWDER FLASK.

Influence of Religion.

One feature which pervades all these peoples, lending them much of their uniformity, is the Mohammedan religion, which so closely affects their lives. Religious phraseology enters into every conversation, even in false and licentious statements, and the Ḳor'án is constantly quoted, even in jest. Islám, it is true, is spoken of by the Moors as decayed, but it is none the less persistently upheld, and Jews and foreigners are only tolerated since they have grown indispensable.

In a work like this any attempt to describe the rise and progress of Islám, or to enter into an enumeration of its precepts, would be out of place, and would

* In chapter xxii.

only serve to add unnecessarily to its dimensions. Readers are supposed to have already formed some acquaintance with the writings of authorities on these points, but it is worth while bearing in mind that Morocco still affords an opportunity of studying Islám in a condition almost unalloyed by foreign influence.

History of Islám.

Here the Arab missionaries had almost their own way among a people ignorant and superstitious, who had no elaborate religion to oppose them, or to become a modifying influence. Notwithstanding the popular idea on the subject, it is certain that whatever smattering of Christianity had found its way among them was but vague, and probably confined entirely to the dwellers on the coast. The introduction of Islám has been dealt with in my *Moorish Empire.** and there remains but to consider the present state of its observances. These are so bound up with social and legal customs, and with every aspect of Moroccan civilization, that it is impossible to treat them as distinct, and no attempt will be made to do so.

Early Christianity.

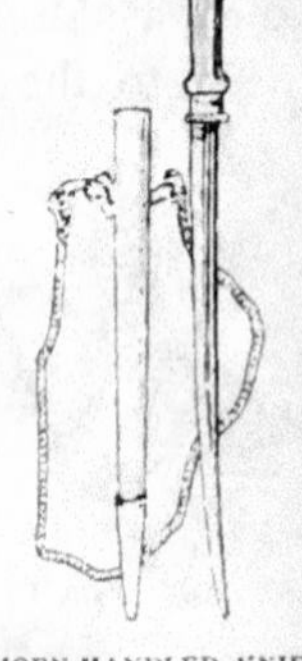

HORN-HANDLED KNIFE AND SHEATH.

The great blot on the creed of Islám is that precept and practice are not expected to go together except as regards the ritual, so that a man may be notoriously wicked, yet esteemed religious, having his blessing sought as that of one who has power with God, without the slightest sense of incongruity. The position of things was very well put to me one day by a Moor in Fez, who remarked: "Do you want to know what our religion is? We purify ourselves with water while we contemplate adultery: we go

Moral Standard.

* Chapter ii.

to the mosque to pray, and as we do so we think how best to cheat our neighbours; we give alms at the door, and go back to our shops to rob: we read our Ḳor'áns and go out to commit unmentionable sins: we fast and go on pilgrimages, yet we lie and kill." An indictment like this from native lips is stronger than anything an outsider could say, and I need only add that as often as I have repeated it to Moorish friends, it has received their endorsement. *

Unfortunate Lot.

Yet it must not be inferred that all Moors are bad or hypocritical, or that they are entirely destitute of noble qualities. Far from it: as men there is much to be said to the honour both of the Berber and Arab races who make up the Moorish nation, to say nothing of the ill-fated but jovial Negro section, for they all have admirable qualities, and I have found among them many estimable friends. But when the effect of their religion upon their characters is considered, it is seen to be a curse and not a blessing. On the whole the Moor is to be pitied rather than condemned, for we may say of him in Cowper's words:—

> "His hard condition with severe constraint
> Binds all his faculties, forbids all growth
> Of wisdom, proves a school in which he learns
> Sly circumvention, unrelenting hate,
> Mean self-attachment, and scarce ought beside." [1]

---

* All that is required of a good Muslim is that he, being circumcised:

(1) Repeat the creed: "There is no god but God, and Mohammed is the Apostle of God;

(2) Pray five times a day;

(3) Keep the fast of Ramaḍán;

(4) Give a certain proportion of his income as alms;

(5) Go on pilgrimage to Mekka, if possible.

[1] *The Task.*

THE MAÔLÛD OUTSIDE FEZ.

Molinari, Photo., Tangier.

CHAPTER THE FOURTEENTH

THE MOHAMMEDAN YEAR IN MOROCCO

DATING from April 19th, 622 A.C., the first day of the moon of Moḥarram preceding the emigration of Mohammed from Mekka (which took place sixty-eight days later, on the ninth of Rabî'a I.), the followers of that reformer, reckoning by the lunar year, are now in their fourteenth century, our new century commencing Ramaḍan 10th, 1318, A.H. As their year consists of only 354 days, 8 hours and 48 minutes, as against the longer solar year, they are always falling behind the seasons to the extent of about eleven days per annum, so that their new year and religious feasts retrograde through all our months in succession. Six of their months having 29 days, and six of them 30, in nineteen out of each thirty years they have to add a day to the last month of the year, to keep pace with the moons, which makes it difficult enough to calculate exactly when a given year began.*

"*Anno Hejiræ.*"

* To obviate this difficulty Mr. A. M. Laredo, of the Italian Legation in Tangier, has published a most valuable series of tables, *Rapport entre les dates du calendrier musulman et celles des calendriers julien et grégorien*, (to be obtained of the author,) of which I have made great use. But Mr. Laredo holds by the popular error, corrected by Caussin de Perceval, which makes the era commence on July 16th, A.D. 622, an error which, however, only affects the first nine years. Similar tables have been published in Europe. An approximate formula for calculating the year only is: if x be the year of the Hejira, A.C. $= x + 622 - \frac{x}{33}$.

The names of the Mohammedan months * are:—

Moḥarram, †	or Es-shahr el 'Aáshûr.
Ṣafar,	,, Sháï'a ,,
Rabi'a el áûlà, (I)	,, Es-shahr el Maôlûd.
,, et-táni, (II)	,, Sháï'a ,,
Jumádà el áûlà, (I)	
,, et-táni, (II)	
Rajab. †	
Sha'abán.	
Ramaḍán. †	
Shûwal,	,, Es-shahr el 'Aïd es-Sagheer.
Dhû'l Ḳa'idah, †	,, Baïn al 'Aïád (Between the Feasts).
,, Ḥajjah, †	,, Es-shahr el 'Aïd el Kabeer.

EL YÔM EL 'AÁSHÛR: "TITHING-DAY."

The "Sacred" Month.

The Mohammedan year commences with a month of mourning, called Moḥarram or "Sacred," from several traditions connected with it. Many fast on the second, third, ninth or tenth day, especially on the tenth, which is the Yôm el 'Aáshûr. Amongst the events believed to have taken place on that day are: the first reunion of Adam (A'dám) and Eve (Hawah) after having been cast out of Paradise (Fardaôs): the exit of Noah (Nûḥ) from the ark; the pardon of the sins of Adam, David (Dáwud) Enoch (Idrees), Noah, Job ('Ayûb) and Jonah (Yûna); and in later times of the death of El Ḥosaïn, Mohammed's grandson. The ancient Arabs fasted on that day long before the time of Mohammed, but as fasting is not then compulsory, it is now seldom observed except by

* Special epithets are commonly attached to the names of certain months: Moḥarram el ḥaram ("the sacred"), Ṣafar el khaïr ("of prosperity"), Rabi'a en-nabáwi ("of the prophet") and Rajab el fard ("the only").

† Fighting among Mohammedans is not permitted during Moḥarram, Rajab, Ramaḍan, Dhû'l Ḳa'idah and Dhû'l Ḥajjah.

the Shî'ï sect, whose head-quarters are Persia, and whose *raison d'être* is hatred of Turks.* The Persians, with their fellows of northern India, having made the death of El Ḥosaïn a perpetual grievance against the Sunni party, every year perform the most extravagant rites, and in their frantic processions lash and torment themselves to frenzy, in the manner approved by devotees of most eastern creeds.

Observance.

In this country the only observance recalling these rites of which I have been able to hear, is the abstention by some few families from washing their clothes during Moḥarram, but many then, as at other feasts, visit the graves of their relatives, carrying with them branches of myrtle to place there. Weddings never take place during this month, nor are public singers employed, and houses are not white-washed. Otherwise the fast becomes almost a feast, partly in consequence of the light-hearted temperament of the people, as compared with the Persians, for instance, and partly because of the attendant pleasure of alms-giving and receiving which form the special feature of the Yôm el 'Aáshûr. In some parts of Morocco the pious distribute drinking-water, for which special earthenware jars are sold at the time; sweets, dried fruits, etc. being also bestowed on the poor.

Curious Customs.

In the mountains above Marrákesh it is the custom to throw water on the passers-by, something after the manner of the water feast in Burma, and elsewhere on the eve of the 'Aáshûr fires are made on the terraces, while in Marrákesh itself I have seen the youngsters parading the streets with an attempt at music, one of their number dressed in a sheep-skin with the head left on. Of these customs

* I have explained elsewhere[1] that the words Sunni and Shî'ï have no party significance in Morocco, where neither sect is known, the Moors holding partly with both.

[1] *The Moorish Empire*, p. 38.

it is extremely difficult to obtain explanations, or even details beyond what one may one's-self observe, for the ignorance of the people is very great, and it is chiefly among the most ignorant that they survive, perhaps from pre-Mohammedan times. In the Shï'ah countries cane and paper representations of the tombs of El Ḥosaïn are paraded and buried, but the nearest approach to this in Morocco of which I know is the carrying round of paper lanterns, called bisáṭ, in an alms-collecting procession. Ordinary musical instruments are discarded during Moḥarram, but great numbers of gaily painted earthenware pipe-shaped drums (agwál) and rude tin or iron castanets of gigantic size (ḳarḳábát) are sold in the streets, and purchased by most of the children, who use them freely. At night little groups with these instruments may be seen round lights in the streets, which are quite enlivened thereby.

The Tithing.

One of the traditions of Mohammed is that "Whoso giveth plenty to his household on the day of 'Aáshûr, God will bestow plenty upon him throughout the remainder of the year." On that morning everyone looks his best, wearing some new garment, and all who can do so give something as alms, if not the full tithe which they should give. So many dues which they consider should come under this calculation are collected by the government, that what remains to be given on this occasion is in most cases small. Yet the importance of the act is appreciated by none better than Mohammedans, among whom the Moors are in their own way fairly generous.

EL MAÔLÛD EN-NABI: "THE PROPHET'S BIRTHDAY."

Two months after 'Aáshûr, on the twelfth of Rabî'a el áûlà, comes the Maôlûd, on account of which that month is also known as Rabî'a el A'nwár, "Spring of Flowers." It is considered one of the most lucky of months, and is the only one beside Ramaḍán whose commencement is saluted with cannon: in the country at the first glimpse of dawn its advent is signalled by the discharge of fire-arms from every house. At the houses of shareefs there is often music and singing on that night, such houses being visited by women who perform at weddings and other festivities: the eve of the Maòlûd, called Laïlat et-tabeet—"Watch-night,"—is entirely devoted by some to such rejoicings. On the day itself, between the maghrib and the 'ashá, a fokih in the mosque reads a portion of the *Maôlûdìyah*, a lengthy poem by the Sheïkh Bûsîri, or a group of pupils round him read a verse on which he comments.

Watch-night.

The women have a custom at this time of painting a vertical stripe of blue between their children's eyebrows, in order to ward off the evil eye. In some parts they cook a special dish called herrberr, known in England as frumenty,* such as is common also at the Old Style New Year. To a basis of wheat, steeped and husked, then boiled with raisins and spices, beans, chick-peas, figs, pumpkin, meat, fish, etc., are added, according to season.

Otherwise there is nothing peculiar in the observance of this feast, except that it is the favourite time for circumcisions, and boys born during Rabî'a I. are considered especially fortunate, being in the country often called Mûlûdi on that account. Previous to the performance of the rite, the parents of the lad, if not in indigent circumstances, generally cause him to be paraded through several streets of the town, dressed in the richest and most gaudy articles of clothing obtainable, with a stiff handkerchief bound like a hat round

Circumcisions.

* Sometimes locally corrupted to "furmity" or "frummity," but from the Latin *frumentum*, corn. See p. 104.

his head; mounted on a handsomely caparisoned horse, often borrowed for the occasion.

Processions.

The horse is led, and on each side of it walk men bearing silk handkerchiefs, with which they continually flap away the flies from the child's face. The procession is headed by native musicians keeping up an incessant din of ear-splitting music. Behind walk the family and friends of the boy. Two boys are sometimes paraded together, and sometimes two are placed on one horse. The procession is frequently accompanied by flags, the object of all this display being to attract the eye and divert it from the child, so great is the fear of the "evil eye." The operation is performed with scissors, either at home or at some shrine of repute.

Offerings.

On the seventh or great day of the Maôlûd it is customary for presents or offerings, called hedîah, to be made to shareefs and other saints, and these are sometimes very valuable. On this day cattle and sheep may be seen paraded through the streets, accompanied by music and flags, with men carrying trays containing wax candles and sometimes money. The beasts are killed, skinned and cut up by the donors at the doors of the saints, and the pieces are divided among their families.

The 'Aïsàwà Stampede.

Another special feature of the Maôlûd en-Nabi is the 'Aïsáwà procession, or rather stampede. Wherever they are to be found, from Morocco to Egypt, the members of the ṭáïfah or congregation of Sidi M'hammed bin 'Aïsà of Mequinez are supposed to make a pilgrimage to his shrine near that city every Maôlûd. A short time before it, according to distance, parties are formed for the journey, passing through the towns in noisy processions, collecting alms which are often not inconsiderable, frequently including articles which they practically demand from the shop-keepers, giving perhaps in return a sip of milk from a well-mouthed jar. At their záwîah in Mequinez they perform a grand dhikr or frenzy dance, and on the second day after the feast set off home. As they pass through each town on the way, the dhikr is repeated, and it is a wonder how they manage to survive. The frenzy is achieved by the constant repetition in concert of a special religious sentence (dhikr), which serves as the secret pass-word of the order. As they are not anxious to enunciate this too clearly, the result to a listener is rather that of a pack of wolves, than the sound of the human voice. Those who are most susceptible (known as saḥäïm) often need to have their hands bound to restrain them: these devour any prey (farîsah)—sheep, dog or serpent—that they encounter, tearing it apart while still alive; and some of them are credited with strength sufficient to slay an ox with two fingers, while others are supposed to be able to fly! *

"In a Fine Frenzy."

For onlookers this stampede forms the chief feature of the feast, and large crowds assemble to watch them pass. Even women, young and old, occasionally join their ranks, and these become worse than the men, notwithstanding the efforts of their friends to calm them by placing their hands on their heads. Yet, after it is all over, it is strange to see those pale, emaciated blood-stained, fiendish-looking figures settle down again to ordinary life, as though nothing out of the way had happened. I have had servants who obtained a holiday for the occasion, quietly returning to work after a day of rest. There seems to be a class of men and women to whom this sort of excitement is second nature, for they have their counterpart with minor variations in the whirling and howling dervishes

A Horrible Sight.

* For a further account of this order see chapter xix.

of Cairo and Constantinople, and the many species of Hindoo and other fakîrs whom I have seen do much the same in other lands.

History.

The special prominence given to this feast in Morocco dates from 1291, when a decree to that effect was promulgated by Yûsef III. "May God have mercy upon him for this innovation, which is due to him," says the contemporary writer who records it.[1] The ameer Ahmad Dhahebi (cir. 1590) used to make much of this feast, instituting processions with innumerable candles and a public royal service, when the history of Mohammed's birth was recited with other poems under the guidance of foḳihs, great gifts being afterwards distributed, and the populace being admitted to the palace, where they could "imagine themselves in paradise."[2]

Laïlat el Mi'aráj.

No great day occurs again till the twenty-seventh of Rabî'a I., known as the Laïlat el Mi'aráj, or "Night of the Ascent," the anniversary of Mohammed's alleged visit to the seventh heaven. Some fast that day and the day before, and there is private feasting at night, but nothing in the way of public ceremonies.

En-Niskhah.

The same may be said of the Yôm en Niskhah or "Day of the Copy," the fifteenth of Sha'abán, the eve of which is supposed to see our destinies determined for the coming year. The Sajrat el Muntahà, "Tree of Extremity," in Paradise, which has a leaf for every human being, with names inscribed, is on that night shaken, and those whose leaves fall die within the year. At this time is the great congregation at the shrine of Mulai 'Abd es-Salám bin Masheesh, to the south of Tetuan.

[1] The author of *Raôḍ el Kartâs*, p. 541. [2] El Ufráni, pp. 237, 240.

RAMAḌÁN.

During no month of the Mohammedan year does the foreigner in this country so fully realize that he is surrounded by the followers of the prophet of Mekka as during Ramaḍán. With those who can afford it night is turned into day and day into night. From before sunrise—when one can distinguish a black thread from a white—till the hour at night when that is again impossible, not a morsel of food, not a drop of liquid, not a whiff of smoke, not a draught of sweet odour or pinch of snuff, passes either the lips or nostrils of the pious Muslim. All who must—the majority of the people being so situated—toil on at their daily duties, faint from hunger and parched with thirst, till the evening gun bursts on their grateful ears, but finds them in such a state that they seldom care to eat at once, sometimes not even to partake of the basin of thin soup which has been ready prepared for a breakfast dish! When it falls in summer, the most trying season, the fast lasts seventeen or eighteen hours.

How Kept.

Poor folk! Towards the afternoon their tempers are sorely tried, and Ramaḍán quarrels are many and sharp, but though fierce battles are fought with words, blows are seldom resorted to, each party contenting himself with madly abusing the parents and ancestors—especially those of the weaker sex—of his antagonist, till they arrive at that pitch of excitement which, if they were English, would mean black eyes, or if Spanish, cut throats. Some well-disposed passer-by will thrust the verbose disputants aside, leaving each to retreat covered by a continuous fire of abuse.

Effects of Fast.

Actual fighting among the Mohammedans during Ramaḍán is strictly prohibited by the Ḳor'án, but it is probable that the "eating-up" of a province too weak to afford much opposition, or from which all the able bodied males have fled, is not considered in this light. A touching incident in connection with this command occurred at Mogador in 1873. Between the death of one sultan and the accession of another the country knows no law: all authority being dependent on the sultan himself, none exists at those times, and the populace accordingly indulges in the wildest forms of excess. Such was the state of things during Ramaḍán of the year named: four kaids of the provinces of Ḥáḥá and Shiadhma had fled before the mob, and having taken refuge in Mogador, that town was besieged by their late subjects. As they did not possess cannon, Mogador could not be entered, and all the besiegers could do was to cut the aqueduct which supplied the place with water, and to set fire to the gardens whence it was supplied with vegetables. But the besiegers had left nothing for themselves, and during the five days of the siege they would have starved but for the kindness of the besieged, who actually opened the gates at night, and allowed some of the enemy to come in and buy food for the rest! It is no wonder that under such circumstances peace was soon concluded.

A "Peace Month" Incident.

In the East, Ramaḍán is made the occasion for generous gifts from the rich to the poor, to enable the latter to purchase the more nourishing food required for such a fast, and every possible arrangement is made to minimize its severity, little work being done, and cool, shady places frequented. In Morocco it is far otherwise, and it is heart-rending to observe the miserable faces of men who have done a hard day's work in a broiling sun on an empty stomach, with nothing extraordinary to eat the previous night.

Generosity.

Mohammedans are commanded to fast each day of

MOGADOR FROM LANDING-PLACE.

Ramaḍán, between the rising and the setting of the sun. The precise moments of the beginning and ending of the fast are marked by the firing of cannon at a signal given by watchers on the minarets or other exalted positions. If anyone is in the act of eating when the gun fires, he may finish the piece which he had in his hand, or in his plate or basin, but may not put forth his hand to take another portion. The sick, expectant mothers, children, prisoners, and those travelling or on the field of battle, are exempted at their option from the stringent rules of the fast, but to claim exemption is considered effeminate and discreditable, and as a debt to be discharged at some future period, so that both old and young, rich and poor, strong and weak, alike strive to maintain its rules to the utmost limit of their endurance. As the age of puberty is considered an appropriate time to commence to fast, the common expression that anyone has not yet fasted implies that he has not yet arrived at that stage. Many keep this fast who neglect their daily prayers, and it is believed that few in Morocco break it in secret. It not infrequently proves fatal to people in delicate health, and it is especially hard upon the poor who labour for the sustenance of themselves and their families, and cannot sleep away the weary hours as rich Muslims do. Christians who employ Moorish servants do well to remember this, for however much religious observances may differ, this is their way of serving GOD.

Strictness of Fast.

On the eve of Ramaḍán (Laïlat er-Ramaḍán) the evidence of twelve Muslims is required to prove that the new moon has been seen, before the fast can be proclaimed, which is also the case at its termination. Either is announced in towns by the firing of cannon, which are echoed by guns in the villages,

Proclamation.

through which the firing rapidly carries the news to a distance. In towns, too, the firing is followed by the blowing of long, straight trumpets (nafeer). Any day during the month, at the moment when the sunset gun fires, people may be seen running about the streets carrying basins of gruel and soup from house to house, handing them one to another as they pass along. Hearty cheers and the ringing voices of children rise from every Muslim house and street the moment the welcome "boom" is heard. The Moorish coffee-houses are soon filled with hungry men and boys, eager for some light refreshment and a cigarette. A little later they partake of the fuṭûr, or breakfast, which is usually as plentiful as their means will allow.

Breaking the Fast.

Then comes the time of prayer, when the mosques are lighted up; but public worship is not well attended. Immediately after the usual 'ashá prayers there is an additional service called tashfîá, at which the Ḳor'án is read, and the two regular rika'hs or series of prayers are repeated. Sometimes two divisions (hizab) of the Ḳor'án are read each night, in order to go through the whole in the month: sometimes it is finished on the twenty-seventh. At the conclusion of this service, which may last an hour—about 11.45 p.m.—the trumpets and oboes (ghaïṭah) are sounded by special men from the mosque towers, and the doors are shut till the ṣuḥûr or second meal-time.

Special Services.

Coffee-houses remain open nearly all night, and many of the lower orders resort thither to hear music and story-telling, and to smoke keef, the intoxicating leaf of Indian hemp. The streets are comparatively deserted until the ṣuḥûr, which is announced about twenty minutes past twelve by trumpets and oboes, and by violent beating of the drummers

Ramaḍán Nights.

(ṣaḥḥárs), each pair of whom parade a certain quarter of the town. The ṣaḥḥár carries a stick wherewith to strike doors unprovided with knockers, as he cries aloud, "O servants of God, rise for the service of God! Eat and drink, and may God preserve you!" The tabil or drum is carried at the left side, and is beaten by two sticks, a heavy-headed one called 'ûd, and a lighter one called ḳaṭeeb.* Some time later the trumpets and oboes sound again to hasten the meal, and a fourth time at the close of the night, warning the faithful to eat their final mouthfuls and prepare for the fast, but few rise at that hour.

Laïlat el Kadr.

One of the last ten days of Ramaḍán is called Laïlat el Ḳadr ("the Night of Power"). It is the night on which the Ḳor'án is said to have been sent down to Mohammed, but the exact date is not known, though a tradition fixes it to be one of the odd dates after the twenty-sixth, and is in favour of the twenty-seventh. This night is called "better than a thousand months," and angels are believed to descend with blessings for the faithful, while, as the gates of heaven are then opened, prayer is held to be certain of success.

Special Observances.

The houses and mosques are illuminated, and the cafés are full, but many prefer to pray all night The záwîahs receive abundant offerings of candles from men and women, and in some of them tea and refreshments are kept going. Meanwhile the ṣaḥḥárs parade the town in quest of gifts in money or kind, wherewith to supplement their regular wage for the month, received from the mosque. At the following fejer, or dawn, a special cannon is fired. But the most noticeable feature of the Laïlat el Ḳadr is that then—that is, after sunset on the twenty-sixth

* For illustrations see p. 203.

day—and then only, all the year round, do the Moorish women attend the mosques, and it is an interesting sight on that occasion to see their shrouded forms as they pay their annual visit in charge of servants with lanterns, and, as one may well understand, with no little stir, although, for a crowd of women, marvellously silent.

During Ramaḍán the Jinn, or Genii, are said to be confined in prison, hence on the last night of the fast, some women sprinkle the floor of their houses with salt, to prevent their return, saying as they do so, "In the name of GOD, the Pitying, the Pitiful."

THE "LESSER" AND "GREATER" FEASTS.

The 'Aïd es-Sag͟heer.

Immediately following Ramaḍán comes the 'Aïd es-Sag͟heer or "Lesser Feast"—a title hardly appropriate in view of the manner in which it is kept in Morocco,—more fitly termed the 'Aïd el Fuṭûr or "Breakfast Feast," since it is in reality but the rejoicing after the fast. Never are more new slippers and cloaks procured, never is better provision of powder made, than for the grand display on the afternoon of the first of Shûwál, when all turn out in their best. From early morn the town is astir with holiday makers, who go about shaking hands and exchanging good wishes, visiting friends or those on whom they think they have any claim for a gratuity. This they do not hesitate to suggest in the case of present or past employers, or of persons of position who have in the past done them one service, and may therefore be expected to do them another. Feasting is in vogue wherever it can be afforded; presents of cakes and sweets are frequently sent, and many shops are shut for the day.

The religious duties of this festival include a special service with sermon in the m'ṣállah or praying-field, which is provided outside every large town for occasions when all meet together, and with the exception of the "powder-play," the gayest scenes are to be encountered as the crowds flock in its direction, or as they return from service. Wherever the sultan may be, he attends this service in state, receiving at its close the provincial kaids and other officials who have come with their tribute and taxes. After some three days of feasting, accounts, or rather estimates, are investigated—as after the two other great festivals, the 'Aïd El Kabeer and the 'Aashûr,—and a fair proportion of these dignitaries are lodged in gaol, or sent back with a warning which entails an extra "squeeze" of their districts, and a fresh remittance to Court.

The Breakfast Feast.

But now all is gay, if not thoughtless, and it is the picturesque and culinary which prevail. Some, having feasted the first day, fast the next two or seven, as in Ramaḍán, considering this a means of special merit. Many women go on these days to the cemeteries to place myrtle branches on the graves of relatives, often taking with them cakes and sweets for distribution among the poor, who also resort thither on such auspicious occasions. A sulḳah or repetition of the Ḳor'án will often take place at a grave, or at least a Fátiḥah; or the chapter Yá Seen will be recited.

Feasting and Fasting.

Two months later comes the "Greater" or "Sheep" Feast, the 'Aïd el Kabeer, on the tenth of Dhû'l Ḥajjah, the last month of the Mohammedan year, for the first nine days of which many fast. It is distinguished by the slaying of sacrifices in remembrance of the ram slain by Abraham instead of his son,—Ishmael, according to Ishmael's descendants, and those who have adopted their religion.* Otherwise

The 'Aïd el Kabeer.

* "The following is the account given by Mohammedan writers: 'When Abraham (the peace of God be upon him) founded Mekka, the Lord

it does not differ greatly in its observance from the lesser feast; new clothes, congratulations, presents, visiting and feastings, with of course "powder-play," the Court receptions, and the visits to the cemeteries. But the distinctive event takes place after the morning service at the m'ṣállah. This is the great day for the pilgrims at Mekka, or rather out in the valley of Mîna, to slay their sacrifices, reference to the account of which by Burton should be made. *

The Early Sacrifice.

As soon as the m'ṣállah prayers are over, a sheep is slain outside the field by the ḳádi, who cuts its throat with the usual formula, "B'ísm Illah"—"In the Name of God,"—the fact being announced at once by the waving of a cloak for which a man on the mosque-tower is watching. He at once waves the signal to the battery, where a salute of twenty-one guns commences without a moment's delay. At this sound every householder who has remained at home for the purpose cuts the throat of the ram at his door. The one which the ḳádi has killed is instantly borne off on the shoulders of stalwart runners to his private residence, a rabble following to see if it arrives before it is quite dead, in which case its bearers are well rewarded, for it is considered a good omen for the coming year.

desired him to prepare a feast for Him. Upon Abraham (the friend of GOD) requesting to know what He would have on the occasion, the Lord replied, "Offer up thy son Ishmael." Agreeably to GOD's command he took Ishmael to the *Ka'bah* to sacrifice him, and, having laid him down, he made several ineffectual strokes on his throat with a knife, on which Ishmael observed, "Your eyes being uncovered, it is through pity and compassion for me you allow the knife to miss; it would be better if you blindfolded yourself with the end of your turban and then sacrificed me." Abraham acted upon his son's suggestion, and having repeated the words, "In the name of GOD, GOD is great," he drew the knife across his son's neck. In the meanwhile, however, Gabriel had substituted a broad-tailed sheep for the youth Ishmael, and Abraham, uncovering his eyes, observed, to his surprise, the sheep slain and his son standing behind him'."—HUGHES.

* *A Pilgrimage to Mekka.*

At the Court celebration the sultan also slays his ram, which is borne off in similar haste to the palace, while His Majesty kisses the standards of Mulai Idrees and other great saints, repeating the Fátiḥah before each. Then ensues a great deal of hand-shaking, called "pardoning," for by that act all grievances of the past are forgiven, and everyone goes home for the feast itself.

The Feast.

At noon the liver and heart of the sheep are consumed, principally in the form of ḳoḍbán, little pieces threaded on skewers, a bit of fat between each, rolled in salt and spices and grilled, a most appetizing confection.* In the evening some families eat of the meat, but others have a superstition that this should be deferred till the next day, the noon meal of which is the head served with kesk'soo. Superfluous meat is salted and cured in the sun in strips called ḳadîdah, which, if afterwards boiled down in fat and oil, are called khalia' and are much in demand as provision for journeys. The poor, too, come in for a share of the feast, and rich men sometimes kill several sheep for their benefit, the accepted principle being that at least one-third should go to relatives, and one-third to the poor. The objectionable feature of the "Sheep Feast" is that the slaughter takes place in the narrow streets, in which blood and entrails are left to corrupt while the scavengers keep the feast. On the second day takes place the game of bû j'lood,† when the chief player is dressed in a sheep-skin.

THE SOLAR YEAR.

In no way connected with their present religion, and certainly ante-dating it in its observance, there is another method of dividing the year in vogue in Morocco,

* See p. 102. † p. 122; cf. p. 241.

according to the solar reckoning and to the European Old Style months, twelve days behind our own. The names employed for these—Yenáïr, Febráïar, Márṣ, Ábrîl, Máîah, Yûnîoh, Yûlîoh, Ghûsht, Shutanbir, Áktòbar, Nowanbir, Dujanbir,—sufficiently proclaim their origin. Besides these, the year is divided into seasons—fuṣûl (*s.* faṣl) Rabî'a or "Grass," commencing Feb. 27th; Ṣaîf or "Gleaning," commencing May 29th; Khareef or "Fruit," commencing Aug. 29th: and Shitwah or "Rainy," commencing Nov. 27th, according to New Style. From July 23rd to Sept. 1st is the S'máïm or time of great heat, and from Dec. 23rd to Feb. 1st is the Liálî ("Nights") or time of great rains.

Solar Calendar.

Two annual feasts appear to be the survival of some more ancient creed, El Hagûz or Láïlat Yenáïr, Old Style New Year's Day; and El A'nṣarah, St. John's or Midsummer Day. On the former occasion in some parts no fires are lighted, notwithstanding the season, and only cold food is eaten. In others special dishes of 'aṣîdah (porridge) or herrberr (frumenty) are prepared and eaten in the mosque, with great rejoicings, the poor being often invited by criers to "Eat GOD's food." On the A'nṣarah general holiday is kept, and a special dish of kesk'soo, beans, chick-peas etc. is prepared. Bunches of figs from the male trees are on that day hung in straw on the female trees, and in some parts excursions are made to the hills, where are lighted bonfires over which the young men jump, amid feasting and games.

Pre-Muslim Festivals.

Although there is a general sameness about the feasts of the Moors, the people themselves enjoy them so much, and there is always something so picturesque about them, that they never seem to pall. Speaking for myself, provided that I am in pleasant company, especially with those to whom the

Interest of Feasts.

scenes are new, I can enjoy the "powder-play" which forms the leading feature of all, or the processions and the feasts, with as much zest as when I first saw them years ago. For most feasts new clothes are worn as far as possible, and everything looks gay with colour in these sunny climes. Notwithstanding all their woes and disadvantages, the people of Morocco take life very easily, and their enjoyments are those of simple folk. The booming of guns, the waving of flags, the beating of tambours, the blowing of oboes, the hurrying briskly to and fro, all of which mark these occasions, help to build up effect, and it must be an apathetic heart which does not sympathize.

A TYPICAL MOSQUE.

CHAPTER THE FIFTEENTH

MOORISH PLACES OF WORSHIP

AMONG Mohammedan nations the Moors are of those who hold their places of worship in most veneration, the mere approach of a Jew or Christian being resented by them: of other religious beliefs they have no conception.* Even the streets surrounding some sacred shrines are protected by chains which no one may pass who has not "resigned" himself to the will of Mohammed, and there are certain towns in Morocco considered so holy on account of the tombs which they contain, that the unbeliever may not even enter their gates. I well remember the curious feelings with which for the first time I gazed at the walls of one of these places, the town of Zarhòn near Mequinez, and knew that I dare not approach. Such places exist all over the world of Islám—Mekka, for instance, the very country round which is prohibited to all but Muslimîn; but few have resisted the march of the times like those in Morocco. Bigoted Persia, Haïdarabád and Tunis are the only countries besides Morocco in which I have

Sacredness.

* The untravelled Moor finds it very hard indeed to believe in the existence of heathen, especially of atheists, all classed under the comprehensive term johálah—"ignorants" or "agnostics." To him the existence of the One God, "Lord of the Worlds, and King of the Day of Judgement," is the predominating fact, with regard to which he can conceive of no question.

been refused admission as a Christian to the mosques and shrines. Throughout the Turkish dominions travellers may enter freely in foreign dress, if wearing "Fez" caps and removing their shoes, or without doing either by using a silver key and the pair of overall slippers usually found at hand along tourist tracks. And it is worthy of note that many places to-day most closely guarded were entered by Europeans in times past without objection, as, for example, the shrine of Mashhad in Persia, or to turn to Morocco, the tombs of the kings[1] and the sanctuary round the tomb of Sidi 'Abd el Azîz at Marrákesh, the latter of which was only decreed ḥaram or "forbidden" in 1893. In Tunisia, on the other hand, the only mosque accessible to Europeans is the great one at Ḳaïrwán, the most sacred of all till the French occupation, but by the invaders defiled and thrown open.

Comparison with the East.

Until about a century ago the suburb of Saffi known as the Rabat or "Camp," was also closed, to the great inconvenience of the European residents, and it was opened only by the action of the able consul for France, M. Chenier, who insisted on riding through.[2] The town of Wazzán, once sacred as Zarhôn, was thrown open by the late shareef, he who had married an English wife, and who made her countrymen welcome: Dr. Spence Watson was even permitted to enter a mosque there. Within a generation it was not permitted to the Jews, even of Tangier, to pass the mosques with their shoes on,[3] but the rule was broken through there by the insistance of Sir John Drummond Hay that his interpreter should share his privileges. Yet the tranquil way in which the brushing aside of all these barriers is accepted, one by one, shows that after all there is no great question of conscience involved.

Restrictions Abolished.

[1] CHARANT, p. 150. [2] JACKSON. [3] MURRAY, vol. i., p. 18.

The trouble arises rather from interference with the vested interests of those who make a living from the offerings, who fear that diminished sanctity will mean diminished incomes. Perhaps they are right, but little by little these changes are taking place, and ere long we may see the mosques of Morocco as open as those across the border in Algeria, but that can hardly be expected while Moorish rule continues. Meanwhile my own investigations have been made in the guise of a Moor of Fez.

Typical Mosques.

Foremost among Moorish places of worship are the mosques or jam'as * in which public prayers are held, and sometimes preaching. These buildings vary in size and construction, of course, as much as the dwellings of the people; more so than the churches of England. Still, there is a typical form, an open court in which there is a fountain, surrounded by a covered portion, its roof supported by rows of pillars. The court is generally well to one side or corner of the plan, with access direct from the street. The mosques differ altogether from those of Turkey—akin to which are those of Tartary, Russia, China, Malaysia and Java—which are practically altogether under cover; and from those of Persian design, as in India, Persia, and Central Asia, where the court is usually larger than the covered space, there often confined to a few arches across one side. The reason for these various styles lies in the variation in climate, extremes of cold and heat requiring greater protection for the worshippers, as in the Turkish

Comparison of Style.

* Jam'a (pl. jûám'a) means ["place of] congregation," and is the only word used in Morocco. The English name "mosque" is a corruption of an eastern name "masjid," *i.e.* "place of worship" or "kneeling," rendered in Spanish "mezquita," corrupted into the French "mosquée," from which we have borrowed our word.

group; greater heat accounting for that of Persia. Variable climate, and cold, wet seasons, bring about the Moorish type, which extends more or less from Egypt to Spain, with numerous exceptions, especially in Egypt, where all but the early erections follow the Turkish idea. Those of Arabia form a mean between the two styles with court-yards, the great mosque at Mekkah consisting almost entirely of a court-yard occupying the centre of the building, while those of Baghdád and the North have the covered part in the midst of a surrounding court-yard. In Turkistán I found the roof confined to one corner: in Bokhára it is almost always so.

A Typical Mosque.

The typical Moorish mosque, such as one also finds and can freely visit in western Algeria, presents on entering long vistas of horse-shoe-arched aisles, low-roofed in proportion to their area, the pillars square and white-washed, like the walls, but covered to some three or four feet high with an effective dado of rush mats, similar to those upon the floor, though usually more elaborate in colour. Here and there along the vaulted roof hang candelabra and lamps or tumblers in which wicks are floating on oil upon water. Otherwise the place is absolutely bare, and it is necessary to approach the miḥrab,—the niche towards Mekka,—to discover any interior decoration. This is generally confined to this niche and the arch above it, with perhaps some scroll-work running across one end. To the right of the niche, close before which the imám or leader prays, is the monbar or pulpit—a wooden erection painted green, by no means elegant, ascended by a flight of steps,—from which the imám or a special khaṭíb (preacher) delivers the Friday discourse. This completes the furniture of a mosque, for the worshippers array themselves in rows upon the ground with their faces towards the niche. Votive candles are frequently burned here on either side, varying from a few ounces in weight to gigantic pillars.

When decoration is employed on a Moorish mosque it is most commonly found on the tower and gate-ways, or in the court-yards, often faced with tasteful glazed tile-work and adorned with marble pillars and a central fountain for ablution. Before a Muslim can say his prayers he must at least perform the lesser purification with water or sand, washing his hands, feet and face at the fountain, while for the more thorough purification needed after certain actions, there are lavatories attached to the mosque. To enter a mosque in Java I once had to wade through a shallow canal which ran round it like a moat, but there, as in Morocco, cold water is ever refreshing, both winter and summer. As the steam-baths are employed for the greater ablutions, they may almost be considered as pertaining to the mosques, and it is for this reason that they are as jealously guarded from outsiders as the places of worship themselves.*

Decoration.

Lavatories.

Baths.

The towers of the mosques,—called by Europeans the minarets, †—which serve the same purpose as those of our churches, are in Morocco square, a smaller tower rising from the centre, sometimes surrounded by three or four super-imposed metal balls, and always furnished with a short projecting flag-staff. From this is suspended a horizontal rod, below which at prayer-time floats a flag-like banner, black or dark-blue on Friday at noon, at other times white. The

Mosque Towers.

* Christians were forbidden to use the baths of the Muslimîn by the khalîfa El Mutawakkil, cir. 860. But in the Turkish dominions generally this is disregarded, and all are there welcome who pay.

† For manárah or manárat, the feminine form of manár, a tower, originally indicating one on top of which nár—fire—was kindled as a beacon.

ascent to the shoulder round the upper portion of the tower is by an inclined plane carried on vaulting, surrounding some six or eight storeys of single chambers.

TOWER OF THE CHIEF MOSQUE, TANGIER.
Molinari, Photo., Tangier.

The campanile of St. Mark's at Venice is of this construction, as also is the tower of the old mosque at Seville, the finest specimen standing in Europe, now a belfry; sister to those at Rabat and Marrákesh. The split tower of Tlemçen erected just a century later, is of the same design.* The walls of these minarets are either plain

* For illustration see *The Moorish Empire*, pp. 64, 77, 83, 101.

white-washed, or faced with tiles set in brick-work panels, but in a few instances the whole is stone-wrought in geometric devices. Storks' nests add a picturesque effect to many of these towers.

Calls to Prayer.

But the feature of the mosque tower which lends it its charm, is the principal use to which it is put, the chanting of the calls to prayer. Mohammed chose well when he preferred the human voice for this purpose to either the trumpets of the Jews, the bells of the Christians or the drums of the heathen. Nothing is more fascinating to the new-comer to Morocco, or indeed to any Muslim country where the chants are executed as they should be, than the weird and long-drawn sound of human voices from a dozen directions at dead of night. To quote the words of Dr. Spence Watson,* "It was this cry in the night which I found so peculiarly impressive. About half-past two in the morning rang forth the deep, solemn sound from many splendid voices, startling the surrounding stillness. As the first burst of harmony died away, you heard it replied to from the distant minarets of the city, and then it was again taken up by the choir above you, sometimes sinking into a low whisper, sometimes swelling to a loud, full, triumphant chorus, ringing clear and strong. Night after night I listened to it with wonder and delight. It was no short call like that which I had previously heard at other places, but a true musical service of a rarely beautiful kind." I think that the finest that I ever heard was from the Ḳarueeïn mosque at Fez, where a special fund provides for singers for several hours in succession, in addition to the regular callers to prayer, those chanting at night being called "the companions of the sick." In other cases the only additional chant is given twice, an hour and half an hour respectively

* *A Visit to Wazzán.*

before the fejer or dawn, this cry being called the ábad or everlasting, as it is an ascription of praise to GOD, commencing, "The perfection of GOD, existing for ever and ever" repeated thrice, and proclaiming His independence, exaltation, bounty, mercy and other attributes. From an early period it has been the custom to choose men of different voices to sing together.[1] In Morocco blind men are not, as in some eastern countries, chosen for the office of muédhdhin or summoner, in order that they may not look down from above on their neighbours' wives, since the towers are generally too high for this to be needful.

Wording of the calls.

Directly the faintest streak of light is perceived in the East, the cry bursts forth, "The night has departed with the darkness, and the day approaches with light and brightness! Praise GOD for securing His favour and kindness! GOD is most great! [twice.] I testify that there is no god but GOD [twice.] I testify that Mohammed is the Apostle of GOD [twice.] Come to prayer! [twice.] Come to security! [twice.] Prayer is better than sleep! [twice.] GOD is most great [twice.] There is no god but GOD [twice.] Arise ("make morning") and to GOD be the praise!* Arise, and to GOD be the praise! Arise, and to GOD be the praise!" This is four times repeated, once to each quarter of the compass. Truly it is an uplifting and an inspiring admonition which all would do well to obey!

At the other four times of prayer only a portion of the above is chanted, beginning with the first "GOD is most great," and ending with the second "There is

* This phrase, peculiar to Morocco, was added by 'Abd el Mû'min, the Muwáḥḥadi, about the year 1150, but was forbidden in vain by Idrees el Ma'mûn, about 1227.

[1] ABD EL WÁHID, p. 250.

no god but GOD," omitting the phrase about sleep. The notes to which the ordinary cry is most commonly set in Morocco are extremely simple and impressive:

Music of Calls.

or:

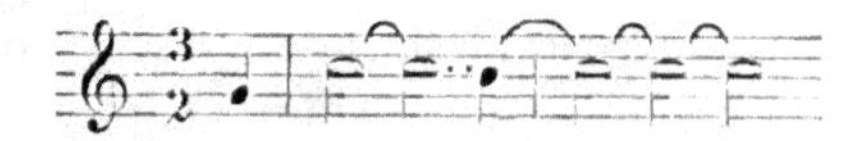

and so on, repeating the air, the second and fourth notes being drawn out to the extent of the mućdhdhin's lung power, swelling and fading away with superb effect.

The more important mosque towers contain European clocks and sun-dials whereby to announce the hours of prayer, but in the majority of cases the stars or the length of a man's own shadow, or the gleaming horizon and cock-crows are the only indications, while in the country it is always so. Europeans have, it is said, been admitted to repair these clocks, on the same grounds as serve to admit asses during other repairs.

Fixing the Prayer-Hours.

In no way second to the mosques in sanctity are multitudinous saint-shrines (záwiahs) scattered all over the country, whether near dwellings or not, the tombs of men who have earned the title of ṣáliḥ, or "holy" in ways which would not earn such distinction with us, and whose intercession with GOD is now supposed to avail where the prayers of ordinary mortals fall short. Many of them have a great reputation, nursed by interested devotees who go about the country preaching their fame and collecting alms, and by pilgrims who flock in large numbers to favourite

Saint-Shrines.

shrines, sometimes preceded by banners and music, especially on the occasions of annual or other festivals. Some were founders of religious brotherhoods, whose interest it is to keep up the establishment, and these have naturally the most important tombs.* In other cases it is the heirs who keep the shrine going, and they often make a good living out of their inheritance.

Development of Shrines.

Unless the departed saint was of considerable note, or able to bequeath sufficient funds for the purpose of a more important start, his grave is often marked by nothing more than a ring of white-washed stones, with a piece of white rag on a cane as a distinguishing flag. In time this may be replaced by a walled enclosure, in its turn to be succeeded by a square, domed construction with one horse-shoe door, known as a ḳûbbah. This is the typical form, the plain octagonal dome being of less area than the walls, to allow a graceful set-off and a crenellated coping: there is seldom any other ornament, but it is brilliantly white-washed when new or in vogue.

Country Shrines.

In the country one occasionally comes across whole groups of these tombs, either those of different saints, or successive editions of the same shrine, each built without destroying the others, probably with the same idea as that which prompts the Buddhists of Siam and Burma to erect such numbers of useless pagodas,—that each builder may claim the merit of his own construction. There are few scenes in Morocco more picturesque than these glistening ḳûbbahs amid the olives or beside some stream in the

* Such tombs become important political as well as religious centres. In 1636 Mohammed es-Sheïkh wrote to the members of a powerful brotherhood, "the sources which furnish calumny, sedition, treason, hypocrisy and effrontery are the záwîahs, rîbats, fandaḳs, workshops, bazaars and prisons."[1]

[1] El Ufrání.

valley, or by some mountain spring. In cities they are sometimes richly decorated with glazed tiles and stucco-work, and the shrine itself, within, is like a huge chest covered with coloured cloth and embroidery, as are also the walls to a certain height, above which hang clocks and texts and hideous pictures of Mekka; while from the roof are suspended lamps and candelabra, ostrich eggs, glass balls and other tawdry ornaments.

Interiors.

A COUNTRY SHRINE.

Photograph by Herbert White, Esq.

Sometimes there is a mosque attached, with or without a minaret, but in any case unless the spot is neglected—that is to say, as long as anyone can make a living out of the alms of the faithful—the regular daily prayers are sure to be said there, and calls to prayer are uttered from the door or roof. Like the mosques, these shrines are forbidden to non-Muslims, and the sanctity of many makes them sanctuaries which sultans themselves seldom dare to

Uses of Shrines.

violate, even in pursuit of a rival: in extreme cases all they can have recourse to is a close investment, starving the inmates.* When the shrine is somewhat removed from the highway it is usual to fix a spot by the track in sight of the guardian, where contributions may be laid, and whenever the pious traveller comes in sight of a distant shrine he places a stone on the way-side cairn which is always to be seen at such spots.

Absence of Priesthood.

Islám has no priesthood. Every man who believes in Mohammed can perform all duties connected with his religion for which he has the requisite knowledge, and it is his bounden duty to do so in default of some one better qualified. Every man is therefore imám or leader in his own house, or wherever else he is in authority, though officials usually delegate this duty to a dependant fokîh or scribe who acts as a sort of chaplain. In the mosques, too, these officiate, though they may be traders, or follow any other profession, as well. Any young fellow who has a fancy for reading, and is of a quiet disposition, can attach himself to some teacher of this sort, adding to his fame by sitting at his feet, and sharing the alms he thus helps to earn, till his own reputation will keep him afloat. It is difficult, if not impossible, for a Moor to conceive of education apart from religion, on which all his studies and law are based, and a man who is seen with a book in his hand is at once put down as a theologian.

The duties of an imám are to lead the prayers with a clearly pitched voice, and to keep order generally.

* Exceptions are, however, on record, as when, in 1602, Ahmad II. proceeded against the son who afterwards succeeded him, then in sanctuary with 15,000 men, dragging him forth; or as when, in 1618, a pretender was shot on the tomb of 'Ali bin Harazam at Fez.[1] Similarly cir. 1730 the keeper of the Zarhôn sanctuary gave up the sultan's nephew for a quintal of silver.[2]

[1] El Ufráni, p. 391. [2] Mairault, p. 107.

On Fridays the khoṭbah or "address" is delivered before the prayers in the more important mosques,* usually in those with towers, which, however, are very rare in the country. This reading is performed by one of the leading foḳîhs, called the khaṭîb, who in consequence receives an allowance from the mosque funds. Holding a staff in his hand as a sword, he ascends the monbar or pulpit, and makes a short declaration of faith and of allegiance to the sultan, whose letters are then read, if there are any, after which advice is given on religious or topical questions of public interest. Sometimes anyone present reads aloud from the *Dálîl el Khaïrát* or "Path of Good Deeds," before the khaṭîb arrives. The only others employed in the mosque are the ḥazzábà, or readers of portions of the Ḳor'án, night and morning. The muédhdhins generally keep the keys and do the cleaning. During the Friday prayers the gates of the towns are closed to prevent incursions of the tribes. According to the *Raôḍ el Ḳarṭás*, this custom originated at Bougie in Algeria in 1184, in consequence of a rebel, El Mazurki, entering the town and massacring the people while at prayers.[1] But on several occasions terrible bloodshed caused by foes within has taken place in Morocco during these prayers.

The Imám.

Seen, or even heard, from the door, the service on a Friday at noon—the only time when there is a full congregation—is extremely impressive, but the effect of being inside is almost overwhelming, as with rhythmic, measured motion, all together in the wake of the imám, whose back is turned towards them, they ascribe all praise to GOD, repeat in unison the

The Friday Service.

* In Tangier the sermon is preached in the Ḳaṣbah, Sidi bin Naṣar, New and Great Mosques in the order given, as in such cases they are taken one after the other by the same man.

[1] p. 385.

simple opening prayer of the Ḳor'án and other prescribed ejaculations; rising and stooping, bowing and kneeling, forehead on ground; the sonorous reverberation of their voices interspersed with sudden pauses giving an exaggerated feeling of solemnity. Personally, I have never known anything like it: all is so very simple, so apparently spontaneous, so devoid of the machinery of books and music, and the words employed are so uplifting, that if it were not for the accompanying testimony to the mission of Mohammed, one could join in heartily, and be the better for it. The grand simplicity and true devotion of the service never fail to strike the thoughtful mind. No gorgeous decorations, no grand music, and no pompous ceremonial divert attention from the GOD whose house it is, not even special clothing, for there is hardly a bit of colour to be seen among the every-day wool-white cloaks of the congregation—all men.

The Noon. Prayers.

As the crier on the mosque-tower gives the summons to the noon-day prayer, the imám within repeats it, and as he concludes, the whole congregation—in one or two instances numbering thousands—join, as they stand with uplifted hands, in the thrice uttered cry "GOD greatest!" Then follow the prayers referred to,—the Fátiḥah—repeated by the congregation with hands held out before the face as if to receive a blessing therein, and the cries, "O LORD, to Thee be the praise!" and "GOD is merciful!" according to the form for private prayer. Then at the close they all silently rise and crowd out, the atmosphere hushed till the street is reached, with its busy cares, for the Mohammedan knows no Sabbath of rest. One of the Murábṭî ameers was so particular in gathering the people to their prayers, that twenty stripes were meted out for every absence, and five for missing part of the service.[1]

[1] *Raôd el Kártas*, p. 184.

At other times Moorish mosques are seldom entirely closed, although the chief doors may be fastened, and they then form a refuge for the weary passer-by who is content to roll himself up on the matted floor in a corner and rest, as I have

Mosques as Guest-houses.

WALL OF THE KASBAH MOSQUE, MARRAKESH.
Photograph by A. Lennox, Esq.

on occasion been glad to do when in Moorish dress. In the country the village mosque, often indistinguishable in appearance from the thatched huts surrounding it, serves as the guest-hall, in which all who come may take up their abode, and, especially if of the pilgrim class, may feel certain of someone bringing in his supper to share. I remember when on one occasion thus enjoying hospitality—it being impossible on account of the mud to pitch my tent,—observing a bag of meal suspended from the roof, on which cobwebs were thick: on enquiry I found that it had been left there long ago by some way-farer, and as the place was considered too sacred for theft, it was likely to hang there still longer. Veneration for the place of prayer is apt, however, to be less strict in the towns, where the theft of the slippers which have to be removed at the door—as at that of every inhabited room,—or at least their exchange, is not unknown, and shrines have at times been robbed, while frequently the mosques have been the scenes of massacres and conflicts. Youths are also not averse to playing pranks in mosques, such as sewing the cloaks of sleepers to the mats, and I have heard of fifteen worshippers having their cloaks stitched together in a row on the Great Night in Ramaḍán.

Maintenance.

The funds from which the mosques and saint-shrines are maintained are derived from property called waḳf, "entailed," bequeathed for the purpose, and entrusted to an official known as the náḏhir. But so little care is taken to make the best of it, and so little supervision is exercised, that much of the waḳf property is let for a nominal rental to be sub-let many times over, or the actual occupier purchases the key at a high figure, paying only a trifle each month.

Mortuary Chapels.

Attached to most mosques of importance is a mortuary chapel or beït el ginaïz, in which a supply of biers for free public use are kept, being replenished by such families as care to incur the expense of new ones for their dead. Here bodies are brought for a short service of prayers and recitations before forming the procession to the grave-yard. Another subsidiary building attached to chief mosques or shrines of the large towns is the morstán or refuge for

Hospitals.

the sick and demented—which serves also as a sort of morgue,—one cannot call it a hospital.

In many cases madmen, in spite of their reputed sanctity, are chained up in its recesses, but these establishments are on the whole so filthy and loathsome as to become death-traps, and many sufferers are brought there only to die, deprived of all medical skill, and nourished scantily from the ill-administered funds bequeathed for the purpose or received as alms.

Courts.

Often the Court of the ḳádi or civil and religious judge is hard by the chief mosque, and also the shops of the notaries public and attorneys.

Mosques as Schools.

A few of the larger mosques serve also between the hours of prayer as college halls, the so-called colleges being seldom more than residential quarters for the students, as elsewhere throughout the strictly Mohammedan world. In that case the various professors have their accustomed aisles or corners in which those who study their subjects assemble, squatting round them on the floor. Schools for the lads are frequently found in adjoining houses, and in the country it is commonly the mosque or saint-shrine itself which does duty as school-house.

A MOSQUE CHANT FROM SUS.

(The blessings of God and peace be on our lord Mohammed, and his family and friends: increasing peace.)

A RELIGIOUS PROCESSION.
(Passing through the gates of Tangier.)

Photograph by Baron Whettnall

CHAPTER THE SIXTEENTH

THE PRAYERS OF THE MOORS

IN common with Mohammedans all the world over, the Moors have set forms and regulations for prayers, as for every other religious duty, and among their co-religionists they may be counted strict in their observance of them. It is rather in the moral obligations of their creed that they consider laxity pardonable, and it is with the idea of balancing their reckoning that they are so punctilious in performing ceremonial obligations: in Islám prayer is relegated to the latter category. Five times a day at least the pious Muslim turns his face to Mekka and the House of GOD there, as he bows in prayer with words and motions beautifully chosen and peculiarly effective. Tradition has it that Mohammed originally ordered fifty prayers a day, which are still performed by some of the religious brotherhoods, but that on the successive petitions of Moses he reduced the number, five by five, till only five remained. In the vast majority of instances, it must be feared, even these are rattled through by rote as matters of custom, without a thought of their real bearing or solemnity. No reference to personal affairs is ever introduced in the recital of the forms prescribed, but added as the worshipper stands upright at the close, with palms outstretched before his face—as though to receive in them the blessing he seeks. Wherever the call to prayer may be heard, it

Strictness.

Petitions.

is the Muslim's duty to obey it in the nearest cleanly spot, provided he be ceremonially pure, or has the means of purification at hand. Thus in the shops and marts, in the streets and gardens, on the roofs and on ship-board, Mohammedans may be observed at prayer, and an impressive sight it is.

Purification.

The ceremonial purification * without which no prayers can be said is called the wuḍoo, and may be complete or partial, according to the nature of the action requiring its performance. This may be either an act of personal necessity, or contact with something in itself unclean, a dead body for instance. † A complete Ḳor'án may not be touched till the reader be purified, but its portions may be. The complete ablutions are most commonly performed at the steam-baths, and the favourite time for this is very early on the Friday morning. For the lesser wuḍoo lavatories are provided at the mosques, or water may simply be poured from any convenient vessel, for which purpose there is in every furnished dwelling a special ewer, long-spouted for ease of manipulation. The Moors, like most other Orientals accustomed to scanty supplies of water, are careful not to wash *in* it, but *with* it, pouring it over the hands, or dipping a washed hand in and throwing the water over the part to be washed. When water is not to be had, the purification may be accomplished with sand, or by merely placing the hands on some clean stone or the ground, and performing a special abbreviation of the ablution motions known as tayammum.[1]

* Enjoined to the Ḳor'án, v., 9.

† Animals allowed for food (halál) are, however, clean at all times and in all particulars (even to their excreta) with the exception of their blood, which is in all animals unclean (ḥaram, *i.e.* "prohibited"). Dogs, though unclean as food, are maintained as pets.

[1] See *Mishkát*, bk.. iii., ch. xi.

Squatting on his bare heels, with his sleeves rolled up, the performer inwardly states "I purpose performing the wuḍoo for prayer." Then, pouring a little water into his right hand, he washes the two together, and performs with the left the sinjá

The Lesser Ablution.

SPRING AND CONDUIT IN A MOORISH GARDEN.

—cleansing of the body, if this has been rendered necessary,—after which he rubs his left hand on a stone, and washes them both. In consequence of this the left hand should never touch food, especially moist food, as it is always reserved for touching anything dirty.* The

* On account of this Mohammedans, when speaking of "God's Hands," employ the word denoting the right, or merely say "the Two Right Hands." Cf. El Ufráni, p. 304.

mouth is next filled with water from the palm of the right hand, the operation being performed three times, and the teeth rubbed once, usually with the left fore-finger. Then water is snuffed up from the right hand, after which the nose is blown with the left, three times. Both hands, filled with water, are next passed over the face three times, after which first the right, and then the left hand and arm are washed to the elbow three times, and the wet hands are passed from the forehead to the nape, concluding with a twist of the fore-fingers in the ears as the profession of faith is made, the hands being drawn back over the face during its second half. Lastly the feet are washed, three times apiece, as high as the ankles, the right first, and if the profession has been omitted before, it is then repeated as an introduction to the prayer which follows.

The Greater Ablution.

For the greater or complete ablution the order is: left side, right side, back and head three times in addition to what has been described.* For the tayamum it is necessary only to go through the motions of washing the hands and face, then stroking the arms from the tips of the fingers to the elbows and back, as though anointing them, the right first, touching the ground between each performance. As far as the hands and mouth are concerned the method of washing after a meal is identical with this, which indeed becomes so much a matter of habit with the Moors, that they seldom wash in any less formal way.

A Moor of the better class who makes any pretension to education carries with him under his arm a coloured

* Mohammed is said to have declared "He who leaves one hair on his body unwashed will suffer in proportion in Hell,"[1] to avoid which danger the Moors shave all abundant hair from their bodies, or make use of depilatories.

[1] *Mishkât*, bk. ii, ch. viii.

felt cloth or libdat el gulûs, on which not only to sit whenever he needs to rest, as its name implies, but also and primarily on which to kneel when he says his prayers. Failing that, a cloak or anything clean may be spread on the ground, or if there is nothing to spread, any spot on which the sun has shone suffices, even though patently foul, though of course the cleanest within reach must be selected. The next thing is to ascertain the ḳublah or direction of Mekka, which if not already known from local surroundings, can be sufficiently calculated from sun or stars. In every mosque or praying place this is denoted by a niche—mihráb,—and in some houses boards with inscriptions are hung up for this purpose. At first Mohammed taught his followers to face Jerusalem, after the Hebrew manner, but as this seemed to unduly favour the Jews, when he found that they did not accept his mission he ordered prayers to be said towards the ancient heathen temple at Mekka, the Ka'abah ("Cube") or Beït Allah ("House of GOD") whose erection was ascribed to Abraham. That his attention may not be distracted during worship, having removed his slippers—since the place of prayer is holy ground—the Moor places them sole to sole with the toes towards him, a short distance in front, in order to fix his eyes on them; and no other Muslim would think of passing before him while at prayer. In the presence of others it is essential to have the head covered, as a sign of respect.

Praying Cloths.

The Ḳublah.

Bare Feet.

Standing erect, with his feet just apart—from which position they must not be moved the whole time,—and with his hands extended outwards from his ears, the lobes of which are just touched by his thumbs, the worshipper exclaims in a clear and reverent voice, "Allahu 'kbar" (GOD is most great!)

Obligatory to Prayers.

an ejaculation known as the takbîrat el iḥram or "glorification of prohibition," after which it is not permitted to look right or left, or to take notice, whatever happens, except between two rika'hs or sets of prayers. This having been repeated a second time, he utters the profession of faith, "Áshahadu, lá ílaha íl Állah; wa áshahadu ínna seyyidîná Mohammed er-rasûl Allah" ("I testify that there is no god but GOD; and I testify that our lord Mohammed is the apostle of GOD"). It is considered profitable then, but not compulsory, to say "Haia 'alà eṣ-ṣaláhi, haïa 'alà el faláhi: ḳad ḳámati eṣ-ṣalát" ("Come to prayer, come to security: the time has arrived for prayer"). Then again the takbeer is offered, "GOD is most great!" and the hands hanging down at each side—the distinctive posture of the Malakí sect, to which the Moors belong—the Fatiḥah is repeated:—

The Fátiḥah.

"Praise be to GOD, the Lord of the Worlds, the Pitying, the Pitiful, King of the Day of Judgement. Thee do we serve, and from Thee we seek help: lead us in the perfect way, the way of those on whom is Thy grace, not of those on whom is wrath, nor of the wanderers. Amen."

Stooping slightly, with his hands upon his knees, one more takbeer is uttered, after which the worshipper rises again to exclaim "Samia' Allahu li man ḥamidahu; Allahuma Rabbaná, wa lak el ḥamd" ("May GOD hear him who praises Him; O GOD our Lord, to Thee be praise!"). The first phrase being said by the Imám or Leader, when there is one, and the second by the people. Then he kneels down, or rather sits on his heels with his knees on the ground, and bowing twice that his forehead may touch it too, between the two palms, he reverently, in a lowered voice, proclaims each time, "GOD is most great," sometimes adding a

Specimen Prayer.

voluntary petition of his own wording. A favourite prayer to introduce here is, "I glorify Thee, O GOD, and give Thee praise, and testify that there is no god other than Thee; and of Thee I ask pardon, and to Thee I confess: I have done evil and injured my soul: O pardon me, since there is none that can pardon sins but Thee," which is repeated three times. This ends one rik'ah.

Standing once more, he repeats the chapters Fátiḥah and Yá Seen of the Ḳor'án, or more commonly only a portion of the latter, as it contains no less than eighty-three verses; or a shorter chapter may be preferred, as El Kaôthar, with only three. Then commences the second rik'ah, kneeling as before, pronouncing the takbeer twice as he does so, saying between the two "Salutation be to GOD; alms be to GOD; good works be to GOD; prayers be to GOD!"

Thus far is farḍ or obligatory, the last expression being that which Mohammed is said to have uttered as he entered each successive heaven on his midnight journey, but often there is added: "Peace be unto thee, O thou Prophet, and the mercy of GOD, the High and Blessed One; Peace be on us, and on the holy servants of GOD. I testify that there is no god but GOD, and I testify that Mohammed is His servant and His Apostle." During the repetition of these two sentences, delivered in a semi-kneeling, semi-sitting posture, the two hands are placed flat out on the knees, with the fingers apart. A distinguishing practice of the Máliki sect,* to which the Moors belong, is meanwhile to move up and down the fore-finger of the right hand, called the "testifier," or "finger of witness." Some here repeat "Glory to GOD!" "Praise to GOD!" "GOD

Optional Prayers.

* One of the four "orthodox" denominations to whom pulpits are allotted in the great mosque at Mekka.

is most great!" a hundred times in all, counting them off on the joints of the fingers; finishing up with the Fátiḥah.

Concluding Salutation.

If only two rik'ahs have to be said, or when the number prescribed has been reached, the worshipper, holding his head down, exclaims to his guardian angels, "Peace be unto you: and unto you be peace," turning his head to the right as he utters the first salutation, and to the left as he utters the second. The final act is to wipe down his face with his palms, kissing his fingers as he does so. If more than two rik'ahs are said, the repetition of more from the Ḳor'án than the Fátiḥah is omitted. It is before the final wiping of the face that private petitions are made, if at all. Notwithstanding all the detail to be got through, four rik'ahs do not usually take more than three or four minutes. In time of war only one half of the army prays at a time, or less.

Hours of Prayers.

The five compulsory hours of prayer commence with the dawn, but do not include the actual moments of sun-rise, noon or sun-set, since the sun is adored by some at those times; and prayers may not be said between those of the 'aṣar or mid-afternoon and sun-set. Soon after the muédhdhin has chanted the fejer or dawn-call to waken—which is regulated by the appearance of the first faint streak of light, or failing that by the position of the three stars known as mishbûḥ, or by the third cock-crow—the faithful recite the ṣbaḥ or morning orisons, two rik'ahs of seven positions which are farḍ or obligatory, and two others which are sunneh or traditional. Between this and the next compulsory hour, the dhohr, it is a sunneh custom for the religious to recite six extra or nafilah rik'ahs, known as the ḍuhá. About twenty minutes after noon the loolî or "first" cry for midday prayers is heard, at which time on Fridays the services in the mosques begin, concluding with four rik'ahs sunneh and four rik'ahs farḍ, called the dhohr, for which also a cry is made about 1.20 p.m. The exact time is marked by the shadow of a perpendicular stick becoming one quarter its length, and that of the next prayers, the 'aṣar, by the shadow becoming one quarter longer than the stick;

A MOORISH PALM GROVE.

it is then time to say four more sunneh and as many farḍ rik'ahs. Some four minutes after the actual sunset the summons goes forth for the three farḍ and two sunneh rik'ahs which go by its name, the maghrib,—identical with that of Morocco, after which a dozen extra prayers are said by the pious before the regular 'aṣha or supper prayers—due when the red gleam after sunset has disappeared,—which consist of four rik'ahs sunneh and four rik'ahs farḍ. These are followed by two more sunneh rik'ahs called eeshfa'a, and at any time after by one to three single rik'ahs known as witeer, considered to be meritorious in proportion as they are late.

Country muédhdhins having no watches or calculations to assist them, announce the maghrib when they can no longer see the hairs on their hands, and the noon and the 'aṣar by the measurement of their own shadows with their feet. The time of the 'ashà may also be told by the same three stars as the approaching dawn, but in all cases it is considered better to be late than early, in accordance with the custom of the country, the excuse being that what is said before the time is only credited as a free-will addition to the previous prayers. For those who have no special inclination that way, it may be well believed that such a series is perfunctorily performed, and it is no wonder that many who do not wish to neglect them altogether work off the whole lot at night, or even a week's accumulation before the Friday.

Methods of Calculation.

In addition to all this there is still another method of prayer employed by the Moors, in common with the Hindus, the Buddhists, the Roman and Eastern Christians, and other creeds, the rosary, which they call taṣbeeḥ. This is composed of ninety-nine beads of wood, bone, ivory, seeds, or fruit-stones, etc., with a sort of small handle in which the cord is joined, and two additional knobs after the thirty-third beads from either end. Many have also ten beads tightly threaded on a short string at the end, along which they are pushed to record the hundreds of vain repetitions up to a thousand. The beads may be of any size, from that of a small pea to that of a walnut, such as is worn as a sort of badge round the neck by begging members of the Darḳáwî brotherhood.

Rosaries.

Many keep their rosaries constantly going, whatever business or conversation they may be conducting, which gives an air of religious abstraction, and often causes no little incongruity in the

Vain Repetitions.

eyes of an outsider, without interfering with bargaining powers, or even of transactions more than dubious. One not infrequently hears, for instance, a shop-keeper mumbling rapidly to himself "Ástaghfir Állah; ástaghfir Állah" ("I seek pardon from GOD") while he assures a customer between the pauses, "Now take it for what I gave for it—so much. (I seek pardon from GOD; I seek pardon from GOD.) No? Well, take it for less—so much—you are such a good friend that I do not mind losing by you. (I seek pardon from GOD: I seek pardon from GOD.) Well, then, if you won't, may you be accursed! (I seek pardon from GOD: I seek pardon from GOD.)" Other common rosary phrases are "There is no GOD but GOD;" "To GOD be the glory;" "Prayers on the prophet;" or any of the pious expressions culled from the Ḳor'án, or employed in the regular prayers. Distances are sometimes roughly calculated by the time it takes to make the round of the string, a place being described as so many rosaries off. It is with the Moors to-day as Ovid in his *Fasti*,[1] wrote of the Romans of his day:

"Et peragit solita fallere voce preces:
'Ablue præteriti perjuria temporis,' inquit.
'Ablue præterita perfida verba die!
. . . .
'Nec curent superi si qua locutus ero.'"

[1] Bk. v., l. 680.

BRINGING IN AN OFFICIAL DINNER.

Drawn by R. Caton Woodville.

CHAPTER THE SEVENTEENTH

ALMS, HOSPITALITY AND PILGRIMAGE

ALTHOUGH the Moors can fully hold their own in a bargain, and are frequently impelled by motives of self-interest to what appears to be generosity, it cannot be recorded of them that they are ungenerous, or that most of them have not kind hearts, and are indisposed to good deeds. In this, as Muslims, they do not lack encouragement, for Mohammed has left them abundant precepts inculcating alms-giving and hospitality, as well as general good works. "Pay your legal alms," says the Ḳor'án: "Be constant in prayer and alms-giving:" "GOD loveth not the proud or vain-glorious, who are covetous and recommend covetousness unto men, and conceal that which GOD of His bounty hath given them, . . . and who bestow their wealth to be observed of men." There is a Mohammedan saying that "Prayer carries us half-way to GOD, fasting brings us to the door of His palace, but alms procure us admission." Mohammed is reported to have said that he who left his legal contributions unpaid should have a serpent twisted round his neck at the resurrection.

Generosity.

Koranic Injunctions.

The legal alms, or zakát,* as distinguished from ṣadaḳah† or free-will offerings, have to be given once a year, at the feast of 'Aáshûr or tithing, and consist in varying proportions of the worldly goods

Tithes.

* Anglicé "sanctification," *i.e.* of property.

† Anglicé "righteousness."

a man possesses at the time, his actual cash being subject to 2½ per cent. of zakát. His stock, cattle, and all property which has been held a year, pay proportions of which the Moors do not seem to have any general knowledge, and about which few appear to be particular. No oversight is exercised, so it is probable that the legal standard is seldom approached.

Alms-giving Seasons.

Besides the 'Aáshúr, alms are readily given at each of the feasts, especially after Ramaḍán, when portions of wheat and other food are collected on behalf of every member of a family, to be given to the poor under the name of fiṭrah or "breakfast dish." Formerly this was gathered and distributed by government, but in 1286 Yûsef III. left it to individual discretion.[1] Fridays are considered special almsgiving days, and so are the fast days at the beginning and end of Rajab, and on Sha'abán 17th, but probably much more finds its way into the pockets of the professionally religious than into those of the really needy. After a funeral food is distributed at the grave, and of course on occasions of rejoicing, such as weddings, the poor come in for their share of the feast. One of the most meritorious methods of bestowing alms in these warm lands is by providing drinking-water, either by erecting fountains or wayside crocks, or by simply paying a water-carrier to go round with a skin-full, calling on all the thirsty to freely drink: "Ho ye that thirst, come and drink: this is the way of God!"

Thirst Quenching.

Beggars.

Under such conditions beggars could not fail to abound, and they manage to make themselves heard as well as seen. At every gateway, by every frequented mosque, and at any other likely point they congregate, uttering wearisome cries with wonderful per-

[1] *Raỏḍ el Ḳarṭás*, p. 529.

sistence and unvarying tones. Most of them bring in the Name of GOD, in which they beg, but many are content to imply it, making mention only of some favourite saint, one of the most common expressions combining the two, "For GOD and my lord 'Abd el Ḳáder!"

BEGGAR AT A MOORISH FRONT-DOOR.
Photograph by G. Michell, Esq.

Petitions.

"For the face of GOD!" cries another, or he simply ejaculates "For GOD! For GOD!—'Al' Allah!"—repeating it slowly at first, then more briskly, and still faster, faster, faster; till, rocking to and fro in time with his cry, he works himself up to a pitch beyond which he cannot go, and suddenly collapses, letting fall his head upon his breast in silence. Others ask that GOD may "leave those who give in prosperity," or "have mercy on their relatives," or "preserve their children," or "give them strength and blessing," or "keep their bag full," while a delightfully suggestive prayer is "May GOD give thee something to give!" Those who are not so inclined, but who are pestered by their importunity, get rid of them at last by replying "GOD bring it!" or "GOD make it easy!" A special polite way is to say "GOD open a way for us and thee to prosperity!" But if a man means to give, it is considered that he loses his reward if he selects a coin of low value from his pocket, the most excellent idea being that he who is truly generous will be content to share what he has, giving whatever comes first, a lesson which all might learn. A man or woman who lives by begging is said to "stand at GOD's door," and what is given to a beggar is described as "for GOD's due"—"ḥaḳḳ Allah." When free supplies are sent to the poor the summons is to "come and eat GOD's food."

The Retort Courteous.

In hospitality the town Moors are well to the front, but do not excel to the same degree as the Arabs. In the country it suffices for a wayfarer to approach any dwelling or the village mosque, to be assured of a place to sleep, and something to eat, though he must not expect too much unless at the hands of some well-to-do individual who makes a point of hospitality. On approaching the home of a tribe, the native traveller ascertains from some shepherd or ploughman the name of the man in the village most reputed for hospitality, and forthwith makes for his home. Arrived there, he proclaims himself "ḍaïf Allah"—"guest of GOD," and is heartily entertained for the night, and told next day for whom to ask in the next village, a companion being sent with him if necessary. Should harm befall him, his late host summons his male relatives to avenge

Hospitality.

the insult, and they at once set out with their guns for the purpose.*

MOORISH HOSPITALITY.
(Welcoming Newcomers.)

Photograph by Dr. Rudduck.

Respect of Persons.

But in this, as in so much else, all depends upon the the social status of the visitor, who, if apparently of the least importance, will probably be made the guest of the local head-man, and fed on the fat of the land. In many parts the governors pride themselves upon their open-handed hospi-

* I am even informed of the existence in Sháwîah and among the Slûḥ of tribes whose notions of hospitality go so far as to lead them to lend their mothers, sisters and daughters, but never their wives, to their guests.

tality at the expense of those they govern, and it is the same with many of the great hereditary saints, who consider as their guest whoever visits their place. As Europeans come in for a share of all this beyond what the Moors do, they are apt to over-estimate Moorish hospitality, which to be rightly judged must be considered from the stand-point of the needy Moor. It is doubtful, however, whether in a comparison on that basis our own hospitality would show up as well as we might expect.

Entertaining Europeans.

Formerly it was the custom throughout the country, and it still is in most parts of the interior, to consider the foreign visitor as the guest of the nation, and to provide him with all that he needs free of charge, though of course the officials and others employed in catering for him at no cost to themselves expect to make something out of it, and presents are not refused. The provisions thus supplied are called môna, and are furnished by the authorities on production of a shareefian,—i.e. "official" letter,—to be obtained from the court of a provincial governor on the application of foreign officials, the nature of the treatment received depending largely on the source of the letter. Even when unprovided with such letters, European travellers who call upon the ḳáïds or governors will often be provided with a good supper, half a pound of tea, a pound of candles and a loaf of sugar, to which for more important folk may be added fruits, milk, sweets, a sheep, and barley for the animals, besides supplies for the servants.

Môna.

"Quid pro quo."

The difficulty in such cases is to know how to make a suitable return for the kindness received, the supply and transport of a number even of small presents being no trifling matter in Morocco, and money seldom being accepted. In the case of embassies, for which everything is provided on the most lavish scale, the country-people are severely "squeezed," and although the value of the supplies they furnish nominally comes out of their share of the taxes, along the high-roads to the capitals it becomes a serious burden. Too often the superabundance is disposed of by night to the people themselves, who repurchase it from the foreigners' underlings. Notwithstanding all the efforts made by most of the ambassadors to put a stop to this, it still goes on, and the people grow accustomed to being bled.

At Meal Times.

At his own meals a Moor seldom cares to be alone, and if able to do so will often invite another to eat with him in order to have company, many officials and others in good position making it one of the duties of their secretary or their steward to take meals with them: those in high authority often demand that their head cook shall partake of each dish and cup for a different reason, to guard against poison. Christians visiting Moorish friends, and known to approve of Moorish manners and food, will often be invited to remain informally for a meal, as well as being bidden to feasts.* Besides this, it is incumbent on anyone eating before others to invite them to join, whether they do so or not remaining at the bystanders' discretion. I have seen one glass of tea, or one cigarette, passed round to a dozen, and have at times felt terribly boorish for having to excuse myself from doing the same with some European eatable which was the only food within reach I could manage, and which I had cooked for one.

When an invited guest is a stranger, or when special honour is to be done, it is customary to send one or

* It is in this connection worthy of note that while Mohammed commanded "O True Believers, take not Jews or Christians for friends" (sûrah v.), he also expressly enjoined in the same sûrah, "the food of those to whom the Scriptures were given is also allowed as lawful to you . . . also free women of those who have received the Scriptures before you."

more of the servants to fetch him, or even a mule or a horse for him to ride, and when a man of low degree invites one of importance to honour his house, he probably goes himself to fetch his guest. Otherwise the guest may have to wait some time at the door, while the women are being stowed away, before his knock will be answered, or if it has been, before the door is opened to him. When his host appears with the blandest of smiles, and a torrent of hearty welcomes, prominent among these will be "Marḥabáṇ" or "Marḥabá' bikum,"—"Welcome" or "Welcome to you," repeated many times amid enquiries after health and welfare, which may be accompanied by "Ahláṇ wa sahláṇ,"—"(Be) at home and at ease," to which is sometimes added a poetical complimentary phrase such as "Ameer el miláḥ wa zaïn el budoor,"—"Prince of the good, and beauty of the stars," or by the simple statement "Anta fi dár-ak"—"Thou art in thine own house!"

Dining Out.

The guest having meanwhile reciprocated enquiries mingled with praise to GOD, according to the customary forms of salutation, he is led—often by the hand—into the guest-chamber, which in large establishments is one of a suite of rooms in which male guests are lodged, or on a private stair, entirely separated from the women's quarters, but which in ordinary dwellings is the family living and sleeping room evacuated for the occasion. Once inside here, the door is closed, or the curtain over it dropped, and the women venture from their retreats till the host gives the signal for them to again retire, without which it would be most impolite even to rise, and more so still to approach the door. The women receive guests of their own sex only when no men are about, the stranger's slippers at the threshold being a warning to them not to approach. Such visits are commonly paid by way of

The Guest Chamber.

the roofs. Many ḳaids have a number of unfurnished guest-rooms in which travellers are entertained, and in towns there are allotted vacant houses or gardens, or some official is instructed to turn out of his quarters for them; or they may be relegated to the Jewish quarter.

A WAYSIDE CAFÉ, THE PILGRIMS' LODGING.
Photograph by the late Dr. Robert Brown.

Among the religious duties of Islám, none is in greater favour among the Moors than pilgrimage, whether to the great Mohammedan centre at Mekka or to some distant city or shrine in the country itself. The ḥájj or pilgrimage *par excellence*—to Mekka, of course—is incumbent on every Moor, as a member of the Máliki sect, who has strength for the journey and power to earn his food by the way. This accounts for the large number of Moroccans who are to be found throughout the length of Barbary, in Egypt,

Pilgrimage.

and in the Levant generally, the most part poor, or who, having settled where they are when unable to proceed further for lack of means, have since grown rich. In Tunis those from Sûs especially abound, forming so reliable a guild—in which all members are responsible for each other,—that they are in great demand as guards. On the pilgrim route from Damascus to Madîna, too, where the wells at each stage have to be guarded by forts, it is only the Moors who can be induced and trusted to remain as garrisons.[1]

Formerly the whole journey was performed by land at immense risk and hardship, caravans yearly making the round from Morocco to Mekka and back,* taking and bringing merchandise as well as pilgrims, uniting business with religion. Now that method is a thing of the past, and the faithful make their way to the coast in irregular shoals instead of caravans. There they camp at the ports till they go on board some foreign vessel, usually a merchant steamer chartered for the run to Alexandria, Port Said or Jedda, by some speculator who packs all he can on board, at whatever rate he can obtain in competition with others, averaging from four to ten dollars (13s. 4d. to 33s. 4d.) a head. At this price it is hardly surprising that luxuries are not conspicuous, and that each one finds his own provisions, even including his skin of water, though when this runs out the ship replenishes it.

The Journey.

Pilgrim Ships.

An ordinary stock of eatables to take includes a pound each of tea, coffee, and candles; a small loaf of sugar, two pounds each of dried meat and rancid butter; and ten pounds each of kesk'sû, biscuits and charcoal, with ten or more loaves of bread: a supply intended to

* From Fez to Alexandria used to occupy four to six months.

[1] See DOUGHTY'S *Arabia Deserta*.

last for some fourteen or sixteen days, and leave something to land with. Besides these, most men take as indispensable utensils, brazier, stew-pot, bellows, tea-pot and glass, kettle, dish, and wooden spoon. The only other special provision needed is that of the new sandals and áḥrám (an unsewn cloak or rather rectangular cotton sheet) which the pilgrim has

A Pilgrim's Outfit.

A CORNER OF THE MARKET.

From a photograph by W. B. Harris Esq.

to wear as he enters the sacred district in which Mekka stands. The round cost to a working man who seeks no more than is absolutely necessary, amounts to about fifty dollars, the return fares being much higher than those quoted. Morocco is left ten or fourteen days after the 'Aïd eṣ-Ṣag̲heer, in order that the pilgrims may assemble on the all-important day of the 'Aïd el Kabeer at the valley of Mîna near Mekka, returning to their home-land if not delayed, about the feast of the Maôlûd.

Cost.

RUINS OF A COLLEGE, RABAT.

Cavilla, Photo., Tangier

CHAPTER THE EIGHTEENTH

EDUCATION IN MOROCCO

MOROCCO is one of those lands in which the ease and cheapness of obtaining an education might lead one to consider it in this respect fortunate, but a very different estimate will be formed when the nature of the education provided is taken into account.

Deceptive Appearance.

Although it may be said that every Moorish lad can learn to read if he likes, and a fair proportion of them pursue their studies as far as they go in Morocco, the best to be obtained amounts to so little that "education" is hardly the word to employ. Everything turns on the splitting of hairs over words that are dead, and not on the practice of what they might teach, or on the making of discoveries. The higher branches of knowledge are entirely wanting, or hold an unimportant place as voluntary studies forming no part of the regulation course, and what smattering of them can be acquired is almost always an antiquated misconception which had better not be taught. Education in Morocco is for this reason at a very low ebb.

From five years and upwards, if only to keep them out of the streets, the lads of Morocco are sent to school, but if they do not display aptitude they are often removed to learn a trade before they have learned their letters, so unessential is reading considered in a land in which there is so little to read, and nothing of much practical value. The first

Early Commencement.

time that a new boy comes to school his father brings him, with a present of some sort for the foḳîh or teacher, to whom he often gives also a small stock of raisins, sweets etc., with which to bribe the pupil's attendance till he grows used to it. After a week or so a little tea or feast in his honour is given by his family to the other boys, who get the afternoon as a half-holiday.

Primary Schools.

These primary schools are held in the mosques, or in rooms about the town belonging to them, called m'seed, in which all sit on the ground, the teacher facing his pupils, whose bare pates are all within reach of the switch in his hand. Instead of books or slates, each one is provided with a piece of thin board, narrowed to the lower end, rubbed over with a sort of pipe-clay on which they write with reed pens, and ink prepared from charred horns, or wool, and water. One of the bigger boys being set to teach them to write the alphabet which they have already been taught by ear, the letters are written out on the boards for them to copy. The lessons are then read aloud by all together, rocking to and fro to keep time, some delighting in a high key, others jogging easily in lower tones, perhaps considerably behind.

School Fees.

The teachers of these schools are seldom men of education themselves, even according to the local standard, though they generally have a reputation both for learning and religion, and are not infrequently imáms and muédhdhins as well, thus earning some ten to thirty dollars a year besides school fees. These consist of small sums or articles, from a centime or an egg upwards, brought each Sunday (when it is called ḥadîyah), or each Wednesday (raba'ïah), and sometimes each Saturday (sebtîyah), as well as at each new moon (sharîyah), and at feast times. It is usual to tell each boy what he is expected to bring, according to his parents' means, especially at the holidays or áwásh-ar. These occur at each of the three great feasts, extending from a week before them to a week afterwards, some times up to twenty days, with occasional single days, as the Yôm el 'Aáshûr, the Anṣarah, etc. Collections are also made for occasional picnics by taking round the writing boards. Thursday afternoons and Friday mornings are half-holidays.

Holidays.

School hours commence in winter before daylight, but in summer after it, somewhere between three and five a.m.—the earlier hours being kept in the country,—and continue till a quarter after twelve, a break for food having been made about nine or ten. From half-past one again they last till an hour before sunset, and some come again before supper. Those who do not learn their lessons in class are kept in till they do so by good foḳihs, but such are scarce. In the case of rich families private teachers are employed to come to the house, and then too, on rare occasions, the little daughters will receive a smattering, but this is rare unless their father is himself their teacher. "Teach not thy daughter letters: let her not live on the roof!" says the native proverb.

Hours of Study.

The whole of the first school course is the Ḳor'án, which has to be learned by heart before anything else can be done, though little of it may be understood. Its language is for the most part far too intricate and high-flown, even where ordinarily intelligible, for their small minds, not to say for those of the average full-grown Moor. As soon as a pupil has mastered the first division or ḥezb—of which there are sixty—he brings an extra present for the foḳih, called a k͟haṭmah or seal, and the whole school, which seldom numbers more than a score, is treated to an

How the Kor'án is learned.

extra "half."* When fifteen divisions are mastered, the father, if he can, gives a feast to the teacher and all the boys, called a zerdah, and at the half a still more important one, for which it is incumbent on him to borrow if he has not the means, a sheep or a cow being often presented to the foḳîh. When the whole has been once gone through, which may be at the end of about two years, the biggest feast of all must be prepared, even if to give it the father be obliged to beg.

Then the operation is repeated, the second reading taking a year or a year and a half. After three or four times the dullest ought to know it right through by heart, and occasionally a bright youth will retain the whole the first time. As each stage is reached a circle drawn on the board by the foḳîh, with ¼, ½, ¾ or "through" inscribed in the centre, is the certificate which the proud pupil is enabled to show to his friends. Sometimes a bargain is struck at the outset with the foḳîh as to what shall be given him on this auspicious occasion. From this time forth education in Morocco is free, as the foḳîhs of greater reputation to whom the ambitious scholar now repairs are anxious to attract all they can around them, since they receive in consequence increased support in alms, the blessings assured by their presence growing in proportion to their reputation. Studies with teachers of this sort seldom proceed beyond the Ḳor'án and some of its commentaries. Thence the student proceeds to college, whenever possible to Fez, but if not, to some provincial town in which the same course prevails, though very much inferior in quality.

Graduation.

The Moorish collegiate system differs little from that of the other Mohammedan countries, and, except in

* Instead of learning the Ḳor'án straight through, after the Fátiḥah (ch. i.) is acquired. the last chapter, as the shortest, is tackled, and so on, backwards to the second, which is the longest.

matters of detail, a description of the Azhar at Cairo, the central school of Islám, or of those of Bokhára—which supply all Tartary and Central Asia, —both of which I have investigated on the spot, as well as those of Fez, would be equally applicable to any. Instruction is in all cases confined to the mosques, the madarsahs or colleges being only residential quarters for the students, who pay nothing for either, though they have to "buy the key" of their room when they enter, and can stay as long as they like, which is usually from three to ten years.

Collegiate System.

In Fez a student (tilmîd) generally makes a start with little money, but with a supply of home-made kesk'soo, perhaps a mudd; of butter perhaps twenty pounds, of dried meat perhaps half a hundred-weight, if he can afford it, and also clothes and a mattress, which completes his outfit, though many a poor youth can provide no more than the price of his key. Those whose families cannot send a supply for the winter each year have to make a living as best they can by copying,* reading the Ḳor'án, writing letters, or even begging breakfast of one and supper of another, to supplement the solitary loaf of good bread which each morning is thrust into every room through a hole in the door at the expense of the mosque, but commonly attributed to the sultan. This distribution takes place only in the madarsahs, which are large three-storeyed houses built round court-yards, on to which, or the galleries round, open rows of small rooms for the students. Each building is in charge of a muḳaddam, who keeps the place clean, and also distributes the bread. The

'Varsity Life.

* The payment for copying varies, according to writing, from 5 ok. to a peseta per kurrás of ten leaves quarto with 24 lines to a page, an average price being 3 rvn. or 6d. Only Ḳor'áns (called mus'ḥaf) are written with vowel points, and these are bargained for at from $2 per copy, paper found, but not ink.

only other resident official is the imám who leads in prayer.

The price of a key runs from twenty to a hundred dollars, or even two hundred sometimes, according to position and demand, the favourite madarsahs being those of the 'Aṭṭarîn, the Sherrátîn, the Meṣbáḥîyah, the Ṣaffárîn, and the Báb el-Gîsah, which are almost entirely devoted to students from the country. The first-named is the most aristocratic, the second being perhaps the most comfortable, attracting chiefly Algerians and Filális. For hard-working students the last three are famous. The less important are those of Abû 'Aïnán and eṣ-Ṣaḥrîj. Women are supposed never to enter a madarsah, and all non-Mohammedans are also excluded, but with this exception no one exercises any control over the students, who, having come up of their own free will, generally take care to maintain a good reputation, especially as the livelihood of so many depends upon their doing so. Any crimes that may be committed are judged by the ḳáḍi, who has also the chief voice in the appointment of professors, but the latter have no control over their pupils outside the mosque.

Fez Colleges.

All who come to study in Fez are supposed not only to know the Ḳor'án by heart, but also to have mastered the outlines of the native system of grammar and rhetoric (naḥu, ṣarf and ájrûmîyah*). On arrival they may resort to what professors they like, finding each in his allotted corner in the aisles of the vast mosque of the Ḳarûeeïn. The more important among the professors, who attract large numbers, are provided with stools or "chairs" (kursi or majlis), while those less sought after have to content themselves, like their pupils, with the matted floor, since other furniture

Matriculation.

* So named from the author of the standard work on the subject, the Sheïkh Ajrûm (Jerome).

there is none. According to their reputed learning they are described as of first, second or third tabaḳ (class).

Terms.

The terms are from the middle of Shûwál to the last week of Dhû'l Ḳa'dah: from the twentieth of Dhû'l Ḥaj-jah to the end of Ṣafar, and from the middle of Rabî'a II. to the last week of Sha'abán, or the twentieth of Ramaḍán.

Curriculum.

An ordinary day's work commences after morning prayers with the study of the Ḳor'án and its commentaries, lasting for an hour or so: then the student will attend a fresh professor for a course of law till eight, and after them a third who will deal with jurisprudence till ten, with yet a fourth till noon, who may perhaps inculcate "minor sciences" such as the taking of astronomical observations, or arithmetic, but there is no fixed order. In the afternoon fewer professors attend, and the subjects may be from 1.30 to 2.30 grammar and rhetoric: the remainder of the time till the 'aṣar prayers being devoted to the so-called sciences. Lastly, the students are supposed to read at home in the evening all they have a desire to know of history, geometry, astronomy, medicine, poetry, etc., as well as to prepare the passages to be elucidated on the morrow. Wednesday is a half-holiday, and Thursday and Friday are whole holidays.

Lectures.

The method of instruction is for one of the pupils, appointed as reader, to go through a short passage aloud, which the professor then expounds, dealing first with the meaning and "weight" of the words, then with their bearing as there employed, and the resulting meaning of the sentence as a whole, quoting lastly the opinions of the commentators on it. No one ventures to interrupt him with a question or a remark, but at the close the learners may inquire for any further explanation needed. Usually the students only carry to their rooms one musannif (section of an unbound book) at a time, by which arrangement a few copies go a long way.* The library of the Ḳarûeeïn, a big room in the Maḳsûrah, near the mortuary chapel, can only be used by well-known foḳîhs, who may take the books home only on the order of the ḳáḍi. Most students have to borrow elsewhere or copy, when too poor to buy at the sales by auction which take place each Friday after the noon-day prayers.†

Professors.

The professors are selected in accordance with the public voice rather than academic honours, which in Morocco consist in certificates given by individual professors, stating that so-and-so has studied such and such books with the signatory, who considers his acquaintance with them sufficient to enable him in his turn to teach. Such a document is called an íjázah or "pass." No examinations mark either entry or exit. There may be some fifty professors in Fez, all told, about twenty being of first rank. They are paid by the State, being sometimes provided with a house, certain clothes, and a supply of provisions,‡ and since many of them hold other posts besides, they are not badly off.

Results.

M. Delphin, Arabic professor at O'ran, who has translated a good account of the system of studies in Fez,§ records that none of those who offered themselves for examination at O'ran could excel the students from Fez in Arabic literature. But it is a ques-

* For a list of the principal authors studied see Delphin. Most are common to the Muslim centres of the East.

† A list of 240 volumes to be found in the libraries of the Ḳarûeeïn and Erseef mosques, obtained by M. Ordega in 1883, is given by Prof. Basset, with some valuable bibliographical notes, in the "Bulletin de Correspondance Africaine," Algiers, 1882, p. 366. (B. Mus. Ac. 5350.)

‡ A first-class professor may receive $30, 40 measures of wheat, an ox, and a suit of fine clothing.

§ *Fas, son Université*, Paris and O'ran, 1889.

tion how far such a course as that described is of real value as education, beyond the mental training required to grasp those subtle distinctions and knotty points which Chinese and Arabian teachers think of more importance than the subject of the writings.

Pilgrimages.

The veneration in which the "learned" are held in Morocco is very great, and their presence anywhere is always believed to bring blessing, so that they are eagerly sought after, all their wants being met by the faithful with more or less liberality, according to the reputation of each individual. An interesting and practical custom is that of the summer pilgrimages which are sometimes undertaken by a professor with a group of his pupils, who are everywhere welcomed by the assembled villagers, for whose benefit he discourses on religious duties and other things which should be "understanded of the laity." For a month or more, master and pupils fare well as the guests of the country people, on whom they have conferred a favour by coming. Thus they move from shrine to shrine in great comfort.

The 'Ulamá.

Those in the cities who have earned a reputation for wisdom go by the name of 'ulamá (*s.* 'alîm) or "learned," and to their judgment all defer. Around the sultan there is always a body of these to advise as to the bearing of koranic law upon questions brought before them, and to support the sultan in measures which might otherwise arouse objection. These are the great obstructionists, and it is through their power that Islám binds Morocco down: so it is in all Mohammedan lands. It is doubtful whether these men or the actual saints of the country receive more honour, but there is no doubt as to which class makes the better thing out of this veneration. Wherever they go in the streets the "learned" are received with applications for blessing, and, dressed in the garb of their class, I have often had my shoulders, hands and ankles kissed by strangers in the street.

The Feast of the Scribes.

In addition to the ordinary holidays, Fez students have a yearly feast which is unique in its way, and owes its origin to the assistance received by Mulai Rasheed II. from the ṭolbah or scribes of Táza when engaged in his fight for the throne in 1664.* It is said that a Jew was in power there, and that the ṭolbah penetrated Táza and assassinated him, in return for which service that sultan and his successors have permitted the students of Fez to choose a sultan of their own for one week in the spring, when they all go out into camp on the banks of the river about a mile from town, and not a few citizens with them. The "little brief authority" of the imitation sultan is awarded to the highest bidder, as it brings the right of asking from the real sultan a favour which is seldom refused, being usually the release of some prisoner, besides which the holder is thereafter freed from taxes. Its value therefore varies greatly, running from $50 to $200. In addition to this sum, contributions are levied on the shop-keepers and house-holders, against whom humourous charges are often brought by the police of the student-sultan, who is surrounded by all the official life of a real Court, and parades the streets in state with music and shouting, shadowed even by a royal umbrella. With the so-called fines and free-will offerings, to which the real sultan adds a liberal supply of provisions, there is sufficient to ensure a magnificent feast, called Nozhat eṭ-Ṭolbah—"the Scribes' Recreation"—and altogether the students have a very good time, with every sort of game and amusement. During the week the real sultan himself pays the camp a visit to tender submission to the power of learning,

A Mock Court.

* See *The Moorish Empire*, p. 138 (n).

and it is then that the mock sultan makes his demand. Before all is over, however, he has to flee lest at the last moment his quondam subjects should rob him.

Scientific Attainments.

Of the quality of the instruction imparted under the head of sciences very little can be said, since the whole system of Mohammedan learning is some centuries behind time, and to describe it would but be to revive the crude ideas of the Middle Ages, common to the civilized World of that day to an extent which enables the Moors in Spain to rank with the foremost. Of algebra and alchemy, whose very names we owe to Arabic, the Moors at least know next to nothing now, and what they think they know is merely fossil lore.* Astronomy, or rather astrology, is now represented only by an array of words, their highest achievement being to tell the time of day.† In medicine their knowledge is remarkably unpractical, although they have some books containing valuable facts on herbal and other treatment, of which, however, the barbers and writers of charms, their only doctors, know nothing. Of history little is read but a few old records of their

* The answer of a learned sixteenth-century alchemist in Morocco to one who wished to learn of him is worth recalling: "The number of radicals in the word ḳimîah is five, as also is that of the fingers; if, my friend, you wish to practise that science, undertake agriculture and toil, for they are the true ḳimîah (alchemy) of man, not that which works with copper and lead."[1]

† Yet M. Sedillot translated an astronomical treatise written by a Moor, Abu el Ḥasan 'Ali, who lived in the 13th century: *Traité des instruments astronomiques des Arabes* (Paris, 1834-5), supplemented by a *Mémoire sur les inst. astr. des Arabes*, (Paris, 1841-5). An interesting description of a Moorish astrolabe made in Fez in 1782, chiefly for ascertaining the hours of prayer at that latitude, is given by M. Delphin, with illustrations, in the "Journal asiatique," March 1891 (B. Mus. Ac. 2098 d.). In the same place he has recorded the names of fourteen Arabic astronomical treatises known in Barbary. See also F. Sarrus, *Description d'un Astrolabe*, 1852, with engravings of a specimen from Fez.

[1] El Ûfrânî, p. 94.

own and other Mohammedan countries, long out of date, and I doubt if Morocco possesses a volume in Arabic touching upon European history which was not printed at the Mission press at Beïrût or elsewhere in the East.

Geography.

The same might be said of geography, of which the very rudest notions exist, and the shape of the Earth is not yet accepted in Fez, where the little World the Moors know, for the most part that of Islám, centres in Mekka, and is surrounded by an encircling ocean, the Baḥr el Moḥaït. The only towns known by name to the average Moor—without an idea as to where they are, unless he has been there—are those of the North African coast; Yanbo'a, Jedda, Madîna and Mekka; Jerusalem, Damascus, Baghdád and Basra; Constantinople, Moscow, London, Manchester, Paris and Marseilles; Madrid, Seville, Cadiz, Córdova, Granáda, Malaga and Gibraltar: beyond this he has heard the names only of some of the countries of Europe, and that of the United States of America, known by their having officials here, and by their protecting natives. Further afield only India and China are known by name, though some have heard of Persia. For this I can vouch through having so often in vain endeavoured to answer enquiries as to my travels, even when I felt sure I was speaking to men who must know. On the other hand, my own experience enables me also to state that excepting in the countries reached by the Morocco pilgrims, and in Constantinople, those in the East who have not received some form of European education, have no idea where Morocco is, and few even know its name. In Persia, Central Asia, Northern India and throughout Eastern Islám, it is included with Algeria and Tunis under the title of El Gharb, or "The West," and elsewhere it is only becoming known under European appellations. These I was surprised to find used even on Arabic maps in Egyptian schools, instead of its own Arabic names, and the same was the case with other North African places, the compilation evidently having been the work of Europeans, a most unfortunate occurrence.

Arithmetic.

Arithmetic is one of the sciences which the Moorish student is left to pick up for himself, though the average shop-keeper, who cannot more than read and write, if he can do as much, is generally successful in obtaining a workable acquaintance with the principal rules, often from some special teacher. One of the first things learned by all, together with the alphabet, is the numerical value of the various letters, remembered by meaningless words spelled in the order they stand to read 1, 2, 3, 4, etc., the equivalent for which forms the first word, "ábajad," by which the whole system is known. The multiplication tables are thus learned by mnemonics, a long string of words which are committed parrot-like to memory.* The same system is employed in recording dates on buildings etc., and in many other ways, where the number is obtained by adding up the numerical values of the letters contained in a rhyme or in a single word or chronogram. †

* The actual values of the letters and the words they form are as under:

ابجد هوز حطي كلمن صعفض قرست ثخذ ظغش

1000, 900, 800 ; 700, 600, 500 ; 400 300 ; 200-100 ; 90, 80, 70, 60 ; 50, 40 30, 20 ; 10, 9, 8 ; 7, 6, 5 ; 4, 3, 2, 1

Which in English read, from right to left:—

"ábajad, haûziṇ, ḥuṭîṇ, kalamin, ṣ'afḍiṇ, ḳurisat, thak<u>h</u>udh. <u>dh</u>ag<u>h</u>s<u>h</u>iṇ."

The multiplication tables are learned thus:—

System of Mnemonics.

5×6—هول (haûluṇ) *i.e.* 5×6 = 30.

4×3—جدبي (jidbîuṇ) *i.e.* 4×3 = 2+10.

7×9—زطحص (zaṭ·ḥaṣuṇ) *i.e.* 7×9 = 3+60.

† For a specimen mnemonic date used in architecture, see *The Land of the Moors*, p. 97. One of the chief arithmetical works in use in Mo-

Moorish addition (jima'a) and subtraction (ṭarḥ) are performed as with us, but Moorish multiplication (ḍarb) is a very clumsy affair, division (ḳismah) being worse. Of the former this is an example:

```
   434
     547
 212128
  1106
  0521
   22
   68
 237398
```

In this style of multiplication the top line is the multiplier, and the operation commences from the right.

Multiplication.

Thus, 4 × 7 = 28, written down as above, then 4 × 4 = 16, the 1 being placed to the left of the 2 as representing hundreds, and the 6 underneath it as tens, and so on. Multiplying next by three, the 1 is placed in the tens column and the 2 in that of the hundreds, with beneath it the 2 of the 12, the 1 going to the top vacant space in the thousands column; under this last goes the 5 of the following 15, with the 1 to the left in the ten thousand column. In the last line, multiplying seven by four, the 8 goes in the hundreds column, the 2 to the thousands; with the 1 of the next 16 below it, the 1 representing ten thousand: lastly, under this 1 is placed the 0 of the 20, the 2 being placed at the top of a new column. It will be seen that the actual operation is precisely our own, the only difference being that here each figure is written down, whereas we simplify matters by "carrying" them in our head, and adding them mentally. The same may almost be said of their division, in which (when

rocco is the *Kitáb el Faraïd el A'sghar, min 'Aïlm Ḥorof el Ghobár*, by El Kalsádi.

rightly worked) the number to be "carried" is placed over each figure as it has been divided, but why the repetition of the divisor below I am at a loss to imagine. "Long" division has to be worked out in the same elaborate manner as the multiplication, far too intricate in detail to be worth explaining. It is, however, of considerable interest to notice that the method of operation precisely reproduces that on the abacus, according to the Chinese or the Russian system, of which the Japanese is only a simplification.

Division.

Here is an example of division worked for me by a leading Moorish merchant:

$$\frac{3456789}{6} = \begin{array}{l} 011452 \mid \underline{5} \\ 3456789 \\ \underline{6666666} \\ 542794 \end{array}$$

It was meant, I suppose, for:

$$\begin{array}{l} 043010 \mid \underline{3} \\ 3456789 \\ \underline{6666666} \\ 576131 \end{array}$$

It is hardly necessary to describe the caligraphy and books of Morocco, which are of the ordinary Arabic style, even when the language is Berber. An extremely graceful writing from right to left, it is easily learned, though when the shorter vowels—represented only by "points" above or below the line—are omitted, those to whom the words are new find reading difficult. The styles of writing vary greatly, according to the uses to which they are put, and the majority of the people who can write do so exceedingly ill, having hardly abandoned the crudeness of the copy-board stage, besides which the spelling is often

Books.

atrocious. On the other hand, the scribes in the cities often excel in the production of extremely neat and tasteful manuscripts. The books, which open from right to left, are mostly bound in red Morocco leather—not the more highly finished European imitation, but almost smooth skin,—neatly tooled with lines and geometrical patterns, with a flap to protect the side edges. The binding is strongly done by hand, but manuscripts intended for study are more often inserted in loose sections in a cover-case. Some years ago Mulai el Ḥasan III. established in Fez a lithographic press on which a number of religious and kindred works have been printed.*

Character.

Otherwise all but manuscripts come from the East. This is an objection in the native mind, as the more running and jumbled hand there employed, though vastly better for despatch, is much less elegant and simple than the purer styles of the Arabians and Moors, which differ little. Another variation is that the Maghribîs write their ķáf thus, ڧ and the Sharķîs or Easterns thus, ق the companion letter fá being ڢ in the West, and ف in the East. As terminals these two, as also nûn ں and yá ى are written without dots, their forms being kept sufficiently distinct to prevent confusion, while the final yá is usually turned back as in Hindustáni, thus ے, and may even be joined to a rá ر a zain ز or a waû و. Other variations are insignificant. In pronunciation the original Arab sounds are as closely adhered to here as anywhere, as will be seen from the table of transliteration which precedes this work.

The dialect varies greatly from tribe to tribe, but in Fez, where the Morocco standard is heard, it is of an astonishingly good quality. At first, like most folk, I was prejudiced against Morocco Arabic, especially as I had heard it chiefly on the coast, but as I travelled

* Most of them are to be found in the British Museum.

into the principal Arabic speaking countries, I became convinced that in Morocco many of the purer forms had been preserved, and that the local idioms and peculiarities were here no greater than much farther east, a view in which I find myself supported by most of those best able to judge. The main fault, if it is one, lies in discarding all but absolutely necessary inflections or forms, and in the contraction of words by eliding most of the shorter vowels.*

Dialect.

A most careful comparison of Morocco Arabic with that of the East has been made by Dr. Talcott Williams,† some of whose observations are worth quotation, as, coming from another country, he was better equipped than the writer for detecting variations. "Besides the slurring of gutturals in the City Arabic," which struck him very forcibly, he notes, "there is also a strong tendency to shorten words, eliminate syllables and clip terminations, which completely changes the vocalization of many words.... Current with this syncopation is a tendency to sharpen and shorten vowel sounds, a tendency apparent in a great number of dialects. There is a constant transformation of the *fatḥa* into *kisra*. This usage is most apparent in the verbal and pronominal forms of the sec. pers. sing., where it leads to the almost universal use of what seems to be the

General Modifications.

* In 250 words comprised in twenty-one passages selected mechanically from a translation of John's Gospel into North Morocco Arabic, made by American missionaries, 95 were found to be those used in the standard Arabic version, 49 were changed in form only, and 106 were replaced by others. Out of 263 words, 197 were found in the ordinary Arabic dictionaries; 35 were from roots found in the dictionaries, but not the exact form; 10 were given in the dictionaries with other meanings, and only 13 were not traceable to any Arabic root.

† *The Spoken Arabic of North Morocco*, in the "Beiträge zur Assyriologie und Semitischen Wissenschaft," Leipzig, vol. iii. 1898, pp. 561—587. To this I have added a critical supplement in the American "Contributions to Comparative Semitic Grammar," which will probably appear in the "Beiträge," vol. iv., pt. 4.

feminine form, but which is in fact nothing but the masculine form with this phonic modification of the final vowel.

"Besides these general modifications, which give the spoken Arabic of Morocco a general system of sound and rhythm widely different to that of the East, it has, like all spoken tongues, those subtle variations due to the accent of a place and to the accepted usage of a class. The Arabic of the official class, as apart from that of the educated, has a peculiar and marked flow of which I can only say that it has the peculiar *cachet* always and everywhere marking a tongue when spoken by those in society, which it is always as easy to recognize as it is impossible to reproduce. It is also always equally easy to note the effect of the reading of the Ḳor'án on those whose official duties bring them in close connection with the mosque. There remain four distinct phases which the ear soon came to note; the ordinary city or trading pronunciation, those of the mountaineer [Jibli], the sedentary Arab, and the Jew, which last comes near being the worst and most obscure *patois* spoken anywhere and dignified by the name of Arabic.

Distinct Phases.

"After the ear has grown familiar with the changes and alterations outlined above, it becomes clear that this dialect, so often spoken of as so corrupt as to be unintelligible, varies very little, as far the vocabulary goes, from the Arabic of the East. I venture the assertion that when its vocabularies come to be prepared, it will be found that not over ten per cent. of the words are different, and of these no small share are older Arabic words than those in use further to the eastward, where the tongue has had a more continuous literary development." All this is perfectly true, and if the visitor is struck by unfamiliar

Comparison with Eastern Arabic.

words, they will more often than not consist of archaic forms none the less pure because they have dropped out of use elsewhere. The deeper, therefore, the visitor's knowledge of classical Arabic, the less apt will he be to consider that of Morocco corrupt. The differences are most apparent to those accustomed to an equally corrupt form in some other country.*

Morocco Arabic.

* Of the students whose attention has been turned to the Maghribi variety of Arabic, Franz von Dombay, an Austrian who held a consular post in Morocco, heads the list. In 1800 he published in Latin a Morocco Arabic grammar and vocabulary, utilizing Arabic types and special blocks. As early as the British occupation of Tangier, a century previous, excellent Arabic type had been used, as, for instance, in the vocabularies furnished by Addison. Dombay's list was freely used without acknowledgment by Hélot in his pocket French and Arabic dictionary, and also without acknowledgment by Marcel in his larger dictionary of Barbary Arabic (1837), which appears to have formed the basis of more than one successor equally careless in acknowledgment. It is noteworthy that this latter employs the Arabic type afterwards so widely used in Algeria and by the Friars in Tangier, one of the most bald and ugly ever invented. The Moors, however, prefer it to all eastern types, or to either of the more open class cast in Beirût. The best adapted to Morocco is that of the great Leipzig edition of the Ḳor'án, or of the French Government press, after which ranks that of the Oxford Arabic Bible.

Foreign Authorities.

Some years later Caussin de Perceval published a *Grammaire Arabe Vulgaire* for Barbary, re-issued in 1880, but its use for Morocco is slight. A small collection of Dialogues was issued in Spanish by Castillo y Olivas for the use of the Spanish troops in 1860, but it is now difficult to meet with. The only serious attempts to form distinctly Moroccan vocabularies have been the excellent *Vocabulario español-arábigo* compiled by the late Fray José Lerchundi, head of the Franciscan Mission in Morocco, which he printed and published in Tangier in 1892, and my own *Morocco Arabic Vocabulary*—in Roman type—which I printed and published in Tangier in 1890.† Fray Lerchundi had twenty years before issued the standard Morocco-Arabic Grammar in Spanish, which unfortunately gives too much prominence to Tetuan and Tangier vulgarisms: this he reprinted in 1891, and an English translation by Mr. J. MacIver MacLeod was published in 1900. The grammar notes prefixed to my vocabulary are the briefest and most concise possible, intended solely as "first aid" to the beginner. I subsequently published a short series of *Morocco Arabic Dialogues* by Miss Carrie Baldwin (now Mrs. M. Lochhead) revised by the late Mr. William

In Morocco, as in most eastern countries, private signatures go for little, functionaries using seals of rude construction which they rub with an inky finger, or merely hold in the smoke of a candle, wetting the paper. Others have recourse to notaries public whose intricate signatures, recognisable only by those acquainted with them, are familiarly known as "beetles," and are always placed in pairs, with that of the ḳáḍi as witness, if concerning a matter of any importance.* In all legal matters these alone are recognised, and as there are few in Morocco above a bribe, the ease with which false documents may be obtained is evident. Moorish notaries are no way behind those of other countries in the intricate wording of what they draw up, or in the use of special phraseology, and in order to insure against fraud it is customary to insert minute if stilted descriptions of those who appear before them with depositions.

Signs Manual.

Ordinary Moorish letters, as well as all books and documents, begin with an ascription of praise to God, generally followed by "The prayers of God be on our lord Mohammed!" or something to that effect, books commencing also with "In the Name of God!" The practice of using the 'alám or superscription, "Praise be to the only God!" was introduced as the watch-word of the Muwaḥḥadi or Unitarian reformers

Letters.

Mackintosh, and at the same time a Spanish edition of the same, *Diálogos español y arabe.* These represent chiefly the Mogador and Tangier dialects, and are very practical.[1] More recently several German scholars have turned their attention to this subject, notably Dr. Auguste Fischer and Herr Luderitz in the Mittheilungen des Orientalischen Seminars (Berlin), vols. i. and ii.

* The legal instrument embodying the concession in the Middle Ages of the monopoly of teaching in England to the priests is confirmed by "a beautiful notarial monogram which must have cost the greater part of a day to draw." (Hist. MSS. Commission, viii., 281-2.)

[1] Tangier, British and Foreign Bible Society's Depôt: London, Quaritch, Picadilly; cloth, 6*s.* and 5*s.* respectively: pocket size, round corners.

along with other innovations in the eleventh century.[1] Instead of placing their seals at the foot, sultans and high officials place theirs at the head, and before perusal the imperial seal is always reverently kissed or placed to the forehead. Letters usually open with some such phrase as "To our (beloved) friend (the wise and learned scribe—or great and glorious governor) Mr. (Pilgrim) Mohammed, son of Ṣáïd the Marrákshi, of Tangier, peace be unto thee, and the mercy of God, and His blessing; and mayst thou continue in and with prosperity as we do, praise to God: after which . . ." letters then proceeding to business in the most pithy and laconic style, unless designed to obtain some favour or to achieve some unexpressed object, when they blossom into poetry and wordiness. They commonly conclude abruptly after a series of sentences all strung together by "ands"—without any punctuation or capital letter—with "and peace: on the . . . of . . . year . . . The signature (or by the hand . . . or order . . .) of So-and-so, the grace of God be upon him; amen." The superscription of the envelope, or the back of the neatly folded and well-sealed paper, usually runs, "To reach, if it please God, the hand of the merchant (or scribe, etc. with epithets as inside) Mr. So-and-so, son of So-and-so (of such and such a place or occupation) at—may GOD forgive (or receive) him."*—

* The following specimens will show to what extent the Moors at times indulge in an elaborate epistolary style.

A BUSINESS LETTER.

"Praise be to the One GOD,
and may GOD bless our lord Mohammed and his (people).

"To him who is (a friend) to us and we to him; and may nothing but GOD become between us and him in this most happy world, to the end (of it), if it please GOD, the witness of his deeds, and that is thee, O fortunate and glorious cavalier, established by the decree of GOD and His justice in His eternity, the wise and learned scribe James, son of the

[1] *Raôḍ el Kartas*, p. 305.

The writing is unpunctuated, all the sentences being connected by "and", though "full stops" are sometimes employed in books.

Materials.

The paper on which Moorish books and letters are written is if possible of good quality, thick and glazed, of quarto size, with an ample margin all round except on the left, and the lines are written perfectly straight, either by folding the paper over instead of ruling, or by pressing it on a board called a misịṭarah or "liner," across which strings are glued where the lines should come. The pens used are cut from sections of the light canes of the country, and the ink, made of charred wool or horn, or vegetable black, is dried by the application of sand, black, if procurable. To prevent too much ink from being taken up, the pot is nearly filled with cotton wool, which acts as a sponge. Some few carry their writing apparatus about with them, using a neat case of horn to contain the whole outfit. Writing is never done on a table, but on the palm of the left hand, or on a few spare sheets forming a pad resting on the left knee, as the writer sits cross-legged, by no means an uncomfortable method, as in camp I have found full often.

merchant, the scribe Edward Meakin; the Peace of GOD be with thee, and the mercy of GOD Most High, and his blessing (shown) in the existence of our lord (the Sulṭán) victorious through GOD: now, after thou hast taken in this, he who salutes thee is the writer, Mr. Slave-of-Peace, son of —— of ——, and I inform thee that we have sent thee a box and a sack to Tetuan with the bearer of this writing, and his pay is 4 pesetas, and we have agreed with him for this amouut, and this is to inform thee of it, if it arrives at the house there, and no harm (has happened) to it, and may GOD bring us together in a near (time) and it *must* be, our friend, and I ask from GOD and from thee, and from thy share of bounty, that thou mayest remember the matter of the sash and plait which are in the house of the pilgrim. May GOD load thee with prosperity. In complete friendship and peace, 15 of First Rabî'a, Year 1307.

"Slave-of-Peace, son of ——, the ——."

AN INVITATION TO DINNER.

"To my gracious master, my respected lord....

"This evening, please GOD, when the king of the army of stars, the sun of the worlds, will turn towards the realm of shades and place his foot in the stirrup of speed, thou art besought to lighten us with the dazzling rays of thy face, rivalled only by the sun.

"Thy arrival, like a spring breeze, will dissipate the dark night of solitude and isolation."

AN INVITATION TO A CAROUSAL.

"To my noble and venerated friend....

"Please GOD, this evening, when the silver circle of the moon fourteen days old will present itself on the surface of the blue sky, spreading all around it rays of love and tenderness, we will hold a gathering in the village of Sidi Kásem that place so full of delight, and all night, until the rising of the day we will indulge in inexpressible pleasures. We do not admit of the delay of the thickness of a hair. Let the force of sails and oars hasten thine arrival, which will be a source of delight for all your friends."

PASSPORT.

"Praise to the One GOD.

"And there is neither strength nor power but in GOD Almighty, the Most High.

"We have granted permission to the bearer,....., to travel in our dominions protected by GOD, and to visit the tribes who are under the control of the Government, but he is not to expose (his life) in parts where they are not under control. We order our governors and obedient tribes to take care of him, and give him assistance, and to receive him with kindness and attention, so that no injury may befall him from any-one: and Peace. Date."

This last is one of those given to favoured travellers by the Sultan. When handed to any of his subjects, it is first reverently applied to his forehead, and then kissed devoutly.

THE 'AÏSÁWÀ STAMPEDE.
(Coming down the Main Street (Siághîn) of Tangier.)

CHAPTER THE NINETEENTH

SAINTS AND SUPERSTITIONS

ANY attempt to number up the saints of Morocco, or to record the multitudinous superstitions in vogue in this country would require the labour of years and the space of volumes. But a few of the most important of both may be briefly touched on, as essential to an understanding of the people and the influences which affect their lives and characters. However foolish many of the tales accepted by the Moors may seem to us, they all have important bearing, and contribute to the moulding of the nation, besides serving to illustrate native life and thought as nothing else can. Many vestiges there are undoubtedly of pre-Mohammedan faiths, perhaps in some instances of that of Christ, but these require special study, and for the moment only those current beliefs which have the support of Islám can be dealt with.

Importance of Superstitions.

To begin with, there are saints, a large and important class, for the most part fools or impostors whose thoughts are supposed to be so entirely engrossed in Heaven that they are considered unaccountable for what they do on Earth. Such are permitted to break all the laws of religion or man with impunity, so great is the veneration in which they are held. However pleasant this may be for lunatics or those who affect to be such, it is sometimes quite another thing for the sober-minded, who do not care to have

Holy Madness.

to submit to every unaccountable fancy on their part, but who none the less have to submit, though actually violent madmen are often confined in chains. But saints are often of important use as peace-makers, and the protection they can afford frequently prevents mischief.*

Signs of Sanctity.

These men are commonly to be met with tramping the country or haunting particular spots, clad in filthy rags, or grotesquely got up in parti-coloured garments, begging or commanding the passers-by to make them presents. Sometimes, on the contrary, they go without a stitch of clothing, as I have met a man in Fez, and have also seen one riding in the train of the late sultan. Wherever such men go they are welcome, and receive all sorts of presents. I have sat at dinner with a governor when one of their number walked in uninvited, and without a word sat down to the dish before us, which we, also without a word, resigned to his exceedingly dirty fingers, and on finishing he silently rose and left.

Hermits.

Occasionally these men retire to a cave and other secluded resorts (khalwah) for meditation, and it is such who obtain the most lasting repute, but they are exceedingly rare. They seem, however, to have been more common in the past. In the *Raôḍ el Ḳarṭas*[1] we read that in 1175 A.C. died "the pivot of his age," Mulai Bu'azzà el Azmeeri, having reached 130 years, of which twenty were spent as a hermit in the mountains above Teenmál in the Atlas, dressed in palmetto, with a ragged jelláb, and a cap in shreds. Of another the same work records,[2] "he fasted and prayed incessantly to combat internal enemies, till only his skeleton remained." He wrote "Love and its desires

* In the Ṭadla district it is sufficient for the great shareef Ben Daûd to send a member of his family with his parasol to ensure his safety on any errand.[3]

[1] p. 383. [2] p. 387. [3] DE FOUCAULD p. 50.

do not exist for me; only breathing agitates me now: I live for death, and my soul lies in my shadow." The popular belief is that such saints, called ḳoṭ'bs or "pivots," are born possessed of the siḳwat er-Rabbánîah or "Divine imitation," but that they are afterwards "filled" by sitting at the feet of another so filled. Those who have founded orders are supposed to have been privileged recipients by relevation from Mohammed of special instructions as to the "way" of life. All such, however, find it equally necessary to preserve or invent a "golden chain" of spiritual ancestry which links them to Mohammed. One of these is given by Rinn,[1] and another is mentioned by d'E. de Constant[2] as being two metres long, in small writing.

"Lives of the Saints."

One really does not know where to begin to recount the stories told of dead saints in Morocco, which vary each time they are told, and which tend to grow in proportion as an interest is shown in them. Even of those whose admirers have formed themselves into brotherhoods or religious orders —ṭáïfah, *pl.* ṭûáïf—records are sadly lacking, and where they are left entirely to the lips of interested parties they are apt to assume astounding proportions. The most important have special seasons for receiving visitors, when their tombs are the centres of fêtes and pilgrimages recruited by criers at similar fêtes elsewhere, who often get parties together and march to the spot with music and flags, attracting additions along the route, and receiving alms to defray expenses from those who cannot go themselves, a feature which un-

CANDLE USED AT SHRINES.

[1] *Marabouts et Khouan.* [2] *Revue des Deux Mondes,* Mch. 1886.

doubtedly accounts for the popularity of such "personally conducted" parties.

Most of the worthies who repose in these shrines are the patron saints of the district or village, or have some particular art or handicraft in their special keeping, or they may be noted for the cure of certain complaints, though Mulai Bû Sháïb, near Azammûr, goes by the name of "The Healer of every Ill," a very convenient reputation, at least for those in charge of his tomb. Women desirous of offspring or of securing their husbands' affection; men in search of treasure; all who have need of some worldly advantage, know where to go with their prayers, if only to some old gun or tree-stump,* rather than direct to Him of whom they are so fond of declaring that "He hath no partner," which they practically make their saints to be.

Patron Saints.

The orders or ṭaïfahs of which these saints are the patrons are for the most part perpetuations of the groups of disciples who surrounded them in their lifetime, presided over after their death by mizwár or naḳib who is often a descendant of the founder, or who has been appointed by his predecessor. The keepers of the zawîahs or shrines are called muḳaddams, and the local heads of the order, sheïkhs.† The idea of joining an order seems to be to secure the saint's good offices in getting into Paradise, at the threshold of which some believe he will meet them, and many to prevent disappointment join several orders,

Religious Orders.

* The tomb of an English woman at Mogador being mistaken for that of a saint, became so much in vogue among country pilgrims that the authorities asked her friends to cover it up, which they did, but to no purpose, for the devotees picked off the cement and chipped the marble, chiefly for the women to make powder wherewith to dust their faces and make themselves fair.[1]

† The word darwîsh—"poor man"—is employed in Morocco in this sense only, not in that of its Turkish form, dervîsh, in the East.

[1] Richardson, p. 104.

though the membership of some, as the Tijánîyah, is conditional on no other order being entered.

Candidates have only to appear before the khalîfa or the sheïkh of the local zawîah—of which each saint of note has many about the country,—with the indispensable present, requesting to be taught the peculiar wärd or motto, usually a verse from the Ḳor'án, or some kindred pious expression—and the dhikr or pass-word—sometimes of peculiar pronunciation or intonation. By the repetition of this dhikr, first slowly, then at an increasing pace, the members work themselves up into a state of religious frenzy held to be highly meritorious. None are refused. Members of the orders are called ikhwán or brethren, and some admit sisters (khawátát).* He who habitually performs the rites of his order becomes looked on as a murábaṭ (from rabaṭa, "he bound"), a word from the plural of which, comes Murábṭîn, the name of one of the Morocco dynasties, corrupted by foreigners into "Almoravides." †

Admission.

In addition to these repetitions, or as their presumed result, some of the orders give way to the most extraordinary practices, and in their frenzy perform deeds which would seem impossible at other times. Foremost among such are the 'Aïsáwà,‡ followers of M'hammed bin 'Aïsà of Mequinez,§ whose annual orgies take place on Mohammed's birthday, when the devotees assembled at his shrine or elsewhere devour sheep and other animals crossing the path of their ra-

The 'Aïsáwà.

* As the 'Aïsáwà, Darḳáwà, etc., but not the more serious and soit-disant spiritual orders,—Sûfîyah.

† From whom again the name of the coin "Maravedi."

‡ *Sing.* 'Aïsáwî.

§ Sidi Mohammed ben 'Aïsà, who lived two centuries ago, in the time of Mulái Ismá'îl, was a poor man who during prayer in Mequinez had money left miraculously at his house, while his wife drew gold coins from the well, so in a vision he was ordered to found a brotherhood.

ving dance, tearing them limb from limb while yet alive, and with savage yells thrusting bleeding portions into their mouths. From a low roof by their side I have watched the whole thing, and as I write the sound of the music and firing with which their procession is accompanied falls on my ears, recalling the scenes of other years on this day, which I do not move from my seat to re-witness. The 'Aïsáwà are said to hate black clothes, and to have sworn to murder their wearers, but in their calmer moments they have no objection to becoming their servants. In other parts of North Africa, over which this order is widely spread, its members eat red-hot charcoal, glass, thorns, etc., and from their ranks are recruited the serpent charmers, for they are said to be able to handle every venomous thing.

Explanations.

To account for this the story says that M'hammed bin 'Aïsà, when out in the country with his disciples * who, having nothing to eat, could not restrain their appetites, gave them permission to devour what they could, with the result that they fell upon every living thing in their way, in commemoration or expiation of which this yearly stampede is held, some holding also that the cries emitted represent those of the animals eaten. Another story is that one day he summoned his hundred disciples to meet their death at his hands, each being in turn invited to enter a house at the door of which he stood with a blood-smeared knife, having in reality killed a sheep inside, but no men. Thirty-nine Moors and a Jew who professed Islám had the courage to enter, and the descendants of those who were afraid to do so now eat anything they can at least one day in the year, while those who passed in have received their reward.

* These disciples had been gathered by the distribution of the gold miraculously provided.

The blood-thirsty Mulai Ismá'îl, fearing the growing power of M'hammed bin 'Aïsà, banished him to where his ḳûbbah now stands, near a spring called forth by a blow from his staff. Then the saint offered to buy up Mequinez itself, and contrary to the sultan's expectations, paid the price demanded, so as a ransom it was agreed that from the 12th to the 19th of Safar only the followers Sidi M'ḥammed bin 'Aïsà should be allowed in the streets, to avoid which embargo all its inhabitants joined his order. On the death of the saint, Mulai Ismá'îl is said to have prepared a pit full of snakes and other venomous creatures as a test of his true followers, commanding the 'Aïsáwà to enter it and eat therein food prepared with poisons. All hung back till Lallah Khamîsah, the wife of one of them, jumped in, when they all followed. It is to celebrate this event and their deliverance from the ordeal, say some, that each year they hold their ghastly orgies.[1]

Treatment of the Founder.

Akin to the 'Aïsáwà are the followers of Sidî 'Alî bel Ḥamdûsh, whose white ḳûbbah or shrine peeps out from the hill of Zarhôn towards Mequinez, and after whom they are called Ḥamádshà.* This order was instituted at a later date, and their special feast is also a few days later than that of the 'Aïsáwà: their forte consists in catching stones and cannon-balls upon their heads, or in belabouring their craniums with iron-studded sticks, while many play on the ginbrî, ṭarîjah, ghaïṭah and t'bil.[2] During the self-inflicted blows (the result of which is minimized by practice) they repeat, "Who pardoned our past sins will pardon those of the future." †

The Hamádshà.

* *Sing.* Hamdûshî.

† A good account of the Ḥamádshà performance is given in *the Times of Morocco*, No. 62, from Capt. Hood's account of the British Embassy to Mequinez in 1861.

The following graphic description of a Ḥamdûshî séance is from

[1] De Neveu, pp. 68—86. [2] See pp. 202 etc.

Acrobats and Musicians.

The patron saint of acrobats is Sidî Ḥamed û Mûsà of Sûs, nephew of Mulai Abd es-Slám bin Masheesh, who lived about the year 1200. The performances of his followers do not partake of the nature of those described, although by repeating their orgies for money the 'Aïsáwà, Ḥamádshà and kindred orders do undoubtedly make a living.* These men are well-known in the circuses of Europe and America, forming part of almost every show of import-

the pen of Mr. Geo. C. Reed:—"Two lines of men and boys are drawn up, one facing the other, and near by are musicians with drums and discordant pipes. The musicians begin to play, slowly at first, and the two lines jump up and down, backward and forward, to the time of the music, and as directed by three or four leaders between the lines. Faster and faster beat the drums; higher, harder, and wilder grows the dance, and louder and louder the shouts, until the men in the middle are in a frenzy. One dances about brandishing four of the broad-bladed axes which are the special emblems of this sect. Two of these axes have double blades about six inches in breadth, another has a single blade a little larger, while the fourth is a huge instrument more than a foot from point to point. He lays them on the ground, and bowing low, calls out some invocation, then is up again and round about in the open space between the lines. The dancers shout, he yells, and grasping the axes firmly in both hands, raises his arms high above his head and leaps into the air. As he alights, he brings the blades down full upon his head. He staggers, howls, jumps higher and chops harder, and again and again, until his head, face and shoulders are covered with blood. And now another one begins the head chopping. The drums beat furiously, the pipes shriek, and the frenzied dance becomes wilder. One man rushes out, seizes an earthen water jar, dashing it upon the top of his head, smashes it and hurls the fragments high in the air. Another is now mopping his head on the ground to wipe off the flowing blood, and a third seizes a big cannon-ball, puts it on his bleeding head, and balancing it there, dances about from side to side. Two others lock arms and run about wildly, then, breaking away, rush to the edge of the surrounding crowd and throw themselves flat on the ground at our very feet, with their faces in a large basket of oranges. They lie there a moment, then each seizes an orange in his mouth and away they go."

* A valuable paper on the Sidi Ḥamed û Mûsà acrobats was contributed by Herr Quedenfeldt to the *Zeitschrift für Ethnologie* of Berlin, vol. xxi., (1889), pp. 572—586. (B. Museum, PP. 3863 b.) It contains much interesting and original information.

ance.* Musicians are considered under the especial protection of Mulai Bushṭa of Fishtàla, at whose shrines they are recommended to pass at least a night in practice, while the sellers of sweets by the wayside call on Mulai Idrees in a manner which, in the words of an able writer, would lead one to "imagine that the founder of the first Moorish dynasty commenced life as something in the retail confectionery line."

But no saint of Moorish birth is so much in repute in this country as the Persian 'Abd el Ḳáder of G͟haïlán, buried in Bag͟hdád in the twelfth century,—whose surname has become corrupted into Jiláni and Jellálli—on whom the beggars and wayfarers call. It is said that once he visited Morocco, and inhabited a cave in Jebel Kôrt, in the G͟harb, which may perhaps account for the singular favour in which he is held here. Many Moors who have accomplished the Mekka pilgrimage find their way across to Bag͟hdád to visit his tomb, where I found a goodly number of them living in the rooms surrounding the courtyard till they should have collected sufficient to warrant moving farther, and several times on the Syrian desert I encountered groups of them on foot, with whom it was a pleasure to converse in the familiar dialect, seeing their faces light up when I referred to their homes, most of which I knew. On my return to Morocco that visit eclipsed all else I had seen or done on my travels, and was a never failing subject of enquiry. The ṭaïfah which Mulai 'Abd el Ḳáder founded eight hundred years ago, is renowned among all the Mohammedan sects,* the members being known in the East as Ḳádirîyah, and

Mulai 'Abd el Kader.

* The translation of a most important Arabic document, giving the "spiritual genealogy of this order, its traditions, its forms, a catechism thereon, the descent of its founder, and a patent appointing a muḳaddam," is given by M. Mercier in the *Recueil de la Société Archéol. de Constantine*," vol. 13, (1869) p. 409, etc. (Brit. Mus. Ac. 5349.)

in the West as Jellállà, with some distinctions, one of which is that the former do not pray so loudly: to them the sultan of Turkey is said to belong.*

Mulai 'Abd el Ḳáder is described as the sulṭán es-Sáliḥîn—"Emperor of Saints"—and on account of his virtues he is considered a ghaûth or "helper," one who bears three-fourths of the 300,000 misfortunes which descend each year in the month of Safar, half of the remainder being borne by twenty holy men called áḳṭáb (*pl.* of ḳoṭ'b), and the final eighth shared by ordinary mortals. The ghaûths who are overwhelmed with this burden do not die, but pass into an abode between the third and fourth heavens, where they are attainable by prayers recommended by small offerings to their followers on earth. †

Qualifications.

Besides the widely spread orders depending on individual saints like these, there are the Darḳáwà, of whom

* A full account of the ritual of this order would be very long and uninteresting, but some particulars may be mentioned. The members of the brotherhood are instructed to repeat the confession, "There is no god but GOD," 165 times after each of the five prayers of the day; "May GOD pardon me" 100 times; and "O GOD, give the blessing to our lord and master Mohammed, in quantity ten thousand times greater than the atoms of the air" 100 times.

In praying they must sit cross-legged on the floor, the right hand open, palm upwards, on the right knee, the left hand lying on another part of the left leg. In this position the worshipper enunciates calmly and slowly the Name of GOD, until all thoughts of persons, things, time, and money—are got rid of. This will require from 1000 to 2000 repetitions, in which special stress must be laid on the last syllable—"Allah-*u*." Then, turning the head from left to right, he repeats "Allah-*a*" until good thoughts come. Finally, bowing the head, and letting go all good thoughts, he says "Allah-*i*" until but one thought absorbs the mind—GOD.

† It has been suggested, not without some show of reason, that the origin of the Ḳádirîyah may have been the effort to repel the first and second Crusades, which took place during the founder's life-time. The order was probably Ṣûfi or mystic in its original conception.[1]

[1] See LOUIS RINN'S *Marabouts et Khouan.*

TOMB OF MULAI 'ABD EL KADER EL JELLALLI, AT BAGHDAD.
(The domes are resplendent with blue, green and white tiles, and are crowded with pigeons.)

Photograph by Colonel Mockler.

there are several branches in Morocco. The members of this order are chiefly beggars who tramp about with staves in their hands, and giant rosaries round their necks, some wearing green turbans. Their chief saints are Mulai el 'Arbi ed-Darḳáwi, buried at Bû Briḥ in the mountains of the Beni Zerwál near Fez, and Sidi Mohammed bin el 'Arbi el 'Alawi of M'daghra, N.E. of Tafîlált. The Darḳáwi wărd, as written for me by one of their sheïkhs, is "O GOD, may prayers and peace be on our Lord Mohammed; and upon his family and friends be peace increasing."* The particular Darḳáwi teachings lay special stress upon the first half of the Mohammedan creed—the unity of GOD—which alone they recite aloud, considering the part about Mohammed, which they repeat mentally, to be less important, though essential. Only GOD, they say, should receive public praise.

The Darḳáwà Order.

According to Captain de Neveu, [1] the Darḳáwà acknowledge GOD alone as their sovereign, opposing every man ruling over his fellows, hating all non-Muslims; inhabiting towns only from necessity; sleeping, eating and speaking as little as possible; never listening to slander; travelling bare-foot in desert places and blindly following their leader when required for a religious war. The Moorish sultans are approved by them as shareefs, not as ordinary rulers. Novices are received only by a general assembly, swearing certain oaths. This order is distinguished from most others by an element of secrecy.

Peculiarities.

M. Isaac Darmon,† quoting a work called El Mashîshah,

* To which another added further blessings on Mohammed and the names of his various relatives.

† *Etude sur la secte .... dite les Darkawa .... compte rendu de l'Ass. fr. pour l'Avancement des Sciences*, Congres d'Oran, 1888, p. 339. Also Walsim-Esterhazy, *Domination turque .... en Alger*, p. 187.

[1] p. 155.

attributes the foundation of this order to Mulai El 'Arbi ben Ahamed es-Shareef es-Shadîli ed-Darḳáwi, who was born in Fez about 1737, being brought up in the village of Darka among the Beni Zerwál. In 1768 he became the disciple of 'Ali el Jemel ben 'Omrán es-Shareef el Fási,* who could trace his spiritual ancestry back to Mohammed and Gabriel. This Mulai el 'Arbi was a member of the Shadelîyah order,† a branch of the Ḳádirîyah, of which therefore the Darḳáwà are an offshoot. He died near Fez about 1815, and his tomb at Bû Briḥ is marked by an important shrine, where a festival is held each 13th of September (O.S.)‡

History.

Less numerous in Morocco is the order of the Tijánîyah, founded at 'Aïn Máḍi, near Taghwát in Algeria, by Ahmad et-Tijáni, a learned and travelled teacher who had acquired a great reputation for sanctity. Their prescribed dhikr is to repeat one hundred times each: "GOD is pitiful!" "May GOD pardon me!" "There is no god but GOD!" and "O GOD, give Thy graces and accord Thy salvation to our lord Mohammed, who has opened that which was shut and closed that which preceded, and who causes the truth to triumph by the truth. Give also unto his family all the merit due unto them!" Another prayer about ten times as

The Tijánîyah.

* Buried at the Rumîla in Fez. He taught respect to Christians and Jews, and kindness to animals.

† Founded by Si Aḥsan 'Ali es-Shadîli, born in Morocco in 1175, whose master was a student of Abu Median, the friend and disciple of Mulai 'Abd el Ḳáder, spread his order in the Maghrib and Spain. Es-Shadîli died on his way to Mekka at Homaïthara, near Suakim, where his imposing shrine has ever since attracted pilgrims.[1]

‡ In 1805 serious trouble was caused in Algeria by the Turkish Bey's having put to death a member of this brotherhood, whereupon the Bey attempted to secure their sheikh, who fled, and the natives rose against the Turks—those of Tlemçen in vain demanding the protection of Mulai Sulaïmán of Morocco.[2]

[1] See *Revue des deux Mondes*, vol. 74, March 1886. [2] Ez-ZAÏÁNÎ, p. 185.

long as this last one must be repeated twelve times. The members are to be recognized by the division of their rosaries into six sections by pieces of red wool. It is one of the strictest and most earnest orders. Their centre is at the oasis of Bû Semghûn in Southern Algeria.*

The order most recently formed in Morocco is that of the Shingîaṭà, the founder of which, Sidi Má' ul 'Aïni es-Shingîaṭi, is already an old man, famous for his writings and his sanctity. Mulai el Ḥasan III. and his chamberlain "Ba Ahmad" both belonged to his order, and when visiting Marrákesh, where a fine zawîah has been erected, Má' ul 'Aïni was received with almost regal honours, and was sent away loaded with presents. His home, Shingeeṭ, of which his brother Mohammed bil Musṭafà bin Todl bin Mámeen is sheïkh, lies in the extreme south-west of the Empire, towards Timbuctoo. He has made a study of the other brotherhoods, the result of which he has embodied in an important volume, *Na'tu 'l Badáïah wa Muntaha 'l Ghâïah.*

Shingîati Order.

Another notable religious following, though not exactly an order, was formed by Mulai Ismá'îl in giving his imported black troops Moḥammed ibn Ismá'îl el Bokhári† to be their patron, after whom they are known as Bokháris. This widely venerated saint was the author of the first collection of seven thousand of Mohammed's traditional sayings, known as the Jam'a es-Ṣaḥḥeeḥ—the "Reliable Collection,"—which is almost as much revered as the Ḳor'án itself, and is read through every year by the sultan and the

The Bokhárîs.

* The Senûsîyah, whose centre is at the forbidden Jerbûb, south of Tripoli, and who have given the French so much trouble by their agitation against foreign rulers, have not made themselves felt in Morocco, where their special teaching has no *raison d'être*, their founder was educated in Fez.

† He died in 870 A. C. or 256 A. H., near Samarkand, where I was informed that his tomb is still to be seen at a distance of some parasangs, but time did not permit me to visit it when there.

'ulamá. On the march a copy precedes the "black guard" on a richly caparisoned horse, and at night it is carried respectfully into the sultan's quarters.*

Mulai 'Abd es-Salám.

Among the chief saints of Northern Morocco is Mulai 'Abd es-Salám bin Masheesh, who was born in the twelfth century, while Mulai 'Abd el Ḳáder was at Kôrt, according to tradition, and was sent for by that saint, who kissed the child and declared that he should be his successor.† Subsequently, while at school, he found himself enabled to communicate with him of Bag͟hdád—to which in the meanwhile the saint had returned—by moving his foot, and later gave remarkable proof of his saintship by commanding the intervening hills to bow, that, to determine a dispute about the hour of prayer, a glimpse might be had of the flag on the mosque at Mekka. His tomb is in the mountains of the Beni 'Arôs, south of Tetuan, to which in the middle of Sh'abán great crowds repair, as also at the Great Feast, on the day when the pilgrims at Mekka go to 'Arafát.[1] Hay believed it to have been the site of a pagan temple,[2] which is very probable.

Mulai Bûselhám.

On the coast to the south of Laraiche, in the tribe of Aôlád Miṣbaḥ, is the famous shrine of Mulai Bûselhám, close to the mouth of a lagoon up which the sea is said to have come at his bidding, to show his superiority over his companion, Sidi 'Abd el Jaleel et-Tîjár, whose feat consisted in catching a fish on each hair of his hand, and whose ḳûbbah stands across the stream. From this point Mulai Bûselhám is said to have been able to maintain a conversation

* The great work of El Bok͟hári has been published both at Leipzig and Bûlaḳ in three folio volumes.

† His genealogy is given in *The Moorish Empire*, facing p. 116.

[1] See p. 256. [2] p. 132.

with Mulai 'Abd es-Salám, sixty odd miles away. His real name was 'Abu Sa'ïd el Miṣri or "Egyptian." He and his companion lived as hermits in a cave on Jebel Bûhalál above Wazzán in the time of the founder of the present glories of the Wazzán family, Mulai 'Abd Alláh Shareef (died 1675 A.C.), who did not yet know himself to be a ḳoṭ'b, but was sent by his teacher to supersede them in their cave.

Lallah Maïmônah Tagonaût.

The great time at the tomb of Mulai Bûselhám (said also to be that of Alexander the Great!) is his dha'af in the spring, when the devotees on their way thither from the north halt for the last night about thirty miles inland, at the shrine of Lallah Maïmônah Tagonáût. This "beautiful and pious" damsel was so attracted to Mulai Bûselhám that she prayed to be made a hideous negress in order to be free to serve him, which was granted, though at night her natural form returned. The motto of her order is "God knows Maïmônah, and Maïmônah knows God."* Near the mouth of the Wád Sûs is the shrine of another female saint, Umma Ta'zzah Manṣûr, whose protection from all perils of the sea is sought from far and near.[1]

The Wazzán Shareefs.

Sidi Mohammed bin Yimlaḥ, ancestor of the Wazzán family, having asked in marriage the daughter of his uncle, Mulai 'Abd es-Salám, she would not consent to the match unless the whole of creation went surety—dámin—for their provision, which it did, whence the Wazzán shareefs get their title of Dár Damánah, "House of Surety." Two of their descendants, Tayyib and T'hámî, sons of Sidi Mohammed bin 'Abd Allah es-Shareef, were the founders

* In the parish church of Wissant, Pas de Calais, I was struck by the sight of a statue representing a bearded woman. Being a nun, she had prayed for a beard to prevent the attention of the local great man, and was canonized as St. Wilgeforte.

[1] Bû'l Moghdad, Rev. Mar. et Col., May 1861, p. 493.

of the extensive orders of Tayyibeeïn and Tuhámah, which are popular throughout Algeria, especially in Constantine and at Dár Záwia, near Nedrôma.* Of the former order the shareefs of Wazzán are the hereditary

A NORTHERN MOROCCO VILLAGE.
(Swáni, near Tangier.)
Photograph by Dr. Robert Brown.

mizwárs: it is especially strong in the Tûát Oasis, where its members are distinguished by one of their rosary beads being of coloured stone, or by a ring of brass on the rosary. The order was founded in 1678 to support the throne, the sultan of that date, Mulai Ismá'ïl the Blood-thirsty, enhancing the prestige of his relative for this purpose.

* On this account Marshal Bugeaud endeavoured in 1843 to obtain their favour, through the Consul-General at Tangier, but his presents were refused.[1] Subsequently, however, when the British refused protection to the Wazzán Shareef, Háj 'Abd es-Salám, it was joyfully afforded by the French, who educated his two sons by his English wife.

[1] De Neveu, *Les Khouans*, p. 51.

Other important shrines of Northern Morocco, each with its group of disciples and a living representative, are those of Sidi Ben Dáûd of Bu Ja'd near Ṭadla, a powerful house in constant request for arbitration between the Berber tribes of the district. Not far off, at Fishtála, lie the remains of Mulai Bûshtá el Khammár, referred to as one of the disciples of Mulai 'Abd es-Salám. These remains boast two tombs, the "great" at Fishtála and the "less" at Ṣaghîra, the contentions of rival claimants being satisfied by the admission that as he was so holy a man, he may be in both. He left no descendants: hence, doubtless, the importance of his remains. In life he was a water-carrier.

Double-Tombed Saints.

Another double-tombed worthy in the Gharb is Sidi Ḳassem, round whose place of burial quite a town existed two hundred years ago,[1] in which Europeans were not allowed, though now but a village remains, with a great autumn feast. Sidi Ḳassem was a highwayman, who, having entered the hut of a dying saint whom he went to rob, caught his spirit and changed his business to such effect that when he died there was a fight for the possession of his body, the unsuccessful party eventually stealing it from the tomb of their rivals, who to their surprise found it still there! The two tombs are known as Mûl' Aḥarôsh and Mûl' el Ḥeri.

A Remarkable Conversion.

A story interesting in this connection is related by Prado in his History of Ceuta. The Moors having landed by night and carried off to Tetuan an image of the Saviour on the Cross, it was recovered by a clever ruse conceived by a converted Moor. It was believed that in the hills above Ceuta there was an unmarked grave of a great saint, and the convert having gone out by night and buried part of a

Mediæval Reprisals.

[1] Braithwaite.

skeleton, left the ground as though he had just dug up the remainder. Returning to Ceuta he announced that he had got the bones of the saint, and these the daring thieves were glad enough to ransom with the crucifix and a considerable payment.

Sidi 'Omar el Ḥádi, who lies on a mountain close to Ḳariat ben 'Oda, has the unique distinction of having lived a bachelor. His festival falls in August.

Morocco's Great Saints.

Mulai Idrees the elder, buried at Zahôn, and Mulai Idrees the younger, buried in Fez, respectively the great missionary of Islám in Morocco, and the founder of the kingdom, both enjoy unrivalled honours, and their tombs are perhaps the oldest in the Empire that are well authenticated. Southward, in Tafîlált, lies Mulai 'Ali es-Shareef of Yanbo'a, the ancestor of many venerated saints whose tombs are near. One of these Tafîlált worthies is credited with having stopped a fight by transporting the wall on which he was seated between the combatants. His followers climb palms unclothed, declaring that if they are pricked the tree will bear no fruit.[1]

Mulai Ya'kûb.

In the hills above Fez are the sulphurous springs of Mulai Ya'ḳûb, kept boiling, according to some, by his giant slave-woman underground, though others aver that his daughter, Lallah Shafîah, having been buried alive in the shrine on the top of the hill, has something to do with it. Crowds repair from all parts of Morocco with the best results, but to avoid extremes of temperature the patients must keep repeating "Cold and hot, my lord Jacob; cold and hot!" The saint himself is said to have been buried in Jebel Amáwi in Syria.

Marrákesh is often described by no other name than "The Seven Men"—Es-seba'tu Rijál—because in the

[1] Erckmann.

special care of that number of saints, the chief of whom is that redoubtable worthy Sidi bel 'Abbás, whom some have endeavoured to identify with St. Augustine.* Of him it is related that while living in Ceuta he foretold that the Christians would possess it, and went through the form of selling it to a Jew for the price of a loaf of bread, with which he set off for Marrákesh, where he arrived naked, having bestowed his clothes on the poor by the way. But Marrákesh being already stocked with saints, he showed them there was still room for him by floating a rose on the brimming bowl of water which the resident saints had sent him as an intimation of this fact.[1] Others say that he showed his power by overturning a bowl of milk without spilling a drop. But a written charge having been brought against him before the ámeer, of betraying the girls who came for his blessing, he caused the accusation to be changed into praise by merely receiving the closed letter from the hand of the ámeer and returning it. It has been alleged that a French steamer was once saved by a Moor's throwing over his dagger in the name of Sidi bel 'Abbás, whereupon the sea calmed, and the dagger was discovered in the alms-box of the saint at Marrákesh.[2] He is also the patron of trade, and his zawîah occupies quite a district by itself, with its mosque and ḳûbbahs, college and sick-house, streets of sanctuary and inalienable property, although his original settlement was on the picturesque crag of Gîlîz, outside the town.

Sidi bel 'Abbás.

* The origin of this idea is apparently a statement made by Gramaye in his *Africæ Illustratæ*, (1622) that a certain saint at Tagaost in Sûs, being thought to be an Augustine monk, Thaddeus—otherwise Matthew—or Bartholomew of the Canaries, in 1525 the Augustinians of Teneriffe sent a deputation to make enquiry, but could not obtain the books the saint was said to keep there. He was believed to have worked miracles, and to have put an end to a plague. Those who would propitiate him must be kind to Christians.

[1] Harris. [2] Erckmann.

"Another of the lustrious seven, the Imám es-Swahîli, assured his colleagues that as long as he remained in the city, hunger would be kept out. Annoyed at what they deemed his presumption, they hunted him from the place; and a pretty sanctuary in the space—half cemetery, half washing-ground—outside the Rubb Gate, attests the melancholy fact that he never re-entered Marrákesh; hence the frequent famines."[1] After Sidi bel 'Abbás the Marrákshîs pay respect to Mulai Ibráhîm, the lovely situation of whose shrine on a hill above the Ghegháyah valley on the slopes of the Atlas, just a day's ride from the city, doubtless helps to make it popular. A day beyond, at the head of the Aït Mîzán valley, just at the foot of Tizi-n-Tagharat (often called "Miltsin"), is the insignificant but highly venerated shrine of Sidi Shimhárôsh (a very Hebrew sounding name), said to have been the king of the Jinns.

The "City of Seven Men."

Many of those who have obtained a great reputation for sanctity have started as hereditary "nobles" or shareefs (*pl.* shorfá) or descendants of Mohammed, of whom there are large numbers in Morocco. So highly are these esteemed, that in questions of rivalry he who is not a shareef has little chance against him who is one. Even the relief of vituperation so much in favour must be restrained in quarrelling with shareefs, since all the choicest anathemas are of an ancestral reflective character, and would in that case arrive at Mohammed himself. The pedigrees of all the leading families are known, but the vast majority claiming this rank have nothing whatever to show for it. The oldest established family is that of the 'Dreeseeïn, founded by Mulai Idrees, one of the chief branches of which is that of Wazzán. Second to them is the 'Aláwi family, intro-

Shareefs or Nobles.

[1] JOHNSTONE, *Moorish Lotos Leaves.*

duced into Tafîlált from Yanbo'a in Arabia, three hundred years ago; besides which, Arabian shareefs have from time to time been induced to settle in the Dra'a and other parts, on account of the blessings they are supposed to bring, by which means the stock is replenished, and the glory of nobility revived. The reigning dynasty is of this Tafîlált or Fîláli line, descended from the Mulai 'Ali es-Shareef from whom it derives its name of 'Aláwi, and to whose arrival with the returning pilgrims from Mekka was ascribed so great an increase of the date crop that his power became supreme. The same phenomenon, however, had been observed when other shareefs had been brought, and Mouëtte relates the adventures of a foreign captive who escaped from Tripoli in the disguise of a saint, and on reaching Tafîlált had the greatest honour paid him for the excellent crop of dates secured by his presence!

The Aláwî Family.

Among the curious beliefs of the Moors may be mentioned the expectation of the Imám el Mahdi ("Directed Leader"), an expectation shared with all the Mohammedan world, which in centuries past has afforded excuse for as many impostors in Morocco as anywhere, and from time to time there are fresh ones rumoured. Some expect the Mûl' es-Sá'ah—"Lord of the Hour,"—called, like their prophet, Mohammed bin 'Abd Allah, to bring the whole World to the feet of the latter: some opine that the Mahdi will arise at Massa in Sûs, joining with Christ and Elijah (Iliás) to spread what they consider to be the truth, after which the end of the World will come; but they all look for the second coming of Christ. Massa is already celebrated in Morocco as the landing-place of Jonah, for does not one of the jaws of the fish lie yet on the shore?

The Expected Mahdi.

But the attributes of sanctity in Morocco are by no means

confined to human beings, for certain rocks, trees, guns, etc., obtain their share of veneration, and, if one may say it, of sacrifice and offerings, though these are gathered by men in charge. It is not uncommon in the country to see one of these revered objects covered with bits of rag torn from the garments of those who have come there to pray; a sort of reminder. Near Saffi is a giant wild olive tree (zibbûj) known as Lallah Zibbûjah, held in great esteem. Oaths may be sworn on cannon. Sometimes even a horse has been canonized, as one which saved the life of Mulai Ismá'il, and was maintained on camels' milk and kesk'soo.[1] Storks, swallows, crows and nightingales—all share a sort of sanctity which at least secures immunity from wholesale destruction.

Inanimate Saints.

With these superstitions are intimately mingled beliefs in 'afreets, jinns and ghools, for all of which Mohammedans have the sanction of the Kor'án. The belief in the constant presence of angels (malákût) is fundamental in their religion, for they are taught that all through life a guardian angel stands on either hand, the office of the one on the right being to record one's good deeds, and to prevent the one on the left, whose office it is to record one's bad deeds, from doing so till evening, that before then their protégé may have an opportunity of wiping them out by the due performance of prayers and alms-giving. These angels are known as the "illustrious writers"—kátibeen kirámeen—and are changed every day. After death the conscience-account is made up at the grave-side by the inquisitor angels, Munkir and Nákir, with results which cause many to turn in their graves.

The Spirit World.

In order to protect themselves from the attacks of evil spirits who are supposed to inhabit all empty or

[1] PELLOW, p. 253, orig.

uncanny places—as well as the world-encircling mountains of Ḳáf, where they keep company with Gog (Yájûjah), Magog (Májûjah) and Anti-Christ (Maseeḥ ed-dujjál), —careful persons mutter as they enter such places, "In the Name of GOD, the Pitying, the Pitiful," on hearing which the spirits move 300 years' journey off. They are said to mount on one another's backs till they reach Heaven, that they may hear what the angels say, falling stars being missiles hurled at them by GOD to make then desist. Sometimes they are called Iblálîs, plural of Iblees, another name for Shaïṭán their chief, but there are also believing Muslim jinns, and some of them are Jews and Christians. The most powerful for evil are said to be Shaïṭán Mareed.

Exorcisms.

An Arab proverb says "At nightfall hide your children, for then the devils are out." In this belief, it is a common custom to place dishes of food in likely places at dusk to propitiate the hungry "jinn", just as is sometimes done when there is a suspicion that the ghosts of departed relatives are wandering supperless. In any case it is very seldom the plate is found unemptied in the morning! In some parts such offerings are put outside at night beside fountains and wells to feed the devils and keep them away from the houses, and some keep a piece of bread under their mattresses with a similar idea, while meal and oil are sometimes thrown into the corners of new houses before occupation to propitiate the jinns, or knives and daggers are placed under the pillows of the sick in order to prevent their approach. All these and many other customs which might be cited are much more common among women than men, but their great upholders are the female slaves, who doubtless bring many of them from their native lands.

Hungry Devils.

There is no telling in what shapes these jinns (good or

bad) and 'afreets (bad) may appear, but it is usually in the form of some animal the idea of which held by Mohammedans as agreeable to the character of the spirit possessing it: g͟hools, on the other hand, whose pastime it is to feed on the dead in grave-yards, and on the living too, if they can catch them, are represented as appearing in all sorts of suitable monstrous shapes.* The cloven hoof is commonly attributed to beings of this class.

"Genii" and "Ghouls."

The power of the "evil eye"—'aïn el ḳabeeḥ—is firmly believed in by all, the most effectual charm against it being the out-stretched palm, which is in consequence rudely depicted on the doors of the Jews, who share this and other superstitious beliefs, while some, on the number five being mentioned, will exclaim "îadak!"—"thy hand!"—by way of precaution. If five people happen to be together they are described as "four and one." No living thing must be stroked or patted with the palm, and if a living thing is to be admired, an ascription of honour to God must be introduced.

The "Evil Eye."

Among minor superstitions the number seven is considered unlucky (sa'ïbah), and persons bargaining will often endeavour to obtain a little more or give less, on the pretext of not agreeing to seven exactly. Tuesdays are held to be unlucky, but Mondays, Thursdays and Saturdays are considered propitious for the beginning of a journey, though new clothes should not be donned on Tuesdays, Saturdays or Sundays. To break a dish in anger with a wife is expected to bring about dire results, and many other actions, such as blowing food to cool it, blowing a light out,† spitting

Luck.

* Some are believed to appear at sunset in the smoke of alum in an incense-burner.

† The Moors therefore extinguish their candles by a quick vertical pass of the hand.

in the fire, or brushing the teeth horizontally, are considered unlucky.

Charms.

Not only as a protection against the subtle malign influence to which is attributed every form of evil, but also as a means of cure from sickness, ḥajabs (charms) or "writings" of pious sentences are in great request, and many ṭálebs or scribes make a living by prescribing them, often having a book from which to copy the correct expressions for every case. Pieces of cane filled with earth from the tombs of saints, or crushed scorpions, are also hung round the neck by way of ḥajab. These charms are usually sewn up in little leather pockets to be worn by man or beast round the neck or arm. Sometimes "writings" are prepared to act as spells, and one writer records having seen a bundle of these tied to the feet of pigeons and fowls to keep them moving, that the mind of the one against whom the spells were directed might be kept in a state of constant ferment.

SILVER CHARM CASE.

Fortune-Telling.

In a land with so many willing beliefs it is surprising that still more is not made out of popular credulity than is the case. Fortune-telling (ḍarbat el fál),* for instance, though freely practised, does not seem to be in general demand, perhaps from fear of too intimate relations with the demons who are believed to possess the bodies of many. There are, however, by the Wád Sijerah, near Mequinez, two tribes who are addicted to the practice, the Aôlád Naṣáïr (possibly a corruption of Naṣárà, *i.e.* descendants of Nazarenes) and the Sidi Menî'a, but I have never come in contact with

* Also called, from the name of a prominent professor of the art, ḍarb ez-Zanáti.

them. Women sometimes pose as witches, though usually not quite as old as western etiquette demands, freely tattooing chin and wrists, and binding their heads with dirty rags, the rest of their garments being sheets or blankets suspended by cords which leave the arms bare. Assemblies of pilgrims, festivals and markets are their favourite haunts. Or, staff in hand, and a big leather bag behind, one of these will parade the streets, looking into doors and crying, "Shall I cast lots, my Beauty?" or some such request. If this is acceded to, she is called in and supplied with a fine silk sieve and a handful of flour.

Darb er-Raml.

"What dost thou need to know?" she asks; "about thy husband that is to be, or thy health, or what?" On being informed, she shakes the flour on the up-turned sieve, and noting the lines it forms, remarks, "There are those who love you, those who dislike you, and those who hate you. The first who come, go not with them, with the second go eat and drink," and so on, finally giving a roundabout answer to the question put, though by this time her mumblings sometimes grow unintelligible, but nevertheless she demands and receives her fee of a farthing to a halfpenny, or some food. This performance is called darb er-raml or "sand-striking," as it is also performed with sand, which form is common in the East.

"Sortes Koranienses."

In cases of doubt many have recourse to an istikhárah or "request for direction," opening a Ḳor'án at random after having thrice repeated the Fátiḥah, and *ch.* vi., *v.* 59, the latter commencing "With Him are the keys of secret things: none knoweth them but He." Whatever sense can be made of the seventh line of the right-hand page gives the answer, according as its tenour is good or bad; or the letters khá (representing kháïr, good) and sheen (for sharr, evil) are counted, the majority deciding. If none are left, the answer is negative, if two, indifferent, if one, affirmative. Others use el ḳarî'at el ánbîyáh, or the "sharing of the prophets," a square on paper subdivided into a hundred compartments, in each of which a letter is written. After the repetitions before referred to, the eyes are shut, and the finger is placed at random on a square from which each fifth one gives the successive letters of an answer, pro or con.

Magic.

With regard to magic, known as siḥr or 'ilm el jidweel, there does not seem to be much of this in Morocco, though some forms common to the East are encountered, that in which the aid of good spirits is invoked being called ismá from the invocation of the Ism el Adḥeem or Dimyati, the Great, Unknown Name of God, as opposed to siḥr, which is accomplished by the invocation of evil spirits, enchantments being called s·ḥûr, and the magician saḥḥár.

A Moor once described to me the form of jidweel known to us through Lane's account as the "Magic Mirror," and the performance he had witnessed in Fez differed from that described by Lane as he had seen it in Egypt * in minor points only, while in many of the minutest details it was the same. Briefly the Moorish account was as follows.

The "Magic Mirror."

Some incense being placed on live coals in a brazier, a lad not yet arrived at puberty was summoned from the street and made to sit beside it while the performer drew on his palm a m'ḥallah (*i.e.* camp) or square subdivided by parallel lines, into a large central square in which he dropped a blotch of ink for a mirror, with eight other oblongs and squares

* *Modern Egyptians*, ch. xii. An interesting point about the experiment is that Lane's "Magician" was a Maghribi, a term which, however, might, when used in Egypt, mean Moor, Algerian, or Tunisian.

around it. In these divisions were written in Indian figures—never used in Morocco—the numbers

4	9	2
3	5	7
8	1	6

forming the magic square, round which was written a verse from the Ḳor'án,* "This our book is declared unto you in truth, since we were desirous of a copy of what you were doing."

The boy being asked if he could see his face in the ink, and replying "Yes," the performer held his hand while he repeated seven times part of the 21st verse of the Sûrat Káf, "We have removed from thee thy veil, and thy sight to-day is piercing,"† which he had also written on a piece of paper and placed inside the boy's cap. He then inquired if the lad saw anything in the ink, especially if he saw any men, to which he replied that he saw a sôḳ or market full.

"Then tell them to bring a bull."

"It is there," answered the boy, "it is a black one."

"Tell them to kill and eat it."

The boy did so, adding, "They are eating it."

"Then tell them to bring the judgement seat for the sultan."

Next the boy was told to summon the suspected thief before the sultan—for this spell is seldom used in Morocco for any other purpose—and on the thief appearing with the stolen property in his hands, the boy at once named him, thereby concluding the trial, which is commonly known as the ístinzál.

Astrology, 'ilm et-tanjeem, is almost a dead letter among the Moors.

* Sûrat el Játîyah. † Words referring to the Day of Judgement.

RABHAH.

A former slave-wife of a native British agent at the Moorish Court, now free.

Freyonne, Photo., Gibraltar.

CHAPTER THE TWENTIETH

MARRIAGE

MARRIAGE being, in the words of one native proverb, "half of Islám," and in those of another, "perfecting religion," it is not to be marvelled at that every Moorish youth of eighteen to twenty who can possibly afford it with the aid of parents and friends, is settled in matrimony. And as four wives are allowed to every man who can keep them, irrespective of the unlimited number of concubines he may purchase, while divorce is simple and expeditious, this condition is readily entered into on the advice of others, without the parties most concerned having ever met. In occasional cases they may have secured a glimpse of one another, or a stolen interview may have lent inducement to arrange a match, for when it has the chance love runs the same course in Morocco as anywhere else. I have known of one or two genuine "love-affairs," but in each case only where the restrictions of town-life were somewhat or altogether relaxed: in one of them it was to me that a dusky suitor came for permission to marry a coal-black slave whose liberation my father was attempting to obtain. Having introduced the subject by a general assertion that he wanted a wife, and would be glad of my assistance in procuring one, he steadily excused himself from considering any of those I suggested, pointing out in each the lack of some good quality conspicuous in the object of his choice. One was not fat enough, one was too tall,

Importance.

Love Affairs.

one could not cook, another had too many relatives, and so on, till his whole face beamed as I mentioned Rabḥah, now long since his wife, to whom he had for some time been paying marked attentions, making presents at every feast.

But for a well-bred Moor there is only one door open, for the whole thing to be arranged by his mother, with or without the help of the professional match-maker, or khaṭṭábah, who goes about from house to house on various errands, and receives commissions from both sides when she brings about a suitable match. Her office in the matter is to report to the mothers where they may hope to find partners for their children, praising each to the relatives of the other, and, if need be, arranging an introduction. Then the boy's mother may call with one or two cousins or aunts, who, having satisfied themselves in a business-like way as to the personal charms, the dowry, and other matters involved, report the verdict to the youth or his father, that if it be considered with favour the latter may "put the question" to the father of the girl, and, if possible, strike a bargain. This bargain is not, as many have sought to maintain, a mere matter of purchase—though undoubtedly it often has that look—since the ṣ'daḳ, or payment stipulated for, becomes provision for the bride, unless foul play or pressure divert it, as is sometimes the case, into the pockets of her father or other relative, under the name of a loan. This payment is compulsory in Muslim law, the lowest sum permissible being from sixty to eighty methḳáls, or ducats, of ten ôḳîyahs, the total being worth to-day about a pound sterling. In the Gharb $13 or $14 is a common sum, and wives at that "price" are easily divorced after bearing three or four children. In any case the sum seldom exceeds $100.

Professional Match-making.

The Marriage Portion.

Of the sum agreed upon by the waḳîls, or attorneys of the contracting parties (the woman's nearest adult male relative, or in default her legal guardian if still a child, or her nominee if of age, and the nominee of the bridegroom by affidavit before notaries), half is paid down when the contract is signed, the other half to be held in reserve till the husband's death, or till she is divorced against her will (when it must be immediately paid); or it is given to her by instalments, so much per annum, this of course being only when it is considerable. Or it may be payable after twenty years. In cases of widows or women divorced, only half the usual amount is paid. Whenever possible, brides are found among family connections, both from a clannish instinct, and because Muslim law precludes the alienation by bequest of more than a third of a man's estate. Alliances are frequently contracted with families of lower social position on account of the greater facility of divorce, with no powerful relatives to offend. During a long engagement presents are exchanged by the parties at feast times, the lady sending principally eatables, and receiving slippers, handkerchiefs, etc., on the tray when returned.

Contracting Parties.

All things being thus in order, preparations are made for the wedding, always a grand affair from the point of view of their social position when the bride is a virgin, though a very simple matter-of-fact affair if not. In the first place, there is the collection of the household gods, of which the man generally supplies the crockery, cooking utensils, candle-sticks, trays and hardware generally, with the carpets, mats and bedding, while the first instalment of the dowry from the husband, added to that received from her father, goes to procure the wife's share, the lighter and more ornamental portions of the outfit, which, together with

Furnishing the House.

her wearing apparel and jewels, remain her peculiar property, and are taken away with her if divorced.

The Trousseau.

In wealthy families a professional dress-cutter is employed at the bride's house to the accompaniment of music and singing, the various garments being sprinkled with anise for luck, before being made up. The bridegroom is expected to include among his hedîah or presents, a white silk veil (kimbush); one scarf (shimbur) of red crêpe, and another of cloth of gold; a striped silk and gold kerchief (dirrah); a pair of gold-embroidered velvet-slippers (sharbal); a rich silk girdle (hazzám), and slippers or handkerchiefs for each of her near female relatives. Of all these things notaries make a list at the home of the bride on the actual day of the wedding, when the bulky things precede her, and the valuable ones accompany her to her future home.

Preparing for Festivities.

Sometimes a feast is given at the time of signing the contract, but there is always a week of feasting when the wedding comes off; that is if it can be afforded. For this, in the country, there is a fixed understanding as to the share in the provisions to be given by the bride or the bridegroom, though the friends of each give separate entertainments, those of the bride to women, those of the bridegroom to men. On such occasions the family barber acts as master of the ceremonies, attending to all details of preparation, borrowing or hiring the extra utensils required, presiding at the feast, and allotting the guests positions according to social status. In a large establishment separate rooms are allotted to the various grades, each in charge of an assistant who finds sitting room for all upon the mattresses around the walls, and places samovars and tea-trays before suitable persons. When the house is large enough the men may be entertained on the ground floor, while the women are accommodated above.

Seven days or thereabouts it takes a Moorish couple to get married, and mightily tired they must be of it all before it is over, with its incessant round of feasting and firing and music, which, however trying to the neighbourhood at large, is evidently welcome to the multitudinous guests. Although the details of the customs followed vary in different parts of the country, the general system is the same, and the description of what takes place in Tangier will serve as an example of most.

The Marriage Feast.

A MOORISH GIRL.
(In our garden on Tangier Wall.)
Photograph by L. W. Elond, Esq.

A week before the wedding intimate female friends are invited to assist in preparing cakes and sweetmeats for the approaching festivities, and five days before the great event the bride goes to the public bath at midnight with her friends, attended by musicians; there, amid much fun and rejoicing, she is specially washed and perfumed, after which she retires to bed for the rest of the day, while her friends feast below.

Next day (n'har ed-dabîhah) a sheep or bullock presented by the bridegroom's friends is killed at the door of the bride's house, with abundant drumming and other "music," while in her own apartment the bride prepares for her first reception by having her hands and feet dyed with ḥenná, musicians performing from time to time. With candles burning in their hands, the maidens and brides who have been invited invade the lady's chamber, raising a dirge-like

Elaborate Preparations.

chant while a powerful negress envelops her in a ḥáïk and carries her downstairs on her back. While the ḥenná is being applied in the manner elsewhere described, * bride and visitors call to mind their departed friends, and set up a terrible wailing.

Next morning and evening more feasting and drumming, and at night fresh application of ḥenná. During this day (n'har el jawári) the bride receives her maiden guests, who bring presents for her or her mother, or throw them to her as she sits on her mat in state. Some bring with them loaves of sugar, candles, tea, clothes and ornaments, or send a lamb or cow before they arrive, all of which go to help out the feast. Such gifts are indispensable, and constitute a debt which the bride has perforce to repay when each donor is married, so that they might be more correctly described as loans. As the donor enters the precise nature of each is announced by a professional negress, who adds "God bless her, and may we soon be doing thus in her honour!" A careful list of givers and gifts is kept for future reference and settlement.

Wedding Presents.

This is followed by another day of reception by the bride, who is again decked out, this time in white, for the entertainment of her matron friends, who come in much more gorgeous attire than is permitted to maidens, even if it has to be borrowed. Recently wedded brides make their first public appearance on these occasions, dressed and painted as for their own weddings, reducing the amount of facial decoration at each subsequent wedding till they settle down into "old stagers." Presentations are then made as on the previous day, the mothers of bride and bridegroom leading off with gifts of money, which go to the musicians and dancing women.

The Bridal Reception.

* See p. 70.

Meanwhile the bridegroom has been receiving his friends—men only, of course—at his own home. The curious custom of loosening his belt after placing before him a meal of perhaps thirty courses is first performed by his grandmother or oldest female relative present, as he sits with his hood drawn over his head. Later a show is made of applying ḥenná to the little finger of one hand, and some times a spot of blue paint behind the ear, to avert the "evil eye."

Bachelor Festivities.

In the evening numbers of his friends pay him visits, enlivening the streets with their lanterns, and after partaking of tea and cakes, powder is often distributed on behalf of the bridegroom, to ensure abundant firing on the next, the great day (n'har el 'âmmarîá). This is always on a Thursday, if possible, but if not, on a Monday, other days being considered unlucky.

The Bridegroom's Preparations.

At daybreak or before, the bridegroom goes to the steam bath, after which he submits to be shaved all over save his beard and moustache, the latter part of the performance taking place at home, to the accompaniment of music both in house and street. Then he is attired in his wedding garments —often the gift of the bride—including the turban which he probably wears for the first time on this occasion. All the guests present throw coins into a handkerchief at his feet, half to provide for a picnic two days later, and half to be divided between the barber and the musicians.

The Bride's Preparations.

In the bride's home a similar performance has been taking place in the presence of intimate friends, but the girdle is omitted for the present. The bridal head-dress is composed of muslin and silk handkerchiefs over a closely plaited queue, and a thin veil-like ḥaïk of silk is thrown over all. On the morning of this day, two notaries come to the house of the bride to make the inventory of her belongings, but otherwise there is a well-earned measure of rest to all concerned till the evening or latter part of the afternoon, though sometimes music and receptions continue in the home of the bride.

Fetching the Bride.

Then comes the great affair of the wedding, the bridal procession. The bridegroom's family and friends set out soon after the 'aṣar prayers, (according to the distance) with music introduced by two drummings which serve as a summons, to fetch the bride home in the 'ammariá. This is a square, steeple-roofed frame or box covered over with cloth or coloured cottons and muslin, surmounted by a kimbush, or cloth-of-gold scarf, which serves as a carriage, being lashed on the back of some beast of burden. To steady it on the way, a lad is usually placed inside, and it is furnished with a loaf of bread, a candle, a few raisins, and a piece of loaf sugar, sometimes contained in a leather model of the 'ammariá itself. On arrival at the home of the bride, this box is placed at the door of her room by her nearest male relations, who retire while one of the big negresses in request on these occasions, if not a slave of the house, lifts the bride bodily off the bed on which she has sat bedecked all day, and places her inside the box, carefully closing its curtains.

The Bridal Procession.

Enter the men once more and lift the load to its place, while the negress attendant, known as the nagáfah, is sent on ahead in charge of the box containing her mistress' jewels and marriage "lines"—âḳd en-nikaḥ—which include the inventory of her property. Then commences the full power of the music, and in the country the powder-play, which continues to the door of the bridegroom's house. On the way a number of halts are made at the mosques or shrines

WOMEN OF THE LATE SULTAN'S HAREEM ON THE MARCH.

Drawn by R. Caton Woodville.

to say a Fátiḥah, and often a circuitous route is chosen to include some special sanctuary. In Fez it is the custom for the bride to walk to her new home, if a maiden, just before sunrise, if a widow, after supper, accompanied by friends and relatives, but not by her father, and by women slaves carrying her belongings and enormous wax candles.

Sometimes the bridegroom joins the procession; at others he awaits it, and on its arrival stands at the door of his room with his hand or sword extended, that his wife may pass beneath it as a token of submission to his will, for Morocco is not as yet distraught by questions of women's rights. I am informed that in Sûs he fires a shot over her head with the same idea, the bullet being left in the wall, by way of reminder. The men then retire, leaving the bride in charge of the nagáfah, who, with a lighted candle in her hand, proclaims the charms of the new-comer, whom she may poetically describe, if fair-skinned as "fresh butter," if tinged with "colour" as "a piece of amber." A bowl of milk is placed to the lips of the pair by a female relative of the bridegroom, who then also retires, and light refreshments having been prepared inside, the door is shut, and the "happy couple" are left to make each other's acquaintance over a cup of tea.

Marriage, Courtship and—Love?

One of the peculiar customs of country weddings is that as the bridal procession approaches his house, the bridegroom is found riding out to meet it. When he does so the Fátiḥah is repeated: then he heads the procession, at the end of which comes the bride, who is left alone in her room till her husband comes to her at night, when the guests have left.

Next morning the bridegroom intimates his satisfaction with the match to the nagáfah, who informs their waiting friends, and the fact is announced to the public by a discharge of fire-arms, usually three shots. If, however, as sometimes happens, the bridegroom does not find his bride the maiden she was represented to be, it depends upon his fear of retribution from her family whether he exercises his legal right of sending her home at once, or next morning, or not at all; but the scandal caused by such a proceeding is in most cases sufficient reason for getting it done with as little disturbance as possible.

A Strange Custom.

In some parts the custom prevails in the country of taking the bride in an initial procession outside the village and back, or to the bath, friends and relatives coming in from the villages round for a feast, of which a sheep or ram is the *pièce de resistance*. Next day the bridegroom sends to the bride's house, accompanied by music, presents of bread, oil, raisins, figs, onions, capsicums, candles, etc., and slippers, ḥenná, wood, charcoal, etc., with a bullock or calf for the feast. There is feasting also in his own house, where amusements of various descriptions proceed, such as sitting round a table on which are a bowl of ḥenná and two unbroken eggs beneath a silk handkerchief: in the bowl are coins which may be retained by those who get them as they dip in their hands to be stained, though at the same time the guests are expected to make contributions. Occasionally some of the men will dance with the basin on their heads, till it drops, when they will snatch off the bridegroom's ḥáïk and run off, returning later to eat again, for this feasting, both among men and women, lasts four days. It is usual for separate days to be fixed for the reception of married and unmarried guests, or brides of a year, the way the time is passed depending on the class of guests: the married people sometimes take away slippers, to bring them back full of raisins or other gifts. The bride

Country Ways.

generally gets worn out by all the festivities, and may often be seen with tears upon her cheeks amid the fun, for the strain upon her must be very great.

After the wedding, the bridegroom is supposed to stay indoors for a week, and the bride for a year, which means pretty close confinement when, as frequently happens, she finds herself in charge of a one-room ménage. But it affords excellent opportunity for the addition of the fatty charms so admired of the Oriental, to enhance which prospective brides go through a regular course of stuffing after meals with paste of parched flour, honey and sesame.

Afterwards.

On the seventh day the feasting recommences with the first assumption of a married woman's garb by the bride, whereat her friends assist again. Moorish maidens dress as simply as Moorish matrons dress richly when they can afford it, and now for the first time she dons rich cloth-of-gold and gold brocade. The special feature of the costume is a heavy triple tiara of cloth adorned with pearls and jewels, beneath which hang the fringes of gay silk kerchiefs, and over which is thrown the rich kimbush. On this occasion too, for the first time, the young wife has her face painted, a red shield-shaped device being traced on each cheek, and filled in with blue, green and white dots. Patches are stuck on where they may draw attention to her best features, and gums, lips, eyes and eyebrows are treated as elsewhere described.

Thus adorned, the poor bride has to sit in state for five long days, never opening her eyes or speaking, while her friends and relatives feast before her, each in turn taking a peep beneath the veil and making her comments aloud. The street-door is left open all the time, that any woman passing may enter and convince herself of the bridegroom's good

First "At Homes."

fortune. On the first day all this is done to music, and on the fourth the ḥenná is renewed in preparation for the fifth, for which special invitations are issued to witness the ceremony of assuming the girdle. On this day her mother pays her first visit, bringing with her two tables, one laden with cooked food, and one with tea, sugar and candles, and in return receives from the bridegroom a piece of dress stuff or kerchiefs. In the evening the girdle is wound round the bride by two little boys, as she stands over a platter containing eggs, almonds, dates, raisins, walnuts and maize, which are afterwards distributed among her friends. Then she is led round to inspect her new home, each woman carrying a lighted candle, and vociferously ululating or beating drums. On the bride's arrival at the last room a show is made of scraping a fish over her foot, in token of her assumption of household duties, after which she is escorted to her own apartment, there once more to receive congratulations, and to remunerate the musicians and tire women who have attended her during these twelve weary days.

Married Life.

On the fortieth day the dressing and ḥenná-staining is gone through for the last time in public, and when ten months have passed one more reception is held, this time for young brides like herself. Her future lot will depend on the influence she maintains over her husband, to be measured not only by good looks or by accomplishments, but by the number of sons she bears, and the competition of possible rivals. The laws of divorce do not differ from those of other Mohammedan lands, being merely those of the Ḳor'án.

Divorce.

On the slightest provocation a man may dismiss his wife, but she can only divorce him by process of law, on certain stated grounds, of which Moorish women seldom venture to avail themselves. They are, however, constantly divorced, the only obligation on the husband's part being the payment of the balance of the dowry, providing also for the wife's maintenance for a hundred days, and for that of the children till able to fend for themselves. Twice a wife may be treated thus and taken back again, but not a third time unless marriage has been meanwhile consummated with another and annulled. Or if a husband in his wrath pronounces a triple divorce, the same position is reached at once. A woman who obtains a divorce has to return the dowry paid.

The estimation in which Mohammedans hold the common sense of their women may be judged from the advice of the Imám et-Taraï, "It is desirable for a man, before entering upon any important undertaking, to consult ten intelligent friends; or if he have not more than five such friends, let him consult each of them twice; or if he have no more than one friend, he should consult that one at ten different times; if he have none to consult, let him consult his wife, and whatever she advises him, let him do the opposite: so shall he proceed rightly in his affair, and attain his object."

Wifely Counsel.

MOORISH GRAVE-YARD AT TETUAN.

Cavilla Photo., Tangier.

CHAPTER THE TWENTY-FIRST

FUNERAL RITES

APPROACHING death has no fears for the Moor, who is content to rely on God's mercy to those who have accepted Mohammed as His apostle, and who have attended to at least the more important ceremonial precepts of his system. If they have doubts as to the side on which their conscience account stands, they and their friends take care to lay in a precautionary stock of merit by the distribution of alms, and the recital of prayers or extracts from the Ḳor'án. The name of a deceased Moor is never mentioned by those who knew him without the addition of the ejaculation "May God have mercy on him!" but this in no sense casts a reflection upon his character.

Anticipation.

When death becomes imminent, it is customary to moisten the lips of the dying person, and to remove the pillows, covering the face with a cloth, and as soon as life appears to be extinct the fact is announced by the cries of those present. This makes it quickly known in the street, bringing to the door such friends as can come to condole with the bereaved, and spend from half an hour to two hours repeating prayers for blessings on the departed, and fortitude for the survivors. As they leave, they enquire what time the funeral (ginázah) will be, as, if death has occurred in the morning, it usually takes place

Announcement of Death.

the same afternoon, or else next day. No other announcement is made.

Hired mourners are not employed by the Moors and the signs of bereavement are here less marked than in most Oriental countries. The women of a family which has lost its head give way, however, to piercing shrieks, and in some parts behave like the demented, tearing their cheeks with their nails, rending their garments, and placing ashes upon their faces, hands and clothes. These customs are mostly confined to the Arabs and Shlûḥ, who sometimes also attire themselves in old clothes (sack-cloth), and throw old pots and pans out after the deceased has been carried forth. In the case of virgins, bachelors, or women who have died in child-birth, cries of joy are sometimes uttered as the corpse is carried out of the door.

The Death Wail.

The men do not mourn, though for a near relative it is customary to abstain from feasting for a period of "ûḳár" which may last as long as a year. Except in the case of widows, no change is made in the dress of either sex, but the women abstain for a time from adornment and finery, even from washing their clothes, and weddings or feasts are very quietly celebrated. On the death of her husband a widow is at once rolled up in a ḥaïk until new calico garments can be brought to her, as she must wear this material exclusively for four months, eleven and a half days, and must do her own washing apart from that of others on Saturdays, when alone she is permitted to use the steam bath, taking care to be back home by the time of afternoon prayers. Although she may visit her friends, she may attend no festivities, and must take particular care not to go bare-foot.

Mourning.

Immediately after death, the body of the deceased is washed with warm water and rose-water, sometimes also with soap, usually by some ṭáleb or 'árîfah accustomed to the task, who binds up the jaws with a strip of selvedge, inserting cotton wool into the ears and nostrils, also under the arm-pits, and between the legs; and ties the big toes together. This is performed on a special board called a maghsil, kept for public use. Shirt, drawers, socks and sash having been put on, with turban or kerchief according to sex, all new, the body is laid in the shroud or k'fin, a white cotton sheet which is knotted at head and feet. Sometimes the body is placed in the mortuary chapel adjoining the mosque, to have once more the privilege of hearing prayers. If the body remains in the house overnight, it is left in a room alone with candles and incense burning. Often it is sprinkled with water of orange-flower, cloves, marjoram or musk. The clothes worn at death are usually given to the poor, or to a ṭáleb who assists in the funeral rites. Some carry shrouds with them when travelling, and in the army these are furnished by the government.

Last Offices.

One of the biers called na'ash—kept at the mortuary chapel for free use—being brought, or else a new one having been made which will afterwards be presented to the mosque for free use, the body is laid therein, generally after sprinkling it with saffron water, and sometimes the shroud also with water from the well of Zemzem,* and a blanket—ḥáïk—is thrown over, or sometimes the flag from a saint's shrine, or the girdle of the widow, if she has been left enceinte. The bier of a woman is distinguished by an arched erection of cane, over which are thrown a blanket and a light white curtain, if married, or a coloured handkerchief if unmarried,

The Funeral.

* In the mosque-court at Mekka, believed to have been that revealed to Hagar and Ishmael, the water of which is brought back by pilgrims, being reputed of miraculous virtue.

the bier being decorated exactly as the bridal cage, 'ammaríá. Occasionally, in the towns, coffins called tabût are employed, especially for women—plain boxes with bottoms of open lath-work. The bearers are commonly the friends or admirers of the deceased, or merely such as desire to perform a good work, and relieve one another at frequent intervals; but sometimes they are paid, especially in the large cities, when they are called zarzáyah. If possible the procession includes a slave or

A FUNERAL PROCESSION.

two freed by the will of the deceased, or purchased and manumitted by his heirs, holding the certificates of freedom aloft in a cleft stick. At times the ṭálebs go first, but at times the bier, because it is said in the Hadeeth or sayings of Mohammed that the Angels led the way. The bodies of children are carried by a man in his arms, wrapped up, or in a small bier on his head.

As they slowly march with little attempt at order,

someone strikes up the profession of faith in GOD and Mohammed, which is weirdly chanted, sometimes with too much of a nasal stress to be agreeable at close quarters, but exceedingly effective at a distance, especially in the case of one or two really magnificent tunes. In most the chant is antiphonal, one half singing the first part of the creed, the others commencing the second simultaneously with the last syllable of the first; or the whole is gone through first by one half and then by the second, so that no pause or break occurs the whole length of the march, or till the interment is over. This chant or dhikr is not, however, always used, and unless someone strikes it up, the funeral proceeds in silence. The following is one of the best; but the effect can only be produced by voice or violin.

Funeral Chants.

From the house the procession makes for the mortuary chapel,—beït el ginaïz—where the bier is placed on the ground with the face towards Mekka, while a muédhdhin proclaims at the door leading into the mosque, the prayer for burial, "and he a man; may GOD have mercy on him, and all Muslimín have mercy on him!" (Or "and she a woman.") A fokíh then leads the congregation in the prayer for the dead.*

Burial Service.

* Having opened with a declaration of his intention, and a takbeer or statement that "GOD is most great," standing with his hands extended on either side of his head, with the thumbs against the lobes of the ears, he recites the Fátihah followed by a second takbeer. He then recites: "O GOD, bless our lord Mohammed the illiterate prophet, and his family and companions, and save them!" A third takbeer having been uttered, he continues, "O GOD, verily this is thy servant and the son of thy servant: he hath departed from the repose of this world and its business, and from what-

Arrived at the grave-side, the bier is deposited on the ground at the head, in a line with the trench, which is fairly wide, but only three or four feet deep, with a narrower trough at the bottom into which the body can be almost slid by the nearest friends. In the case of a woman two or three relatives stand round with out-stretched ḥaïks, while the father, brother, or in default of them some man of piety and standing, lowers the body. This having been laid on the right side, with the face towards Mekka, the shroud is opened at head and foot, lest at the resurrection the deceased should find himself in the same predicament as Lazarus. Two are never placed in the same grave, from a fear that they might mistake one another's bones on that occasion. Boards or stones—called laḥd—having been placed across the ledges formed by the lower trough, the earth is filled in, water being poured on if it is very dry, in order to

Interment.

ever he loved, and from those by whom he was loved in it, to the darkness of the grave and to what he [there] experienceth. He testified that there is no god but Thee alone; that Thou hast no partner, and that Mohammed is Thy servant and apostle: and Thou knowest all about him. O GOD, he hath gone to abide with Thee, and Thou art the best with whom to abide. He hath become in need of Thy mercy, and Thou hast no need of his punishment. We have come to Thee supplicating that we may intercede for him. O GOD, if he were a doer of good, over-reckon his good deeds; and if he were an evil-doer, pass over his evil doings: and of Thy mercy grant that he may experience Thine acceptance; and spare him the trial of the grave and its torment, and make his grave wide to him, and keep back the earth from his sides, and of Thy mercy grant that he may experience security from torment, until Thou send him safely to thy Paradise, O Thou most pitiful of the pitying!" After the last takbeer, from which this prayer is known as that of "the four takbeers," he concludes with "O GOD, deny not to us our reward for him [*i.e.* for having prayed for him] and lead us not into trial after him: pardon us and him and all Muslims, O Lord of Creation!" His guardian angels on either side having been saluted as after ordinary prayers, the foḳîh requests those present to furnish testimony regarding him, to which they reply, "He was of the virtuous," wherewith the service concludes.

make it solid, as it is believed that the wicked suffer torment from the pressure of the earth. Sometimes palm or myrtle leaves are strewed on the bottom, or a light mat. The same procedure takes place whether there is a coffin or not.

Cemeteries.

The graves of the Moors differ considerably in different parts of the country, the most common practice being merely to surround the heap of displaced earth with a circle of stones which are seldom cut, but in the case of a reputed saint are often whitewashed, when a white flag on a cane will probably be set up at the head. A more elaborate style is a low, whitewashed wall all round, lower on the side towards Mekka, which is often made to include a number of graves of one household. At other times a dome is erected, especially when there is a hope of receiving zîárah, the offerings of pious visitors. Elsewhere head and foot stones are in vogue, or the former only, but inscriptions are rare.* The only common sign is an upright stone at one end or both, not a flat one, called a mish'hád or "witnesser." A woman's grave may be distinguished by one or two saw cuts in the top of that at the foot.

Grave-side Service.

The dhikr having ceased, a muédhdhin utters his cry, and the ṭálebs or scribes who have attended sit down to recite certain chapters of the Ḳor'án for a consideration, while alms are distributed to the assistants, especially to the poor, who consequently are not slow to get word of an important funeral. In Algeria, even in European dress, I was once included in the distribution at a funeral I had attended to obtain a closer view than I could attempt in more bigoted Morocco. The alms include bread and water, but never

* Dr. Addison said (p. 206) that epitaphs were out of fashion, but that Leo Africanus once made a collection of them which he presented to a brother of the King of Fez.

meat, which would be considered of an unpropitious resemblance to the dust returned to dust, and even the national dish, kesk'soo, is not in the best of favour, as so many have helped to make it. The idea is to purchase merit, for which dried fruits such as figs and raisins are more highly esteemed, the former specially so, as every seed contained in them is believed to earn its own blessing.

Offerings and Libations

Each subsequent morning for three days the males of well-to-do families gather with scribes at the grave and distribute more bread with figs and dates, and after they have retired the women, who have waited at a short distance, approach with branches of myrtle and palm, and flowers which they lay on the grave, then paying many times its value to a water-carrier to pour out a skin-full of water thereon. Sometimes the whole family gathers on the fortieth day, when more eatables are distributed and scriptures read, flowers and branches strewn, and water poured out,* after which, the materials being ready, if a tomb-stone or enclosure is to be erected, the work is at once put in hand.

Women Mourners.

Women do not attend the funerals in towns, though they do so among the Arabs and Shlûḥ, who often disregard Mohammed's objection to wailing at the grave, or even to praising the deceased. In Fez it is considered a disgrace for a woman to weep thus, and some think that unless their tears are caught by their veils they injure the deceased. But the elder women may visit the grave next morning, called the ṣ'báḥ el ķubûr, or "tomb morning," and on Friday afternoons it is customary for them to repair to the graveyards with sprigs of myrtle to lay on the graves.

* Perpetrating, perhaps, a heathen libation.

which being almost their only outing except to the bath, gives frequent occasion for scandal.

If the funeral has been delayed over night, fokîhs will have been employed to recite a portion, if not the whole, of the Ḳor'án, either on the spot or at their own homes, the latter being cheaper and costing from three dollars upwards, according to the social position of the deceased. The figure quoted is at the rate of a *real vellon* (billion) for each of the sixty sections into which that book is divided, but to perform this sulkah or "passing through" as it should be, all the fokîhs should sit together, each taking up the recital where his predecessor leaves off. So essential is some form of this recitation considered, that for the penniless it is done in the morsṭân at the charge of the Government, which in that case meets all expenses, but if possible breakfast is provided for the fokîhs, when the recitation has been by night. In the house, too, is often repeated part of a poem in praise of Mohammed, called the "Borḍah," consisting of 165 verses by the Sheïkh el Bûṣeeri, buried in Alexandria. Frequently the whole Ḳor'án is repeated again at the grave, and also portions of the Sûrahs "Áhli I'mran," "En-Nisá," and the whole of the Sûrahs "Yá Seen," "Tabárkah," or the last fourteen short Sûrahs. Commonly these recitations are prolonged for three days—the third day being the most important,—and sometimes even for six months or a year.

Reciting the Ko'rán.

The proven cases in which voices have been heard issuing from the ground after burial, and those in which bodies unearthed have been found contorted, are accounted for on the best of Islámic authorities by the belief that the two angels Munkir and Nákir come on the night after the funeral to examine the dead (whose spirits return for the ordeal)

In the Silent Grave.

and cast up their conscience accounts. But into the details of that superstition it would be out of place here to enter, as they may be found in full in any work on the tenets of Islám. Most of the grave-yards are unenclosed spaces outside the towns, though saints are frequently buried within, but ordinary corpses are not allowed to be brought inside the walls, so are taken first to one of the shrines which almost invariable stand in such localities, their sanctity forming a strong attraction. Whenever the Moors see a funeral pass, of whatever creed, they stand and repeat the takbeer thrice, but they never attend Jewish or Christian funerals.

PART III—SUPPLEMENTARY

AT THE FOOT OF THE ATLAS.

CHAPTER THE TWENTY-SECOND

THE MOROCCO BERBERS

PROBABLY few outside nations have played more important, yet withal less prominent, parts in the European historical drama than that very little known people, the Berbers of North Africa. A hardy race, dwelling in mountain strongholds, they have preferred their bracing hill-top breezes to all soft allurements of the plains, and they remain there as masters. Holding intact the highlands along the whole southern coast of the Mediterranean, many nations have they seen rise and fall, many foreigners have laid hold on their coast-line, but none have ever penetrated far their cherished home. Egyptians, Phœnicians, Grecians, Romans, Vandals and Arabians, all who have come in contact with them, have been the better for it. Powerless to completely subdue those warrior tribes, the strangers have all been gainers from infusion of their busy blood, and have returned from Africa with gathered force. With armies recruited among them Carthage fought Rome, and under Hannibal they made their first great recorded invasion of Europe.* They made their second under Arab leaders when they conquered Spain.

Importance.

* When Hiero sent a thousand archers and slingers to help the Romans against Hannibal, the envoy explained that they would be found "aptam manum adversus Baliares ac Mauros pugnacesque alias missili telo gentes." [1]

[1] Livi. xxi., 57.

Arab Influence.

The conquering Easterns inter-married with them from the first, accepting as brothers those who "resigned themselves," and appropriating the women of those who did not. The settlers on those fertile plains were suckled by the mountain wolf, a beast they could never tame. So years rolled by, and centuries, but the Morocco Berbers changed not. They remain to-day what they were in the days of Jugurtha —we might almost go back to the Pharoahs,—save in one most vital point: they have all embraced Islám.

Religion.

What all invaders from the north had failed to do, one earnest, hungry band of desert wanderers did.* Their Arabian cousins had an influence which no outsider could obtain, and by at once assimilating with their conquered converts, reaped new life and vigour to push on the cause. Then it was that their religion progressed, but it was not till nearly two hundred years after Mohammed had fled from Mekkah, that the Morocco Berbers had all accepted his creed.† By the time that they were ready to swarm across into Spain, the Muslims were no longer a handful of nomad adventurers, they were a horde of sturdy hill-men, the Arab and the Berber blended in the "Moor," the latter element predominating. These were the people who over-ran Spain, and whose northward march was the terror of Europe, people among whom science flourished and art reigned supreme.‡ Had it not been for

* See Fournel, *Les Berbères*, Paris 1875, 1881, 2 vols; "a most valuable and erudite work."

† They were only completely reduced to Islám by Mûsà ibn Noṣaïr on his way to the conquest of Spain.[1]

‡ Ibn Khaldûn devotes an important chapter to the enumeration of the kings and great men who down to his time (cir. 1300 A.C.) had come of Berber stock.

[1] Ibn Khaldûn, vol. i., pp. 189 and 215.

this potent factor, the Peninsula had never known the Moor.*

Physique.

As might well be expected of such a race of mountaineers, the physique of the Berbers is splendid, and among them are to be seen a good proportion of fine-featured men. They are of fair height, often tall, strong and wiry, capable of sustaining great exertion. They are well-knit, spare in flesh, and though as a nation fair of skin, often tanned by the sun. Those who inhabit the Sûs province—the Shlûḥ †—are as a rule much shorter than those of the north, and those of the Dra'a Valley and anti-Atlas—the Dra'wîs—whose mingled origin apparently includes some negro strain, are considerably darker, more thickly set, and shorter, though none the less genial—perhaps even more so,—and are certainly no whit less enduring than their brethren of the colder regions. The darker families are recognized as Ḥaráṭîn (*s.* Ḥarṭánî) *i.e.* or Mulattos, as having one negro parent, but the majority object most strongly to this description. Some of the Dra'wi countenances are most striking, being of very pronounced type, keen eyes, jovial mouth and white teeth. Their brain power, to judge from the outward appearance of their craniums, should be in no way deficient, but I do not fancy that the thickness of the skulls in any degree equals that of the negroes, though I believe I have seen lads of this race also play at "billy-goat," butting at each other's pates with an astounding crash.

Following the custom of the country generally, with certain exceptions, as the Beni S'baḥ, Shinágatà, part of

* *The Moorish Empire* contains the following references to the Berbers: pp. 4, 6, 10, (and n.), 11, 12; their position in 7th century, 21-3; revolt of A.C. 739-88, 28-30; in Spain, 30-2.

† A word said to be a corruption of áshlûḥ (*pl.* íshláḥ) a camel-hair tent.

the Aït Bu 'Amrán, and the Ida-û-B'lál—the last named believed to be of Arab origin,*—all the males shave their heads, though several tribes leave a patch on one side to grow into a queue called kurn, or if from the centre, guṭáyah. The reason for this I have never been able to ascertain, though every tourist learns "all about it" from his guide. Judging from some of the Egyptian sculptures, they would seem but to perpetuate an ancient custom of that country. The guṭáyah is almost always worn by members of the 'Aísáwi brotherhood. Harris speaks of the Berbers of Tafilált being distinguishable from the Arabs, who preserve the beard and trim the mustache, by removing the latter entirely, and leaving only a small point of the beard linked to the ears by a close-cut line on each side.[1]

Distinctive Hair-Dressing.

Other tribes are known by tufts called nûádir ("sheaves") on either temple,† but it is noteworthy that in this case the hair is always curly. Perhaps it is intermarriage with negroes which accounts for this "woolliness." The Udáià, part of the hereditary body-guard of the sultans, now bear few other traces of the Berber beyond their splendid physique. An able German student of Morocco,[2] has contended that they are partially of Jewish descent, and it is at least striking to notice the similarity of their tufts to those worn by some of the Atlas Jews. The word Udäïà is supposed by him to be from Yáhûdîah (Jews).

Although debauchery is less common among the Berbers than among the dwellers in towns, there is in some

* Part of this tribe, which lives in Sûs, is recognized as Berber, but part is to be found in the ḳaṣbah of New Fez or at Meshra er-Ramla in Shrárda, near by.

† As the Gerwán, Ben M'tîr, M'ját, Zemmûr Shilḥ, some of the Beni Hasin, the Shrárdà and the Udáïà.

[1] Tafilet, p. 65. [2] Quedenfeldt.

ways a great deal more licence without reproach.* Among the unmarried, for instance, the fullest liberty is tolerated until a child is born, when the parents must perforce wed, the man having no option as to the dowry demanded. If unwilling to pay and marry, his property is sold by the tribal council (jima'), and if he still prove contumacious, he will be shot by one of the woman's relatives. It is the duty of the husband to slay the adulterer, and if he slay also his wife he is blameless, the fear of incurring the vengeance of her relatives alone restraining him.

Morals.

The marriage contract is verbal only, but is entered into before the jima', and made public by festivities. The bridegroom pays what is for him a heavy sum down to his bride's family, half for her trousseau, and half as caution money on deposit, to be forfeited if he gives ground for divorce—which rarely takes place on the woman's demand,—or to be returned to him if she is divorced for good reason. It is this payment which is popularly regarded as the "price" of the wife, as her relatives hold out for a sum in proportion to her personal charms, their own position and the consequent value of the alliance, and her financial expectations. If the wife be ill-treated they can demand her divorce on repaying the deposit, but as a rule this is spent as soon as received, so that in practice only her family benefit from the arrangement. In case of divorce the children remain with the father.

Marriage Customs.

In the Rîf district, in order to forestall loose living, marriages are contracted between children of eight years old, the girl being brought home to live with the lad at his parents' home till she expects to become a mother, when a separate home is provided

A Rîfi Custom.

* I am assured that a woman is not infrequently permitted to spend the night with the fokîh in the village mosque.

for the young couple. In consequence the Rîfis maintain a commendable standard, and form one of the finest types of the Morocco Berbers, if not the finest. Certain tribes, however, expect no more virtue among the fair sex than among the men. Several are noted for their beautiful women; others for their love of ornaments, usually silver bracelets, anklets or brooches, and amber, bead or coral necklets. I have also seen marble bracelets.

Weddings.

Monogamy is in most parts far more common among the Morocco Berbers than polygamy, but prosperity brings an increase of luxury in this respect as in others. When a marriage is celebrated in orthodox style, it is made the occasion of a great deal of innocent rejoicing, and a large quantity of powder is "made to speak" in exhibitions of "powder-play," performed, for the most part, on foot. When the bride is a widow but little fuss, if any, is made. Intermarriage between the tribes is not so common as it might be, owing to their constant jealousies. The same bars of relationship obtain, of course, as throughout the Mohammedan world. Syphilitic complaints, so common in the cities, are rare among the Berbers, and are said to be unknown beyond the Atlas; even to be cured by going there!

Festivals.

The Berber festivals are mainly those of Islám, though a few traces of their predecessors are observable. Of these the most noteworthy is Midsummer or St. John's Day, still celebrated in a special manner, and styled "El 'Anṣarah." In the Rîf it is celebrated by the lighting of bonfires only, but in other parts there is a special dish prepared of wheat, raisins, etc., resembling the frumenty consumed at the New Year. It is worthy of remark that the Old Style Gregorian calendar is maintained among them, with corruptions of Latin names, and it would be very interesting to know whence they obtained it. Some opine that once, as a nation, they were Christians, but this I believe to be quite a mistake.*

Traces of Christianity?

The influence of the various bishoprics established along the North African coast was never very far-reaching, and in many cases they were little more than nominal. The special estimation in which the Virgin Mary is held in some parts, and certain ceremonies maintained here and there, are often adduced as proofs of a former profession of Christianity, but I am inclined to doubt the whole thing.† Space will not permit any description of these relics, of whatever they may be, and I have never had the opportunity to give either them or the folk-lore of the people the attention which they deserve. It is often difficult to say where Arabs' beliefs end or those of the Berbers begin.‡

Dress.

The dress varies as much in different localities as anything else.[1] Far in the interior it is almost entirely of wool, needles and thread being unknown. In the extreme south a piece of oblong white blanket or dark blue cotton § with a longitudinal slit in the centre

* See *The Moorish Empire*, p. 307 *et seq.*, and p. 309, note.

† Crosses are sometimes tattooed on the foreheads and necks of women: in childbirth Mary is called upon—"Maná Maryam!" When wheat sprouts, in some parts a procession takes place with a big doll called "Mata," which has been described already in chapter ix.

‡ Hay[2] mentions as peculiar to the Berbers a legend that the sea was at first made sweet, but growing proud it overstepped its bounds, and all livings things except the fish were drowned. Gnats were then created to drink it up, and afterwards bring it up again, whence its saltness. At the top of Jebel Aghmer in the Atlas, near Tikirt, (also called Jebel Unîla) is a perennial pond to which sheep and goats are yearly offered to prevent drought.[3]

§ Called khunt ("Guinea cloth"), mostly from England, being an imitation of a better quality made in the Ṣûdán, which costs several times as much.

[1] Cf. De Foucauld, pp. 44 and 81.

[2] *Western Barbary*, p. 111.

[3] De Foucauld, p. 95.

for the head—called in Mexico a "poncho,"—is thrown over the shoulders, the lower corners simply knotted at the waist, round which another cloth is tied on the left hip. The women often secure these cloths in their places by massive silver brooches of a peculiar pattern, pinned at the shoulder, and wear a waist cord.* Cotton of cheaper European manufacture is steadily finding its way to supersede these more primitive garments.

A toga-like arrangement of a light blanket serves as

A BERBER IN AKHNIF AND THREE MOORS IN HAIKS.

overall for the men, with another small piece of flannel or dark blue cotton or camel-hair cord twisted about the shaven crown. The most distinctive garment in Sûs is the ákhnîf, a thick, waterproof, black goat-hair hooded cloak, with no arm-holes.

Typical Garments.

* Brooches of precisely the same peculiar pattern are found in parts of Scotland and Ireland, and specimens are to be seen in the Dublin Museum.

Across the back is a striking yellow embroidered assegai-shaped patch, the variations in which denote different clans. Drawers are seldom worn except by the rich. Leather sandals are in vogue towards the desert, but only among cavaliers. In the Rif they are made of halfa grass. But as no description of the Berber wardrobe will serve for two districts, I had better not intrude farther.

Art.

Cooking utensils, saddlery, arms, musical instruments and other articles of native manufacture, if rude in some parts, have attained in others what may be considered, with regard to their resources, a state of perfection. In their decorative art considerable talent is displayed, and in the more remote districts, where Arab influence is less felt, the affinity of design and colour to those of Central Africa is strongly marked. This is especially the case with the black and blue-green leather work. To the south-west the comparative proximity to Guinea makes itself felt in the same way. As compared with the more refined Oriental productions, however, everything is extremely rude.

Architecture.

It is a striking fact that far away on the other side of the Great Atlas is to be found an architectural taste quite remarkable among a people usually setting so little store upon the beauty of their dwellings. Ornamentation is to be seen on every hand, and instinctively the question is asked how far these people we call Barbarians are accountable for the prosperity of the arts under Moorish rule in Spain. While the Arab or Moor of the plain is content to dwell in the meanest of huts or a tent, and the strongholds of governors are of roughly rammed earth, their exterior a shapeless mass worn by wind and rain, these Berbers dwell in comfortable houses with projecting eaves to their flat roofs, and the citadels which dot the Atlas are crenellated like mediæval fortresses, wearing quite an imposing appearance.* In some districts strong store towers (tigimi) are observable on every hand, which in time of war serve as forts. They have usually four towers, and walls thirty feet or so high, sloping inwards. By contrast, west of Jebel Gláwi fortified villages called agadîr are preferred.†

Dwellings.

The people dwell in homes as various as their dress. It is believed that, like the Arabs, they were originally nomads,‡ and many still live in huts which they are nothing loth to quit and live elsewhere. Sallust's comparison of their thatched homesteads to the upturned keels of boats is well-known,§ but is not a very good one, and does not at all apply to the square-built homes of the mountaineers. On ascending the northern slopes of the Atlas, huts disappear entirely, and are replaced by erections of stone and mud, roofed with sticks spread over with trodden earth, built up against the hill-sides. For protection, as the villages are seldom walled, unless of some size, all the doors are turned to the centre, and the walls are windowless. Some districts are peculiar in having dwellings each in the centre of its owner's plot of cultivated ground.**

* Harris (Tafilet, p. 102) suggests a Phœnician origin for these erections, which reminded him of nothing so much as of the elevations given in the works of Pierrot and Chipiez.

† This has been erroneously taken by foreigners in some cases as the name, instead of only as the description, of a town, as the port of Agadîr (Santa Cruz). Evidently this was the original name of Cadiz, for M'BAALI AGADIR ("the Agadir of Baal") appears on coins found there;[1] whence Gadeira and Gades.

‡ Berber nomads were still mentioned in the eleventh century, when these Arab tribes arrived, previous to which El Bekri says there were Arabs in a few parts of the plains alone.[2]

§ *De Bello Jug.*

** As the Aït Bû Zîd, and parts of Háhá.[3]

[1] RAWLINSON'S *Phœnicia*, pp. 290 and 67, 68.

[2] IBN KHALDÛN. [3] DE FOUCAULD, p. 73.

Built mosques are infrequent, though saints' shrines are common enough—sometimes the only white-washed structures to be met with,—and often an ordinary hut or room has to do duty for both school and church. For ovens they build a sort of dome with a hole in the top, which is first well heated by lighting a fire in it, the bread being put in while it is still hot. Adjoining every village, or not far from it, is another occupied solely by Jews. These live almost as slaves to their respective Berber protectors, and are subjected to indignities of all descriptions. They lose no opportunity, however, of repaying these with the proportion of interest which they endeavour to obtain for their loans by their superior subtlety and cunning.

Public Buildings.

The food of the Berbers is of the simplest, and very nearly vegetarian. Wheat or barley porridge, 'asîdah—in the Rîf, zanbu—eaten with oil or butter, is in Sûs esteemed a great delicacy, and takes the place of the kesk'soo of the plains as the national dish. Meat is the portion of great men only, except on market days or festive occasions. Agriculture is much neglected, and fruit and vegetables become exceedingly scarce in the country. Dried turnips, eaten raw, form an important provision. Toward the desert dates are a staple article of diet, and walnuts are plentiful in the mountains.

Food.

A specimen daily round of meals is: on waking, a bowl of vegetable broth; at eleven o'clock, a dip in the family dish of porridge; at sunset, a similar share of 'asîdah or kesk'soo, made, perchance, as I have tasted it, of barley with fresh broad beans or turnips on the top. A favourite breakfast for those who have cows is sour milk and dates, for, making a virtue of necessity, most of these dirty people like their

A Day's Menus.

milk sour.* Honey is much used, and the wax is chiefly reserved for votive candles or for export.

Supplies.

Salt is found in abundance in certain regions, while further south it becomes extremely valuable. Soap—always soft—is unknown far inland,† cinders and herbs replacing it, though where it is made—solely by the Jews—it has a good sale. In many parts even cows are scarce, as well as horses, and the steeds which are found in the mountainous districts are, like the mules, small, and wonderfully agile. Had they not possessed the latter qualification, I doubt whether I should have been alive to-day, for sometimes on those roadless mountain sides one has to ride, as the Moors say, "liver in mouth." The sheep are also small, many of them black, and in some districts the black wool is used by the men and the white by the women.

Personal Habits.

Several of the tribes have a predilection for smoking, using pipe-bowls of hard black wood from the Ṣûdán, or hollow bones. Their tobacco is sold by the leaf, and most of it is home-grown. Snuffing is still more common.‡ I do not think that Indian hemp is so much patronized further south as it is on the plains of the north. Intoxicating drinks—usually thick syrups—are prepared from dates, figs and raisins, but inebriety is nowhere general.

Laws.

As Mohammedans, the Berbers are nominally ruled by the Ḳor'án, but it is only natural that certain ancient usages belonging to an earlier faith should have survived among such conservative folk.[1] Genuine Berber civil laws, called îserf, are, like the

* As English people learned to like "high" game before the introduction of fast trains and ice chambers enabled them to procure it in wholesome condition.

† Not south of Tikirt.[2]

‡ De Foucauld says that in the south the habit is confined to the Jews.

[1] See ERCKMANN, p. 115. [2] DE FOUCAULD, p. 93.

customs, entirely traditional, and are upheld by an assembly, called the unflûs. A verbal summons before witnesses on the part of the plaintiff is all that is necessary to secure a trial. No one is amenable in the first instance save to his own tribe, unless for a wrong committed among others, but he may demand a fresh trial by another unflûs if dissatisfied with the first, though bribery alone is successful in practice.

Seeking Justice.

If a complaint be not immediately attended to, the suppliant for justice can generally secure attention by offering a sheep as sacrifice—'ár—before a jima' or "gathering" of from two to any number of leading residents whom he may discover in any place, as he may easily do of an afternoon, when much time is spent in gossip beneath the lee or shade of some wall or tree. But justice can be counted on only by free men of the place, not by strangers, unless under the protection of an influential resident. Even among the members of the tribe it is the number of relatives who can be called upon for assistance, or who would revenge an injury, which constitutes power, and assures fearlessness: small families or sections are always oppressed. When the accused pleads "not guilty," and there is no positive evidence against him, he will be acquitted without himself swearing, if he can find ten brothers or other male relatives to swear on his behalf, but the accuser must always swear to the charge.

Fine Distinctions.

Theft by day is not regarded by these people as dishonourable, rather the reverse, especially if accomplished at some personal risk; a man may be seen boastfully exhibiting property so stolen to its lawful owner, demanding payment to return it, and chaffing him for not having shot the thief. Highwaymen are in great repute, and plunder of passers-by is looked upon as a respectable means of subsistence.

Excursions are constantly made to the lowlands or to the outskirts of some city for this purpose, or to carry off droves of steeds or oxen which have been sent out to graze. But petty larceny, thefts under cover of darkness, and abuse of trust, are viewed quite otherwise, and the thief, if caught, will receive scant mercy. In such cases in some parts criers are sent round to the markets to offer rewards, and houses may be searched; but if in vain, compensation must be made, which is prohibitive of the extension of the practice.

Penalties.

The penalties imposed are not, as a rule, severe, though much suffering is often inflicted by the great people of a tribe by imprisoning offenders or enemies in underground granaries unfit for human habitation. The bastinado is also employed, though not so commonly as further east, but thieves are sometimes blinded with a red-hot ram-rod or other iron. Strangers caught thieving are shot on sight, but members of the tribe are spared to be further dealt with, both from policy and fear of reprisals. The Rîfis will tie such a thief up to a tree and shoot him, as they will a man presuming to wreak his vengeance on a market, which, with the roads leading to it, is regarded as privileged, but the Shlûḥ of the south permit the exercise of the vendetta anywhere. Otherwise capital punishment is rare, with the exception of cases in which the culprit is handed over to the avenger of blood to do what he will with him.

Feuds.

All criminals are subject to the *lex talionis*, of which the vendetta is a natural sequence. This continues till it is stopped either by some superior civil or religious authority, or by the practical extermination or expatriation of one side. The blood-money (dîyah), which has to be formally demanded before declaring the feud (ṭolb or ḳîṣáṣ), is usually an impossible sum, perhaps all the man is worth, as no small odium attaches itself to those who are willing to settle in that way.

Quarrels.

The blood feuds which result from the operation of this law are among the chief sources of the continual fighting between the tribes, although a simple raid or highway robbery frequently gives rise to a quarrel in which some thousands are eventually

BERBER CULTIVATION IN THE ATLAS.

The darker portion is irrigated, the lighter is barren: the clear division between them is the course of the highest stream. Below it the hill-side is built up into "fields" a few feet wide.

Photograph by Dr. Rudduck.

embroiled. Another fertile source of quarrels is the right to the use of streams for irrigation purpose. A curious custom for recording time has been noted in certain districts, the standard measure being the time a certain basin with a hole in it takes to fill and sink.

Every tribe differs from its neighbours in some point or other. For instance, one will be found extremely religious, with saints' shrines and teachers in abundance,* and next to it will be a tribe in which Islám is a mere form, and even the rite of circumcision is but scantily practised.† In one spot the grossest ignorance prevails, while hard by is a tribe of which many even of the women can read. I remember the mother of one Berber ḳaïd[1] who not only spoke Arabic as fluently as her own tongue, but also read it with ease, and could discourse most intelligently, the only intelligent native woman in Morocco with whom I ever conversed. One general custom, or rather absence of it, is to allow the women to go unveiled, except where more Arabicized, while on the borders of the desert the men wear a veil (lithám) as protection from the sand and glare. A pall of gross superstition, however, casts its gloom over all.

Religious Fervour.

Like hardy mountaineers all the world over, the Berbers are essentially an independent and warlike race. One of the greatest insults to be offered to any of them is to say, "Your father died in his bed!" In some districts the coward is paraded in a Jew's cap till he has retrieved his character by some brave deed. Flight from the enemy is sufficient to enable the wife to obtain a divorce, on the ground that she cannot remain the spouse of a Jew. The petty warfare which is incessant among them renders their tenure of life very uncertain, and there is a saying that while the Arab fears hunger and is starved: the townsman fears death from too fast living and kills him-

Warlike Qualities.

* As at Tîsnît, where Arabs are looked on almost as pagans, and most men read.

† As at Tatta, Akka, etc. whence few pilgrims go to Mekka, and as few can read or recite the prayers. (De Foucauld.)

[1] The Ait Yussi.

self thereby: the Berber fears murder and is assassinated. Where every one goes armed, ready to defend or attack as occasion offers, repeated gun-shots are universally taken as summons to an affray.

The quiet plain-dwellers have a wholesome dread of these highlanders, and nothing could be more comical than the awe of one of my servants at the sight of an Aberdonian, after having been duly instructed that he belonged to one of the Berber class of Great Britain! Such dread is only too well founded, for not only do the Berbers prevent the low-landers from encroaching on their fertile valleys, and prey upon their flocks and caravans, but they also at times press them into their service. One method of preventing the escape of a lowland cow-herd is to tie him bare-legged on the bare back of a bull which has been kept several days without water, and is suddenly let loose to rush with him to a stream. The result incapacitates the unfortunate rider from riding again. Although this brutal practice is well vouched for, it is to be hoped it is not common.

Tyranny.

En-Noweiri makes Count Julian give 'Okbah a fine character of the Berbers: "They are a people without religion, they eat carrion, they drink the blood of their beasts, and they are like brutes, because they do not believe in God, and do not even know Him."[1] Leo Africanus, quaintly translated by Pory, says of them, "No People under Heaven are more addicted unto Courtesie than this Nation. Mindful they have always been of Injuries, but most forgetful of Benefits.... The greater Part of these People are neither Mohammedans, Jews nor Christians, and hardly shall you find so much as a Sparke of Pietie in any of them." They certainly display untamed cupidity, and

Character.

[1] J. As. 3, xi., 124.

are ignorant of truthfulness and honesty to a degree most truly Oriental. Yet in all my dealings with this race I have found that while they were extremely suspicious of foreigners, they were yet ready to become good friends when they had proved the stranger to be true, and were not altogether ungrateful. I consider them superior to the Arabs both in physique and in moral character.

Recommendations.

Evidence of this is afforded by the employment of Berbers from Sûs as night watchmen and guards for all the stores and railway stations in Tunisia, in preference to any others, on account of their reliability, and similar guards are to be found at the caravan stations along the route from Damascus to Mekkah.* Their callousness to extremes of heat and cold is astonishing, and their powers of endurance are remarkable. They have in some districts been noted for their acrobats, as far as history extends.[1] Herodotus speaks of these, and Egyptian monuments also record their visits from the West under the fourth dynasty.[2] Of recent years companies from Sûs have played in Europe and America.

Independence.

The Berbers pay but little respect to the authority of the sultan, whose chief power and influence are religious, for on them the religion of Arabia sits lightly, and in consequence the districts which they inhabit are practically closed to Europeans. Every summer the late sultan undertook an expedition against some of them for the extension of his rule, or the collection of tithes. United, these wiry mountaineers could easily overcome him, but their inter-tribal rivalry has ever been their weakness. This alone enabled the wanderers from Asia to master them one by one, and it is the experience gained by the Moorish government of to-day, in pitting one against the other, which gives

* See DOUGHTY'S *Arabia Deserta.*

[1] See p. 336. (Sidi Hamed û Mûsà.) [2] BRUGSCH BEY, *Egypt under the Pharaohs.*

it so much success in employing the same tactics towards European nations.

It is strange that so vast and so distinct a people should own no leader round whose standard to rally in the face of a common foe. It would seem as though, rightly or wrongly, the curse of Ishmaël had descended upon them. Among themselves there is always warfare. No traveller is safe from pillage unless protected or accompanied by a member of the tribe through which he may be passing, of sufficient importance to guard him from injury, by fear of retribution. Travellers must always pay zeṭáṭah to be provided with mezrág, or protection, the latter word meaning literally a lance, as the sending with them of a chief's lance used to be their guarantee. Harris says that the Dáds tribe can travel safely anywhere in consideration of their granting safe passage within their borders, through which lies the high-road from east to west.[1]

Safe-Conducts.

The hospitality of these people, if not so profuse as that attributed to the Arabs, is sufficiently extensive, once fear and prejudice are removed. Were it not for their lack of a stable government, and the tempting ease with which crime of all sorts may be committed amongst them, even the present system of escorts would be unnecessary. In some districts all visitors make for the mosque, whence the m'ḳaddam sends any number up to ten, who may come on the same day, to be guests of a certain resident, if he be able to entertain so many. Each "householder" takes his turn, which alone counts, not the number entertained.

Hospitality.

The methods of self-rule followed by the Berber tribes vary considerably.[2] In some cases the governing body is a gathering of representatives of the various sections, veritable little republics, as near the

Government.

[1] TAFILET, p. 98. [2] DE FOUCAULD, p. 91.

democratic ideal as possible. The more original custom, however, seems to have been to entrust supreme power to an ámghár, or "elder," who corresponds to the Arab sheïkh. These generally realize that the less they oppress the people, the more secure their position will be. There is a third style, in which the assembly nominates a sort of governor.* Some tribes are split up into families with their own hereditary sheïkhs, or ámghárs,† and others elect sheïkhs yearly for each district.‡

Habitat.

The greater part of the Atlas Mountains, and right away across North Africa, that back-ground ridge of snow-capped mountains, is the Berbers' dwelling-place,§ and though many of the hill-tribes are of such mixed origin,** that it is difficult to assert off-hand the nationality of this one or that, yet so closely are they linked together by their language and their customs, that there is no possibility of confounding the vast majority of their tribes with those of other origin.

Antiquity of Tribes.

Of most of the Berber tribes mentioned by the early Morocco chroniclers,[1] no trace is now to be found, but a few stand out as having held their own to this day. Such are the Hawárà, the Ghomárà and the Miknásà. Among them also were the Zanátà, who were long to play so important a

* As at Tîsnît and Tatta.

† As the Aït oo M'rábit, Ida oo B'lál, Isaffen, etc.

‡ As the Aït Siddrát, Imerghán, etc.

§ El Bekri tells a quaint story of Alexander, who, he says, told it to Aristotle, that he had a certain mare which never neighed till she had drunk the waters of the Atlas, which, the sage declared, should be regarded as a warning, showing what sort of men dwelt there.[2]

** As the Aït bû Amran, Beni Marîn, etc. The Aït Atta, Berbers in language and dress, but by exception horsemen—famed since Leo's time for their skill in racing horses on foot,—one of the most powerful and warlike tribes south of the Atlas, claim descent from the Koreïsh tribe of

[1] *E.g.* Idreesi, p. 66; Ibn Khaldûn, En-Noweiri, etc. [2] *Rev. Afr.*, 1892, p. 269.

ASGHIN, AN ATLAS VILLAGE.

Photograph by Joseph Thomson.

part in the nation's history, the Ketámà and Sanhájà, or Zenága, who give their name to Senegal, apparently their head-quarters. That of the Zanátà appears to have been to the south of O'ran, and they were among the claimants of Arab origin,* though it was alleged by the Arabs that they were descendants of Goliath, *i.e.* Philistines or Phœnicians. The Ghomárà, who form the main body of the Rîfis, and whose kinsmen are the Beni Ḥassán, are of the Maṣmûda family, with which indeed the greater number of the Morocco Berbers were connected,[1] though Mannert describes the inhabitants of the Rîf, called by Pliny Metagonitæ, as a mixture of native Numidians, Carthaginians and Phœnicians.[2] Among the Masmûda tribes enumerated by Ibn Khaldûn, five hundred years ago, are the still recognizable Hantátà, Nafîsà, Urîkà, Ghegháyà, Dukallà, Ḥaḥà, Mesfîwà, Siksáwà and Idau Tanán tribes, other important divisions being the Harghà, Tînmalál, Gedmîwà, Hazmîrà, Assadîn, Beni Wazzît, Beni Magîr, 'Aïlánà, Maghûs, Doghaghà, Zeggen and Lakhás, many of whom have quite disappeared. The Tûáriḳ or Tûáreg (*sing.* Targa) "veil-wearers"—in Arabic

Arabs. Their women differ from the Berbers in wearing a shawl of red black and white stripes.[3] Idreesi awards the distinction of Arab origin to the Hawárà, and refers to the Beni Yûsef, Fandaláwà, Bahlûl, Zawáwà, Majásà, Ghaïátà and Salaljûn as Arabic-speaking Berbers. Ibn Khaldûn thinks the Sanhajà and Ketámà could make good this claim,[4] which became general when islám had embraced them all. As a general rule the prefix Aït ("Confederation") to the name of a tribe indicates Berbers; that of Aolád, Arabs, and that of Beni (the last two meaning "Children") the mixed Jibli or mountaineer people. The Arab nomads did not reach Morocco in any numbers till the fifth century of the Hejira.[5]

* Ibn Khaldûn has discussed their claims and the origins of their names at great length in vol. iii., p. 184, and vol. iv., p. 597.

[1] Ibn Khaldûn, vol. ii., pp. 134, 135.

[2] p. 536.

[3] Harris, *Tafilet*, p. 208.

[4] Vol. iv., p. 185.

[5] Ibn Khaldûn, vol. iv., p. 492, notes. See *The Moorish Empire*, for a full discussion of this question.

Muliththamîn—of the Algerian Sahara do not extend to Morocco.*

Race.

No decision has as yet been reached as to the family to which the Berbers belong.[1] Some hold them to be Hamitic,[2] but I am inclined to think that while certain portions, notably towards the south-west, have largely intermingled with, and become modified by, the sons of Ham, they are themselves of another stock. Several hold that they cannot be Semitic,[3] and some ask why should they not be of Aryan blood.[4] There may be something after all in the well-worn theory that these people were descended, at all events in part, from the tribes expelled from Palestine by Joshua.[5] Idreesi says the Zanátà were descended from Goliath (Jalût), son of Dháris, son of Jána.[6] Ibn Khaldûn quotes this story from one Mohammed ibn Jarûr et-Tábari (838—923), adding that the name of their leader Ifrikos was given to the country of Ifrikîyah, or Tunis, which we have corrupted into Africa. Others, he tells us, say they were descended directly from Shem through Canaan, Mazîgh (whence one of their names), Temla and Berber (whence the other name),† while others again believed them to be Amalekites, descended from Esau. One statement made by Ibn Khaldûn which is specially worth nothing, is that the Copts (*i.e.* Guptîs or Gyptîs—Egyptians) would not let them remain in Egypt.[7] But hav-

* De Foucauld speaks of the great tribe between Wád Zîz, Wád Dáds and Wád Dra'a, divided into two branches speaking Berber only, the Aït Aṭṭa and the Aït Yufilmál (or Aït Z'dig), as the most powerful tribe in Morocco.[8]

† They are also said to have been descended from one Ber, son of Kish, son of Ailam, probably of the family of Ham; otherwise from the founder of the earliest Egyptians, Ber son of Mazîrg, son of Canaan, son of Cain.[9]

[1] See MERCIER, *Revue Africaine*, No. 90, Nov. 1871, pp. 420—435.

[2] *E.g.* HARRIS in *Tafilet*, and CUST in *Modern Languages of Africa*, p. 97.

[3] *E.g.* HANOTEAU.

[4] Gen. FAIDHERBE is inclined so to class them.

[5] PROCOPIUS, *De Bello Vandalico*, (ed. 1531), lib. ii, p. 222. See *The Moorish Empire*, p. 10.

[6] p. 65.

[7] Vol. iv. pp. 175—6.

[8] GRÅBERG, p. 72.

[9] p. 362.

ing quoted them, the able Berber historian sums up and dismisses all these theories, because the Berbers were already numerous in these countries as far back as records went. He finally decides his people to be of the race of Shem, and kinsmen of the Agrîgesh [Gergasines? Greeks?] and Philistines, whose kings were called Jalût.[1]

The name by which these Berbers know themselves, Amazîgh * (language Tamazîght), lends colour to the supposition, based on traditions of old writers, that their forefather was Meshech, the son of Japheth, which would give the Ayran theory a chance. The name Philistine (Pilistin) is recorded by several authors as used in different districts, both as denoting Jews and Berbers, and I have heard it applied by Jews in the Atlas to the surrounding Berbers, but this may have been no more than a figurative use, as in the mouth of Mathew Arnold. Some Berber tribes are doubtless partially of Jewish blood. † It has also been suggested that possibly some of the conquered Hyksos may have passed into the Maghrib. ‡

Names.

The fair complexion of the Berbers has led to some remarkable theorizing. Procopius early called attention to this fact, and wrote of people in Mt. Atlas with white bodies and yellow hair.[2] According to Tyler,[3] "the earliest recorded appear-

Complexion Theories.

* Gråberg finds "the root of this name, Mazig, in many Greek and Latin writers, as Mazyes, Mazisci, Mazyces and Mazich."[4] See also his "Remarks on the Language of the Amazirghs;" London, 1836. The Latin writers referred to include Lucretius, Suetonius and Ptolemy.

† Gråberg, also mentions a tradition among the people themselves that their ancestors were Jews.

‡ Abu'l Feda, Ibn Khaldûn[5] and Ibn Abi Zarga—the latter in the *Raôd el Kartás* (1326),—say that some of the ancestors of the Berbers of El Maghribel Akṣà were Jews, some Christians, and some Zoroastrians, but how the last-named got from Persia to Morocco is not explained.

[1] *l.c.*, p. 184. [2] Bk. ii., c. 13 (Bonn Ed., p. 400). [3] *Anthropology*, p. 309.
[4] p. 69. [5] Vol. iv., p. 177.

ance of fair-whites may be in the paintings where Egyptian artists represent with yellowish-white skin and blue eyes certain natives of North Africa, a district where remnants of blonde tribes are still known." These were, in the words of Laing,[1] "the Lebu (Libyans), a fair-skinned and blue-eyed white race, whose descendants remain to this day as 'Kabyles'* and Berbers in the same localities of North Africa."† The Arabs seem early to have admired them, for En-Noweiri tells of the sale in the East of one of their girls for a thousand gold mitkals or ducats.

European Influences.

"It was formerly believed," says Gibbon,[2] "that the boldest of the Vandals fled beyond the power or even knowledge of the Romans to enjoy their solitary freedom on the shores of the Atlantic Ocean." But Ibn K͟hallikan quotes an ancient writer to the effect that in the twelfth century the Berbers of the Atlas complained to the Mahdi Ibn Tûmart that the rosy cheeks and blue eyes on which he had remarked were due to the intercourse of European mercenaries in the ameer's service with their women.[3] Modern writers have imagined traces of Roman and other foreign physiognomy among these people,[4] but though these admixtures may have influenced to some degree the local types, it is unlikely that distinct effects are still to be observed. Whatever peculiarities exist in certain districts, are much more likely to be due to the settlement at comparatively recent dates of bodies of European slaves.[5] General Faidherbe went so far as to surmise that a fair race from the Baltic or Northern

* An erroneous French expression meaning "Tribes," in Arabic ḳabáïl.

† An essay on this subject by Paul Broca was published in Tissot's *Monuments Megalithiques et les Populations Blonds du Maroc*, Paris, 1876.

[1] p. 399. [2] *Decline and Fall*, vol. v., p. 120.

[3] Vol. iii., p. 211. See *The Moorish Empire*, p. 241. [4] JACKSON, p. 135. SHAW, etc.

[5] See *The Moorish Empire*, pp. 301—2.

Gaul invaded the North African littoral some three thousand years or more ago, and M. Mercier considers that perhaps the ancestors of the fair strain among the Berbers were the tenants of the Celtic graves found here and there throughout the land. [1]

Possible Kindred.

There is a strong supposition that the mysterious Iberians in the Peninsula were of Berber stock, * [2] and I am inclined to believe, from internal evidence, a theory which at first sight struck me as very far-fetched, that they were closely allied to the "little black Celts," † the genuine Celts being a tall, red-haired people. If so, they were ancestors to part of the population of the western parts of Cornwall, Wales, Ireland and Scotland, to say nothing of Biscay and Finisterre, and the builders of those rude stone monuments which exist as well in Barbary as in Britain. Professor Brenton makes out the old Etruscans to have been Berbers, [3] and Professor Keane holds the Berbers to be of Caucasian stock. [4] Whoever in Europe may or may not have claimed kindred with them, the fact remains, as stated by Latham, that the Berbers, or more strictly speaking the Amazîgh, still occupy the largest area of any race in Africa. ‡

* Sir J. W. Dawson [5] says of the identification of the Neolithic men with the Iberians by Professor Boyd Dawkins might have been carried farther, to the identification of these same Iberians with the Berbers, the Guanchos of the Canary Islands, and the Caribbean and other tribes of Eastern and Central America. Dr. Bertholon considers that the Iberians still furnish three-fifths of the population of North Africa. [6]

† "Black" being only a comparative term for "dark."

‡ Essays on Berber Ethnology have been published by Dr. Ricque (Paris, 1864): Ernest Mercier (*Rev. Afr.*, no. 90): Sabatier (*Rev. d'Anthrop.*, July, 1885: and Quedenfeldt (*Zeit. für Ethnologie*, 1888, etc.), the last named dealing with the Shlûḥ.

[1] *Rev. Africaine*, No 90, Nov. 1871, p. 431.

[2] TUBINO, *Los Aborigenes Ibericos*. 1876.

[3] *On Etruscan and Libyan Names*. Proc. Am. Philos. Soc., vol. xviii., Feb. 1890.

[4] *Africa*, p. 65.

[5] *Story of the Earth and Man*, p. 404.

[6] *Revue Générale des Sciences*, Nov. 30th, 1896, p. 972.

Although the Berber tongue has a strong affinity with the Semitic in the construction both of its words and sentences, and especially in its verbs,[1] its vocabulary is so entirely different that it can hardly belong there.*[2] Mr. Renan holds that the Berber

Language.

BERBER HOUSES, ARROMD, GREAT ATLAS.
Photograph by Dr. Rudduck.

tongue "does not belong to the family of Semitic languages: it stands with regard to them as does the Coptic,

* De Slane, in his notes to the Berber historian, Ibn Khaldûn,[3] points out the following features of similarity to the Semitic class; its tri-literal roots, the inflexions of the verb, the formation of derived verbs, the genders of the second and third persons, the pronominal affixes, the aoristic style of tense, the whole and broken plurals, and the construction of the phrase; whereas it differs from it in the dative of the third personal pronoun, and in the mobilization of the pronominal affixes. It differs essentially from the Coptic and Haussa languages in conjugations, declensions and vocabulary.

[1] See NEWMAN, *On the Structure of the Berber Language*, in PRITCHARD'S *Researches*, vol. iv., 1844.

[2] See HODGSON, *Trans. Amer. Philos. Soc.*, Philadelphia, 1831, vol iv., p. 48, and *North Amer. Rev.*, vol. xxxv., p. 54, also *Notes on Northern Africa*, New York, 1844.

[3] Vol. iv., pp. 504 and 524.

which may well be the principal idiom of a Hamitic family, to which the Berber would belong."[1] Prof. Basset sets it down as Kushite or Hamitic, or Proto-Semitic, probably connected with Libyan and Numidian.

Some have imagined that the ancient Punic bore some relation to this tongue, but this has been disproved, though it is almost certain that Jugurtha and his people spoke it, and it must have been well-known to the Carthaginians. De Slane considers that there is practically nothing Phœnician, Vandal or Roman in the language.[2] M. de Rochemonteix has pointed out that the same pronominal roots, the same methods of inflecting them and the substantives, and of forming derivatives, as are met with in the Berber of to-day, existed in the ancient Egyptian. There is a strong belief that the Guanchos of the Canaries were Berbers, and evidence of at least an intimate connection is afforded by the similarity of many of their words and grammatical forms, as shown by a study of the language of Teneriffe.[3]

Next-of-Kin.

It has been suggested with some show of reason that the present form is an older and less perfect language, moulded grammatically on the Arab model. The vast number of Arabic words which have been incorporated into the modern Berber, estimated by some writers, I do not think excessively, as a third,[4] have all been more or less modified to bring them into harmony with the original rhythm, but I believe that from one dialect or another all the real Berber words might be collected. This task would, however, be a useless, though an interesting one, as in no part would the whole be intelligible. The proportion of Negro words in use towards the south, though large, is not so great as that of Arabic words in the north.

Arabic and Negro Influences.

[1] *Les Langues Sémitiques.* [2] Notes on IBN KHALDÛN, vol. iv., p. 564.

[3] MARQUIS OF BUTE, Paper read in the Anthropological Section of the British Association, 1891. [4] DE SLANE on *Ibn Khaldûn*, vol. iv., Ap., p. 497.

Foreign Students.

Several well-known students have from time to time occupied themselves with the Berber language, mostly treading on one another's heels, instead of faring afield.* Among those who have done real service, mention must not be omitted of Professor F. W. Newman, (publications on it from 1836 to 1887)† and Venture de Paradis,‡ who have studied at such disadvantages; of Delaporte and Hanoteau with their Algerian Berber grammars; of Brosselard § and René Basset with their dictionaries, or of De Slane with his able translations. Professor Basset has been at work on the subject for some twenty years, and has produced a comparative vocabulary of several dialects, as well as a collection of fables in those of no less than twenty-three tribes.** M. Louis Rinn has issued a pains-proving work, in which he makes the Berber language and character parent to a Greek, Latin and French family.†† His work is more ingenious than conclusive.

A Comparison.

The great difficulty with Berber is that it is a language without a literature, only one or two dialects possessing any writings at all, these being chiefly of small account, and in adapted Arabic char-

* Thirty-three works on the Berber language are quoted by D'Avezac, Paris, 1840. See also Basset, *Manuel de la Langue Kabyle*, pp. 1*—9*. Zacharia Jones wrote a *Dissertatio in Linguâ Shilhense* in a work by Chamberlayne, *Oratio Dominica*, Amsterdam, 1715. Gråberg, in 1836, published *Remarks on the Language of the Amazirghs, commonly called Berebbers*. Dr. Cust has collected some information on the subject in his *Modern Languages of Africa*.

† Perhaps the most important is his *Libyan Vocabulary*, London, 1882.

‡ *Grammaire et Dictionnaire de la Langue Berbère*, Paris. 1844; Bonn, 1845.

§ *Dictionnaire Français Berbère*, Paris. 1844.

** *Poème de Çabi en Dialect Chilha (Sous de Maroc)*, Paris, 1879. *Relation de Sidi-Brahim de Massah dans le Sous*, 1882. (Treated also by Newman and Hodgson.) *Lexicographie Berbère*, (Rîf Dialect) Paris, 1883. *Recueil de Textes et Documents relatif à la Philologie Berbère*, Algiers, 1887. These are collected in the *Loqmân Berbère*, Paris, 1890.

†† *Les Origines Berbères*, Algiers, 1889.

acters. A ready comparison of Rîfian Berber with the Morocco Arabic is afforded by the following transliterations of the Lord's Prayer.*

Rîfian: Bábáth-nakh wunnî dhî ·ijnathin adhitawaḳaddas· ·isim
Arabic: Abá-ná alladhi fi es-samawát liataḳaddas ism-ak

innish, addîas ir-hakamth· innish, atîrî ir-khaḍir· innish
lîáti malakût-uk, litakun mashîyatuk

mammish gujinná· hamîá kha-th-·mûrth: aghrom idhakhaïrizmïn
kamá fi es-samá kadálik 'álà el arḍ: khubza-ná kafáfa-ná

ûksha-natht aïḍá·: thagh-fer thanakh dhanûb·-innakh mammish
á'aṭi-ná el-yôm: wa aghfir laná dhunûba-ná kamá

ghánaghfer· nishshin thanîan· ir-mudhnibîn· in-naḳh; wa-ra-khsîdif
naghfir naḥan aïḍán lil-mudhnibîn ilai-ná; wa-lá tudkhil-ná

dhî ·tajrîb, ·lakin sinjmanakh izg-lbrîs, ·liánna gharik
fi tajribat, lakin najji-ná min esh-shirrîr, lián lak

ir-murk· dhir-kûwith· dhir-majd· ghar-dáïm, Ameen.
el mulk wa el-kûwat wa el majd ilà el-abad. Ameen.

The Rîfi version is from that prepared for the British and Foreign Bible Society by the late Mr. William Mackintosh of Tangier. The only other volumes of any importance in either of the Morocco dialects, of which I am aware, are the *Tûwáḥḥid* ("The Unity"—of God), a very rare and highly prized treatise, believed to be the oldest African work in existence, except in Egyptian or Ethiopic, written by the Muwaḥḥadi pioneer, Ibn Tûmart the Mahdi, also the author of

Literature.

* The Arabic version as pronounced in Morocco is placed under the Rîfian, word for word. To simplify comparison, hyphens are used to separate words from particles, though not so separated in writing. A point (·) before or after a portion of a word indicates that portion as corrupted Arabic, but points have not been inserted in the case of particles.

a work called *Morshídah* ("the Directress"), an attempt to convince the Berbers of the truth of his creed, in which he was successful,[1] and of the *'Azzu má Yaṭlab.**

Among the Berbers, who think highly of it to this day, the *Tûwaḥḥid* was held in greater reverence, if possible, than the Ḳor'án itself. Ibn Tûmart's followers, the Muwáḥḥadìs, went so far as to commit his works to memory. As the Maṣmûda tribe, the first to support this Mahdi, could not speak Arabic, he counted the words in the first chapter of the Ḳor'àn, and calling as many men, seated them in a row and named each one with a word. Then, each pronouncing his name in order, they repeated the chapter. At the same time the officers of the Ḳarûeeïn Mosque at Fez had to be dismissed because they could not speak Berber.[2] Berber translations of the Ḳor'án are, however, mentioned by El Bekri; one by Sálih ibn Ta'arîf, a prophet, cir. 744, and one by Hamîm, a Rîfi, cir. 925. De Slane mentions two more translations of the Ḳor'án into Shilḥah, said to have been made in Sûs during the present century, the authors of which were beheaded and the Mss. burned.[3]

The Berbers and Islám.

Traces of an ancient alphabet are to be found in some districts of Southern Algeria, and these have been collated, showing that there were thirty-two letters.[4] In addition to the twenty-eight of Arabic, Berber boasts tseem, چ, jain ژ (like the Persian), zhád ڽ and gáf گ.† Doubtless a careful search among

Characters.

* These three works exist in one volume in the National Library in Paris.

† The Tûáriḳ of Algeria possess no 'aïn.

[1] See *The Moorish Empire*, p. 69.

[2] *Raôḍ el Ḳarṭás*, p. 538.

[3] Notes on *Ibn Khaldûn*, vol. iv., p. 534.

[4] JUDAS, *Sur l'Ecriture de la Langue Berbère dans l'Antiquité et nos Jours.* Paris, 1863. Dr. E. T. HAMY, *Inscriptions Gravées... près Figuig*, Paris, Rev. d'Etbnog., vol. i., 1882: also DE SLANE on *Ibn Khaldûn*, vol. iv. 1882.

the female ornaments would discover something akin to these characters in Morocco. As a rule the women speak less Arabic than the men, but among the Tûâriḳs it is said that more women read than men, and the writings discovered have usually been but inscriptions of various sorts, chiefly on ornaments.

Among the peculiar grammatical features of Berber may be mentioned two numbers (no dual), two genders and six cases; verbs with one, two, three and four radicals, and imperative and aorist tenses only. Basset says that in Algeria there is no article, but I agree with De Slane[1] that the prefix "tha" of Morocco represents a lost article, or rather that it is an article which has lost its determinate value.

Dialects.

The many dialects into which the language has in process of time become subdivided are attributable to the lack of a literary standard.* The difference is indeed so great between distant parts as to have led many to suppose that they were different tongues. It may yet be proved that some are as distinct as Spanish and Italian. St. Augustine, however, recognized their fundamental unity, for he wrote,[2] "In Barbary, Africa, we know many people with one tongue." Such comparisons as I have been able to make between the styles used in Morocco have satisfied me that they are essentially one, however they differ in use. When Arabic is spoken of as the language of Morocco, it is seldom realized how small a proportion of its inhabitants use it naturally. Berber is the real language of Morocco, Arabic that of its creed and government.

* A peculiarity of the Rîf dialect is the change of the Arabic "l" to "r," as will be observed in the quotation given, a fact which lends support to the theory that the word Rîfian or Rîfi is identical with Libyan or Lîbi, "b" and "f" being of course interchangeable, through "v." I have no opinion to offer on this point.

[1] Notes on *Ibn Khaldûn*, vol. iv., p. 538.

[2] *De Civitate*, xvi., 6.

The Word "Berber."

The word Berber itself, from which we have formed the word Barbary, is of very doubtful origin. Equivalents, denoting indistinct sounds, seem to exist in Latin, Greek and Arabic, while it is probably not a genuine Berber word. It serves, nevertheless, as a convenient and widely accepted name for the whole race, which is known to the people themselves by a different title in each district. Only certain portions acknowledge the name of Berber (*pl.* Bráber). Ibn Khaldûn says that in Arabic the word denotes "a mixture of unintelligible cries, so that one says of a lion that he 'berbers' when he roars confusedly."[1] De Slane, however, thinks that the ancient Egyptians used it, as also did St. Augustine at a later period.*

Of late years the works of several Berber and North African historians have been translated from the Arabic, such as that of Ibn Khaldûn by the Baron de Slane,—a labour of fourteen years, and several scientists, most of them French, have been paying considerable attention to this hitherto little known people.

* Gibbon, in the *Decline and Fall,*[2] says of the word "Berber" that it was applied, first, in the time of Homer to rude tribes with harsh pronunciation and defective grammar; secondly, in the time of Herodotus to *all* nations strangers to the Greeks; thirdly, in the time of Plautus, Romans "submitted to the insult," and freely gave themselves the name of barbarians; and, fourthly, applied to Moors by Arab conquerors, borrowed from Latin "Provincials," and used in relation to the whole country.

In Sanskrit also the word Berber is said to mean a foreigner. The *Periplus of the Erythean* describes the African coast of the Red Sea as "Barbariké Épeiros," an epithet endorsed by Ptolemy: and Julius Honorius alludes to Berbers near the "Malva Flumen" now the Melwîyah. Knight's Encyclopædia gives "Verves" as the name of one Mauretanian tribe, and "Verbicæ" that of another. The subject is discussed at length by M. Mercier in the *Revue Africaine.*[3] It is noteworthy that the tribes so-called on the Nile and the Red Sea speak a different language from that of Barbary.

Herodotus[4] says that the Egyptians called those not speaking their own tongue Berbers.

[1] Vol. i., p. 168.
[2] Vol. vi., p. 351, n. 162,
[3] No. 90, Nov. 1871. (Brit. Mus., Ac. 6915.)
[4] Bk. 2, p. 158.

COAST JEW AND JEWESS.
(Northern Morocco.)

Photo. by L. L., Tangier.

CHAPTER THE TWENTY-THIRD

THE MOROCCO JEWS

WHILE in common parlance one can hardly include the subjects of this chapter under the loose-fitting title of "Moors," in reality they have quite as good a right to it as any, certainly a better one than many of the slaves from Guinea whose hue in the vulgar mind is regarded as national. A Morocco Jew is as much entitled to describe himself a Moor as an Algerian Jew to pass as a Frenchman, or a Jewish Lord Mayor of London to call himself an Englishman.

Numbers.

Morocco being absolutely without statistics, it is impossible to arrive at any conclusion as to the actual numbers of its Jewish population, or even as to the proportion which they bear to the general population, for they are much more numerous in one part than in another, and their agglomeration in a town frequently means their sparsity in its immediate neighbourhood.* In Tangier, the advantages afforded by the presence of so many foreigners, by the opportunities for trade, and, above all, by the comparative immunity from the indignities inflicted further inland, have all tended to allure considerable numbers, and to keep them there. For these reasons it is probable that out of some thirty thousand inhabitants, of whom some six thousand are Europeans, as many as ten or twelve thousand are

* Gråberg estimated the total at 539,500, Alexander[1] at 340.000, Rohlfs at 200,000.

[1] *Jews*, p. 217.

Israelites. Mogador, which ranks second to Tangier as a busy port, takes the same position with regard to its Jewish population. It has been estimated by men well able to judge that the average proportion of Jewish inhabitants in the towns is one fourth, though out in the country, with the exception of the Atlas district, it is only under the protection of powerful governors, few and far between, that little colonies of the peculiar people thrive. The largest settlement is naturally found in the largest city, Fez, the dwellers in which are reckoned at one hundred and fifty thousand, and include perhaps thirty thousand Jews. In the country, several districts are reported to be without Jewish inhabitants, such as the Berber tribes of Beni M'teer, Beni M'gild, Beni Waghaïn, Aït Yûssi, Zemmûr Shilḥ and Záïr.[1]

Distribution.

With the exception of the ports of Tangier, Azila, Casablanca, Mazagan and Saffi, every town, and almost every hamlet, has its Jewish quarter, wherein alone, enclosed by gates at night, the sons of Israel are allowed to live. The sacred city of Zarhôn they and all foreigners are prohibited from approaching, and in Wazzán they live in rookeries on sufferance. Yûsef I. (bin Tashfin), builder of Marrákesh, prohibited the Jews from living in that city,[2] but since his days it has become one of their centres. It is curious that in 1834 they were not to be found in Agadir or Saffi.[3] Perhaps the fanaticism concomitant with the veneration in which the rabat, or "camp" suburb of the latter port is held had something to do with that case.

Jewries.

The quarters allotted to their Jewish subjects by the Moorish sultans are known either as the melláḥ ("place of salt") or the missoos ("saltless place"). The latter name is given in derision, saltlessness and worthlessness being terms proverbially synony-

[1] De Foucauld, p. 401. [2] Abu'l Féda, vol. i., p. 172. [3] Gråberg, p. 251.

mous. The former designation is explained by the fact that Jewish butchers are forced to pickle the heads of rebels for exhibition above the gates of the towns as a warning to others. Similarly they are summoned to remove dead animals from the streets, to clean drains, or to do anything which the Moors consider defiling. In certain places Jews who can afford it live outside the melláḥs, in the portion allotted to Europeans, but this

GATE OF MELLAH, DAMNAT.
Photograph by Dr. Rudduck.

is not possible everywhere. Even in their melláḥs they have not always been safe, for, as on the accession of the wretch El Yazeed in 1790, they have sometimes been abandoned to the soldiery and populace.[1] But by that time the British Consul reported the Jews as "constantly scribbling to Europe," with the result that they have found good friends there.* As late as 1820

* One of the most interesting efforts on their behalf was the visit of Sir Moses Montefiore in 1864, for the purpose of obtaining some amelio-

[1] MATRA's Reports, *Public Record Office*, vol. 17.

the Jews of Fez were massacred by the Udáïa, then in revolt.

Oppression.

It is probable that the Jewish inhabitants of Morocco have never been free from a certain amount of oppression, and that from the first they have had to suffer indignities which have long been regarded from both sides as matters of course, but which are none the less irksome. It must be remembered that until within the past century "Nazarenes"—a term which in Morocco is equivalent to "foreigners"—were classed with Jews, and the two were treated alike. It is only awe of the superior power of the former which has secured to them the privileges now enjoyed. To this day unrecommended foreigners are forced to dwell in the Jewries of the interior and the closed ports, no Muslim daring to take them in without permission.

Divisions.

The Jews of Morocco are divided into two distinct classes, the descendants of those who first settled in Morocco—now to be found in their unmixed state in the interior only, most of them residing in the Atlas,—and the descendants of those who emigrated to Morocco when in the fifteenth century zeal-mad Spain expelled her Jewish subjects. Those who settled on the Moorish coast absorbed their co-religionists in their vicinity, and thus established what has become the more civilized and important section of the two. Davidson, however, considered those of the mountains "far superior, both physically and morally, to their

ration of their condition, but without much result, though great things were expected of it.[1] En-Náșiri, the latest Moorish historian, describes Sir Moses as an envoy of the Rothschilds, and explains that the decree he obtained (of which he gives a copy), was purposely worded so as to be useless, and only promised them the rights given by God.[2] En-Náșiri voiced the opinion of the leading Moorish jurists in considering the comparative mildness of their present treatment as heretical.

[1] See HODGKIN's account. [2] Vol. iv., p. 156.

brethren residing among the Moors,"[1] but I think that what struck him was only the result of their free country life. It will be well to consider these two sections separately before attempting to draw general conclusions, although it is as one body that they appear to their rulers, and to the outside world.

Language.

The main distinction has ever been the language, for while the one class has spoken Berber and Arabic, the other has spoken Spanish and Arabic. The proportion who speak both Berber and Spanish—always with the intermediary Arabic—is microscopic, if it exist at all. As elsewhere, the Jews have shown themselves apt linguists, ever ready to master French and English in addition to their mother tongues, but the special facilities afforded in some of the towns in favour of the former enable it to be spoken more correctly. The lads in the Tangier Schools put the majority of English boys to shame by assiduity and perseverance in this direction. The merest smattering is turned to account in practice upon visitors, until the progress made is often wonderful. But the Arabic of the Morocco Jews is an atrocious production, and their Spanish, hardly better, is of an archaic pronunciation.

The Atlas Jews.

Of the Berber-speaking Jews of the Atlas, we have yet much to learn. There are stories current of agricultural colonies dwelling beyond the Atlas, which, if true, would add a further interest to an already fascinating subject. The traveller who has given to the world the most complete account of the peoples of that district—a meagre one nevertheless,—is De Foucauld, the prince of Morocco explorers. From him we know that the customs observed in comparatively well-known districts extend to the whole of the vast area embraced by the Greater and Lesser Atlas.

[1] p. 183.

Their condition varies there between that of serfs and slaves. Sometimes they are under the binding protection of the local sheïkh, and at others they belong to private individuals, who have practically the right to sell them. They are not only compelled to do much without payment, but they are imposed upon at every turn. They may not marry or remove their families till they have obtained permission from their so-called protectors, but without this protection they would not be safe for a day. Yet some five-and-twenty shillings has been considered sufficient blood-money for one of these unfortunates! On the other hand, outsiders are permitted to do them no injury, which would be considered as inflicted upon their protector (kási) who makes the duty a point of honour of avenging such. Disputes of this nature between powerful men lead frequently to intertribal quarrels. *

Protected Serfs.

To insure safety in travelling it is sufficient for the protégé to bear some article belonging to his master, written documents being scarce up there, with few to understand them. Yet there are districts in the Atlas where the Jews are forced to go armed, and to take part in tribal fights. The treatment of individual serfs depends entirely on the temper or pleasure of their masters, for their chances of redress for injury are practically *nil*, so that their position is in some respects worse even than that of negro slaves, who, being Mohammedans, may benefit at law from certain rights denied to those who spurn their prophet. Centuries of this oppression have naturally had

Method of Protection.

* A story was once told me on good authority of one sheïkh slaying another sheïkh to avenge the death of a Jewish serf of his in consequence of treatment received from his victim, to whom he had abandoned his "protégé" for a "consideration." The bargain appears to have been struck with the same implied restriction as in the case of Job, "Only upon himself put not thine hand."

a very deleterious effect upon the characters of the victims, who are cringing, cowardly creatures, never daring to answer back, and seldom even standing erect—a people demanding our utmost pity.

From the day of his birth until all trace of his last resting-place has disappeared, the Hebrew of Morocco is despised and scorned. "Dog of a Jew!" is a very mild term to employ in abusing him; the sobriquets of "ass!" and "swine!" stand in equal favour, and in polite society he is not to be referred to without an apology—"It was, yes, my lord, by thy leave, excuse me, a Jew!" But the various indignities to which his race is exposed in daily life differ too much from district to district for any complete list to be of general application. I shall therefore attempt to take notice only of the most important, in addition to those especially connected with the serfdom of the Atlas, already mentioned.

Daily Indignities.

For an unprotected Jew to lift his hand against or curse a Moor would be to bring down untold vengeance on his head. Yet in Muslim Courts Jews may not tender evidence on oath—a disability shared by foreigners,—so that they are obliged by *force majeure* to put up with whatever is inflicted upon them. At one time the slightest retaliation meant death to the avenger, however he might have been provoked, except by violation of domicile, and frequent cases are on record of Jews burned to death for wounding a Moor. Only last year (1900) a native Jew, naturalized as a citizen of the United States, and clad as a European, was lynched by the mob in Fez, for firing on a shareef who had struck him, and his body was only saved from being burnt by a high official, drawn to the spot by the cries. Some months later $1000 blood-money was, as usual, paid by the

Legal Disabilities.

Lynching

Moorish Government for the benefit of his family, and the affair was settled, a much larger amount being wrung from the shopkeepers in the vicinity of the murder. The slightest encouragement would have led the enraged populace to sack the mellâḥ. In 1881 a Jew was lynched in Fez for insulting a ḳâḍi. While in Tangier considerable laxity is allowed, in other parts their treatment is much more severe, and every day unlucky Jews are punished for imaginary offences or to gratify pure spite or greed. Lack of civility to a Moor, or outbidding him on the market, may become an offence, and attempting to obtain the aid of strangers an unpardonable crime. To leave the country the men used to be forced to pay $4, and the women $100, and sometimes the departure of the latter is still prohibited. Even when imprisoned, they are usually thrust into the foulest quarter of the dungeon.

Irregular Taxation.

In addition to the poll-tax, it has always been customary for the Jewish subjects of the sultans to present them with specially valuable offerings on the occasion of family festivals. Though these continue, they are not now the irksome imposts which once they were. Two centuries ago the usual thing on the birth of a son to the emperor, was to contribute gold pendants and earrings set with pearls, with gold plates bearing as inscriptions prayers in favour of mother and child.[1] The value of this jewellery was estimated in 1715 at £15, a much more considerable sum in those days, and in this country, than it represents in England now, and as Mulai Ismâʻîl was credited with some nine hundred sons, and received this amount for each, as well as similar articles in silver (minus the pearls) for some three hundred daughters, he must have reaped a considerable harvest in this field alone. Forced labour

[1] Pellow, p. 23. See *The Moorish Empire*, p. 148.

and the most unreasonable levies of manufactured goods have also been frequently inflicted on this much-suffering people. In public works, such as the building of the walls of Mequinez and Tetuan, we have it on record how they were compelled to toil unpaid beside the European slaves.[1] When Mulai Ismá'íl besieged Ceuta for many years, he was wont to make the Jews supply the powder used on Fridays, when they did the chief cannonading.[2] A thousand Jews are said to have been forced by Mohammed XVII. to take part in the siege of Melilla in 1774.[3] But there is also on record the appearance of a Jew, Samuel Valenciano, in charge of vessels for the relief of Azammûr when possessed by the Portuguese and besieged by the Moors in 1539, as also in command of a successful sortie.[4]

Town Regulations.

Except at Tangier, Jews may acquire no lands or property outside their melláhs, with the result that rents therein are raised abnormally by repeated "farming," and that most of the Jewries are terribly over-crowded, the landlords opposing their enlargement. In most towns, in the day-time, except on the coast, they can only leave their quarter barefoot; until recently, with the exception of the Hazzán (Rabbi) they were not permitted to ride in towns, and outside only on mules. Before certain mosques they must always remove their shoes, and formerly this was incumbent upon the women also, but Mulai Sulaïmán exempted them because, in the words of a quaint writer, "it was indecent and disturbing to devotion to see their tremendous calves."[5] Some governors cause them to remove even their head-dress before them, and when the sultan goes to mosque, as indeed, on the occasion of religious festivities, Jews are wise to keep out of the

[1] JAMES, vol. ii., p. 22. [2] GRÅBERG, p. 195. [3] PEZZI, p. 173.
[4] EL UFRÁNI, p. 122. [5] RICHARDSON, vol. ii., p. 4.

way, or they may be roughly handled, especially by the 'Aïsáwà.

Sumptuary Law.

The compulsory dark-coloured gaberdine of the men is also considered an indignity, and when foreign protection has been obtained is fast being laid aside in favour of European ugliness. Mulai 'Abd er-Raḥmán objected to this, and once ordered all Jews dressed as foreigners to be stripped and put in black again,[1] a hue which no Moor ever wears in any garment. It is most unfortunate that the younger ladies on the coast are so misguided as to reject their own becoming costumes to the extent that they do, in favour of hideous Parisian fashions not to be compared for beauty of grace with those worn by their mothers. Many of the older members of the community are conservative enough to retain the time-honoured style, but their juniors think they know better.

Costume in the North.

The peculiar dress to which unprotected male Jews in Morocco are restricted consists outwardly of a dark blue or black gaberdine of felt cloth, embroidered with narrow silk braid of the same tint, in which is worked on the right-hand side a distinctive badge almost identical with that once worn in England. Below this garment are visible the ankles—bare, or clad in white stockings—thrust into black slippers, while the Moors wear yellow, a colour which, in common with all other bright hues, is forbidden to the sons of Israel.[2] but not to the daughters. At the throat a bit of white material, or what was such once, is visible, and the sleeves, tight when buttoned, may be flapping loosely open. The face, a characteristic one, often marked with small-pox—though not so often as among the Moors,—is surmounted in the north by a proverbially greasy skull-cap, black, of course, while

[1] Richardson, vol. ii., p. 5. [2] Ali Bey, p. 33.

abundant locks crop out all round, left long, and forming an unintellectual fringe in front. The mourning custom of letting the hair and beard grow is strictly adhered to.

Costume in the South.

In the south peculiar bunches of curly, almost "frizzly," hair adorn each temple, such as also form a distinctive feature of one of the tribes of alleged Jewish origin, the Udáïà, part of the royal body-guard. The cap is in those parts replaced by a blue cotton kerchief, spotted with white, which, folded corner-wise, with the ends tied under the chin, gives an "old-womanish" appearance, far from prepossessing. This costume is varied considerably in the Atlas, where a hooded cloak (akhnif) of one piece, thrown back over the left arm, identical with that worn by the Berbers, is much in vogue; and of course everywhere there are deviations from these costumes, down to shirt and drawers alone, or rags and tatters.

Garb of Worship.

The ṣiṣit or sacred vest* with its mystic knotted tassels (kanfôt) representing the "fringe" with "border of blue" enjoined by Moses,[1] is generally worn by day; and at prayer-times the ṭallit—doubtless a relic of a toga-like garment in use before the present guise became compulsory—is worn just as the Moors wear the ḥaïk, but is not considered obligatory.† The phylacteries or tefilin are at the same time bound upon the forehead and left fore-arm,[2] neat little cubical cases of leather containing inscribed parchment rolls ‡—prepared with the most scrupulous care to preserve ceremonial purity,—fastened on by thongs in a pre-

* The ṣiṣit resembles a large pocket handkerchief, sometimes with a hole for the head in the centre, worn over the shoulders; the kanfôt, which alone are essential, hang from the four corners, and if policy prevents the wearing of the garment, they will be preserved, if possible, in the sash.

† Country Jews wear the ṭallit in the morning only, and call it ṣiṣit.

‡ Containing *Exodus,* xiii., 1—10; 11—16: *Deut.* vi., 4—9; xi., 13—20.

[1] *Deut.* xxii., 12, and *Numb.* xv., 38-40. [2] *Deut.* vi., 8, and xi., 18.

scribed manner, each twist and knot with some mystic signification.

Dress of the Women.

The dress of the women affords extreme contrasts. At home, in the morning, it is of the dirtiest and most slovenly, just a skirt and bodice, not unlike their European equivalents, but the latter often very low and loose. On high days and holidays the gorgeous attire worn by the same individual will be overwhelming in value and brightness. Rich, dark velvets, loaded with gold braid, form the costume, while the hair of a married woman, which the public may never see, is enveloped from the forehead in an expensive Lyons silk kerchief, bedizened with costly jewellery, as also are neck and wrists. A fortune is sometimes invested in these chattels, which on account of their value often develop into heirlooms, and are not to be seized for the husband's debts. In the estimation of Europeans the free use of antimony to darken the eye-lashes far from enhances their undisputed good looks.

Among the Berbers, the dress of the woman sometimes so nearly resembles that of the Muslims as to deceive even a native when a stranger. I have a lively recollection of the sudden change of my servant's language from courtesy to vituperation when he discovered one day in an Atlas village that he was addressing Jewesses politely, instead of Mooresses, as he had supposed.

The Mezûzah, outside which is written the Sacred Name,[1] is always to be seen on the door-posts, and is daily saluted with reverence. It is often shielded by a cover of needle-work.

Synagogues.

The synagogues of Morocco are, on the whole, mean and unhealthy, but are only on a par with the habitations of the worshippers. They are commonly called Sla' (*pl.* Sla'wát) *i.e.* "Places of Worship,"

[1] Shaddai, "Almighty," *Deut.* vi., 9; and inside, *Deut.* vi., 4—9, and xi., 13—20.

WIFE AND DAUGHTER OF A JEWISH BANKER OF MEQUINEZ.

Molinari, Photo., Tangier.

but sometimes also, on the coast "S'nôga." I have visited many, but they have a wearisome sameness. I speak now of the typical specimens, without reference to the fine modern buildings erected by subscription or by private liberality in some of the coast towns, as, for instance, the New Synagogue on Tangier Wall, or that of the Nahon family near to hand. The majority are small, with labyrinthine entrances, sometimes passing through distressingly odoriferous dwellings. Many are but private houses fitted up for worship. The Sefarim or Rolls of the Law (Tôrah) are seldom richly caparisoned, and the number in each synagogue is small, perhaps not half a dozen. They are generally paraded, on Mondays and Thursdays, when members of the congregation are called up to read extracts. The lamps are of the poorest quality, most of them wicks in oil floating on the water in huge tumblers.

Accommodation.

The accommodation on the great feast-days is so inadequate that numbers have to stand in the street outside. The segregation of the women is usual where galleries exist, and in some towns the women veil themselves while in the streets somewhat like the Mooresses, but they are poor attendants at the house of GOD. In country towns the condition of the houses of prayer is even disgusting, for they serve also as places in which to eat, to sleep and to kill chickens, not to mention cooking and trade.[1] I have never in any land seen more neglected and unsuitable synagogues in actual use than in Morocco, though those of Persia are almost as bad. In Baghdád they are in comparison grand, as also throughout Palestine, Syria, Egypt, Turkey and Central Asia.

The shôḥeṭ commonly performs his duties in the poultry line at street corners and other public places,

[1] Cf. DE FOUCAULD, p. 400.

where the interesting preliminaries may be studied gratis.* However carefully the slaughtered bird is handed to the bright-eyed maid who stands there to receive it, the final struggles often prove too much for her, when it is dropped to flap about among the passers-by, or the operator holds it under his foot while he examines his blade, preparing for action again. Sheep and cattle are slaughtered in a special yard or corner of the market, the shôḥetim receiving the horns, hides etc. by way of remuneration, a portion of which in some cases goes to the poor-box.

Butchers.

The performance of the mîlah by the môhel occasions the most prodigal feasting, and a still more prodigal display of female attire and jewellery, as well as of female adiposity and flashing eyes. A chair belonging to the community being set up on one side of the father's courtyard or balcony, the other side is thronged with lady spectators, as the venerable rabbi, who combines so many functions, initiates the scion of the house to Judaism, generally performing the meṣîṣah.† In some cases the birth of a daughter serves for little less rejoicing. It is the invariable custom for the mother to lie in bed in state to receive her guests, for in Morocco no distinction is known between bed-room and sitting-room.

Circumcisions.

On the thirtieth day the father of a first-born son either takes the child to the cohen's house, or the cohen‡ comes to his for the ceremony of Pidyon hab-

* The office of shôḥeṭ requires a special study and practice of sh'ḥîṭa, the art of selecting and killing perfect animals, which includes some knowledge of anatomy, and the use of the knife so as to cause no pain. No one can slay for food without a certificate from the local Grand Rabbi. There are two branches of the art, the slaying of fowls and of quadrupeds,—dinei ôfot and dinei behémot, respectively.

† Sucking the part, spitting out the blood, and sprinkling with spirit. Otherwise it is dried with a handful of powder.

Literally the "priest," but applicable to all descendants of Aaron, many of whom employ the word Cohen or Kahn as a surname.

ben, "Ransom of the Son," ordained in memory of the tenth plague of Egypt.[1] This consists in offering the child to the cohen, and in redeeming him by a money payment, the amount of which varies according to the circumstances of the parents, but which is never large. The first-born of an ass is redeemed by a lamb, and those of other animals in like manner. When any son completes his seventh year, when he begins to learn his religious duties, he is invested with the ṣîṣit, and six years later he assumes the tefilin at a special service, by which he becomes a Bar Miṣvah, "Son of Precepts.'

Training of Sons.

But the weddings! If money is foolishly wasted by the Jews of London to make a grand affair of these, their Morocco brethren are no whit behind. The Arabs are credited with a proverb in which lies much truth, to the effect that while the Muslim squanders his substance in religious festivals and the Christian in law-suits, the Israelite does so in nuptial bouts. What shall I say of the days of preparation, of the breaking of a jar of corn at the door of the bride's room to ensure her fruitfulness, of the slaughter of cattle and sheep and fowls; of the festivities at the bride's house, and the jollifications at those of the bridegroom: of the conclave of the previous Sebt er-Raï—"Counsel Saturday"—when all arrangements are made;* of the despatch next day to the bridegroom's house of the dowry and bridal presents; of the special bathing on the Monday; of the customs and fun of the *talamo* or bridal bed, on which young ladies sit for luck; of Tuesday's torch-light procession of the bride to the house

Weddings.

* In Tetuan and some other parts there still prevails an ancient ceremony on the first Saturday, called the Metkál, when the bride, in Moorish dress, is taken on a white horse to visit her friends.

[1] *Exodus*, xiii., 11—13.

of the bridegroom, chaperoned by her mother, who there spends the night with her; of her induction in state next day by two of the most important male guests; of her sitting for hours like a waxen doll with closed eyes from beneath which perchance there steals an occasional tear; of the ceremony of the Sheba' Berakhôt—Seven Blessings—at an hour after noon that day, with nasal chant and chorus, with exchange of rings, the drinking of wine and the breaking of glass; or of the thousand and one minor observances which vary indefinitely here, there and then? Suffice it to say that on every hand hospitality abounds; that in place of the hard-boiled eggs—two apiece—which are customary at the mîlah and minor ceremonies, luxurious repasts are spread, including a series of excellent almond sweets with preserved and dried fruits, of which each guest takes home a kerchief full. * For drinks there are good wines and bad, with an abundance of villainous anise-seed and fig spirit, while the utmost good-humour prevails, even though there is hardly standing room, and the din of the seldom-ceasing native music necessitates abnormal exercise of lung. The guests are dispersed in various rooms according to social position, and woe betide the pushing individual discovered too high up, for he will be unceremoniously relegated to his proper group, while the more modest are as frequently advanced. So are the Jews wed in Barbary!

The Ceremony.

In each community close intermarriage has rendered the relationships between its members complex and confusing. Often unions take place which must be bugbears to genealogists, as when a young

Intermarriage.

* Modern Tangier hosts provide either fancy papers or boxes wherein their guests may carry away what they cannot eat. I shall never forget the ludicrous effect when first instructed to fill my handkerchief at a circumcision: the remembrance of school-day feasts was irresistible.

lad once puzzled me greatly by referring to a certain individual indiscriminately as uncle and grandfather, for it seemed that his grandfather had married his aunt-in-law. Divorce is not difficult to obtain under certain conditions, but the husband seems always to retain some semblance of authority. Bigamy is also legal, though uncommon, especially among the Castilian section of the coast Jews, whose marriage contracts provide that a second wife may be taken only at the request of the first wife.

JEWISH GROUP AT HOME, DAMNAT.
(The kerchief on the head of one of the children indicates that she is married. Her more bashful husband, a man of about twenty, refused to join the group.)
Photograph by Dr. Rudduck.

Child-Marriage.

The greatest evil, however, is the system of child-marriages. These take place in the interior from the ages of six or eight, the "wife" coming to live with her "husband" at his parents' home, from which time she is distinguished by covering her head with a kerchief. At twelve or so she may become a mother, but many children lose their lives at this critical stage. If the lad has grown tired of her ere this, he being rich and she poor, he may put her away in favour of some one else.

On the other hand, the Jews of Morocco set a good example to their Muslim neighbours in the general level of their morals, and as a result the prevalent skin diseases of the Moors are rare among them, though they are cruelly libelled by their neighbours, who accuse them of having introduced these complaints when they came from Spain. In habits of drinking, nevertheless, they lead the way, and sometimes teach the Moors this vice.

Funerals.

The well-attended Jewish funerals in Morocco are imposing both to see and hear, for the sonorous chanting of a procession of male voices, as they slowly pass to their special grave-yard, is very fine. When death is expected, members of the Ḥebrah or Society called Gemilût ḥasadîm, *i.e.* "of Good Works," are summoned to perform the last offices. Such members are selected as are practised in detecting the approach of death, and when the patient is declared *in articulo mortis* the Shema' ("Hear, O Israel; the LORD, our GOD is one LORD,")* is repeated, while immediately after death special prayers are recited. The body being then undressed, the clothes are thrown on the ground as unclean, and are covered up. Some hours later members of the Ḥebrah Raḥîsah, "Washing Society" (men or women as the case may demand), arrive with a special table for the purpose, and with accustomed ceremony wash the corpse and place it in the shroud.

Any friends of the deceased may act as bearers from the home, where hired mourners wail as well as relatives, and the remains are conveyed in coffin-like biers the

* *Deut.* vi., 4. This was what Mohammed adapted in formulating his creed.

property of the community. Jews are buried in shrouds protected by boards, under horizontal stones some eighteen inches thick, which a Moor once suggested to me were made thus heavy by the heirs to keep the dead ones quiet in their graves. The graves are dug much deeper than those of the Moors, on the coast at least the height of the body, somewhat less in the interior. The next-of-kin to the deceased stands in the grave to receive the body, and the earth is thrown in by the Gemilût ḥasadîm. After burial the women shriek at stated times upon the tomb-stones, but especially at the feast of Illûla, on the 14th of Iyar, —the anniversary of the death of Rabbi Simon bar Yohaï, author of the *Zohar*—when a whole night is spent in camp among the graves. The prescribed duty of the next-of-kin, or of all sons on the death of their father, is to say Ḳaddish in the synagogue every day, at least for a month (though really they should do so for eleven months), during which time they allow their hair to grow, and abstain from feasting.

The Interment.

In matters of food no one could be more particular than the Morocco Jews. In large communities there are always special Jewish markets, where kôsher viands may be obtained, while even water-barrels bear this word embranded on the ends. All forbidden viands, and all flesh not certified by the shôḥet is described as trîfah, "unclean." The preparations for Passover take the place of our spring cleaning, and are very thorough, including white-washing outside, while old crocks are broken and new ones brought out. Yet the streets of the Jewish quarters are the filthiest in all the Moorish towns, and are often several feet deep in rubbish, so that visitors descend by steps into the houses.

Food.

Ceremonial washings are of course performed, but

otherwise water is not beloved.* The women are specially careful to maintain their monthly bath of purification, and some of the men take a douche on Fridays, but without soap, though when the sea-bathing is in season, Tangier Jewesses use soap freely in public. When rain is scarce, the Moors make Jews go out with them to pray, and declare that they shall stop outside the walls "until their reeking breath and feet shall so annoy the Almighty, that He shall grant their prayers to get rid of them."[1] It is a comfort to see how readily those who become more or less civilized through their residence on the coast remedy these matters as their eyes are opened.

Washings.

Although the possible existence of agricultural Jews in unknown parts of the Atlas has been hinted at,[2] the means of obtaining a livelihood followed by the Israelites of Morocco do not differ greatly from those adopted in other lands similarly situated. As artificers they are conspicuous in the manufacture of jewellery, and of brass, tin and metal work generally: in the embroidering of slippers: in tailoring and in carpentry, as also in the preparation of a number of useful and ornamental articles produced by the Moors as well. As merchants and shopkeepers, a large proportion of the trade of the country passes through their hands. Perhaps it would be no exaggeration to state that the larger proportion does so, first and last, very much of what is eventually retailed by the Moors having been imported by them. In this particular branch they probably

Subsistence.

* On one occasion, when asked to interpret for a Jew to a medical friend whom he wished to consult for a skin trouble, the question was put as to when he washed last, to which he replied—

"Me wash? Don't think it! Of course I don't, except three or four times a year. Otherwise I only wash my face and hands sometimes."

[1] Cf. PELLOW, p. 257; HAY, p. 126. [2] *E.g.* by DAVIDSON.

do as much as Europeans and Moors together, but in exports the Europeans rank first.

It is where the handling of money comes in that our Hebrew friend ranks *facile princeps*. At the street corner you may see him squatted on the ground, in dirty gown and dishevelled hair, complacently passing through his bony fingers a peck or two of copper "change" in a basket set before him. From the deep recesses of his ample leather wallet, slung across his shoulder to the left, he can produce a quantity of silver coins, from dollars down to pieces worth but 2d., which he gives or receives in change at the current rates of the day. Or in the seaports you may see his fellow trudge from house to house, negotiating cheques, bills and what-not, for a microscopic commission. Or you may see him appear before the Moorish notary with a starveling Arab who has borrowed twenty dollars from him, at exorbitant interest, perhaps 240 per cent. per annum. Powerful governors are sometimes the debtors, who have borrowed to purchase their posts or to secure them, and occasionally they have Jewish partners, each playing into the other's hands.

Money Changers.

But the highest ambition of the Jew in Morocco who means to rise in the world is an interpretership to a foreign legation, which not only secures a comfortable living, with unlimited opportunities for "palm oil," but also gives a certain rank and importance which may be made the means of stepping higher. Many of the principal Jewish bankers and merchants of the coast towns owe their present position to this initiatory lift, enjoyed either by themselves or their fathers, and some hold foreign vice-consulships. Several are decorated with European orders, though it sounds a little strange to see a Jew wearing the "Cross of the Order of Jesus," or some similar institution.

Foreign Employ.

It is a matter of deep regret that in speaking faithfully of a portion of the grandest nation upon Earth, of a people among whom I count so many friends, I am obliged to note so many serious faults. Let me, therefore, at the outset make it plain that I consider them less as innate qualities than as the outcome of adverse circumstances; as the result of evil surroundings, and of great inherent talents misdirected. In painting the shadows I shall not use my own words, but draw first on those of De Foucauld,[1] though it must be remembered what trying times he passed through in their company.* "Gifted with a lively faith," he writes, "they scrupulously fulfil their duty towards GOD, and repay themselves upon His creatures." Extending this dictum elsewhere,[2] he says: "The Israelites of Morocco observe with the utmost rigour the exterior practices of their religion, but, as we have said, they conform in nothing to the moral duties which their religion prescribes to them. Not only do they not follow them, but they oppose them. Wisdom they call deceit, lying and breaking of oaths: justice is vengeance, hate and calumny: prudence is avarice and cowardice: idleness, gluttony and drunkenness are the happy faculties bestowed by GOD."

Character.

Another writer[3] says that the mothers, Rebekah-like, consider the education of their sons deficient till they can cheat their fathers, adding that the poor Jews believe it no sin to rob Moors and Christians safely, and that the Moors regard their treatment of Jews and Christians in the same light. Dr. Addison, the father of the essayist, remarks that the Moors taunt the Jews with having been exiled from their own country for usury, and use the expression "as de-

Evil Training.

* He travelled in the disguise of a Jerusalem rabbi, thus eluding the vigilance of the Moorish authorities.

[1] p. 14. [2] p. 398. [3] RICHARDSON.

ceitful as a Jew," to which the latter retort "as unfaithful as a Moor." The Moor is said to thank GOD that he is not a Jew, and the Jew that he is not a woman. This may be true so far as concerns principles of honesty, of which these neglected people—ignorant on the whole of any but the ceremonial teachings of the Pentateuch—know little, but it applies far less to their social morals. The Moorish Jew is hospitable, and his family genial: if his habits are dirty and his probity is weak, he stands as far ahead of the Moor in his sexual relations as he is behind him in other respects.

Extenuating Circumstances.

Before condemning him it must be remembered that he has had no chance to learn better. I have no hesitation in adding, as a rider to what I have quoted, that many miscalled "Christians" consider themselves fully justified in defrauding both Moors and Jews. There are people who, equally to blame themselves, refuse to hear anything good about natives of either class. Nor would I have it supposed that by these quotations I wish to imply that such a character is universally deserved by the Moorish Jews. Though it undoubtedly is so by the majority, there are those who stand out the brighter for the surrounding darkness, and whose credit is the greater for the hindrances with which they meet.

Oaths.

Some curious distinctions are observed with regard to their oaths. It is considered a light matter to break an oath sworn by one's own head or conscience, but more serious if the rabbi has added warnings and maledictions, while if sworn with the hand on the Sefar, or Scroll of the Law, it ought to be inviolable. This is sometimes practised with special ceremonies, such as stripping the "deponent," and laying him out in a shroud with the Roll in his hands while the prayer for the dead is recited. Death within a year is believed to be inevitable if such an oath be broken, or the best-loved son may be taken.[1]

HISTORY.

At what period to date the first arrival of Israelites in Morocco it is difficult to say, though Josephus tells us that some three centuries before Christ, after the death of Alexander, Ptolemy Soter exiled them in large numbers—some said thirty thousand—to Egypt.[2] The people themselves have no intelligent idea of their past, beyond that at some stage or other their ancestors hailed from the Holy City, yet many declare that they know to which tribes they belong, including the ten that were lost. Some have opined that one of the earlier dispersions sent them forth,* and possibly there are in Morocco a few thus descended; but it is probable that the bulk of the emigrants belonged to a later period.

Prehistoric Settlers.

The utmost I can attempt to do is to bring together a few scattered data gleaned from various sources, which, with no pretence at completeness, may serve as beacon-lights along their history. The earliest authentic references I have come across are in connection with the invasion in 682 A.C. of the Arabs, who found Jews already established in this country. Several references to this fact occur among the native historians,[3] and in one of the legends which recount in so many ways the founding of Fez, about 808 A.C., a native Jew plays his part.[4] As soon as the town began to rise, a number of Jews took refuge there, and were allotted a quarter to themselves, on the payment of thirty thousand dinars a year tribute in lieu of military

* Some say that the original colonists were furnished by the tribe of Naphtali, scattered after the expedition of the Assyrians, and talk of ancient burial-grounds in Wád Wûn. See HAY, *Journal*, p. 103.

[1] DE CUEVAS, p. 237.

[2] JOSEPHUS, liv, xii; BASNAGE, *Histoire des Juifs*, vol. vii., c. 7.

[3] *E.g.* IBN KHALDÛN and *Raôd el Kartás*, p. 16.

[4] *Raôd el Kartás.*

service. This tax continues to be levied, not only in Fez, but throughout the Empire, and of course the sum has many times increased during these centuries.

Tribute.

Owing to the late sultan's generosity it has been paid quite irregularly, and in some parts has fallen in arrears. The designation always applied to a Jew* in Moorish legal documents is Dhimmî,—"Tributary" literally "Payer of Blood-money"—instead of Yahûdi or Hebráni, the former of which is a conversation applied to the people, and the latter to their language. They were also at one time known as the muáḥad or "guaranteed" race, that is those who paid to be protected.

In 1276 the mob rose against the Jews of Fez, and fourteen had already been slain when the Ameer Ya'ḳûb II., riding himself to the spot, succeeded in quelling the tumult. He forbade any Moor to approach the Jewish quarter, and next morning laid the foundation of New Fez, in which he allotted them the district they still inhabit. Those who wished to enjoy the special safety of the new quarters paid double taxes. Previous to this time it would seem from the record *Raôḍ el Ḳarṭás*,[1] that their home was in the centre of the old town, for in 1133, when the famous Ḳarûeeîn Mosque was enlarged, the adjoining property of certain Jews had to be seized and paid for at a valuation.

Jewry of Fez.

It is interesting to notice that when the Moors invaded Spain, the Jews there not only welcomed them, but in 711 admitted them to Toledo,[2] which had already become a hot-bed of persecution, and it is certain that under Muslim rule they fared much better than under that of so-called Christians. Within a century, in 616, they had been allowed a year to conform to the Romish teachings or to leave the

The Jews of Spain.

* It is equally applied to Christians under Mohammedan rule.

[1] p. 75. [2] Dozy, *Mussulmanes d'Espagne*, vol. li., p. 35.

country, whereupon some ninety thousand had received baptism, but still in secret practised circumcision. So fierce was the feeling that the Sixth Council of Toledo decreed that no king should be crowned who had not sworn to execute its edicts against "this abominable race."[1] At last, in 694, the Jews of Spain and Morocco, to which many had already been exiled, and where some of the Berber tribes professed their faith, were preparing to revolt with the hope of erecting a Jewish kingdom in Spain, a movement which helped to prepare the way for the Moors. In consequence of the discovery of this plot, a fresh council of Toledo reduced the Jews *en masse* to slavery, sparing only children under seven, who were not allowed to marry among themselves, but only with Christians.[2]

Under Moorish Rule.

Their only breathing time was under the Moors, on whose expulsion the Inquisition arose to plague them and to drive them across the Straits. To this day, though to so large an extent permeated with Jewish blood, Spain has practically no acknowledged Jewish population, and those who attend its fairs do so under the name of Moors, against whom there is no such feeling. Nevertheless there were times of persecution under the Moors, as, for instance, under the great Yûsef bin Tashfîn—cir. 1100,—who summoned the inhabitants of Lucena, all Jews, to perform a contract alleged to have been made with Mohammed by their forefathers that they should embrace his creed after five hundred years, a document containing which was declared to have been discovered. But as usual a respite was granted for a sum of money.[3]

Whether any of the Jews expelled from Italy in 1342, from Holland in 1380, from France about 1403, from

[1] DOZY, *Mussulmanes d'Espagne*, pp. 26 and 27.
[2] *Acts of the 17th Council of Toledo*, MANSI, vol xii, p. 94, etc.
[3] HOLÁL, fol. 33, r. and v. IDREESI, vol. ii., p. 54; also in art. *Lucena*.

England in 1422, and from Portugal in 1496,[1] found refuge in Morocco, I must leave others to determine, but it is very likely that to such some of the Moroccan families owe their origin. From Spain came many, chiefly in 1391, 1414, 1492 and 1610. At the expulsion of 1492, a large number embarked on board a Spanish fleet for the coast of Morocco, and landing at Azîla, which was then a Christian settlement, they proceeded to Fez, where a considerable body of their co-religionists resided. On their way they fell in with heartless robbers, at whose hands they were so mercilessly used that many were unable to reach their destination, and, starved, wasted by disease and broken in spirit, they retraced their steps to Azîla, consenting to be christened in the hope of being permitted to re-visit their native land. The number of these poor deluded creatures was so considerable that the priest who officiated was obliged to make use of the mop with which the Romanists were wont to scatter the holy drops "whose mystic virtue they believed could cleanse the soul."[2] Those who sought shelter with the Moors from the outset suffered treatment hardly better than that which had driven them forth, and the story of their sufferings is a harrowing one.

Refugees from Europe.

In spite of the subservient position enforced upon these "Tributaries" by their cousins the Arabs, their inherent astuteness is no less manifest in Barbary than elsewhere, and those who have oppressed them have also taken care to avail themselves of their business qualities. At times the rulers of the Empire drew their chief advisers from this race, and Ibn Khaldûn speaks of a Jew of Fez as the chief confidant of one of the ameers, and the greatest subject

Pages of Honour.

[1] ANDRÉE, *Volkskunde der Juden*, p. 195.

[2] PRESCOTT, *Ferdinand and Isabella*, vol. ii., p. 127.

in the kingdom. The influential posts once held by Jews under Moorish masters in Spain, and the renown of many of their learned men during that period of comparative enlightenment are sufficiently known to need no recapitulation here, but it may be well to recall the names of some of the famous Israelitish diplomats of

A JEW OF FEZ.

the Moorish Empire in Africa. During the last quarter of the fifteenth century Shoomel el Barensi rose to power as minister of the ameer Sa'ïd el Waṭṭáṣ, and his influential position opened the Court of Fez to many a co-religionist. This was the hey-day of the Moorish Jews, as one after another of their number became a sort of privy councillor, notably during the reign of Mohammed XI., (1574—76) coeval with the massacre of St. Bartholomew. As controllers of finances the successive sultans had the same experience of them as have European potentates, and they have also employed them as ambassadors. In 1610 Shoomel el Farrashi (Palache) was sent by Mulai Zîdán as his representative to the United Provinces, and his son David was received as Moorish envoy in Paris in 1631, but was disavowed by his master, though appointed to Holland on the death of his father.[1] He was succeeded in 1675 by Yûsef Toledano, whose brother Haïm was ambassador to England. In 1688 Mulai Rasheed had a powerful Jew of Táza to contend with in his fight for the throne, and caused the Grand Rabbi and others to be burned when he succeeded, while his viceroy in Marrákesh destroyed all its synagogues, then twelve in number.[2]

Formidable Rivals.

Few ever exercised more power at the Moorish Court than, at the close of the seventeenth century, did the favoured Maïmarán, without whose money and influence the brutal Mulai Ismá'îl would never have reached the sultanate.[3] He virtually ruled over his poorer brethren, but had a formidable rival in Moses ben 'Aṭṭár, whose inhumanities reflected those of his master. Maïmarán offered the sultan so much cash for his rival's head, and the millionaire Moses of those days, being informed of the bid, offered twice as much to reverse the bargain, which then became his. But the sultan, having pocketed both sums, commanded the two he could so ill spare to become friends, Maïmarán to give his daughter to Ben 'Aṭṭár, who henceforth stood supreme.[4] An instance of both the power and cruelty of the latter was afforded on the occasion of the British Embassy of 1720, when he had his Gibraltar agent brutally maltreated and all but

[1] *Revue d'Hist. Dipl.*, Paris, 1888, p. 27.
[2] PUERTO, p. 56. See *The Moorish Empire*, pp. 138 and 318.
[3] See *The Moorish Empire*, ch. viii. [4] WINDUS, p. 197. PELLOW, p. 262.

strangled for cheating, without the interference of any other authority, or the semblance of a trial.[1]

It is this man's signature which appears with that of the Moorish plenipotentiary at the foot of the treaty of 1721 with Great Britain, the basis of every subsequent agreement with European nations, which also laid the foundation of the "Protection System."* It is a curious and interesting fact that a Jew should have, on the Moorish side, permitted the entrance of the thin end of a wedge which has since entered so much further as to have become not only the *sine quâ non* of intimate European relations with Morocco, but also the one hope of the Jews in this country almost ever since that time.

The Protection System.

In 1750 the Moorish ambassador to Denmark was a Jew, and thirty years later Ya'ḳûb ben Ibráhîm, of the Beni Idder, came to London in the same capacity, being succeeded in 1794 by one Zumbal, who had been in charge of the sultan's finances, and was high in favour.[2] St. Olon found him thus when he went soon afterwards to Marrákesh as envoy from France. Ya'ḳûb ben 'Aṭṭár, who acted as secretary to Mohammed XVII., had the credit of speaking English, French, Spanish and Italian—presumably in an original style,—and of being a great rogue.[3] Then in 1827 Meir Cohen Maḳneen arrived in England on a special mission from Mulai 'Abd er-Raḥman. In 1859 an English Jew from York was captain of the port at Mogador, and it is stated that one sultan had a Jewish cook.[4]

Jewish Envoys.

To-day, while no son of Israel holds office of note under the sultan, many of those whose parents enjoyed European protection, and who have become to a greater

* For an account of this system see *The Moorish Empire*, pp. 416 *et seq.*

[1] WINDUS, p. 10. PELLOW, p. 223.
[2] THOMASSY, p. 264.
[3] LEMPRIÈRE, p. 173.
[4] RICHARDSON, p. 64.

or less extent Europeanized, occupy positions of influence, both among natives and foreigners, such as hardly a single Moor has attained, and two Tangier families have obtained hereditary protection for services rendered, the Benchimols by France (Treaty of 1863) and the Abensurs by England under the "most favoured nation" clause.*

Hereditary Protection.

There exist among the Moors a number of curious traditions concerning Berber tribes who are affirmed to have been originally Jewish. Unfortunately these are too fragmentary and scattered to be of real service until they have been collated, compared and condensed by some pains-taking student of folk-lore. To such an one there is little doubt that they would afford abundant interest, and at the same time furnish historic clues of importance. In a similar way other tribes in the Anti-atlas are reported once to have been Christian, and an entangled series of myths is current about them all. To unravel the most prominent would be a worthy undertaking, but a toilsome labour of love. On the other hand, it has been suggested that many of the Atlas Jews are descended from early converts from heathenism to the Mosaic teaching, some of whom subsequently embraced Islam.

Folk-Lore.

One writer states – but apparently without authority— that Mulai Idrees II., the founder of Fez, was considered a saint because he secured the conversion of so many Jews to Islám.[1] The unfortunate Davidson, who half a century ago, rashly attempted to cross the Atlas unprepared, and lost his life in consequence, was told of such a tribe whose origin was betrayed by their features, and who, according to the

Jewish Perverts.

* The Act of Parliament required in the latter case was passed in 1896, and was extended to the wife only on proof that the marriage contract practically precluded bigamy.

[1] PELLOW, p. 59.

Moors, had a Jewish odour about them. They engaged in commerce only, or acted as clerks, and although Mohammedans, never attained to high civil or religious positions, nor did they observe the Friday as the "day of the Congregation."

Side by side with these rather doubtful reports of conversions, is a series of accounts of advantage being taken of some thoughtless word to secure punishment for alleged apostasy. In 1820 a Jew, in a tipsy condition, was caught entering a mosque, and was induced to testify belief in the Divine mission of Mohammed. Realising, when sober next day, what he had done, he went to the governor to explain the matter, but word being sent to the sultan that he had recanted, the answer came, "On the arrival of the courier, off with the Jew's head and send it to me." Within half an hour after the message arrived, the head was on its way to Court in a leather bag.[1]

Alleged Conversions.

The story of Sol Hachuel is far more touching, and is indeed one of genuine heroism. Two Moorish women swore in 1834 that this Hebrew girl, who had fled to them on account of domestic troubles, had agreed to "resign herself" to the will of GOD as taught by Mohammed. After imprisonment for some time, she was sent to Court, where her extreme beauty obtained for her a promise of the imperial hareem with every honour, if she would but confirm her presumed change of creed. But her noble courage brought her to a martyr's death, for she was beheaded outside Fez.* It is hardly possible that such a tragedy should

Faithful unto Death.

* For a detailed account of this occurrence see *El Martirio de la joven Hachuel.*, by Eugenio M. Romero, Gibraltar, 1839, The *Archives Israélites* of 1880 (vol. xli., Nos. 22—24) and *The Times of Morocco*, Nos. 46—48, 1886. It has also been made the subject of a play by Antonio Calle, *La Heroina Hebrea*, Seville, 1852.

[1] GRÅBERG, p. 424.

be repeated now, notwithstanding that in theory the same threats exist for perverts from the faith of Islám. Richardson, writing in 1859, tells a story, then fresh, of a Jewish lad who went to his ḳáïd and proclaimed himself Mohammedan, but this official, with greater sense than usual, sent him to prison until the next day, when he had him beaten and sent back home.[1] This was quite an exceptional case, for the Moors are always delighted to make Jewish or any other converts, and offer inducements to those who adopt their religion, though despising them inwardly. From time to time perversions occur from interested motives, and the perverts pass beyond the ken of their erstwhile brethren, anathematized and abjured, but for a short time feasted and made much of by the Muslims. One such convert to Islám, however, Samuel ben Judah ben Azariah of Fez, who lived in the twelfth century, better known under his Mohammedan names of Abu Naṣr bin 'Abbás, or Yaḥya el Maghribi, became famous as a philosopher, mathematician and doctor, travelled widely in the East, and to explain his position wrote a treatise entitled *Ifham el Yahûd.**

Political Status.

As stubborn Jews under a purely Moorish *régime* without even the most elementary rights in the native tribunals, they are tolerated as serfs rather than treated as citizens. Those instances in which their high intelligence and skill have won great power for single individuals have seldom to any extent affected the well-being of the race. Had Morocco remained for ever closed to outside influence;

* The occasional conversions of Morocco Jews to Christianity are dealt with in *The Moorish Empire*, p. 324, where particulars are given of a remarkable treatise attributed to a Christian Rabbi from Fez, Samuel "Marrochianus," published at York in 1649 under the title of *The Blessed Jew of Morocco*, or *the Black Moor Made White*.

[1] Vol. i., p. 198

had the concessions wrung at intervals from the unwilling sultans by the European Powers not opened up a pathway for the Jews, their lot upon the coast to-day would be what it still is in the interior. The possibility of sharing foreign rights and privileges has, however, changed all this for those who come within its range. The treaties assuring protection to the native agents of foreign officials and merchants have been taken far greater advantage of by Jews than by Moors: firstly, because they feel the need of protection in a higher degree, and secondly, because they are more astute in obtaining it. Since a Jew, whatever his outward circumstances, has always a larger amount of cash than his Moorish neighbour, in proportion as he excels him in point of brain, he here scores a decided advantage, and is able to secure far better protection.

Abuse of Privileges.

This may be an abuse, but it is slight when compared with the enforcement of unjust claims, and the imprisonment of debtors under the ægis, and through the influence, of foreign Powers. Though too many foreigners commit the same abuses, and are equally blameworthy,—nay, more so, on account of their superior education and opportunities of learning better,—it is the Hebrew community which, from its numbers, gets credit for the bulk of these misdeeds. The sin of grasping usury, for which, even in the early days of the Exodus, their nation had to be so sternly reprehended, flourishes and cankers in Morocco to the full. I might fill a volume with disclosures of the oppression meted out by Jews in this country to their Mohammedan fellow-subjects: I might go even further, and proclaim what grinding of the face of their own poor, more grievous still in its nature, goes on in the barbarous melláḥs. But I will not dwell on this unpleasant side of things; suffice it to hint at what will ever breed retributive oppression from the Moor, while incurring also the wrath of GOD.

In Morocco two causes have for centuries acted and reacted one upon the other to produce the existing strained relations between Moors and Jews. The steadfast independence which has cut the latter off from intermixture with the former, and their greed of gain, have fostered enmity and hatred in a populace quite as dishonest, which have brought about reprisals and revenge. These have been repaid with the amount of interest they make their victims pay; so fire has kindled fire. The misgovernment of the Empire permits and encourages this in a manner unknown in England, though even there that page of history has had its parallel. It is idle for us to demand emancipation for the Jew, unless we are prepared to raise his social level, and to educate his powers.

Causes of Condition.

Until dishonesty, as a universal characteristic of the country, gives way to honesty, peace cannot be hoped for. If foreign protection could be secured for every son of Israel in Morocco, it would rather expose him to the fury of the populace, and threaten serious war, than attain its primary objects, if the immediate results were only multiplication of the present holders of that privilege without raising their tone. The presence of civilized and well-instructed Jews, with the polish and air of Europe; men whom the foreign schools have drawn from their ranks and placed by the side of Europeans, proves their capabilities, and forms one of the brightest hopes of Morocco.

What is needed.

The schools of the *Alliance Israélite*, and those of the Morocco Relief Fund, under the Anglo-Jewish Association, have already worked wonders, and they need abundant extension everywhere. Many of the leading citizens of the Moorish ports—not only as members of the despised community, but also as members of their cosmopolitan society—have been their pupils, who have completed their education abroad, and returned to do honour to their nation at home.* These, even when poor and unprotected, suffer so little indignity at the hands of the Moors, that they might almost be born Europeans, and according as the whole Jewish population of Morocco can be rendered like them, the greatest inducements to oppression will vanish, and day will have broken on the horizon of the Morocco Jews. Yet in the interior it has been hard to overcome the opposition of the ignorant and bigoted leaders of the Jewish communities to the extension of these schools!

The Most Promising Feature.

They need not only united political influence on their behalf among their brethren in more favoured lands to secure from their Government what is their due as free-born men, but they also need awakening themselves, and raising till they shall be worthy of the position in which we fain would see them. The fact must not be overlooked that no royal or imperial rescripts, no shareefian mandates, can afford the Morocco Jews the friendship or respect which they desire. Nothing but their own behaviour can secure these privileges for them, but it will be long before the evil impressions of ages can be removed.

The "Sine quâ Non."

* In 1894 a most promising organisation was formed in Tangier, the "Association des anciens élèves de l'Alliance Israélite Universelle," which has already done much good work in awarding prizes in the local schools, establishing a modest library and gymnasium, promoting social gatherings of former pupils, encouraging new handicrafts and the study of agriculture in Tunis, assisting emigration to America, relieving the needs of poor scholars, and opening work-rooms for girls, in which they acquire a means of subsistence with their needles, turning out most exquisite embroidery: a local Jewish periodical is also contemplated.

CHAPTER THE TWENTY-FOURTH

THE JEWISH YEAR IN MOROCCO

IT would be presumption for one who has the misfortune to be classed among the Goyim to attempt a detailed comparison of the religious customs of Israel in Morocco with the better known rituals of other lands. Yet they are worth describing, especially as so many who visit this country are entirely unacquainted with Jewish ceremonies and their meaning, and until they are brought face to face with active Judaism are accustomed to regard its observances as of the past. Even if they have had Jewish friends at home, they have probably been of a class which has so far modified the observance of the Law that much of the interest of its forms has been lost. In contrast to this, in Morocco we have a people living, as regards social and religious customs, as their forefathers did in the Promised Land, and in proportion as the conditions of life in Morocco approximate more closely to those under which the Mosaic festivals were instituted, so much is their observance more literal and primitive. In this consists its special charm. Probably no Israelitish communities are more strict in the fulfilment of their ceremonial duties than those now under consideration.

Primitive Customs.

In many ways their ritual is allied to, and in some parts is identical with, that of the Spanish and Portuguese communities in other lands—known as the Sephardim,—but the more primitive usage is to be sought for with the more primitive life, as also the better pronunciation of Hebrew where it exists beside its sister tongue, Arabic. A volume might be written on this point alone, but it must suffice to glance in passing at a few of the special features of the greater festivals or fasts.

The Sabbath.

Nowhere could the Sabbath be more strictly adhered to than among these people, and on Friday everything is "redded up." The great jar containing the Sabbath meals (ha dafina) is prepared with the se'ûdah shelishît—"third meal," *i.e.* Sabbath supper—snug down at the bottom. This consists of chick-peas or beans, which have already been steeped in water with wood-ashes, and which stand long stewing, together with eggs in their shells, meat, herbs, vegetables and sometimes rasped biscuit. The uppermost layer is eaten on Friday after several hours' cooking, a second attack being made on the Sabbath morning, but the third and last is the most important. A carefully built fire of lump and pounded charcoal surrounds the jar, keeping it hot for thirty hours, to avoid the need of touching fire. No Morocco Jew would think of lighting a lamp or smoking, or even of opening a letter on the Day of Rest, though he will play cards for hours, and often get drunk during its course with clear conscience, uttering the Ḳiddûsh, or blessing of meat, with great punctiliousness.

New Year Festival.

The civil New Year's Day (Rosh ha Shaná)—the first of Tishri, seventh month of the ecclesiastical year—is "a solemn rest . . . a memorial of blowing of trumpets, an holy convocation,"[1] on which no servile work is done. It falls about our September. The previous evening—when the Jewish "day" begins,—after the synagogue prayers the table is spread with new fruits and cooked vegetables; meat-soup, mutton

[1] *Leviticus*, xxiii., 24.

and wine. The head of the house blesses the food and thanks God for it, tasting the first fruits, whereupon supper commences. The following evening the same ceremony takes place with the remainder of the food.

GROUP OF ATLAS JEWS.
Deputation of rabbis and merchants of Dammát, who in 1884 sought assistance from Europe to secure the removal of a brutal governor. Taken on the roof of *The Times of Morocco* Office, Tangier.

L. Davin, Photo, Tangier.

In the afternoon of that day, about three o'clock, it is customary to go down to the sea, to a river, or even to a well—to the largest body of water at hand—there to thank God for His mercy in providing it. Sometimes stones are thrown in, the symbol of desire to cast away sins.[1] Both these days are holidays, but the third day is the fast of Gedaliah, observed by pious Jews from sunrise until sunset, when Micah, vii., 18—20, is recited.

[1] See 2 *Kings*, xxv., 25, and *Jeremiah*, xli., 2.

The tenth day (after our reckoning) is, however, much more important. By the Law of Moses it is directed that "It shall be unto you a sabbath of solemn rest, and ye shall afflict your souls: in the ninth day of the month at even, from even to even."[1] "And ye shall offer an offering made by fire unto the Lord: and ye shall do no manner of work in that same day: for it is a day of atonement."[2] "And this shall be an everlasting statute unto you, to make atonement for the children of Israel, because of all their sins, once in the year."[3] It is further threatened that whosoever does not duly observe this day, "shall be cut off from his people."[4]

The Day of Atonement.

The eighth and ninth days of Tishri are days of preparation, on which every Jew must slay his sacrifice, usually a fowl, large numbers of which are brought in from the country. The sex of the bird must be the same as that of the offerer, who is not allowed to kill his own, but either takes it to one of the shôḥetim—officials whose special duty it is to slay animals for food—or summons the shòḥet to his house.

Sacrifice.

After carefully examining the victim, according to the prescribed method, to see that it is without blemish, the throat is cut with a very sharp knife reserved for the purpose. Should the knife be notched, or have caused the animal pain, the victim is rejected, and must be replaced. The livers and lungs of large animals are also examined before the carcase is pronounced kôsher. The blood either falls on the ground, or into a basin with earth in it, but in either case earth is thrown over it. The sacrifice is eaten by the offerer and his family. Fowls for those who cannot afford them are sometimes purchased by their more wealthy brethren. On the ninth a good meal is partaken of an hour

[1] *Leviticus*, xxiii., 32. [2] Ibid., *v.*, 27. [3] Ibid., xvi., 24. [4] Ibid., xxiii., 29.

before sunset, and at sunset there is a special service in the synagogues until about nine p.m., when the duties of the day are ended.

Early on the following morning, the great day of Kippûr, the synagogues are again filled—every male is bound to attend unless ill,—and the worshippers remain till the stars appear, when a horn is blown, and after a few minutes of the ordinary evening prayer, they return home to break a fast of at least twenty-six hours. On the way to their homes numbers gather together in open spaces whence the moon is visible, and thank God for it. One alone can do so, but it is preferable when there are many. This ceremony is known as the Birkat hal-levana.

Atonement Services.

Like Mohammedans, the Jews practise almsgiving and other good works more during the first ten days of their new year, than during all the rest of it. Mohammed is supposed to have copied from them the custom of the 'Aáshûr.* A Muslim writer[1] relates that when Mohammed came to Medina, and found that the Jews fasted on the day of 'Aáshûr, he asked them their reason; they told him that it was because on that day Pharaoh and his people were drowned, Moses and those who were with him escaping: † whereupon he said that he bore a closer relationship to Moses than they, and ordered his followers to fast on that day. He afterwards declared that if he lived another year he would change the day, and fast on the ninth.

Tithing.

The Feast of Tabernacles, commemorating the forty years' sojourn of the Israelites in the wilderness, and that of the Passover, recalling their exodus from Egypt, are the two chief festivals of the Jewish year. That of Sukkôt, ("Tabernacles,"

The Feast of Tabernacles.

* See p. 240. † Evidently a mistaken idea. See *Exodus,* xiii.—xiv.

[1] El Kazwînî.

or more correctly "Booths,") also known as Ḥag ha-asîf, ("Feast of In-gathering,") commences on the fifteenth of Tishri, five days after the Day of Atonement. "Ye shall keep the feast of the Lord seven days," runs the command; "on the first day shall be a solemn rest, and on the eighth day shall be a solemn rest. And ye shall take you on the first day the fruit of goodly trees, branches of palm trees, and boughs of thick trees, and willows of the brook, and ye shall rejoice before the Lord your God seven days. . . . Ye shall dwell in booths seven days; all that are home-born in Israel,"[1] in commemoration of the deliverance of their forefathers from Egypt.

Every house must therefore have its booth, and as in the days of Nehemiah, when the people "made themselves booths, every one upon the roof of his house, and in their courts,"[2] so it is to-day in this country.

The Festal Booths.

For some days previous to the feast, large numbers of canes are brought in from the country, and on its eve great bundles of evergreens, for the construction of the booths. These, averaging some ten or twelve feet square, and about eight feet high, are usually erected in the patios or open courts of the houses, and are frequently ornamented with real or artificial flowers. For eight days all meals are taken in the booths, except in rainy weather, when a blessing is asked in them on the food, which is partaken of under shelter. It is not, however, considered obligatory on the women to eat in the booths.

Duration.

Strictly speaking, this feast lasts only the seven days, but the following day being "a solemn rest," it is commonly reckoned as the last or eighth day, and the following day is the "Rejoicing of the Law." *

* In Jerusalem this feast lasts seven days, but the count of the days having once, it is said, been lost, the custom arose in the West to double the first and last days, leaving four days between.

[1] *Leviticus*, xxiii., 39—42. [2] *Nehemia*, viii., 16.

The first two and the last two days are special holidays, in which no servile work may be done, but those who are obliged to work in order to earn their living are permitted to do so on the four intervening days.

Holy-days.

Being holiday time, in which the command is to "Rejoice before the Lord your God seven days,"[1] very little business is done, even when it is allowed, and the boys endeavour to get a ride on those days, each one according to his means, if only for a single hour, a favourite diversion with them on such occasions. Holiday dresses and feasting are the order of the day, and every one makes merry, but no marriages are contracted during this period, or on the Day of Atonement. Plutarch, in his account of this feast, imagined it to have been in honour of Bacchus.

Peculiar Ceremonies.

Each day of the feast the males carry to the morning prayers palm branches (looláv) the "fruit of goodly trees"—and citrons (etrôg)—both of them unbroken and unbruised, with sprigs of willow etc. When in the synagogue, the citron is carried in the left hand, and other things in the right. As the etrôg must be without blemish, it is encased in paper and wool, lest a scratch should render it worthless, and high prices are sometimes paid for large specimens. The looláv consists of the long shoots from the centre of the palm, perhaps 2 ft. 6 in. long, and an inch thick at the base; it must be quite straight, and without blemish. At the base are tied round leaves of 'arabah—weeping willow,—and of hadass, a kind of myrtle.

A Night of Mourning.

On the evening of the sixth day (the commencement of the seventh) men who have recently lost father, mother, husband or wife, sit up all night praying, and are joined by their friends. This custom continues as long as ten persons gather, so that

[1] *Leviticus*, xxiii., 40.

almost every male is engaged in such prayers.* This ceremony is repeated at Pentecost.†

Festival of Branches.

Each day of the Feast the Sefarîm or Scrolls of the Law (Pentateuch) are carried in a procession round the synagogues by members of the congregation, followed by the rabbis and the people, who, on the seventh day, singing Hosannas, carry

GROUP OF COAST JEWESSES.

Photograph by A. Lennox, Esq.

the branches from which the festival derives its name. The bearers of the Sefarîm are sometimes chosen by the authorities of the synagogue, sometimes by auction, that is to say, the honour is conferred upon those who

* In 1672 it was announced in Salli that the Messiah was expected to be born that year in Holland, whereupon a second Feast of Booths was held, followed by an eight days' fast.[1]

† Strictly speaking this ceremony is obligatory for all, but those who are in mourning avail themselves especially of the occasion as described.

[1] MOUËTTE, p. 31. Cf. ZANGWILL, *Dreamers of the Ghetto*.

will give the most to some charity to obtain it. They are followed by the Ḥazzán (Prayer Leader) reading.

At the Rejoicing of the Law—Simḥat Tôrah—which follows that of Tabernacles, and is the ninth day, this Sefarîm procession, called Haḳafôt, is performed seven times at night and seven times in the morning. Two men are chosen as Ḥatanîm, or "bridegrooms," and each is placed with a Shoshbin or "best man" in a decorated seat of honour prepared for the occasion. The first Ḥatan (Messayem) reads the last two chapters of *Deuteronomy*—the blessing of Moses, called "Vezôt hab-Berákha"—and the second Ḥatan (Mat·ḥil) the first thirty-three verses of Genesis—called "Bereshît," "In the beginning." During this reading the women in the gallery above throw sweets or flowers at them. While the Scrolls are open, boys come up and read a few set verses. When they are closed, one of the "best men" reads a chapter from one of the prophets. In the evening, the Ḥatanîm usually give a feast at home, to celebrate an honour which they sometimes purchase.

Rejoicing of the Law.

In the sabbatical year the Law was read at this feast in the presence of all the people.[1] This is carried out to some extent by the readers first summoning a man of the surname of Cohen (descended from Aaron), next one surnamed Levi (descended from Levi), and then six of any tribes to hear one of the ḥelakîm, or sections, into which the Pentateuch is divided,* and to utter the blessing called Birkat hat-Tôrah. This custom is called 'Alîat hat-Tôrah. The last of the six, having heard his portion, reads a corresponding extract from the prophets, called

Reading the Law.

* There are fifty-four parshîyôt in the Pentateuch, each of seven ḥelakîm. Each parshah has its distinctive name.

[1] *Deuteronomy* xxxi., 10—13; NEHEMIAH, viii.

haftárah. On this day all who have sons under a year old take them to the synagogue, sometimes carrying a large candle and an offering for the poor, when they receive the blessing of the rabbi on themselves and their children. In the evening it is the custom for women to make visits to the synagogues, occasionally for prayer.

Prayers for Forgiveness.

On Yôm Kippûr God is supposed to decree what people are to have during the coming year, and from Ellul the first the Jews pray for forgiveness. On Hosa'anah Rabah, the seventh day of Sukkôt, God is supposed to sign this decree, so the males sit up all night.* Then is read the last portion of the Seliḥôt, or prayer for forgiveness.† This night before the Seliḥôt prayers, there are also read passages from each book of the Bible, if only the first and last chapters, or a few verses, with extracts ‡ also from the *Talmud*, both *Hag-Gadah* and *Hal-Lakhah*, and *Kab-Balah*, as the *Zohar*. After the last Seliḥôt on the morning of Hosa'anah Rabah, the men carry in their hands twigs called Hosa'anah, § which they break by striking them on the floor, as a sign that their sins are remitted.

Hanuka, the Dedication.

Readers of history will remember how the Feast of Ḥanuka, or "the Dedication" was instituted in 164 B.C. by the great Judas Maccabeus, then head of the heroic family of the Hasmoneans. Antiochus IV. (Epiphanes), the cruel and wicked king of Syria, had taken Jerusalem by storm, carried away the sacred utensils and treasures, appointed a governor of his own over Judea, placed a Syrian garrison in Mount Zion, forbidding the exercise of religious rites

* An idea reflected in that of the Laïlit el Ḳadr among Mohammedans, see p. 253.

† Or, where the Spanish rite is followed in Europe, on the Sunday before the New Year.

‡ These extracts are read at Shabu'ôt (Pentecost) too, but not the Seliḥôt.

§ Hosa'anah = we ask help.

by the Jews and commanding them to sacrifice to idols, to profane the Sabbath and to discontinue circumcision—making resistance to these commands a capital offence,—and had destroyed all the books of the Law which he could find, murdering those who secreted them; polluted the Temple a second time, and placed an altar to Jupiter on the Great Altar. On the twenty-fifth of Kislev, 167 B.C., on account of this barbarous treatment of the Jews by their conqueror, the Temple sacrifices ceased.

Origin of the Feast.

At this juncture the princely house of the Hasmoneans, headed by Mattathias the priest, came to the rescue of their people, raising a formidable army to break the usurper's power, a task which was completed under the son of Mattathias, Judas, who in 165 B.C. became master of Judæa. His first care was to purify the Temple, which he did on the third anniversary of the cessation of its sacrifices, Kislev 25th, 164 B.C. In commemoration of this act, the feast of Ḥanuka was instituted.* Its duration is eight days, from Kislev 25th to Tebeth 2nd inclusive, the chief feature being the lighting of the Ḥanuka lamp.

The Ḥanuka Lamp.

In this country the Ḥanuka lamp is usually a flat brass plate, often triangular, hanging on a nail on the wall, with a small protruding lip for oil and wick at the top—called the shammash or "attendant"—and eight similar ones in a row along the bottom.† On the evening of the twenty-fourth of Kislev, which by Eastern reckoning is the beginning of the twenty-fifth day, as night falls after the evening

* It is customary to read up the incidents commemorated during the feast, from the *Megillat Antiochus* This feast falls a week or two before Christmas.

† The most common form is largely made in Shefsháwan. In other countries candlesticks of seven branches with a central burner are used, the original having doubtless been the famous candlestick of the old Temple.

prayers in the synagogue, the head of every Jewish house performs the ceremony of lighting the Ḥanuka light. First he lights the upper burner, then from it the left of the lower ones, while the males of the family offer a berakhah, or blessing, and pray a set prayer ('Al hannisîm—"for the miracles"—) referring to the act com-

A STREET IN THE MELLAH OF DAMNAT.

Photograph by Dr. Rudduck.

memorated. The next day the top one and the two lower ones to the left are lighted with the same ceremony, and each day one more, till on the eighth all are lit. The lights must burn for half an hour daily, and the lamp must be hung near the door or window to be seen from without, not higher than twenty Hebrew yards. During the feast it is customary to eat a sort of sponge fritter, fried in oil, which is sold in the streets,* called by the Arabs after the Greek, *sfinj*, by the Spaniards *buñuelos*, and by the Americans "dough nuts."

A Benedictory "Social."

The next event of the Jewish year in Morocco is little known, because it is not shared by the community at large, but only by the Chief Rabbi and a few of his colleagues and learned friends. It occurs on the fifteenth of Shebat, and marks the nominal division between winter and spring. On that day the trees are said to commence putting forth their buds. All sorts of fruits that it has been possible to collect during the year, dried or fresh, are spread on the rabbi's table with red and white wine, to be blessed, each kind in turn, by one of those present, the wines being so treated and partaken of separately, or mingled several times, with singing and the recitation of Scripture. Altogether it may be supposed that the reverend gentlemen have a pleasant time, and there is something attractive in the idea, but it would be of interest to know whence they derive the custom.

Pûrîm.

In the following month occurs the feast of Pûrîm or "Lots," whereby is still commemorated how the designs of Haman against the Jews under the rule of Ahasuerus, or Xerxes, were frustrated, for "the Jews ordained, and took upon them, and upon their seed, and upon all such as joined themselves unto them, so as it should not fail, that they would keep these two days according to their writing, and according to their appointed time every year, and that these days should be remembered and kept throughout every generation, every family, every province, and every city."[1]

Pûrîm is essentially a feast of thanksgiving, and more than all other days in the year it is devoted to alms-

* For the recipe see p. 104.

[1] *Esther*, ix., 27.

giving. Pûrîm proper is preceded by the Fast of Esther —Ta'anît Esther—which is remarkable for nothing but the fast all day, representing the three days' fast of Esther and her maidens. In the evening, however, at prayers, the hazzán reads through the scroll—*Megillah*—of Esther, and every time the name of Haman occurs, the men stamp on the ground and the boys rap the seats vigorously with pieces of wood—something after the style of the hissing with which an unappreciated actor might be received. When his fate is described, they let the *Megillah* roll fall to one side in their hands, and when they come to the fate of his sons they stamp more loudly still, and shake the rolls which many bring with them. Women do not attend at this time, but it is the duty of heads of households to read the story at home. For a fortnight or so previous it is the custom to indulge in masquerading, when calls are made after dark *incognito*.

Reading the Story.

On the occasion of Pûrîm every male Jew is expected to pay two pesetas (nominally 1*s.* 7*d.*) to the rabbi of the synagogue for the benefit of the poor.* These payments are made on the evening of the thirteenth or of the fourteenth. The morning service on the fourteenth lasts from six to ten a.m., and during its course many collections are made, for which each brings a supply of coins in his tefilîm bag. Two respectable members of the community are chosen by the rabbi to collect for each separate charity for

Business-like Collections.

* This is believed by some to commemorate Haman's offer of ten thousand talents of silver to Ahasuerus, if he would allow him to destroy "a certain people scattered abroad and dispersed among the people in all the provinces" of the kingdom: when he declared that it was "not for the King's profit to suffer them."[1] It has been calculated by some means that this sum would have been at about the rate of half a shekel, or two pesetas, a head for the purchased Jews, so that is the sum which each pays now.

[1] *Esther*, iii., 8

which funds are to be raised. Thus there are funds for the local poor, the blind, the orphans, the widows, the sick, the poor of Jerusalem or elsewhere, and while one passes the box round before the members of the congregation, announcing its object, the other, usually of a higher social status than his companion, carries a bag to receive the contents of the box when full, and to give change when required. After a pair of collectors has visited one synagogue, they go to another, while their place is supplied by collectors for some other object, and when the synagogues have been visited, the round of the houses is made. It is likewise customary for the adults of the families to give presents in coin to the younger members, so that a considerable amount is bestowed in the course of the day, especially as individual beggars make the same efforts as the collectors, both in synagogues and homes. Some of those from Tangier even make their way for the occasion to Gibraltar, where beggars are fewer, and successful Jews are numerous.

A Liberal Feast.

All three days—the Fast of Esther, Pûrîm and Shushan Pûrîm—are high holidays, the last two being devoted to making ample amends for the first day's fast, so feasting, gambling and drinking are the order of the day. It is usual for plates or trays of sweetmeats to be sent from house to house, and especially from young men to their lady-loves. A famous dish on this day is a kesk'soo prepared with milk, sugar, butter and cinnamon, of which plates are sent round to friends. The quantity of milk used causes it to become very dear, as every one tries to secure some. In the afternoon about five o'clock the big dinner—se'ûda—takes place, to which friends and relatives are invited, after the fashion of our Christmas dinner. On these occasions fowls, or larger birds, if procurable, form prominent objects. Special songs are sung; anyone who comes in is compelled to sit down and eat, and the majority get more or less intoxicated before the meal is over. Sometimes a pile of money is placed on the table for distribution.

Shushan Pûrîm.

Shushan Pûrîm differs from Pûrîm only in the fact that the feasting becomes somewhat irksome, and alms-givers have no need of troubling their hoards. It commemorates the extra day of rejoicing kept by the Jews in Shushan on the fifteenth of Adar. Thus is the story of Haman's plot and the wonderful deliverance of the Jews, handed down from generation to generation, "according as Mordecai the Jew and Esther the Queen had enjoined them."

The Passover.

Notwithstanding the lapse of thousands of years, the memorial ceremony of the Passover, instituted on the occasion of the delivery of Israel from Egypt, is still observed by every Jew, and in an altered form more frequently by every Christian. * Although in the latter case only the bread and wine remain, and the bread is usually leavened, in the former case every item mentioned in the instructions given in the book of Exodus is represented separately, though even they are not exactly as prescribed, but rabbinical law has marked out with characteristic minuteness every detail in the observance of the feast. †

* "Christ, our Passover, is sacrified for us: therefore let us keep the feast, not with old leaven, neither with the leaven of malice and wickedness, but with the unleavened bread of sincerity and truth." [1]

Unfortunately the teachings of Christ are disregarded at this season in the ports of Morocco, by the unseemly shooting and burning of effigies of Judas.

† It is to adjust our calendar to that of the Jews, that our "Tables to find Easter" are needed, since Easter Sunday is, or should be, the one in Passover week. The position of "Good Friday" is therefore an anomaly, as we know from the Evangelists that the Crucifixion took place on the afternoon before the "Preparation," whatever day of the week it

[1] PAUL to the *Corinthians*, i., v., 7, 8.

For many days previous to its commencement, the houses of the Jews are literally turned inside out, white-washed from top to bottom, and every nook and corner swept, cleansed, and searched for the smallest particle of leavened bread, even to the very mouse-holes, which are carefully stopped, so that if any of these busy little animals should happen to have a

Preparation.

SPANIARDS "BURNING JUDAS" AT EASTER.
(Tetuan.)

Photograph by W. W. Hind-Smith, Esq.

store of crumbs, they must keep it absolutely to themselves. But this is not sufficient for the table and kitchen utensils which are to be used during the fast. These must either be perfectly new, or kept from year to year for this occasion,* and in consequence for some

might have been. The calendar shows that it fell that year on a Wednesday, which was therefore the day of the Crucifixion. Christ rose, as He had prophesied, after three days and three nights in the grave, on the Saturday evening, the commencement of the first day of the week, on which His tomb was found empty.

* *Glasses* used at other times are nevertheless permitted.

time previous a brisk trade in these lines is done up and down the streets as well as in the shops. During Passover some Jewish confectioners "sell" the keys of their shops to Moors, to repurchase them afterwards, not to be held responsible for any leaven they may contain. Strict Jews will neither drink nor eat in a strange house during Passover, though they will not refuse chick-peas.

Purging out the Leaven.

The ceremony of "purging out the old leaven," which takes place on the evening of the thirteenth of Nissan, —'Ereb Pesaḥ—when the fourteenth has just commenced, is a very curious one, the final touch to all the purifying, when the master of the house plays "hide and seek" with his wife for crumbs which she has concealed. Till this is done they may not eat, and no bread is taken after breakfast on that day until the purging is concluded. Having pronounced the Berakha, the master commences his round, sometimes carrying a candle, and with a brush of feathers sweeps the pieces when found into a spoon covered with a cloth. This cermony is known as Bi'ûr Ḥames, and the careful burning in the street as Serifat ḥames. This must be accomplished next day before noon, after a special prayer in Chaldee, called Kal Ḥamîrah. Sometimes rubbish is burned with the pieces of bread, so that one often hears the expression "Keep that till Serifat ḥames." On this day it is customary for first-born sons to fast, or for their fathers to do so on their behalf if they have not yet reached the age of Bar Miṣvah.

The Meal.

On the afternoon of the following day, while the men are away at the synagogues (in which, by the bye, services are held thrice daily throughout the year), the women of the house prepare the special supper-table—Séder,—which is laid on the first two nights. The actual Passover meal is of course the chief event of the fast of Pesaḥ or Ḥag ham-maṣôt, ("Passover" or "Unleavened Bread") and after the piece of "lamb roast with fire," the cakes of unleavened bread —maṣôt—are its main feature.*

The Unleavened Bread.

Nothing could be more scrupulous than the preparation of these articles. Often the care over them extends as far back as the sowing by Jews of the wheat, from the produce of which the flour is made, and they are never touched by women. The corn must be perfectly dry, and ground in a mill which has been specially cleansed for the purpose. The water used in the preparation of the dough must be very cold, taken from a pure spring, and filtered at sunset through an unstarched cloth. No other ingredient is used in the composition of these cakes, which are about ten inches in diameter, and about a quarter of an inch thick. With the exception of six special cakes, marked I to IIIII, which are set apart, three for the first and three for the second night, all are perforated with the thumb in regular circles. The cakes in these special sets of three, which must be without flaw, are called respectively "Cohen," "Levi" and "Israel."

Baking the Cakes

It is a curious sight to see the poorer Jews kneading these cakes in the streets outside the public bake-houses, as they must be baked as soon as kneaded to prevent the slightest chance of fermentation. Even the oven has to be purified by fire a few days before. Such "maṣôt shemùra" are reckoned ninety per cent more "kôsher" than the others: rabbis and "holy" men have theirs made the day before Pesaḥ, superintending the operations themselves. Many of them are prepared during the preceding thirty days, after the feast of Pûrîm. Their special dish, or ki'arah, is usually

* In the Middle Ages the custom of using simnel or twice-baked bread —*i.e.* "biscuit"—during Lent still obtained in Christendom.

the most valuable one in the house, and the cloth which covers the three special cakes is of the finest. There is also another kind of Passover cakes, kneaded with eggs, sugar and orange juice, which are not necessarily baked for several hours after they are kneaded; they are very palatable.

The Table Spread.

In the centre of the table, or to the right of the master, is placed a large tray containing a piece of the fore-leg of a sheep or an ox—zeròa or ḳorbán "the Sacrifice"—"roast with fire," and one egg (béṣah) lies on top of the maṣôt to the left. Upon the tray are also some lettuce leaves and celery—the "bitter herbs" (maròr), some small balls of ḥarôṣet, a compound of apples, raisins and dates with spices, very carefully prepared during the previous summer, —representing the clay without straw, of which the Israelites in Egypt were forced to make bricks,—and a small basin of vinegar—or salt and water,—to remind them of the passage of the Red Sea. There are also many other eatables, besides a number of bottles of wine, glasses, and so forth.

At the Passover the poorest Israelite makes himself easy, resting upon any cushions that may be available, because, though his ancestors were bondsmen, he is free. The presence of a Gentile, of whom it may be said "he loveth our nation," is not objected to, so that I have had the privilege of joining the family circle of a friend on this solemn occasion, and of partaking of all but the wine, though it also was pressed upon me.

The Ceremonial.

The various ceremonies of the Séder night are very strictly observed and maintained by committing to memory in their proper order the Chaldee words italicised in the account which follows. When all are seated, one of those present cries "*Kadesh!*" whereupon each pours out wine for himself or herself, and all stand up. The master, who has previously washed his hands with scrupulous care, utters the Ḳiddûsh, or sanctification, and all drink more than half a glass. Then all ceremonially wash their hands, a performance known as *r'ḥaṣ*, after which the master, dipping a piece of celery *(karpas)* into the vinegar, offers thanks to GOD for it,

ISAAC AND REBEKAH.

Photograph by Dr. Rudduck.

handing it to each of the party. Then he takes the middle cake of unleavened bread from the pile, and breaking it in two, says: "As I divide this, so GOD divided the Red Sea, on the night when he delivered Israel from bondage." This ceremony is called *yaḥaṣ.*

He replaces one piece on the dish and "reserves" the larger—called áfìkômen—under the upper of the two table-cloths used on that night. The cups are then refilled, and celery dipped in vinegar is passed round.

The master next rises and passes the tray with the meat over the heads of the party, and after re-seating himself, recounts at the request of the children the exodus of his ancestors from Egypt, reading from the Hag-Gadah, a book containing a special account. This reading is called *Magîd*, and is performed in Hebrew alone the first night, but in Spanish also on the second. * Then wine is blessed again, and the ready-filled cups are handed round: next, after all have washed their hands—the *roḥṣá* ablution, with a special benediction,—the upper biscuit of the pile is broken, with another special benediction, and eaten, together with a piece of the middle one, a ceremony called moṣi.

The Story.

Taking some of the' 'bitter herbs" *(marôr)*, the master makes a sop of the ḥaròṣet in vinegar with a spoon, and dipping the herbs in this, he hands it to each in turn.[1] The third and last cake—*korekh*—is then partaken of with lettuce and celery, after a special instruction of Hillel's. The ordinary meal being now declared "served" *(shulḥan 'orukh)*, it is proceeded with. When the meal is ended, the half biscuit—áfìkômen—is taken from under the table-cloth, broken and divided. The pieces are partly eaten, and no more food may be taken that night. In remembrance

The Sop.

* It is one of the metrical accounts of the Exodus given to children to learn on this occasion, when they are instructed to enquire "What mean ye by this service?"[2] which has been corrupted into the well-known nursery rhymes of the old woman trying to take her pig to market, and of "The House that Jack built."[3]

[1] JOHN, xiii., 26. [2] *Exodus*, xxi., 25.

[3] See the *Seder Hagadah*, 1831, vol. 23, and PATERSON SMYTH, *The Old Documents and the New Bible*, p. 141.

of the Red Sea, the remainder *(ṣafôn)* is considered a charm against ship-wreck, if thrown over-board in a storm, and it is sometimes hung on the walls of synagogues.

The third cup of wine[1] is now drunk, after the ordinary thanks (birkat ha mazôn) are offered for the supper. Then follows the singing of certain Psalms, as the 114th to the 118th, with other passages, and after a while the company separates, drinking more wine as they stand up ejaculating "*Nirṣah!*" ("Accepted"), the expression of a wish that what they have done may be acceptable to God. But with so many prescribed drinkings there is, unhappily, a tendency to drunkenness, to which many give way, especially upon the Séder night.

The Hymn.

During the Passover, trays containing unleavened cakes, preserved oranges and dried fruits, generally covered with a purple or red silk handkerchief, are sent as presents to Christian and Moorish friends. The trays and plates must be emptied, and returned to the senders unwashed. On the last day of the feast a return present is made, but instead of unleavened cakes, the tray contains a raw fish, new vegetables, fruit, milk, eggs, young corn and leavened bread—first fruits—and always flowers. These are placed upon a table prettily laid out, and in the evening the family sits round the room to receive congratulatory visits from their friends, who help themselves unasked to sweets, fruits, liqueurs, or wine. On the same day they have in some parts a curious custom of going to the gardens to say the Birkat ha Illanôt or "Blessing of the trees."

Friendly Offerings.

Pentecost, or the Feast of Weeks, was instituted as a thanksgiving feast for the harvest, which in these lands

[1] LUKE, xxii., 20.

begins after the Passover, at which feast the first sheaf was to be offered to the Lord, while at Pentecost or Shabu'ôt two loaves of fine new flour were among the appointed offerings. As its name indicates, it occurs fifty days after the first day of the Passover, or a "week of weeks" from the second day, "from the day that ye brought the sheaf of the wave offering,"[1] "from the time thou beginnest to put the sickle to the corn," "the morrow after the seventh sabbath."[2] It falls on the sixth of Sivan, and is celebrated for two days, in which no servile work is done. The days between the two feasts are called Omer, and are regarded as semi-mourning, so that no marriages are celebrated during that period. As at the Feast of Tabernacles, the first night (which is the beginning of the first day) is devoted by the pious to the study of the Law.

The Feast of Weeks.

At the special noon services in the synagogues during this feast, a book called *Azharôt* is brought by those who can read, who each do so in turn, a verse apiece; but should anyone make a mistake, those who observe it immediately call upon him to re-read it more carefully, and this is repeated until the reader gets through without error. Those who fear reading a difficult verse are careful to escape it by changing their seats. Another custom more generally observed, which was common in Tangier till recent years, is for Jews to repair to their windows or roofs, armed with syringes and a plentiful supply of water as ammunition, therewith grievously to assault and batter such of their co-religionists as duty calls forth from their abodes. *

Peculiar Customs.

* A similar custom, known as the "water feast," which obtains in Burmah at the return of the rainy season, afforded me the most pleasant hot day I spent in that country.

[1] *Leviticus*, xxiii., 15. [2] *Deuteronomy*, xvi., 9.

Curiously enough, the bathing season is supposed to commence immediately after this feast, though even in Tangier English residents find the sea by no means cold from the beginning of April, and take care to enjoy it accordingly.

The Fast of Ab.

As the Dedication of the Temple is commemorated by a feast, so is its destruction by a fast, known as Tish'ah be-Ab, on the ninth of the month Ab. In the first nine days of that month no meat is eaten, lentils being substituted for it, nor are bathing and hair-cutting permitted during this time, abstention from them being regarded as a sign of mourning. Eggs are sometimes used as well as lentils, these two articles being chosen, it is said, because there is no wrinkle on them. A good meal is eaten before sunset on the previous evening, after which fasting is general. After the ordinary evening service in the synagogues the book of Jeremiah's *Lamentations* is read, followed by additional lamentations *(Ḳinôt)*. Next morning, after the service, various other lamentations are read, whereat the women cry, and sometimes the men. This least of the fasts of the Jewish year is also the last.

INDEX AND GLOSSARY

Part III.—EXPERIMENTAL.

Price Fifteen Shillings.

London: SWAN SONNENSCHEIN & CO., Lim., Paternoster Square, E.C.

"THE LAND OF THE MOORS:"

EXTRACTS FROM PRESS NOTICES.

"A very excellent piece of work."—*New Liberal Review.*

"The best general description of Morocco that has come under our notice."—*Field.*

"There is no lack of local colour in a lively record . . . an admirable book." —*Standard.*

"The most complete and exhaustive account we have yet seen . . . Mr. Meakin is to be congratulated upon his achievement."—*Travel.*

"Packed with information presented with great clearness . . . The book is fully and well illustrated from photographs, and has further an excellent map."—*Academy.*

"Of the new volume, no less than of the 'Moorish Empire' it must be said that it is encyclopædic and invaluable. It is as complete a description as either the general reader or the specialist student of detail could desire."—*Pall Mall Gazette.*

"More interesting, though not more valuable than the first . . . Mr. Meakin is, as usual, full and accurate in his information . . . Mr. Meakin's admirable accounts are a mine of information . . . A useful and elaborate volume."—*Literature.*

"Mr. Meakin has done a great service . . . the volume is of higher value than anything else which has been written ; . . . of the highest immediate and permanent value."—*Newcastle Daily Chronicle.*

"Eminently readable . . . Only Mr. Meakin (with the friendly co-operation of his allies in the country) could have produced such a book, which he too modestly introduces . . . Compressed and filtered by an accomplished expert."—*Literary World.*

"We have there the master hand of one who has made practically a life study of the subject, and who is building up a series of books which no one with special interests in the country—religious or commercial, certainly no missionary library—can afford to be without."—*Christian.*

"His handsome volumes resemble cisterns full to the lip of carefully stored rain water . . . To have limned for us Morocco, with such imposing accuracy and with so massive a dove-tailing of references . . . must be admitted to be something of a triumph . . . His work is admirably lucid and concise."—*Bookman.*

"In this new volume the country itself is dealt with in a similarly thorough manner . . . It contains also much valuable information obtainable only from recondite sources . . . as well as much drawn from Mr. Meakin's own large experience of Moorish residence and travel."—*Scotsman.*

"At once a generous and an important contribution to the history of a little-known people, compactly full of useful facts . . . The reading public at large, and students . . . owe a tribute of thanks and appreciation to this industrious historian for his Moorish records."—*Athenæum.*

"Scarcely less interesting and perhaps even more valuable than the previous one, on which we commented so favourably in these columns . . . Extraordinarily complete, full of curious and out-of-the-way knowledge. A most admirable book —cautious, full, learned, and interesting."—*Guardian.*

"Mr. Meakin has already contributed largely to our knowledge of Morocco, and his new volume should be appreciated by all who wish for a careful account of a country the fringe only of which is at all familiar even to well-travelled Europeans."—*Yorkshire Post.*

"The subject is handled with an accuracy, care and skill which will, we feel sure, gain for it the first place as a work of general reference for the student and foreigner resident in the country, and as a trustworthy handbook for the traveller."—*Glasgow Herald.*

"The physical features and animal life of the country and other possibilities of sport and travel are so well described that I can recommend anyone in search of new experiences to look through the 'Land of the Moors' for information and advice before his next holiday."—*Daily News.*

"All sorts of amusing and instructive facts illustrative of Moorish character. In view of the certainty of international complications sooner or later in Morocco, Mr. Meakin's monumental work deserves the most careful attention, and even the desultory reader may rely on finding incessant satisfaction in its perusal."—*Traveller.*

"An almost cyclopedic account . . . a thorough book, and published in excellent taste, this has the convincing note of authority, which the impressions of a mere traveler, or the conclusions of one who is only a scholar, must lack . . . Not only valuable for the information it contains, but readable throughout."—*New York Times, Saturday Review.*

"Certain to have a wider reading, appealing, as it does, to the traveller and sportsmen, than either the purely historical work that preceded it, or the ethnological compendium that is to follow . . . An appalling task, the magnitude of which would have alarmed anyone less enthusiastic . . . Mr. Meakin's description bears the test of close examination . . . his book is a monument of research." —*Morning Post.*

"An admirable account of the country and its characteristics . . . The pains expended on the production of the work must have been enormous. The most cursory perusal is enough to give assurance of the unremitting labour and complete knowledge of his subject which Mr. Meakin has brought to his task. At the same time, while his learning is so sound, the author has a very light and readable style . . . and his chapters are never dull . . . It is difficult to see how he could have turned his unrivalled opportunities to better account."—*Westminster Review.*

"To Mr. Budgett Meakin Morocco was a problem that he set himself to solve. He mastered its language and geography, its history and politics: patiently and industriously be fashioned the history of old times from records to which few have access . . . He has gathered information from the north and the south, from the east and from the isles of the sea; he places the student of Morocco under a heavy load of obligation, and has much to say even new. The map of Morocco brought down to the year 1900 with routes marked and towns set down accurately, is a model of careful, accurate scholarship and research."—*Daily Chronicle.*

"It is questionable whether any European who is competent to tell the world what he knows has such an intimate acquaintance with Morocco and the Moors as Mr. Meakin has gained by years of study, bookish and practical. The literature relating to the country is at his fingers' ends. He feels instinctively the historical suggestions of every part of the country. He knows the record of every white man's travels . . . The competence of Mr. Meakin to act as the interpreter of Morocco to the outside world is unquestionable. He has exceedingly varied knowledge, is a shrewd observer, and writes easily and in an interesting vein. Mr. Meakin has produced a valuable, substantial, readable book, which, with his other works, will constitute the traveller's manuals that everybody who wishes to understand Morocco must read."—*Sheffield Independent.*

"THE MOORISH EMPIRE:"

EXTRACTS FROM PRESS NOTICES.

"It would be impossible to praise this handsome and erudite volume too highly. Mr. Meakin brings to his task enthusiasm, knowledge, experience, a keen eye, and the pen of a ready, but not irresponsible, writer... A remarkable and captivating study it is. The author ... is a singularly judicious critic... There is an extraordinary wealth of romance, of mediæval lore, of adventures in the chapters which Mr. Meakin has found the art of combining into a luminous whole. The author has joined that small but illustrious company who believe in knowledge as the only safe prelude to action."—Dr. William Barry—*Bookman.*

"An exceedingly interesting volume. It is far and away the best book on its subject. The chapters on Moorish Government, diplomatic relations, capitulations, Christian slavery and Salli piracy are full of interest, and we must not omit to mention an excellent critical bibliography of books on Morocco which will be most useful to students. It is a work of much research and labour, and fills a place that was conspicuously empty."—*Spectator.*

"Mr. Budgett Meakin is to be envied for his discovery of a wide gap in historical literature, and congratulated on his success in filling it... The value of the work is enhanced by elaborate historical and genealogical tables and maps, and its interest is increased by a large number of excellent illustrations... The historical section will be of real service to serious students, for whom it is obviously intended. The authorities are ample and trustworthy, and the author has been at great pains to consult the best. His numerous references testify to his research... The book is a mine of curious details, and must have cost its author infinite labour... The subject—likely to become a 'burning question' before long—will probably be almost exhausted if the other volumes are as thorough and complete."—*Literature.*

"This will take rank as a standard work upon Morocco. There is no more competent authority upon the life and habits of the Moors than Mr. Budgett Meakin, therefore students will welcome this book as clear, concise and full of plain facts . . a veritable storehouse to which students of many subjects may turn with success... He has succeeded in compiling an elaborate chronological chart, which will be found extremely useful and accurate... In the space of this brief article it is impossible to convey all the sound arguments adduced by the writer. Those who are interested in Morocco and the Moors should themselves turn to the book, for they will find it replete with genuine interest." William Le Queux.—*Literary World.*

"An excellent compilation from the best available material, historical and descriptive: it is, moreover, pre-eminently up to date in all its details. Much pains has clearly been bestowed on its production, and the amount of matter compressed within a small space, and the quantity of authorities laid under contribution, must command respect... Mr. Meakin is not only familiar with the literature concerning Morocco, but knows the country itself as well, perhaps, as any European, a qualification which enables him to speak with a confidence that carries conviction."—*Athenæum.*

"An excellent attempt to bring into public notice a subject of considerable importance in connection with European history, and to commend it to the attention of students. The volume is packed with information, and is amply illustrated, some of the illustrations being copies of rare plates."—*English Historical Review.*

"We have nothing but praise for this most scholarly volume. A work singularly complete, dealing with the history of the Moors from the period of nebulous tradition to the present day."—*Pall Mall Gazette.*

"It will no doubt rank as an authority to which students will be compelled to refer."—*Saturday Review.*

"Mr. Meakin has no need to be unduly diffident. As a chronicler of a little-known land he proves himself clear in style, critical in the selection of his authorities, and withal distinctly readable."—*Academy.*

"A very interesting book on a very important and distinctly novel subject. It touches the skirts of what is in all probability a problem destined, sooner or later, to set the world on fire ... *The Moorish Empire* is in its way emphatically a scholar's work ... We feel, as we read his pages, a tolerably sure conviction that the author has weighed and balanced his judgments, verified the main lines of his facts, and given little or nothing from doubtful or second-hand sources. For the book itself we have little but praise ... Mr. Meakin captivates our interest ... We shall look forward to his future writings on his interesting and novel subject with the greatest anticipation."—*Guardian.*

"An encyclopædia of information ... witnesses to patient industry on the part of the author ... His long residence in Morocco, his command of the language and his devotion to the task, have enabled him to draw largely from his personal observation and from original native sources. Copious references also testify to an acquaintance with general history which enables him to appreciate Moorish history as a chapter in universal history ... The record is of real interest ... The picturesque illustrations add to the attractiveness of a book of solid interest."—*Times.*

"Mr. Budgett Meakin has ... succeeded in enriching literature. Mr. Meakin is specially fitted for his task ... neither a mere tourist, nor yet a scholar accurate as to dates and facts but ignorant of the daily life of the people of whom he writes, but a man who, on the one hand, knows the people of Morocco from his youth upwards, and on the other hand, has perfected himself in Oriental studies in other and more cultivated Oriental countries. The present instalment of the series is the most complete compendium of the subject which we yet have, and which no student of Morocco can afford to be without ... well thought out and arranged." Cunninghame Graham.—*Daily Chronicle.*

"Mr. Meakin's superb volume ... as a monument of painstaking research in the light of intimate acquaintance with some aspects of the Morocco of to-day ... and as a simple and unvarnished record of the history of a most interesting race ... is deserving of warmest praise. Certainly the abundant foot-notes, as well as the valuable bibliographical summary ... bear testimony to the enormous material studied." F. G. Aflalo.—*Morning Post.*

"Mr. Meakin deserves credit for his success in keeping so much live flesh about his skeleton history ... His 'Moorish Empire' is a most useful and convenient reference book, ... just the sort of book that writers and readers of the Moorish 'question' will like to have within arm's reach."—*Daily News.*

"'The Moorish Empire' has undeniable claims ... Mr. Meakin is in fact, an Oriental scholar ... who has broken new ground in this important book, for there has not hitherto been in any European language a clear and exhaustive estimate of the Moorish Empire in its glory and decline ... Scholars at least will appreciate, not merely to-day, but to-morrow, this intimate, true picture of a Barbary State in mediæval times and under modern conditions."—*Leeds Mercury.*

"An exhaustive and elaborately illustrated history of the rise and fall of the Moorish empire. The material is excellently arranged."—*Review of Reviews.*

"To the general reader the remarkable volume entitled 'The Moorish Empire' will seem like a fairy-tale. Its author, Budgett Meakin, writes with a full knowledge of his subject . . . He has made an important contribution to the history of the country . . . The book is unique in its class, and will certainly be accepted as a reliable authority . . . It was no easy task to furnish a condensed history of Morocco for twenty-two centuries, yet Mr. Meakin has accomplished this task in most creditable manner. His literary style is fluent, but not verbose, and he has the art of selecting the salient features of a reign or of a period and delineating them so as to make his narrative extremely interesting . . . It has prefixed a remarkable comparative chart of the Empire . . . arranged in excellent form."—*Dundee Advertiser*.

"This full but concise epitome . . . One valuable feature is a unique chart measuring over four feet, in which the progress of the Moorish Empire from the eighth century to the present time can be compared with the contemporary progress of the peoples of the East and West . . . It is an attractive and well-arranged compendium, containing a mass of historical, chronological, geographical and genealogical data, and showing the relations which exist between them. Characteristic features of the chart are displayed also in the accompanying narrative, which has inset dates wherever needed, and does credit to the methodical genius of the author . . . Mr. Meakin's aim is the construction of an historical epitome, but he succeeds in giving us in the space at his disposal something more than the dry bones of history . . . A good epitome is not to be epitomised, and this is about as good as it could be . . . Mr. Meakin's monumental work. We have no work of reference on the subject to compare with it, and its profusion of well-chosen illustrations should secure for it a general and hearty welcome."—*Sheffield Daily Telegraph*.

"There is probably no man living who has a better acquaintance with the literature of the subject than the author, who has also had a prolonged first-hand knowledge of the empire of which he treats . . . the internal evidence which the book affords as to its trustworthiness . . . The comparative chart is an extremely useful feature."—*Manchester Guardian*.

"Mr. Budgett Meakin has given us a concise history of the Moorish Empire, a task which few people would be equally competent to accomplish, for he brings to his work not only a very extensive knowledge of Moorish ideas and customs, and a wide reading of original authorities, but also a considerable historical acumen which makes his book valuable, not only to those who want a history of Morocco, but also to those who study history as history, independent of time and place . . . It is a book which should be known to every student of Morocco, and with the two companion volumes will form a veritable encyclopædia."—*Birmingham Daily Post*.

"It seems to us that he has been extremely fair all round . . . The reader must be referred to the book, concerning which we can give the assurance that interest will not flag in the course of its perusal . . . As the primary purpose of this book is not to entertain, but to inform, it is the one practical students want . . . The reader perceives that while accuracy as to dates and facts is a primary aim, they have that clothing which can only be furnished by one who has dwelt among the Moors, who is familiar with their language and habits, who has to a large extent fathomed the, to us, extraordinary contradictions in their character, and who has perfected his understanding of them by life and study in the more Eastern lands whence they came."—*Liverpool Courier*.

"Mr. Meakin is doing for Morocco a work as complete and careful as Edward Lane once did for Egypt."—*Christian World.*

"The genius for taking infinite pains is made evident in every page, and the book will doubtless be a standard work on the subject."—*Independent.*

"A welcome treasure... The author treats like a discriminate historian. In the mood and mode of the statesman and trained diplomat he traces the course of the external relations of the Moors right up to the present time."—*Newcastle Chronicle.*

"The chapters on foreign relations, diplomatic usages and commercial intercourse merit close attention... so that the book will be valuable to political students as a trustworthy record no less interesting to the general reader."—*Western Morning News.*

"As complete a study of the Moorish Empire, both historically and in its present relations to the Powers, as we are likely for some time, at any rate, to possess. 'Picturesque touches,' 'glimpses of feeling,' and 'knowledge of the people,' its politics and government, Mr. Meakin certainly gives us."—*Methodist Times.*

"Mr. Budgett Meakin will receive universal thanks... The author is to be congratulated upon the completeness and terseness of his text. We seldom meet with such evidence of painstaking success in a field so difficult to garner."—*Sheffield Independent.*

"The most complete work of its kind we have yet met. The general reader will find that there is enough of romance in these pages to warrant his attention, for Moorish history presents to us no lack of singular, and, in a way, impressive, figures... But the book is most valuable for its comprehensive survey of Moorish history and the relations of Morocco with other countries."—*Yorkshire Post.*

"How severe has been the duty of condensation... may be judged from the fact that the references to authorities number 1175, and that the third part reviews 223 volumes of Moorish Literature. The author has part of his reward in having produced a work which should be of standard value and permanent interest... Another feature is a large and elaborate comparative chart."—*Scotsman.*

"A work whose value will increase both with the lapse of time and the accretion of that detailed knowledge about Morocco which time is sure to bring. Mr. Meakin, who has had unique opportunities of knowing Morocco, its history and its people, has organized lines of genealogy and chronology, which will spare much further confusion... his pages abound with local colour... a copious bibliography of Moroccan literature... Mr. Meakin's book is fully and beautifully illustrated, and in form, type and every detail, leaves nothing to be desired."—*New Age.*

"This valuable and instructive work gives an interesting account of Morocco since the foundation of that Empire. It provides us with some pleasant reading... It is quite evident that the author has a thorough knowledge of his subject... This 'standard work' should shortly be found in every public library and private reading room."—*Gibraltar Chronicle.*

"The author appears to have so thoroughly saturated himself by observation and reference to old documents, and study of the works of other writers, as to enable him to place before his readers well nigh every item of interest worth knowing of his subject... every page abounds in interest... With the present ever-increasing interest in Africa Mr. Meakin's work ought to find a place in every bookshelf and public library. Whether as a book of reference or to take up in odd half-hours, it is equally interesting. In either case, its pages will be found as full of interest as its subject is attractive even to fascination... But to fully appreciate the matter in Mr. Meakin's work, one needs to travel through its pages with, if possible, the spirit of the author."—*Al-moghreb Al-aksa*, Tangier.

"All travellers in Morocco should read Mr. Budgett Meakin's new book on the history of that fascinating country."—*Travel.*

CPSIA information can be obtained
at www.ICGtesting.com
Printed in the USA
BVHW031135031221
623166BV00001B/15